PRAISE FOR *SQUARE HAUNTING*

"A very readable and enjoyable book, *Square Haunting* is at once a tribute to Virginia Woolf's powerful concept of a woman's need for a room of her own and an exploration of the contradictions and messy compromises so often involved in fulfilling that need."
—MARGARET DRABBLE, *The New Statesman*

"Captivating . . . superb . . . [Francesca] Wade has pulled off a remarkable feat of intellectual and social history with her erudite yet juicy first book. . . . An engaging narrative, movingly bookended by descriptions of the obliteration of a world she so vividly evokes . . . This impressive feminist history stands as an elegiac love letter to a bygone time and place that offered brilliant, iconoclastic women a unique opportunity for freedom and self-expression." —*The Wall Street Journal*

"Serious, stylish . . . It is a pleasure to fall into step with the eloquent, elegant Wade as she stamps the streets of literary London. I would give a copy to every young woman graduating from university and wondering who and how to be." —LAURA FREEMAN, *The Times*

"Powerful . . . Just as Harrison and Power rewrote history to include the lives of forgotten women, so Wade reestablishes the importance of thinkers like Power and H.D., whose legacies have been eclipsed by those of their male contemporaries." —*The New Yorker*

"Original and erudite . . . Wade is adept at evoking the gritty texture of the times, taking us seamlessly from the interior lives of her subjects into the world they inhabited and back again. . . . Wade distils half a century of social and literary history into these five women's lives with a marvellously light touch. This is biography as fresh and engaging as you are likely to find." —ARIANE BANKES, *The Spectator*

"A remarkable, even stirring story." —DAPHNE MERKIN, *The New York Review of Books*

"Rich and powerful." —RUTH FRANKLIN, *Harper's*

"Gripping . . . a compelling study of the quest for creative freedom . . . Wade is an astutely empathetic storyteller who never lets her considerable research get in the way of her elegant writing."

—ANN KENNEDY SMITH, *The Times Literary Supplement*

"An eloquent, pellucid, sometimes poignant study of five female intellectuals, each of whom disdained convention to fulfill their potential. . . . Wade is interested in ideas, in the great movements of history, and, above all, in the spirit of curiosity and adventure that binds these women together." —JOHANNA THOMAS-CORR, *The Observer*

"A superb literary history of five extraordinary women based in London between the wars (in which you will meet Hope Mirrlees, Virginia Woolf and Jane Harrison all figuring out how to invent a life that allows them to write and love freely)." —DEBORAH LEVY, *The Telegraph*

"Richly researched, elegantly written . . . [Wade] moves from the geographical and socially precise locus of Mecklenburgh Square to a glancing history of women's creative, economic, and intimate lives in the early twentieth century." —BRIAN DILLON, *4Columns*

"A fascinating voyage through the lives of five remarkable women . . . moving and immersive." —EDMUND GORDON,
author of *The Invention of Angela Carter: A Biography*

"Elegant, erudite, and absorbing, *Square Haunting* is a startlingly original debut, and Francesca Wade is an author to watch."

—FRANCES WILSON,
author of *Guilty Thing: A Life of Thomas De Quincey*

"Outstanding . . . I'll be recommending this all year."

—SARAH BAKEWELL,
author of *At the Existentialist Café*

"I much enjoyed Francesca Wade's book. It almost made me wish I belonged to the pioneering generation of women spoiling eggs on the gas ring and breaking taboos." —SUE PRIDEAUX,
author of *I Am Dynamite!: A Life of Friedrich Nietzsche*

SQUARE HAUNTING

SQUARE HAUNTING

Five Writers in London Between the Wars

FRANCESCA WADE

CROWN
NEW YORK

2021 Crown Trade Paperback Edition

Copyright © 2020 by Francesca Wade

Published in the United States by Crown, an imprint of Random House,
a division of Penguin Random House LLC, New York.

CROWN and the Crown colophon are registered trademarks of
Penguin Random House LLC.

Originally published in hardcover in Great Britain by Faber & Faber Ltd, London,
in 2020. First published in hardcover in the United States by Tim Duggan Books, an
imprint of Random House, a division of Penguin Random House LLC, in 2020.

LIBRARY OF CONGRESS CATALOGING-IN-PUBLICATION DATA
Names: Wade, Francesca, author.
Title: Square haunting / Francesca Wade.
Description: First edition. | New York : Tim Duggan Books, 2020.
Identifiers: LCCN 2019055631 (print) | LCCN 2019055632 (ebook) | ISBN
9780451497802 (trade paperback) | | ISBN 9780451497819 (ebook)
Subjects: LCSH: Women authors, English—Homes and haunts—England—
London. | Women authors, English—20th century—Biography. / Mecklenburgh
Square (London, England) / Women and literature—Great Britain—History—20th
century. / London (England)—Biography.
Classification: LCC PR110.L6 W33 2020 (print) | LCC PR110.L6 (ebook) | DDC
820.9/928709421—dc23
LC record available at https://lccn.loc.gov/2019055631
LC ebook record available at https://lccn.loc.gov/2019055632

Printed in the United States of America on acid-free paper

crownpublishing.com

2 4 6 8 9 7 5 3 1

Book design by Susan Turner

"I like this London life in early summer—
the street sauntering & square haunting."
—Virginia Woolf, diary, April 20, 1925

CONTENTS

SQUARE HAUNTING

PROLOGUE

A few minutes past midnight on Tuesday, September 10, 1940, an air raid struck Mecklenburgh Square. From number 45, John Lehmann heard gunfire rumbling in the distance, the hum of airplanes at an insistent crescendo until "three whistling, ripping noises" directly overhead were followed by the unmistakable tinkling of breaking glass. Climbing out of bed, he opened the blackout curtains to find his windows shattered and the London skyline obscured by flames. His friend Stephen Spender's house on nearby Lansdowne Terrace, usually visible from his second-floor window, appeared to be enveloped in a burning cloud. "Well," Lehmann found himself thinking, surprised at his state of calm, "poor old Stephen's the first to go."

Lehmann left his room and hurried downstairs, shouting out to his sleeping landlord as he passed. Before he could open the front door, he felt the building tremble with another explosion—"the house seemed to clench itself like a fist for a moment, then silence," he later recalled—and as he tentatively peered outside, he was met with the sight of "an enormous bellying cloud of grey dust advancing down the road toward me like a living thing." Instinctively, Lehmann ran into the square—the searchlight had broken, plunging the area into total darkness—and collided with neighbors in pajamas rushing the other way. An acquaintance from number 46, wearing a tin helmet, explained that an unexploded time bomb was lodged in the square's garden, and the shelter there had been evacuated.

Five houses on the east side of the square formed Byron Court, a block of residential accommodation for nurses from the Royal Free Hospital on Gray's Inn Road. As his eyes accustomed to the dark, Lehmann thought that it looked rather odd, then realized after a few seconds that he was seeing a tree beyond—the building had been smashed to bits, one side standing sliced open like a doll's house.

For the first time in the war, death felt very close to Lehmann. But for the moment, there was little he could do. He sat on a doorstep and chatted to a woman in Auxiliary Territorial Service uniform while the residents of Mecklenburgh Square waited for dawn to confirm the end of the raid. Couples lay in the road entwined for warmth under improvised coverings; someone produced a Dostoevsky novel and began to read as the sun rose; a group of young women, rescued from Byron Court, huddled together in a stairwell. At last, the all-clear sounded and the makeshift party dispersed, back to their flats if they dared, or to find shelter in nearby churches, underground stations, or hotels.

When Lehmann returned to Mecklenburgh Square later that morning, broken glass glittered on the pavement while firemen's hoses snaked across the garden. Rain had dissolved the dust that had coated the bushes at dawn, but the grass was scorched with the detritus of incendiary bombs. A squad of firemen was trying to control the smoke still pouring out of Byron Court, while ambulances and blood-transfusion units stood by alongside hordes of police. Numbers 30, 31, and 32 had been demolished by a delayed-action high-explosive bomb; seventeen residents had been admitted to the Royal Free, with people still being stretchered out at 11 a.m. Six nurses died. All day the square was busy with arrivals and departures, as London's Blitz bureaucracy cranked into its hastily established routine: gas inspectors searching for leaks, the electricity board collecting meters and cookers, deliveries of chloride of lime to disinfect the remaining houses, the PDSA inquiring about distressed animals, and the overworked mortuary van, drawing up to collect the dead. A warden was instructed to authorize and record all comings and goings in the square, as residents returned to pick up post and retrieve business papers, bedding, and ration cards. "09:26 Mr. Jackson, No. 8 Mecklenburgh Square, fed cat." "13:50 Mrs. Harrington, room 52 Byron Court searching for property—left 14:17 none found." "15:40 Mrs. Golding given permission to empty wardrobe in road." "20:13 Dead body removed. Female."

Virginia and Leonard Woolf, John Lehmann's neighbors and colleagues in the Hogarth Press, arrived from Sussex that afternoon to find a crowd gathered in Doughty Street, the entrance to Mecklenburgh Square cordoned off, and access to their flat at number 37 forbidden. Virginia could see that her friend Jane Harrison's former home, yards away at 11 Mecklenburgh Street, was "a great pile of bricks . . . Scraps of cloth hanging to the bare walls at the side still standing. A looking glass I think swinging. Like a tooth knocked out—a clean cut." A neighbor told the Woolfs that the previous night's explosion—the culmination of three nights of German air raids aimed at nearby King's Cross station—had blown him right out of bed. Leaving the square and wandering, dazed, around her usual haunts—from Holborn, where the streets gushed with water from smashed pipes, down the gridlocked Chancery Lane, where her typist's office was destroyed, around Lincoln's Inn and over to Regent's Park—Virginia saw smoke rising from gaps in the streets, a shell of a cinema with its stage visible from the road, a beaten-up restaurant ruefully offering wine to passersby. As she and Leonard drove away that evening, a siren went off and people began to run; the Woolfs raced through empty streets, dodging past haphazardly parked cars and frantic horses released from their shafts.

A week later, on September 16, the time bomb exploded, bringing down the ceiling of the basement room which housed the printing press, blowing several doors off their hinges, breaking every window and all the Woolfs' china. Sparrows fluttered in through holes in the roof and perched on the rafters; the pipes issued spurts of water at unpredictable intervals that cascaded down the stairs. On her next visit, Virginia returned to a Bloomsbury utterly altered from the one she knew. Her old home at 52 Tavistock Square was destroyed ("rubble where I wrote so many books. Open air where we sat so many nights, gave so many parties"). Number 37 Mecklenburgh Square was uninhabitable; a chalk cross she found marked on the door gave Virginia a shivering vision of the Black Death. Sirens wailed outside while the Woolfs and John Lehmann, along with the grimly cheerful overalled clerks from the solicitors' office upstairs, shared cold sausages and attempted to sort the salvageable (the works of Darwin, the silver, some Omega Workshops plates) from the irreparable (most of their crockery and the gramophone) while the wind blew through the splintered windows. A local gardener was enlisted to help excavate the carpet with a spade. On her hands and knees, Virginia scrabbled through the shards of glass and plaster powder, emerging, momentarily triumphant, with twenty-four volumes of her diaries—"a great mass for my memoirs." She never lived in London again. And Mecklenburgh Square—home, through its two-hundred-year history, to pioneering activists, lawyers, doctors, artists, and writers—was now in ruins.

IN THE SQUARE

Personally, we should be willing to read one volume about every street in the City, and should still ask for more.
—VIRGINIA WOOLF, "London Revisited" (1916)

Marooned on an island in the middle of a busy junction, a stone woman stoops to fill an urn with water. The drinking fountain on which she kneels has long since run dry; the steps leading down to the public lavatories behind her are boarded up; the elegant parade of Georgian buildings to her right is severed by a busy construction site. She breathes the fumes of cars passing down Guilford Street, which connects Bloomsbury with Clerkenwell and London's east, while workmen perch on her pedestal to eat their sandwiches. She is a remnant of the past frozen in the present, her name and story buried like the Fleet river on whose banks Guilford Street was built.

Cities are composed of roads and buildings, but also of myths and memories: stories which bring the brick and asphalt to life, and bind the present to the past. For Virginia Woolf, this unassuming statue just outside the entrance to Mecklenburgh Square—the Woman of Samaria, commissioned by a group of sisters in memory of their mother and designed by Henry Darbishire in 1870—was "one of the few pieces of sculpture in the streets of London that is pleasing to the eye." In a city decorated liberally with images of hoary statesmen in celebration of their service to the Empire, Woolf was intrigued by this anonymous woman, who seemed to represent an alternative, hidden history. "I would venture to guess that Anon, who wrote so many poems without signing them, was often a woman," Woolf wrote in *A Room of One's Own*. In that book, she describes wandering the streets of London and observing women talking, walking, shopping, and selling; their everyday animation reminds her of "the accumulation of unrecorded life" which historians—in their habitual focus on "the lives of great men"—were yet to chronicle. For Woolf, the statue paid subversive tribute to the forgotten women of London's past, a small but significant reminder of the figures who have been left out of books, or whose talents were never allowed to reach their full potential, simply because they were women.

In May 1917, T. S. Eliot described for his mother a visit to the American poet Hilda Doolittle, his new colleague on the *Egoist* magazine. "London is an amazing place," he wrote. "One is constantly discovering new quarters; this woman lives in a most beautiful dilapidated old square, which I had never heard of before; a square in the middle of town, near King's Cross station, but with spacious old gardens about it." Somehow, Mecklenburgh Square has remained a quiet enclave out on Bloomsbury's easternmost edge, separated from the better-known garden squares by Coram's Fields and the brutalist ziggurat of the Brunswick Centre. It is bounded by a graveyard (St. George's Gardens) and the noisy Gray's Inn Road, while its central garden—unusually for Bloomsbury—remains locked to nonresidents and hidden behind high hedges. But for D. H. Lawrence, a one-time lodger there, Mecklenburgh Square was the "dark, bristling heart of London."

At the turn of the twentieth century, Mecklenburgh Square was a radical address. And during the febrile years which encompassed the two world wars, it was home to the five women writers whose stories form this book. Virginia Woolf arrived with her bags and boxes at a moment of political chaos; she deliberated in her diaries "how to go on, through war," unaware that another writer had asked exactly that question in the same place twenty-three years earlier, as Zeppelin raids toppled the books from her shelf. Hilda Doolittle, known as H. D., lived at 44 Mecklenburgh Square during the First World War, and

hosted Lawrence and his wife Frieda while her husband Richard Aldington was fighting in France. In 1921, three years after H. D. had left
the square abruptly for a new start in Cornwall, Dorothy L. Sayers
created Lord Peter Wimsey, the swaggering hero of her first detective
novel, in the very same room where H. D. had begun work on the
autobiographical novel cycle that would occupy her for the rest of her
life. From 1926 to 1928, Jane Ellen Harrison, the pioneer of classical
and anthropological studies, supported a Russian-language literary
magazine from the square, working among a diverse milieu of diaspora
intellectuals. And at number 20, between 1922 and 1940, the historian
Eileen Power convened socialist meetings to chart an anti-fascist
future, scripted pacifist broadcasts for the BBC, and hosted raucous
parties in her kitchen.

   These women were not a Bloomsbury Group: they lived in Mecklenburgh Square at separate times, though one or two knew each other,
and others were connected through shared interests, friends, even lovers. H. D. and Sayers lived in the square when their careers had hardly
begun, Woolf and Harrison at the very ends of their lives; Power lived
there for almost two decades, Sayers and Woolf just one year each. But
for all of them, in different ways, their time in the square was formative. They all agreed that the structures which had long kept women
subordinate were illusory and mutable: in their writing and their life-
styles, they wanted to break boundaries and forge new narratives for
women. In Mecklenburgh Square, each dedicated herself to establishing a way of life that would let her fulfill her potential, to finding relationships that would support her work and a domestic setup that would
enable it. But it was not always easy. Their lives in the square demonstrate the challenges, personal and professional, that met—and continue to meet—women who want to make their voices heard.

   Though I've lived in London all my life, I'd never heard of Mecklenburgh Square until I walked through it by chance one summer evening in 2013. Gazing up at the firmly drawn curtains above H. D.'s
weather-worn blue plaque (the only commemoration of any of them
there today), I tried to imagine the conversations that had taken place
just a few meters away, almost a hundred years earlier. Later, at home,

reading about this mysterious square and its illustrious roster of past inhabitants, I was astonished to learn that so many other women writers—some of whose names were unknown to me, but whose lives and work sounded as fascinating as the more famous ones—had made their homes here around the same time. I wanted to know what had drawn these women here, and what sort of lives they'd lived in these tall, dignified houses, where they had written such powerful works of history, memoir, fiction, and poetry—often recreating the square itself in their work. Was their shared address simply a coincidence? Or was there something about Mecklenburgh Square that had exerted on each of them an irresistible pull? They all seemed, on the surface, such

The Woman of Samaria, Guilford Place, in 1912.

different characters, preoccupied by divergent concerns and moving in separate, if occasionally overlapping, circles—but was there anything fundamental that united them, beyond the simple fact that they had happened to alight, at some point, in this hidden corner of Bloomsbury?

The next time I found myself nearby, I took a detour to Mecklenburgh Square. As I wandered around looking for gaps in the thick hedge through which I might glimpse the garden, I remembered Virginia Woolf's famous declaration of 1929: "A woman must have money and a room of her own if she is to write." Turning back for a last glance at H. D.'s balcony as I headed toward Russell Square tube, I wondered if Woolf's extraordinary essay might help me understand the texture of these women's lives here, the prejudices they were fighting and the opportunities they grasped. I began to suspect that what H. D., Sayers, Harrison, Power, and Woolf herself were seeking in Mecklenburgh Square was everything Woolf had urged women writers to pursue: a room of their own, both literal and symbolic; a domestic arrangement which would help them to live, work, love, and write as they desired. Perhaps, I thought, it was this which attracted them all, in the interwar years, to Bloomsbury: a place already with a literary heritage, close to the British Museum Reading Room and the theatres and restaurants of the West End, where a new kind of living seemed possible, and where radical thought might flourish amid a political atmosphere founded on a zeal for change.

In *A Room of One's Own*, Woolf writes powerfully of the way women have been deprived of the conditions, material and emotional, under which artistic work can prosper. For centuries, she explains, women were barred from education and the professions, told that their worth depended on their marital status, and mocked or disparaged for any attempts to express opinions in public, let alone earn money for their work. No wonder, she writes, women's lives are "all but absent from history." The essay begins with Woolf on a visit to Cambridge, walking through a men's college as she waits to meet a friend. The experience solidifies Woolf's feeling of exclusion from the scholarly establishment: a productive train of thought is interrupted when she is sternly reminded that the library is closed to women, its stores of knowledge jealously guarded. But later that day, as she wanders the grounds of a women's college in the spring twilight, Woolf is struck by the phantom appearance of a bent figure, "formidable yet humble, with her great forehead and her shabby dress," striding across the terrace engrossed in thought: "Could it be the famous scholar," asks Woolf, in awe, "could it be J—— H—— herself?" Her vision is of Jane Harrison, the classicist whose groundbreaking work on ancient religion influenced a generation of modernists, and who had died in her home on Mecklenburgh Street just months before Woolf delivered, at Harrison's former college, the lecture that became *A Room of One's Own*.

This ghostly apparition offers the first moment of hope in this dispiriting tale of sneers and locked doors. Fortified by Harrison's example, Woolf's despondency shifts to anger, as she investigates the corrosive effect on women's imaginations of their confinement to a domestic sphere where they were expected to keep quiet, comport themselves correctly, and deviate from conventional living arrangements at their peril. "We think back through our mothers if we are women," writes Woolf, lamenting women's absence from the canon of literature and the usual narrative of history. Jane Harrison offered a rare model of the sort of intellectual freedom Woolf wanted for women. Born in 1850, Harrison was one of the first women to establish, after decades of rejections and setbacks, a reputation as a professional scholar. After leaving university, the academic posts she applied for went first to her male peers, then to the male students of her male peers; it was not until she returned to Newnham College, at the age of almost fifty, that she found an all-female community which gave her the validation, time, and money she needed to produce the works which made her name—and which paved the way for female writers and public thinkers, such as Woolf, Power, Sayers, and H. D. Now, as I examined their books, pored over letters in their archives, and started to notice connections between their lives and work, it occurred to me that Mecklenburgh Square itself might hold within its history a female tradition of exactly the sort Woolf was looking for. These five women who lived there between the wars all pushed the boundaries of scholarship, of literary form, of societal norms: they refused to let their gender hold them back, but were determined to find a different way of living, one in which their creative work would take precedence.

Apart from Harrison, the women in this book were born between 1882 and 1893, into a world where the lives of middle-class women like them were changing fast. The accepted notion that a woman's ultimate goal should be an advantageous marriage was not only starting to sound socially antiquated, but was also increasingly acknowledged as unrealizable for many: a population imbalance, with women significantly outnumbering men, was first revealed in the 1851 census, and it grew steadily across the century, to the horror of some commentators. An 1862 article entitled "Why Are Women Redundant?" suggested that girls should be deported to the colonies to seek husbands there, or be taught flirtation by prostitutes; otherwise, the author warned ominously, these women might, "in place of completing, sweetening, and embellishing the existence of others," be "compelled to lead an independent and incomplete existence of their own." Others, more pragmatically, counseled a widening of women's horizons. Schooling for Victorian girls had been geared toward a domestic life, focusing on the rudimentary grasp of languages, music, and sewing, while higher-status subjects like mathematics and classics were omitted from the curriculum. But from the middle of the century, new schools and colleges began to open, based on the belief that women should be educated on equal terms with men in order to gain the grounding necessary for employment, economic security, and political influence. The demographic imbalance peaked after the First World War, skewed by the number of men killed in that conflict, and the 1921 census noted almost 1.75 million "Surplus Women." (The tabloid hand-wringing caused some amusement: "Good God," wrote Eileen Power to a friend, "am I a surplus woman because I am not tacked on to a man?") But new options were starting to emerge. On February 6, 1918, women's suffrage became part of British law, if at this point only for property-owning women over thirty. The following year, the Sex Disqualification (Removal) Act opened up many professions previously closed to women, stating that "a person shall not be disqualified by sex or marriage from the exercise of any public function."

As women's public roles were changing, so too was the way they lived their lives in private. When Woolf came to write of the liberating effects of work and education, it's striking that she chose as her metaphor a modern room, immeasurably different from the drawing rooms where "women have sat indoors all these millions of years, so that by this time the very walls are permeated by their creative force." A renovation of traditional living arrangements, she suggested, was not only an outward sign of women's evolving freedom, but actually a prerequisite for it. In the Victorian middle-class imagination, the home was a serene, feminine haven completely separate from the world of work. John Ruskin, in 1864, described the home as a "sacred place," a peaceful domain guarded by the "incorruptibly good" wife, who was educated "not for self-development, but for self-renunciation," and who ministered to her husband on his return from a day of toil. In her essay "Professions for Women," Woolf described this cloying ideal of Victorian womanhood as the "angel in the house," the nurturing spectre from whom, she insisted, the modern woman writer must liberate herself. Years earlier, Jane Harrison had expressed a similar point. In her lecture "Scientiae Sacra Fames"—delivered in 1913 before the National Union of Women's Suffrage Societies—she argued that the "deeply depressing" arrangements of a traditional middle-class home offered a telling illustration of women's subordinate status. The drawing room, Harrison wrote, was designated the wife's territory, yet remained a public space, as "the room into which 'visitors are shown'—a room in which you can't possibly settle down to think, because anyone may come in at any moment." The husband's study, by contrast, was "a place inviolate, guarded by immemorial taboos," where the man of the house "thinks, and learns, and knows"; there were, Harrison noted, "rarely two chairs" in the room. The presence in almost every house-

Jane Harrison at Newnham College, circa 1912.

hold of these two polarized rooms, she suggested, served as an allegory for society's refusal to take women seriously. "The house where you don't and mustn't sit in the study is to me no home," wrote Harrison. "But, then, I have long known that I am no 'true woman.' One of the most ominous signs of the times is that woman is beginning to demand a study."

In her 1938 essay *Three Guineas*, writing of "the inanity, the pettiness, the spite, the tyranny, the hypocrisy, the immorality" of Victorian family life, with its emphasis on duty and the subjection of women to the whim of a father or husband, Woolf argued that women's oppression in public life is inextricable from their stifling experience in the traditional home: "the public and the private worlds are inseparably connected . . . the tyrannies and servilities of the one are the tyrannies and servilities of the other." If women are to play a meaningful role in society, Woolf insisted, their domestic arrangements have to suit and support them.

Whenever she wrote about the liberation of a shift in surroundings, as she did throughout her life, in fiction and in essays, Woolf was recalling her own departure, aged twenty-two, from her family home at 22 Hyde Park Gate in Kensington—a dark, dank Victorian house, its muffled furnishings suffused with the must of wine and cigars, and the memory of her parents' deaths—for a "new beginning" in a large house in Bloomsbury's Gordon Square, where she and her siblings agreed that "everything was going to be different." At 46 Gordon Square—the walls painted a fresh white, the front door a bright vermilion—Virginia no longer had to sit demurely in the drawing room, serving tea to her father and his eminent guests, or be led by her proprietorial half brothers around parades of potential suitors at dull society parties. Instead, she had the private sitting room she had dreamed of, while downstairs mixed groups of friends lounged into the early hours, discussing philosophy, art, and sex over whiskey or cocoa. Her friend Violet Dickinson gave her an inkpot as a housewarming gift, and within months Woolf published her first book reviews in a clerical weekly called the *Guardian* and the *Times Literary Supplement*. "Now we are free women," she wrote happily on receiving her first payslip. Woolf delighted in making her own living, risky as it was. (The siblings anxiously sold off pages from their parents' Thackeray manuscripts in order to keep up their rent payments.) The release provided by this house move—much mythologized in her autobiographical writing—shows how intimately a change in living situation can alter perspective; in moving to Bloomsbury, Woolf felt she had exchanged the "respectable mummified humbug" of 22 Hyde Park Gate for a new world of open conversation and professional possibility.

It's fitting that the story Woolf told of her birth as a writer and "free woman" should also be the story of a change of address. As their careers began and developed, as they contemplated their futures at times of private disarray, all the women in this book thought carefully about the sort of home they wanted to live in. Though they arrived at Mecklenburgh Square at different stages in life, moving there provided each of them with a fresh start at a critical moment: the way they each chose to set up home in the square was a bold declaration of who they were, and of the life they wanted to lead. It may seem paradoxical to use women's private homes as a starting point for an investigation into their public lives—a lens through which to examine their writing and careers, their politics and relationships. But each woman came to the square with firm hopes and ambitions—and as she asked how she personally wanted to live, she was also confronting the question of what kind of society she wanted to live in. Each was committed—in her personal life, and as a political position—to the importance of what Woolf called "intellectual freedom": "the right," she wrote, "to think one's own thoughts and to follow one's own pursuits." They didn't want to replicate the traditional pattern laid down for women's lives—that of Woolf's own mother, who "passed like a princess in a pageant from her supremely beautiful youth to marriage and motherhood, without awakenment." Instead, they resolved to earn their own livings, and to order their lives around their work—even if it meant forgoing a traditional family life in the process.

These women knew that, as Woolf wrote, "intellectual freedom depends upon material things": that the ability to write and live experimentally is contingent on practical circumstances not always in one's own control. They wanted and needed to find sustainable ways—through their writing, through teaching, translation, or editing—to earn the £500 a year which Woolf considered indispensable for a writer, to afford the rent for their rooms and maintain the independence for which they had fought. Each of them experienced significant advantages of class, race, and education; some were helped financially by inheritances or allowances from supportive families, though none so substantial that money was not a constant source of anxiety. But they knew that, despite these benefits and their own convictions, their positions as intellectuals remained tentative and insecure. In the interwar years, educated women were still seen as an aberration; popular cartoons portrayed "bluestockings" as wizened and haggard, smoking cigarettes and crushing men beneath their hobnailed boots, while scandalized *Daily Mail* headlines attributed the fall in the birth rate to women's flagrant neglect of their natural role. All these women were, at some point, denied the life they sought: refused access to the same educational opportunities as their brothers, pigeonholed into lower-status jobs or paid less than their male counterparts, marked out as second-class by universities that refused them official degrees, or encouraged to serve as muses to male authors. All were determined to research, write, and publish, but such acts of self-assertion were charged with the possibility of rejection: they had to convince others that their work was valuable, while also needing to convince themselves.

Biography is inevitably written—and read—from a position of authoritative hindsight, when a person's achievements are already acknowledged. It's hard to remember, from that perspective, that these lives might have turned out otherwise; to feel the note of desperation in Virginia Woolf's voice when, in 1911, she sums up her prospects as "to be 29 and unmarried—to be a failure—childless—insane too, no writer," or to appreciate H. D.'s and Dorothy L. Sayers's sincere fears, well before their legacies were assured, that their writing was not as good as that of the men around them who belittled their work. Sayers's greatest novel, *Gaudy Night*, would turn on the question of how women "cursed with both hearts and brains" might preserve their indepen-

dence and find intellectual stimulation without relinquishing the pleasures of partnership—a dilemma that occupied all the women in this
book. Although they expressed their investigations in very different
terms, they had to address the same questions while they decided
where and how they wanted to live as independent women: whether it
would be easier to reject marriage altogether than find a relationship
that wouldn't compromise their work; whether motherhood would
curtail the opportunities they had fought for; what creative sacrifices to
make in exchange for financial security. The exhilaration of taking
control of their living arrangements was only the beginning. "The
room is your own, but it is still bare," insisted Woolf, laying down a
gauntlet to her audience of women students. "It has to be furnished; it
has to be decorated; it has to be shared. How are you going to furnish
it, how are you going to decorate it? With whom are you going to
share it, and upon what terms? These, I think, are questions of the
utmost importance and interest. For the first time in history you are
able to ask them; for the first time you are able to decide for yourselves
what the answers should be."

But what brought these women to Bloomsbury, of all the places where
they might have lived? London, between the wars, was a fast-developing
metropolis: private houses were being knocked down to make way for
glass-fronted shops and blocks of smart flats, while electric trams and
motor cars edged out horse-drawn hansoms on the streets, the stench
of manure replaced by the hazards of motorized traffic. Central London, the heart of a global empire, was a microcosm of wider Europe,
with Little Italy in Clerkenwell, a French colony in Soho, and a German community—though depleted after riots and internments during
the First World War—in Fitzrovia. But the center of London's intellectual life—a radical hub of scholarship and literary production—was
Bloomsbury. University College London, soon branded "that Godless
Institution on Gower Street" for its refusal to make religion a criterion
for entry, was founded there in 1826, offering an affordable education
based not on theology but on science and the arts, while Bloomsbury

housed the first higher educational establishment for women (the Ladies' College in Bedford Square) and colleges opened specifically to provide evening classes for workers. Publishing houses congregated on side streets, while the area was well known for its bookshops, from Jacob Schwartz's Ulysses Bookshop on Bloomsbury Street, stocked with manuscripts he bought from Samuel Beckett, to the notoriously esoteric Birrell and Garnett's in Taviton Street, or Harold Monro's Poetry Bookshop on Devonshire Street (now Boswell Street), where crowds climbed a rickety staircase to the attic to hear famous poets debut new work over sherry. At the heart of Bloomsbury was the British Museum Reading Room, open for all to read and study with no admission charge. The library was lodged within the first public national museum in Britain, which had opened in 1753 in Montagu House, one of the area's seventeenth-century mansions. In 1857, thanks to the efforts of Keeper of Printed Books Anthony Panizzi, it unveiled a great library, its gilded ceiling painted to resemble the sky in swirls of blue and cream, its high dome—under which Virginia Woolf would stand feeling like "a thought in the huge bald forehead"—modeled on the Pantheon in Rome. The Reading Room established Bloomsbury as a democratic and welcoming place for writers, "having for its centre and its symbol," wrote *The Times* in 1894, "the great national storehouse of the learning of all ages and the arts of all mankind."

Early in the twentieth century, Bloomsbury was a byword for left-wing politics and modern culture. It was home to numerous artists and models from the Slade School of Fine Art on Gower Street, who crowded at night into each other's studios to dance the foxtrot around half-finished canvases and dusty assemblages for still lifes. Bloomsbury was known by the 1920s, of course, for the famous group who "lived in squares, painted in circles and loved in triangles," and for the general excesses of bohemian living, such that Stella Gibbons could refer in *Cold Comfort Farm* (1932) to "those Bloomsbury-cum-Charlotte-Street lions which exchanged their husbands and wives every other weekend in the most broad-minded fashion." The Trinidadian socialist C. L. R. James spent part of the 1930s in a Bloomsbury boardinghouse which was "aesthetically speaking one of the worst places in the world": nonetheless, he was struck by his perception of the "Bloomsbury girl," characterized by her wide reading, independent judgment, and determination that "men should treat her as an individual and not as a woman in the Victorian sense of the word." "If you want to live the intellectual life," he concluded, "Bloomsbury is the place."

Renowned for its affordable hotels, the area was particularly popular among travelers from overseas: in its pubs, lecture halls, and boardinghouses, Fabians met with Hindu progressivists, Australian students with Christian socialists. It was home, as a 1935 guidebook stated, to "learned people from all over the world"—from Tambimuttu, Tamil poet and founding editor of *Poetry London*, to the Chinese dramatist Lao She, who taught at the School of Oriental Studies just off Russell Square, to Krishna Menon, the Labour politician, leader of the India League and original editor of Penguin's Pelican series. Mulk Raj Anand, the Indian novelist and activist, came to Bloomsbury in the 1920s to study at University College London. By day he worked on philosophy in the British Museum; after hours he repaired to cafes and pubs—usually Bertorelli's, Poggioli, or the Museum Tavern—where he would share shortbread with Aldous Huxley, ponder Indian nationalism with T. S. Eliot, discuss race relations with Nancy Cunard, or debate the merits of *Ulysses* with a friendly bus conductor. "Bloomsbury appears in these conversations," he later wrote, "to be a much wider area than Virginia Woolf's drawing-room in Tavistock Square."

Bloomsbury's reputation was largely the result of an accident of architecture. In the eighteenth century, the area had been a pastureland, punctuated by occasional mansions set within elaborate pleasure gardens and rolling fields. But in 1800 the Duke of Bedford, who owned much of the land, instructed developers to mold it into an upper-middle-class suburb, comprising squares—modeled on Covent Garden's handsome piazza—of majestic townhouses with uniform facades. These were carefully designed for a traditional nuclear family: the father who went out to work via the carriage he kept in his mews at the back of the house; the central drawing room where the lady of the house presided, tended by servants who lived in their own basement quarters. Trade and business were to be prohibited on the estate, while private central gardens would promote an ambience of health and serenity. But the duke's ambitious building program quickly ran into difficulties. The wealthy tenants he had envisaged—lawyers and bankers seeking a sanctuary away from the city—were now competing for homes in the fashionable centers of Mayfair and St. James, near the royal parks and exclusive shops. The building of railway termini at Euston (in 1837) and King's Cross (1852) connected Bloomsbury directly to the wider world, but solidified the upper class's preference for the fresh air of the newly accessible outer suburbs, if not the leisured luxury of West London. The new mansions languished empty, and work on further squares ground to a halt. While the satirical press

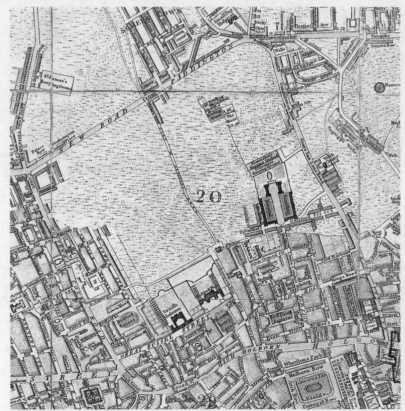

Map of Bloomsbury, John Cary (1795).

mocked Bloomsbury as a "remote and half-discovered region," a gauche wilderness inhabited only by the "semi-fashionable" middle classes, the duke began embittered lawsuits against illegal subtenants and makeshift private hotels.

Mecklenburgh Square was built between 1804 and 1825, on fields owned not by the Duke of Bedford but by the Foundling Hospital. This had been established in 1739, by the seafarer and philanthropist Thomas Coram, as the first home in England for orphaned and abandoned children. Women, often survivors of rape or suffering dire poverty, left their babies—sometimes just days old—in a basket hung at the gate, bearing a token by which the child might be identified at some later date, if a reunion ever proved feasible. Within a decade, the hospital provided a home for over four hundred infants on a site on

Map of Bloomsbury, Edward Stanford (1897).

Lamb's Conduit Field, a former duelling ground at what was then London's northernmost boundary. Coram had purchased the land from the Earl of Salisbury, who was persuaded to sell only on condition that the hospital bought all fifty-six acres, which it did with financial assistance from Parliament. But by 1789, the hospital was losing money fast; donations had dwindled and, despite fundraising efforts augmented by gifts from George Frideric Handel and William Hogarth, the governors were struggling to feed and clothe the rapidly growing number of children in their care.

After much deliberation, despite fears for the children's health in a "noxious" urban environment, the governors commissioned the architect Samuel Pepys Cockerell to develop an estate on the hospital's extensive freehold. Its main features were to be two large residential squares—Brunswick and Mecklenburgh—each with buildings on three sides only, to maintain an impression of expansive countryside. Cockerell's pupil Joseph Kay oversaw the ornate stucco architecture of Mecklenburgh Square's east side, with its Ionic columns and recesses in the style of John Nash's Regent's Park, which the Foundling governors admired so much that they paid him a bonus of eighty guineas and pledged to bury him on his death in the hospital's chapel. The houses were built around a large private garden, its flower beds bursting with roses and lilacs, and planted with plane trees, many of which still flourish today, some of the oldest in the city. A barrier, manned by a uniformed beadle, guarded the east side of the square, where residents complained they were "exposed to insult" from Gray's Inn Road. Despite occasional reports of prostitutes knocking on doors and using "such indecent and improper language that the wives and daughters of the inhabitants cannot but hear it while sitting in their parlours and drawing-rooms" (even by 1873, the square's by-laws forbade "improper or unbecoming language," as well as dogs, fireworks, and games of cricket), the Foundling Estate managed to attract residents impressed by its serenity and its respiratory advantages. As Isabella in Jane Austen's *Emma* informs her hypochondriac father: "Our part of London is very superior to most others! You must not confound us with London in general, my dear sir. The neighbourhood of Brunswick Square is very different from almost all the rest. We are so very airy!"

Nevertheless, Bloomsbury's status as a desirable residential quarter remained in doubt for decades. When Woolf and her siblings moved to Gordon Square in 1904, her family was scandalized by their "bad" choice of district, having read William Makepeace Thackeray's 1848 novel *Vanity Fair*, which portrays Bloomsbury as an "odious vulgar place" to be avoided at all costs by the socially ambitious. But the westward swing of fashion over the nineteenth century established the area as a shabby bohemia associated with the marginalized and the revolutionary. Low rents enabled philanthropic and political projects to take root in the huge, unoccupied houses, run by activists who studied and taught at the universities and free hospitals which had opened nearby. The area's association with feminism was longstanding: Mary Wollstonecraft wrote her *Vindication of the Rights of Woman* (1792) while living on Store Street, and a century later the leading suffrage campaigns made their headquarters in Bloomsbury. Itself home to several prominent suffragettes, Mecklenburgh Square became the site for the beginnings of Virginia Woolf's feminism in 1910, when she lent her efforts to the cause by addressing envelopes for the People's Suffrage Federation in an office she described as full of "ardent but educated young women, and brotherly clerks . . . just like a Wells novel." Established in 1909 with nearly five hundred founding members including Jane Harrison, Bertrand Russell, and Beatrice Webb, the PSF demanded votes for all, with no restrictions based on property ownership. It shared offices at 34 Mecklenburgh Square—a building known unofficially as "Reform House"—with groups offering legal advice to workers, campaigning against low wages and unfair labor conditions, and organizing strikes: a former resident remembered the square as constantly abuzz with "a colony of workers," enacting reform for women and the working classes.

As well as creating a physical network of progressive organizations, the housing surfeit in Bloomsbury inadvertently enabled women who were seeking an alternative and fulfilling way of life to find an affordable home there, surrounded by opportunity and like-minded neighbors. As the Foundling and Bedford Estates struggled to fill their houses with families, they reluctantly allowed the uninhabited mansions to be broken up into flats, or knocked down to make room for housing cooperatives offering convenient accommodation for single people. In 1889, Charles Booth's *Maps Descriptive of London Poverty* found that Mecklenburgh Square had "principally one family to each house, 2 or 3 servants normal, sometimes 4 or 5." But in 1909, the Foundling Estate relaxed its rules prohibiting boardinghouses in its prize square, and most of the buildings became multiple-occupancy. And this concession occurred at a moment when household organization was at the center of heated debates about society, modernity, and how to live.

At the turn of the twentieth century, large numbers of newly educated single women, who wanted to enter a career rather than move straight from a father's house to a husband's, needed living spaces that would allow them to pursue that ambition and demonstrate their rejection of the traditional domestic role. Not only were they demanding a study, as Harrison had suggested; they also wanted to revolutionize what a home could be. In the Victorian mindset, which kept work and home as far apart as possible, Bloomsbury was deemed too close to the

Mecklenburgh Square, east and north sides, circa 1904.

city's commercial center to be an appropriate residence for a genteel family. But for modern men and women who aspired to live outside that paradigm, Bloomsbury now offered a chance to live alone or with a friend in rented flats or boardinghouses, usually presided over by a landlady who lived on the premises and provided meals (of varying quality) for her tenants. Residents would sacrifice total privacy for the convenience of furnished lodgings; some embraced community living, while others relished the ability to dash into town whenever they pleased, to entertain friends casually, and to be self-sufficient. While newspaper advertisements for Mecklenburgh Square in the early 1800s had tried to emphasize the area's respectability ("a genteel, commodious, and remarkably cheerful family residence, desirably situated"), those a century later struck a very different tone: "high-class service flatlets, prices include breakfast"; "Boarding House for lady workers and students: breakfast and dinner, full board on Sundays: gas fires and rings on own meters: moderate terms." The writer Thomas Burke portrayed these packed houses as "nests of the sorrier sort of bordel," while an article in the *Saturday Review* criticized Bloomsbury as having "sunk in public estimation to a dreary patch of second-rate boardinghouses." But others saw this new form of living as a pleasing symptom of the way women's horizons were beginning to widen. A 1900 study entitled "Women Workers: How They Live, How They Wish to Live" declared Bloomsbury "the beloved, the chosen of working women." At last, here was a district of the city where a room of one's own could be procured.

Today, Bloomsbury flats sell for millions, well out of reach for any aspiring writer without independent means. But in the interwar years, as Anand suggested, the area was by no means the exclusive preserve of a wealthy elite. In 1889, Booth had classed most of Bloomsbury as "middle-class, well-to-do," but noted that the eastern side in particular was marked by patches of grave poverty, where slums and brothels had taken over the empty buildings. For Dorothy L. Sayers, who set several crime novels in the area, Bloomsbury was a violent underworld where "people are always laying one another out," and where "births and drunks and wife-beatings are pretty common"; in Margery Allingham's 1938 story "The Case of the Longer View," Bloomsbury is "a sort of halfway house. If you lived here you were either going up or coming down." At times of uncertainty in their own lives, the women in this book were attracted to Bloomsbury for its sense of anonymity and transience, as well as its literary reputation—but all were aware that such freedom was contingent on economic stability. For others who congregated around the area's cheap boardinghouses, a bedsit might be less a sanctuary than a prison. Several of Jean Rhys's novels depict vulnerable women who scrape together the rent for their dingy rooms "in Paddington or obscurer Bloomsbury" with funds accrued from men, mostly with homes and wives, in tacit or explicit exchange for sexual favors; in Katherine Mansfield's story "Pictures," independence is a precarious burden for Ada Moss, an out-of-work actress at perpetual risk of eviction, whose "room, a Bloomsbury top-floor back, smelled of soot and face powder and the paper of fried potatoes she brought in for supper the night before." If freedom requires a room of one's own, maintaining that room requires money and a support network to give one the confidence to flout society's disapproval: safety and success, in Bloomsbury, were never to be taken for granted.

But for women able and eager to subvert domestic norms, Bloomsbury signaled possibility. When she first arrived there in 1904, Woolf instantly felt "at the centre of things": the roar of traffic, the hum of barrel organs, and the shouts of vegetable-sellers through the windows, after "the muffled silence of Hyde Park Gate," gave her a delicious feeling of freedom and proximity to the outside world. In Woolf's 1919 novel *Night and Day*, Katharine Hilbery (who lives with her parents in Kensington, where her passion for mathematics is stifled by domestic duties) looks up at the bedsit window of her friend Mary Datchet (a suffrage worker), who is hauling her furniture against the walls to make space for the meetings of "a society for the free discussion of everything." She instantly sees how Mary has flourished in this casual set-up: "in such a room one could work—one could have a life of one's own." One of the greatest twentieth-century articulations of Bloomsbury's liberating potential is Dorothy Richardson's *Pilgrimage* (published between 1915 and 1938), a modernist novel sequence that was trailblazing in its stream-of-consciousness form as well as in its plot. After her father's bankruptcy and her mother's suicide, Miriam Henderson, a dental secretary, boards alone in a cramped Bloomsbury attic, where she can "live, in freedom, hidden, on her pound a week," and considers her "triumphant faithful latchkey" a symbol of her independence. She enjoys having her own door, to open or close at will, and is able to leave her things "half unpacked about the floor," and read her books while London shines through the window. The writer Bryher, who lived with H. D. from 1920, described Richardson as "the Baedeker of all our early experiences." As was the case for all the subjects of this book, Miriam's search for a new home encapsulates a more fundamental search: for a place in society where she can be free to express herself as an individual, rather than abdicating her identity to the conventions of her sex.

If these changes in the home mirrored a change in women's public roles, they were also a symptom of a wider shift in attitudes, which Woolf connected, in *A Room of One's Own*, with the way women wrote, and the way they were written about: "This is an important book, the critic assumes, because it deals with war. This is an insignificant book because it deals with the feelings of women in a drawing-room." Assessing the pernicious forces which had long prevented women's writing from being taken seriously (despite men consistently extolling their mysteries and allure in fiction and verse), Woolf called on her audience, having killed the "angel in the house," to write openly about their own lives, about their mothers and grandmothers and their friendships with other women, and ultimately to "rewrite history." Her own final, unfinished project, begun amid the air raids at 37 Mecklenburgh Square, planned to offer a history of English literature which would uncover a range of "anonymous" voices from the past. As she worked on her book, Woolf reread the work of Jane Harrison and of Eileen Power, whose erudite, imaginative history-writing performed exactly the sort of excavation Woolf herself wanted to read and to write.

Square Haunting takes up Woolf's call for a different sort of history: it is a biography of five great women, about feelings and drawing rooms, but also about work, politics, literature, and community. And, indeed, about war, which affected each of these lives deeply. In his autobiography, H. D.'s husband Richard Aldington described the years between 1918 and 1939 as "the long armistice": a time of upheaval, of unease, of international tension, but of artistic creativity and experimental living too. These decades were haunted by the aftermath of the First World War, and by increasing anxiety about an impending second conflict, while Britain wavered between nostalgia for the Victorian past and a keen impulse toward modernity. Developments in psychoanalysis, birth control, and art; industrial strikes; and greatly increased possibilities for travel were beginning to expand people's understanding both of themselves and of the wider world. Revolutions in China and Russia provoked passionate debates about the future of democracy, while campaigns for Home Rule in Ireland and in India called into question the legitimacy of the British Empire. Once women's suffrage had been achieved, then extended in 1928 to all women over twenty-one, feminist activity continued on subjects such as abortion, divorce law, and equal pay, but many activists now turned their energies toward work for peace, placing faith in the League of Nations' vision of international cooperation.

Each chapter of this book offers an account of its subject during the time she happened to live in Mecklenburgh Square. My portraits are not cradle-to-grave biographies, nor are they comprehensive. Instead, they offer snapshots of significant moments in these lives which might, in a broader narrative, be skated over. By examining these separate lives together, through the prism of their shared address, I hope to unearth resonances which deepen an understanding of each individually. These chapters capture each woman in a moment of transition, of hope tempered by uncertainty, as she left behind a version of herself in the home or community she was abandoning, and sought to reinvent her life in a new place. For Dorothy L. Sayers and Eileen Power, arrival in Mecklenburgh Square was a moment of pure invigoration; for H. D. and Virginia Woolf, it was a disruption marked by serious ambivalence. During the time all these women spent there—whether months or years—they grappled with problems and ideas which occupied them throughout their lives; they produced ground-breaking writing, initiated radical collaborations, started (and ended) significant relationships, and thought deeply about their values and ambitions. This book began as the story of one small Bloomsbury square, but the more I learned about each of these women, the more I realized how far afield their loyalties, influences, and interests stretched: through Russian literature, French art, Chinese politics, to their peers and friends from all over the world. They were all interested in personal freedom, but were alert also to the ways in which their private struggles intersected with those of others, across place or time, race or class. And their lives in the square were in no way insular, their influence not confined to its boundaries. The concerns and events of the wider world, at this fraught time, were not just a backdrop to personal dramas: they affected every aspect of life in Mecklenburgh Square, as these women worked to shape a more equal future.

We enter Mecklenburgh Square at a time of significant turmoil, in and outside its walls: a time of endings and beginnings, of fleeting hope and of serious despair. In his novel *Kangaroo*, D. H. Lawrence wrote that "it was in 1915 the old world ended. In the winter of 1915–1916 the spirit of the old London collapsed, the city, in some way, perished, perished from being a heart of the world, and became a vortex of broken passions, lusts, hopes, fears and horrors." We begin in 1916, with Zeppelin airships droning over Mecklenburgh Square, a flickering candle illuminating a half-finished manuscript, and an abiding dread that "the war will never be over."

H. D.
(1886–1961)

44 Mecklenburgh Square
February 1916–March 1918

Changing partners, changing hands, dancing round, in a
Bacchic orgy of war-time love and death.

—H. D., *Bid Me to Live* (1960)

When Hilda Doolittle left her Vienna hotel one afternoon in the autumn of 1934, she found the street littered with golden strips of paper, folded in half like the mottos from Christmas crackers. She stooped to unravel a handful, and saw they were printed with short messages: "Hitler gives bread," "Hitler gives work." Startled, she dropped them in the gutter and continued to Berggasse 19 for an appointment with her psychoanalyst, Professor Sigmund Freud. Barbed wire barricaded the streets, and soldiers with guns lurked on corners, reminding her of grainy photographs of the American Civil War. On the pavement, leading right to the professor's door, were chalked swastikas.

In *Tribute to Freud* (1956), her memoir of this period, H. D. wrote that her sessions were intended to confront "my own personal little Dragon of war-terror" and fortify her to face the likelihood of a second world war. But she had also entered analysis in the hope that working with Freud would help her clear the "psychic weeds" that were stifling her writing and had driven her to the cusp of a breakdown. Freud encouraged H. D. to let her mind wander unfettered: to take herself out of his room—crammed with ancient objects among teetering piles of books and letters: shards of red Pompeiian stone, Egyptian cloth, painted wooden coffins, a statue of a sphinx—and travel back in time to the bomb-stricken London of 1916. As the professor probed her unconscious, seeking the origins of her mysterious block, H. D. found that she kept returning to a brief period of the First World War when she had lived with her then husband, Richard Aldington, and various others at 44 Mecklenburgh Square. In letters from Vienna to her partner, Bryher, and later in her memoir, H. D. described how Freud persuaded her to contemplate an era with which she had "carefully avoided coming to terms," the resurfacing of which "made a violent purple-patch in my analysis." Sensing that this spell remained an obstacle for H. D., Freud advised her to resume work on the autobiographical novel, set in her Mecklenburgh Square flat, which she had begun in Cornwall in 1918. To Bryher, H. D. confessed that Freud "seems to believe . . . that it would be best for me to make this vol. of mine about 1913–1920 explicit." "Evidently," she wrote in resignation, "I blocked the whole of the 'period' and if I can skeleton-in a vol. about it, it will break the clutch . . . the 'cure' will be, I fear me, writing that damn vol. straight, as history."

Over her long career, H. D. achieved a reputation as one of the greatest poets of her generation. In 1960, she became the first woman to be awarded the Merit Medal for Poetry by the American Academy of Arts and Letters in recognition of her innovative, complex body of work, which interrogated gender and myth, language and modernity, in restless pursuit of pattern and meaning. At her death in 1961, she was lauded as a genius and promptly forgotten about, until she was rediscovered amid the second-wave feminist project to reclaim lost "mothers." Her poems appeared in new editions, several works of scholarship and biography emerged, and her unpublished novels—which foregrounded her intimate relationships with women—were released, with moving biographical introductions by her daughter, Perdita Schaffner.

Yet still H. D.'s life is often told as the story of her relationships with men: her youthful engagement to Ezra Pound, her turbulent marriage to Richard Aldington, her strange liaison—an affair? a creative disagreement? a wholly fictionalized encounter?—with D. H. Lawrence. She has been pitied as the victim of a series of painful sexual rejections, or admired askance as the ethereal fantasy whose beauty and eccentricity inspired great work by great men. But more than that, her life is the story of her attempts to step out of their shadow and establish an identity on her own terms—a struggle rooted in Mecklenburgh Square.

"All your life," says the narrator in H. D.'s novel *HERmione* (written around 1926 but not published until 1981), "you will retain one or two bits of color with which all your life will be violently or delicately tinted." The years she spent in Mecklenburgh Square during the First World War were so critical to H. D.'s sense of herself that she spent the next four decades trying to make sense of them. She worked compulsively on a cycle of autobiographical works that she considered one single novel, in which she transposed the dramatic events of that time to different settings, experimented with perspective, style, and narrative form, altered characterization, motive, and timescale. On most of her finished manuscripts, she wrote the word "DESTROY." H. D. began working on "the novel" in July 1918, shortly after she left Mecklenburgh Square, and continued to rework the material, in versions more or less distinct, until 1960, when a book was finally published under the title *Bid Me to Live*. When the earlier drafts—*HERmione*, *Asphodel*, *Paint It Today* (the latter two written around 1921, and both published in 1992)—finally appeared in print, they revealed H. D. as a writer of elegant modernist prose as well as verse, but further complicated the picture of her life. H. D. never wrote the story "straight," as she had apparently intended, but had composed multiple contradictory versions which could not possibly all represent the truth of events. Each of these strange and fascinating novels—repetitive, fragmentary, laden with dream imagery and classical allusion—explores one character's inner life across a series of ambivalent relationships. She encounters idealized but arrogant men who threaten to challenge her development as an artist, and women who seem to offer comfort and understanding, yet who hold within them an alarming power to engulf and obliterate her. All turn on the protagonist's efforts to dispel past trauma and rediscover her ability to write. In writing about her past, H. D. was trying to take control of her public presentation, to challenge the myths that others had always created about her. But if writing was to be a way for H. D. to present her own story, she still had to establish exactly who she was.

In her novels, in her analysis, in letters, and in interviews, H. D. would offer wildly inconsistent accounts of herself and those around her. Although she claimed that all her protagonists "are of course . . . the same woman," each of her novels is attributed to a separate writer, their various names listed clearly on the manuscripts, as if to distance herself not only from the character within, but also from the authorial persona. She wanted *Bid Me to Live* to appear under the pseudonym Delia Alton, but her publisher insisted that it would be advantageous for publicity to use the famous name H. D., to which she very reluctantly agreed, though she drew the line at supplying a photograph of herself to accompany the text. The use of initials had been Pound's idea: in 1912, she had shown him a sheaf of early works over buns in the British Museum tearoom, an event which became famous as the founding myth of Imagist poetry. "But Dryad," exclaimed Pound, "this is poetry." Seizing a pen, he altered some words, slashed through some lines, and—when satisfied—scrawled at the bottom the assignation which would both propel and constrain her career: "H. D. Imagiste." She was flattered to be held up as the figurehead of Pound's new movement, and glad to shake off the sluggish implications of her surname as well as the associations of her gender. But despite the acclaim she won under this name during her life, she never felt comfortable being known as the protégée of Pound. "H. D.," to her, always remained a name linked to her early poetry, and to a literary scene she came to find suffocating. She felt the signature—bestowed without her consent— restricted her to a fixed identity that she would spend her life attempting to escape.

With the publication of *Bid Me to Live*, she made a dramatic break with the past. The novel—a compelling work of late modernism, shot through with a dreamlike surrealism—is an evocative portrait of Mecklenburgh Square in wartime, and a dissection of the unlikely ménage that occupied the flat. H. D., then seventy-three, provocatively told an interviewer from *Newsweek* who visited her in the Swiss sanatorium where she was living that the book was "completely autobiographical": "It's just that, word for word," she told him. "It is a *roman à clef*, and the keys are easy enough to find. I even thought there might be some libelous material in it, but some lawyers said no. I am Julia. And all the others are real people." It was clear enough to knowledgeable readers that Rafe Ashton, the bumbling husband, was a portrait of Richard Aldington, whom H. D. had married in 1913; that Bella was his lover, Arabella Yorke; that debonair Frederico and his wife Elsa were D. H. and Frieda Lawrence; that the "huge drawing-room in Bloomsbury" was the first-floor room at 44 Mecklenburgh Square. But the "truth" presented in the book is cocooned in layers of fiction; in finally publishing an account of these years, H. D. was motivated by something deeper than a desire for documentary realism. In 1921 she had shown her friend John Cournos an early version, insisting that it was "not intended as a work of art—at least, not as it stands. It is a means to an end. I want to clear up an old tangle."

For a biographer, the palimpsest of fictions surrounding H. D.'s life is as frustrating as it is intriguing. Time spent sorting through the novels, cross-referencing their characters and descriptions, comparing plot details with contemporary letters and with the fiction and memoirs others wrote about the same events, reveals more mysteries than answers. The impetuous bonfire Richard Aldington made (and later regretted) of a shabby suitcase, stuffed with a bundle of H. D.'s wartime letters from him and Lawrence and abandoned in the basement of 44 Mecklenburgh Square after its inhabitants had dispersed, has ensured that an account of this period can only be partial. A biography offers one version of a life, and H. D. lived several. But whether or not the events, conversations, and betrayals described in *Bid Me to Live* actually happened in the way she evokes, or even occurred at all, its composition was clearly essential for H. D. Not only did this work help her come to terms with complex relationships and emotions rooted in the war years, it also provided a space for her to address deeper questions about writing, gender, violence, and power, and finally set to rest a crisis of confidence and identity which had haunted her since those complicated years in Mecklenburgh Square.

From her childhood, Hilda Doolittle felt like an outsider. She was born in Bethlehem, Pennsylvania, the only girl among five brothers: two sisters had not survived past infancy, and like Virginia Woolf she later became keenly aware that her very existence was contingent on the premature demise of her father's first wife. "Why was it always a girl who had died?" she asks ominously in *The Gift*, a memoir which begins with the young Hilda weeping for the women she had never met, and wondering whether she too was fated to a life of thwarted potential and limited horizons. Her mother, Helen, was descended from one of the original members of the mystical Protestant order known as the Moravian Brethren, a sect shunned by the traditional church for its arcane rituals. Helen had been informed by a fortune-teller that she would have one child who would be especially "gifted," a prophecy which left her daughter feeling a failure. "How could I know," H. D. later wrote, "that this apparent disappointment that her children were not 'gifted' was in itself her own sense of inadequacy and frustration, carried a step further?" Helen was a keen musician who gave up singing after her husband complained about the noise, and was convinced that only her brother had inherited the vision and talent that, in Moravian belief, passed down through the generations. Like Woolf's mother, Julia, Helen was the archetypal "angel in the house," whose devotion to her husband's work and deference to his opinions came to represent, to her daughter, the suffocating confines of traditional femininity. When she thought back through her mother, H. D. was confronted with a disheartening heritage of silence and "morbid" self-effacement: nonetheless, she came to believe that she derived her own "imaginative faculties" from her mother's squandered inheritance.

When Hilda was nine, the family moved to Philadelphia, where her father, Charles Doolittle, had been appointed a professor of astron-

H. D. in Mecklenburgh Square, 1917.

omy; to his daughter's wonder, he would go out at night to observe the stars, and concentrate so hard that sometimes his beard would freeze to his telescope. Having studied at various Philadelphia schools and seminaries, Hilda entered Bryn Mawr College in 1905, but dropped out after three semesters and dedicated herself instead to her writing. She began, her schoolfriend William Carlos Williams recalled, by splashing ink all over her clothes "to give her a feeling of freedom."

Williams had always admired her "provocative indifference to rule and order"—her masculine dress, her love of walking in storms, her spontaneous laughter. But her triumphant rejection of one sort of authority only ushered in another. "I don't suppose it was the fault of Bryn Mawr that I didn't like it," she wrote in 1950. "My second year was broken into or across by my affair with EP." She had met Pound at a Halloween party in 1901, when she was fifteen; he was a year older, dressed as a Tunisian prince in a green robe. Over the next few years, he appointed himself responsible for Hilda's cultural education, taking her to operas, compiling reading lists for her (Ibsen, Balzac, Rossetti, Bernard Shaw, and his own sonnets, which he composed daily while brushing his teeth) and introducing her to Brie ("You have no palates," he sneered when she confessed she didn't like it). He called her "Dryad," and as a silent woodland muse she haunts his earliest poems, later published as *Hilda's Book*.

Pound's cosmopolitan company provided a thrilling alternative to her parents' home, where she felt closeted and misunderstood. She knew she wanted a different life, for which her small world offered no example. But when their tentative engagement ended in 1908 with Pound's abrupt departure for Europe, Hilda was secretly as relieved as were her family, who had been suspicious of Pound's erratic tendencies and rumors of his multiple affairs. Pound was imperious and overbearing, and preoccupied with his own ambitions; at this time he was not interested in Hilda's writing. H. D. later reflected that, had they married, "Ezra would have destroyed me and the centre they call 'Air and Crystal' of my poetry." In her novel *HERmione*, based closely on her Philadelphia years, H. D.'s protagonist becomes distracted by the legend of Undine, the mermaid who gives up her voice in exchange for the feet that allow her to live on land with her prince: Hermione realizes that marriage would consign her irrevocably to the role of muse, not poet. The pattern established in this formative affair set the parameters for H. D.'s subsequent relationships: Pound was the first in a series of men whom she later called her "initiators," to whom she made herself desperately vulnerable, yet against whose guidance she had to eventually rebel. Having avoided a future dictated by Pound's arrogance, Hilda now set to enacting her escape from Philadelphia on her own terms.

In July 1911, Hilda also sailed to Europe, planning to spend a summer traveling and seeing the sights. With her was Frances Gregg, a poet, artist, and mystic whom Hilda had met the previous year, and with whom she had fallen deeply in love. H. D. later described Frances as "a sort of alter ego," whose intimacy had filled "like a blue flame" the absence left by Pound. Frances was the sister and soul mate for whom Hilda yearned; they called themselves twins and witches, and the intensity of their bond—developed over long evenings writing, confiding, and incanting spells together in Hilda's tiny bedroom—cemented her longing to defy convention and live a life untrammeled by her parents' narrow expectations. It was not to Ezra but to Frances that Hilda wrote her first love poems, inspired by a translation of Theocritus which Pound had given her.

Accompanied by Frances's watchful mother, the pair stayed first in "a dreadful little place" on the outskirts of Paris—where they were disappointed to find that the *Mona Lisa* had been stolen from the Louvre—before traveling to London and finding lodgings on Bernard Street in Bloomsbury. "Arrive Sunday," wrote Hilda with feigned nonchalance in a postcard to Pound. "Hope to see you some time." Delighted by the prospect of new company, Pound immediately swept the women into the stylish milieu he had established in the city. "Our reception in London was surprisingly cordial," wrote a happy Hilda to Pound's mother, Isabel, "due to the efforts of his friends spurred on by himself." Pound, well known in the London literary scene (and in the tabloid gossip columns) for his experimental verse and flamboyant dress, whisked them to crowded tea parties of fashionable suffragettes at the home of the literary editors Violet Hunt and Ford Madox Hueffer (later Ford Madox Ford), to hedonistic variety shows at avant-garde Soho nightclub The Cave of the Golden Calf, and to glamorous soirées in elegant apartments where Hilda admired the feel of the soft carpets, the scent of flowers, the witticisms of fellow guests, the whispered gossip of stolid footmen.

She spent her days wandering around the city, exploring its parks, alleyways, coffee shops, and galleries; over cocktails in W. B. Yeats's flat, she debated the merits of Georgian poetry, and she visited the studios of artists including Jacob Epstein, Wyndham Lewis, and Henri Gaudier-Brzeska, whose abstract, Egyptian-influenced work, with its emphasis on rough-hewn authenticity, Pound saw as sharing a sensibility with the modern poetry he was championing. She was taken to a suffrage meeting by Lilian Sauter, sister of the novelist John Galsworthy; she turned the thrilling experience into a short story, raw with anger at the injustice of women's position. Enthralled by London's possibilities, Hilda felt she had at last found somewhere she belonged, and tried to persuade Frances to stay on with her and share a flat in Bloomsbury. Already, the area represented to her exactly the life she wanted, one of open-mindedness and literary activity. But in October, Frances returned to America with her mother, and the following April, Hilda was stung by a letter announcing her engagement to a man named Louis Wilkinson. She was bewildered at this renunciation of the life they had devised together as modern women—eschewing marriage, embracing difference and creativity. But she refused to contemplate returning home herself. Like Virginia Woolf's flight from Kensington to Bloomsbury, her departure from America for England had been a way of seeking "freedom of mind and spirit"—the chance to establish a wholly new identity of her own. "I had to GET AWAY to make good," she later wrote to Bryher. "Can you see how London at least left me *free*?" Her abiding sense of alienation would propel her poetry; separated from her strict parents by an ocean, her displacement gave her the courage to begin to work out who she was, or wanted to be.

H. D. would return to America only a handful of times in her life. In the bustle of London's bohemian circles, she found the stimulation that Philadelphia could not provide, and a sympathetic circle of friends whose support diluted Pound's ongoing insistence that he knew what was best for her. "You're a great success," Pound told her admiringly. With her short hair and elegant, waifish figure (to her teenage embarrassment—though to the benefit of the local basketball team— she was almost six feet tall), Hilda Doolittle cut a chic silhouette in the new fashion of flowing Greek-style gowns. Acquaintances were intrigued by her passion for ancient Greek (which she had taught herself), her musical voice with only the slightest transatlantic accent, and the look of "extreme vulnerability" on her face. In her novel *Asphodel* (a sequel to *HERmione*), London fills the heroine with a new confidence, in her work and in herself: when her fiancé insists that she move out of "that infernal Bloomsbury," Hermione staunchly refuses, associating her dingy bedsitter with her first intoxicating experience of freedom. But Hilda did not live alone for long: toward the end of 1911, her new friend Brigit Patmore introduced her at a party to Richard Aldington.

Then aged nineteen, Aldington was six years Hilda's junior, a striking man whom the editor Harriet Monroe described, to his annoyance, as looking like a footballer. He had prematurely ended his English degree at University College London when his father's money ran out. (He would later claim that he had been expelled for an unspecified rebellion.) Friends and family had entreated him to take a well-paid job in a city firm, but Aldington had instead found a position as assistant to a Fleet Street sports editor, which he considered a stopgap until he could establish himself in a purely literary career. By the time he met Hilda, he had already published poems and translations in several journals, and was regularly skipping meals, spending his money on books instead.

Together, they gazed unhurriedly at friezes and manuscripts in the British Museum; since, being under twenty-one, Aldington was not allowed into the Reading Room, Hilda would copy out Greek poetry for them to translate together in cafes or at home. In the autumn of 1912, when the Doolittles arrived for a tour of Europe, Aldington joined the family in Italy. "R. & H. appear to be falling in love with each other somewhere en route from Napoli," wrote Pound in amusement, having met the party in Venice. They shared a deep love of antiquity, poetic aspirations, and a rejection of middle-class values; what bonded them most powerfully was their mutual desire to forge a relationship free of hierarchy and convention. Hilda had been doubtful about the prospect of commitment, but Aldington seemed different from Pound:

a marriage of true equals, she began to feel, would not supplant her own identity but rather enable her to live and write within a creative partnership which could itself be a way to freedom, each inspiring the other to greater work. On October 18, 1913—at the same Kensington registry office which witnessed the weddings of Katherine Mansfield and John Middleton Murry, Nora and James Joyce, and Frieda and D. H. Lawrence—Hilda Doolittle and Richard Aldington were married. Their marriage certificate shows that he was twenty-one, she twenty-seven; while his occupation was given as "poet," hers was left blank, struck through with a line.

For some time, Hilda, Aldington, and Pound had been living respectively at 6, 8, and 10 Church Walk in Kensington. After their marriage, she and Aldington moved to 5 Holland Place Chambers, eager to establish a home of their own—but were somewhat perturbed when Pound immediately took a room across the hall, claiming he needed a place to fence with Yeats. In their flat, the Aldingtons worked side by side on their poetry, occasionally interrupted by Pound bursting in to borrow household items or recite a new verse. Soon, fed up with these intrusions, the pair moved to 7 Christchurch Place in Hampstead, and discovered that their relationship with Ezra improved when they could retain a distance from "Kensingtonian squabbles & intrigues." For Hilda, this move was particularly significant. She was working hard to develop her own poetic style, writing spare, concentrated pieces imbued with dynamic force and a quiet intensity, often taking inspiration from Greek mythology or nature—the beauty of a stalk tangled in wet pebbles, the wind on the ocean. Her long 1912 poem "Hermes of the Ways" opens at the borderline between land and sea:

The hard sand breaks,
and the grains of it
are clear as wine.

Far off over the leagues of it,
the wind,

playing on the wide shore,
piles little ridges,
and the great waves
break over it.

When she showed this poem to Pound that afternoon in the British Museum tearoom, he was ecstatic. With a rallying cry of "Make it new!," Pound was determined to lead a radical literary movement which would loosen poetry from Victorian and Georgian romanticism by a direct treatment of the subject, which centered on clear images and included "nothing that you couldn't, in some circumstance, in the stress of some emotion, actually say." In Hilda's work, Pound saw the voice that could represent his ideal to the wider world. To that end, he sent three of her poems to Harriet Monroe, the editor of *Poetry*, an influential magazine with a reputation for placing newly discovered talent alongside established names. "Am sending you some modern stuff by an American," he wrote. "I say modern, for it is in the laconic speech of the Imagistes . . . Objective—no slither; direct—no excessive use of adjectives, no metaphors that won't permit examination. It's straight talk, straight as the Greek!"

In January 1913, *Poetry* printed "Hermes of the Ways," "Epigram," and "Orchard" by "H. D. Imagiste." The accompanying biographical note remained enigmatic: "H. D.," it read, is "an American lady resident abroad, whose identity is unknown to the editor." Seeing her poems in print under Pound's label left Hilda with a surreal sense of invisibility, as if her work were not really hers; as if, deprived of her name, she might not even exist at all. Tellingly, she decided not to mention anything to Pound directly, but after the first publication she wrote privately to Monroe to ask her to remove "Imagiste" from her name. Thereafter, her poems were signed simply "H. D."

Pound later claimed that he invented Imagism in order to launch the career of his "Dryad," gathering around her a group of sympathetic poets, among them F. S. Flint, T. E. Hulme, and Ford Madox Hueffer. Aldington would come to take a dimmer view: Imagism, according to him, was "simply advertising bull-dust." The movement soon ran into trouble, as Pound's ego began to override the group's literary ambitions. In July 1913 Amy Lowell, an eccentric and aristocratic Bostonian poet with a huge car and a cigar habit, had arrived in London, eager to meet the Imagists. She was willing to expend energy and money on Imagism, and over candied fruit in her suite at the Berkeley Hotel, then on Piccadilly, she offered to fund the publication of a regular Imagist anthology, its contents selected collectively by the group. Pound, his sovereignty under threat, complained that Lowell was turning Imagism into "Amygism," and switched his attentions to a new movement, Vorticism.

On July 30, 1914, Lowell arranged a dinner party at the Berkeley for the remaining Imagists, who appreciated her democratic and undogmatic approach. Later, in his memoirs, Aldington recalled that conversation turned to gossip about a writer recently returned to London after years in Europe, who had been invited to dinner but had not appeared: David Herbert Lawrence. Someone had heard that he was tubercular; in hushed tones, another conspiratorially informed H. D.— who had not yet met him—that he was a charlatan who had run away with a married baroness. His latest novel, someone else lamented, was sex-mad, and was sure to be suppressed. Seeking a moment's peace, Aldington moved away to the window, from where he could make out a headline on a newsstand at the corner of the Ritz Hotel on Green Park: "Germany and Russia at War, Official." As he watched, the proprietor unfolded a fresh poster and tacked it to the stand: "British Army Mobilised." Aldington remembered glancing back into the room, "where friendly people were talking unhurriedly of civilised things." At that point, Lawrence strode in, wearing evening dress. He had just been with his friend Edward Marsh, private secretary to Winston Churchill, then First Lord of the Admiralty. Marsh had told him bad news: Britain was about to declare war on Germany.

On Tuesday, August 4, 1914, H. D. left the British Museum to join the expectant crowd gathered in front of Buckingham Palace. "We want war!" shouted a member of the mob; another yelled back, "We don't!"

At ten past eleven, a somber King George V appeared on the balcony, steeled to offer reassurance to his subjects. A few minutes earlier, following a Privy Council meeting at the palace, Churchill had telegrammed the fleet with an order to commence hostilities against Germany. The golden age, as H. D. would later see it, was brutally ended; her newfound coterie was broken up. The directness the Imagists valued was undermined by a slippery public discourse of rumor and propaganda, while H. D.'s memories of happiness in Europe were obliterated by images of trenches and mud. The official mantra remained "business as usual," but H. D. and Aldington could no longer find payment for their literary work; novels and poems were encouraged to take patriotic subjects, and journals disappeared or were incorporated into propaganda outlets. Many members of the Bloomsbury set tried the patience of the newly established conscientious objector tribunals, but most of the Imagists signed up willingly. Aldington went immediately with his friend Frank Stuart Flint to register as a volunteer, but was told contemptuously that a hernia operation he had undergone in 1910 would rule him out of the army. Leaving the building, he lost his way and ended up in the armory, where a clerk promptly arrested him on suspicion of espionage.

London's cityscape changed dramatically at the outbreak of war. The drawing rooms where H. D. had attended carefree parties were now given over to Red Cross units; posters declaring "Your Country Needs You" were pasted on every street corner, and Bloomsbury square gardens became hospitals for wounded soldiers or grounds for the training of troops. After zeppelin raids began in January 1915, ubiquitous blackout curtains masked any domestic activity from the outside, while signposts were removed and streetlights dulled. Young women stalked the pavements handing out white feathers to men not in uniform, and recruiting sergeants loitered in doorways to snare the vulnerable. H. D. felt estranged, as a woman and as an American, from the military gusto which seemed to override all her values, and when Woodrow Wilson was reelected as president on a platform of keeping America out of war, she felt people begin to treat her with cool suspicion. Furthermore, she was worried about money. The war had affected the exchange rate, diminishing the £200 her parents sent annually from $5 per pound to $7, which reduced her to asking Amy Lowell for loans. And her anxiety was not only for herself: a couple of months after the war began, H. D. discovered she was pregnant. It felt odd to prepare for new life at a time of widespread death, but she and Aldington looked forward to becoming parents: the child seemed to represent hope for a future otherwise impossible to imagine.

But in the spring of 1915, H. D. suffered a loss that created "a sort of black hollow" within her. On May 21, the baby—a girl—was stillborn. H. D. was devastated. She considered the experience her own "near-death"; she would replay this trauma over and over in her fiction, associating her private grief with the public destruction sending thousands of soldiers to their graves. "Khaki killed it," says the heroine of her novel *Asphodel*, in which the child is delivered during an air raid "just like *Daily Mail* atrocities," the "baby-killer" Zeppelins flying overhead like a pack of hornets. H. D. was abruptly cast into the role of grieving mother, yet without the widely peddled comfort that her loss was a noble patriotic sacrifice. In the nursing home where H. D. spent three weeks, she sensed the "cold, nun-like" nurses' disapproval that Aldington, when he visited, was not in military uniform. The head nurse chastised her for taking up a bed which a soldier might need, as if deeming her feminine pain insignificant, silently scornful that she had not done her duty like the other new mothers who were diligently replacing the generation being killed in France. Friends visited bearing strawberries, irises, blue hydrangeas; H. D. thought none of them understood her suffering.

Far away from home and family, H. D. felt isolated as never before. She turned, for respite, to the ancient literature she loved, which now acquired fresh resonance: Greek epic and tragedy, with their heartrending depictions of women wailing as their plumed husbands and sons strode off to fight a meaningless battle, suddenly felt contemporary. War propaganda often played on parallels with ancient battles in attempts to stoke feelings of heroism: from February 1915, the Gallipoli Campaign was fought on an area dubbed the Trojan Plain, while in March, HMS *Agamemnon* was among the British fleet sent to claim the Dardanelles from Turkey. Around this time, Pound and T. S. Eliot both worked on translations of Aeschylus's *Agamemnon*, which focuses on the homecoming hero, returning triumphant with the spoils of war only to be murdered in the bathtub by his unfaithful wife. But H. D. was drawn instead to Euripides, whose Trojan War plays reserve their deepest sympathy for the innocent mothers and daughters whose lives war destroys. During 1915, Gilbert Murray's translation of Euripides's *Trojan Women*—which focuses not on the Greeks but on the humanity of their enemy—became a brief sensation ten years after its publication; it toured across the United States, sponsored by the Woman's Peace Party, and was praised by the *Telegraph* for bringing out "the affinity between the mind of Euripides and the mind of modern Europe." In an unpublished early essay, H. D. praised the "psycho-physical intensity" of Euripides's choral odes, whose pared-down lyrics and vivid evocation of color and landscape reflected her own poetic style. Euripides, she noted wryly, "was unpopular during his life as a free-thinker, and an iconoclast." She admired his ambivalence to conflict, and what she read as his "outright antiwar and anti-social protest": in his work, she found a moving counterpart to her grief.

That November, the avant-garde magazine the *Egoist* published H. D.'s translation of verses from Euripides's *Iphigenia in Aulis*, which tells the story of Agamemnon's sacrifice of his daughter in exchange for a fair wind to hasten the Greek ships to Troy. Her choice to concentrate on passages from the female chorus, singers who comment on the action but are powerless to participate, seems to reflect her own feeling of helplessness, accentuated in these months by the rift gradually deepening between her and Aldington. Since May, her pain at the stillbirth had been heightened by her suspicion that Aldington, despite his protests, was indifferent to her suffering, and had not really wanted the baby as she had. H. D. came to link the child's death with her shock at hearing about the sinking of the *Lusitania*, which had been torpedoed off the coast of Ireland by a German submarine on May 7, 1915, killing nearly twelve hundred people. Aldington had broken the news to her in a way she had perceived as abrupt and insensitive; from that point on, H. D. had begun to associate her husband with the military impulse which had now brought death inside her own body. War, she wrote later, destroyed "the child Amor": the stillbirth signaled the beginning of the end to three years of carefree happiness and mutual creativity.

If Aldington was distracted, it was because he knew the war would soon summon him away from his wife, friends, and work, possibly forever. In January 1916, the Gallipoli Campaign ended in failure, and the Military Service Act imposed compulsory enlistment on all unmarried men aged between eighteen and forty-one. Aldington knew it would not be long before this rule was extended to the espoused, and that his old injury would be dismissed as the war intensified. The following month, seeking a fresh start, he and H. D. left their home in Hampstead—associated with the pain of 1915—and rented a first-floor flat at 44 Mecklenburgh Square, one of the square's new boardinghouses, managed by a live-in landlady, Elinor James. Around a dozen people shared the building, thrust into haphazard intimacy by thin walls and shared bathrooms. Hot water could be procured by slotting a penny in the gas meter downstairs, while milk bottles were left on the landings by a maid.

The house had been recommended by a fellow Imagist, John Cournos, who lived there in a tiny room on the top floor, recently converted from a bathroom to a bedroom, where he was awoken each morning by the suffragettes who shared his kitchen scraping the burnt tops from their toast. Cournos had been born in Ukraine, but when he was ten his Hasidic Jewish family had left for America to escape the pogroms. In Philadelphia, he had sold newspapers on freezing street corners before school, eventually securing a job as office boy to the managing editor, then working his way up the ranks through a mix of book reviews, opinion pieces, and advice columns. In April 1912, like Pound and H. D. (though he had not known them in Philadelphia), Cournos had emigrated to London in search of literary opportunity: he, H. D., and Aldington had formed a close trio, though his devotion to them both would not serve him well. Partial to polka-dot bow ties and elegant walking sticks, yet with a permanent hint of melancholy in his eyes, Cournos was in love with H. D., though she was oblivious, her attention consumed by the troubles in her marriage.

On February 25, 1916, H. D. and Aldington moved their possessions to their new home, then dined with F. S. Flint in a preemptive farewell at the Isola Bella restaurant on Frith Street. But just a few weeks later, seeking a break from the incessant raids in London, they rented a cottage at Parracombe, North Devon, and left Mecklenburgh Square before they had properly unpacked. H. D. was working on the poems that would form her first collection, *Sea Garden*, while Aldington wrote to Flint of the urge he felt to finish a book before his inevitable summons. When they arrived, the countryside was hidden under six inches of snow, but primroses were blooming in the valley. H. D. woke early to write, make marmalade, and scrub her saucepans in the brook which ran past the house and down to the sea. Cournos came to join them, and to visit his friends Carl and Florence Fallas, who lived in a cottage nearby. The group spent weeks picnicking on the beach, chopping trees for firewood, and bathing nude in the sea, determined to forget the war and enjoy their last days of freedom together. But the atmosphere soon grew tense. Since the stillbirth, H. D. had developed a fear of pregnancy, which made her unable to countenance sex with Aldington. "How could she blithely face what he called love," she writes in *Bid Me to Live*, "with that prospect looming ahead and the matron, in her harsh voice, laying a curse on whatever might then have been, 'You know you must not have another baby until after the war is over.' Meaning in her language, you must keep away from your husband, keep him away from you. When he was all she had, was country, family, friends."

Her aversion to physical intimacy left Aldington frustrated, his libido undimmed by his sympathy toward his wife's suffering. In March, Aldington told Flint that he was attracted to Flo Fallas, but wouldn't sleep with her for fear of upsetting H. D. But in June, he admitted that he and Flo had had sex twice. "Don't tell me I'm a scandalous rotter or I shall weep," wrote Aldington to Flint. "You can trust me not to make anyone else unhappy." "Am I blind?" asks H. D. in her poem "Amaranth," written shortly after she learned of the deception. "Was my beauty so slight a gift, / so soon, so soon forgot?" But H. D. found she could suspend her pain by burying herself in writing, hiding from "the blundering world about us" by an immersion in "the living reality of the world of imagination and art." As it became more and more likely that Aldington would be called up, she tried to set aside her sadness by working "like a mad fanatic"—and was glad, if slightly unsettled, to find that new poems came to her more effortlessly than ever before, as if "dictated from without." "The hurt I suffered has freed my song—this is most precious to me," she told Cournos.

On May 25, 1916, the Military Service Act (Session 2) finally ordered the conscription of all married men. A month later, Aldington was inducted as an infantry private in the 11th Battalion of the Devonshire Regiment, and sent to train at Worgret Camp near Wareham, Dorset. From the moment he was conscripted, H. D. resolved to do all she could to ease Aldington's transition into military life. The army isolated Aldington physically and mentally from his friends and interests, and he was distressed by the monotony of days in the camp, where he carried out hours of physical labor, dreading nightfall when he would be ordered to the unventilated barracks and, though exhausted, be too uncomfortable to sleep. He felt his imagination infected with endless visions of blood and death; the copy of Heine's poetry he had taken with him, intending as a small act of resistance to learn German in spare moments, was swiftly confiscated by his commanding officer. H. D. encouraged friends to write to Aldington, to stave off his "spiritual loneliness," and thanked Lowell for her continued efforts to publicize his poetry: "My one struggle," she wrote, "is to make him feel he is not being forgotten, is not dropping out of the world." She took a room at Corfe Castle, to be near Aldington's camp, and wrote to Cournos wondering whether it would "be a good and wise sacrifice and a beautiful sacrifice" if she helped Flo find lodgings nearby, so Aldington could be close to his lover. "I am ready to give my own life away to him," she told Cournos, "to give my soul and the peace of my spirit that he may have beauty, that he may see and feel beauty, so that he may write."

It was an astonishing offer. Aldington, for his part, saw her self-sacrifice as far beyond the call of duty, and even resented the willingness with which she gave him up to her rival: "Hang Flo & damn Carl . . . For God's sake, love your Faun and don't be nobil." But he wrote in August to Lowell: "H. D. has been truly wonderful: her affection and unselfish devotion have been the prop of my existence." Yet even as she offered this solution, H. D. found herself disconcerted at how easily she could subsume her own desires and interests into those of someone else. "I have all faith in my work," she told Cournos. "What I want at times is to feel faith in my self, in my mere physical presence in the world, in my personality."

Her long, digressive letters to Cournos from Corfe—full of mystical allusion and pleas for understanding—show her struggling to establish her boundaries in a marriage which was always intended to prioritize independence and scorn possessiveness. Yet her desire to retain Cournos as confidant and sounding board seems to have overridden her sensitivity to him as a fellow player in the drama. When Aldington left for camp, Cournos stayed behind at the cottage to help a "dreadfully upset" H. D. pack, and in the sitting room, while they were drinking tea, she impetuously kissed him. A few days later, as Cournos recalled in his autobiography, they simultaneously experienced a bizarre sensation: each heard Aldington's ghostly voice call out Cournos's Russian name, "Korshoon!" This brought a halt to proceedings, but Cournos's longstanding feelings for H. D. were no longer concealed. Yet H. D., while accepting his devotion, made it clear that, despite everything, Aldington remained "the very core of my life." Although never rejecting Cournos outright, she gestured at a communion of the spirit rather than the body, and urged him to commit his unrequited passion to the page. "If love of me—absolute and terrible and hopeless love—is going to help you write, then *love* me," she wrote, adding—whether out of ingenuousness or calculation—that she hoped jealousy at their intimacy would inspire Aldington in his work. "If it seems best, I will tell him that you have loved me and passionately. I will tell him that I could have stayed happy with you in that little cottage," she wrote to Cournos, who had returned, in a grim mood, to Mecklenburgh Square. "When I said I could love you, you know what I meant. I meant if it would help R."

• • •

Richard Aldington did not go to the front with the rest of his battalion—luckily, as it meant he missed the Battle of the Somme—but was awarded lance corporal stripes and held back for officer training. Knowing that he might be sent to France at any point, he begged H. D. to leave England and go back to Philadelphia alone: "If I die when Hilda is in America, she will feel it less, I believe," he wrote to Cournos. But H. D. insisted on returning to Mecklenburgh Square. When she had first looked round the flat, knowing that it would be her lonely wartime sanctuary, the landlady had sensed her desolation and suggested, echoing Aldington's entreaties, that she ask a friend to help H. D. leave town for the duration of the war. H. D. certainly had options—Amy Lowell had donated a substantial sum to Herbert Hoover's scheme to repatriate Americans based in Europe—but she refused to leave London, the first place she had felt she belonged. With Aldington away indefinitely, the room at 44 Mecklenburgh Square took on symbolic importance for H. D.: it was a place that was solely hers to work in, a constant while everything around her was uncertain. While it stood, it offered hope for a future where her values would still hold meaning.

The flat was one large musty room, with apricot-colored walls and a blue carpet. A Spanish screen separated the tiny kitchen from the living area, where H. D. slept on a low chintz-covered couch that doubled as a sofa. Scattered candles illuminated H. D.'s version of interior decoration: statues of the Buddha, a brown teapot, its leaves dumped on pieces of newspaper spread open on the carpet, overflowing ashtrays, cups stained with the remnants of black coffee and colored liqueurs, half-wilted roses, and single eggs languishing on a shelf under the bookcase. In the evenings, she could hear the munitions girls from the top floor clattering downstairs on the way to their night shifts. Another occupant of the house was Alida Klemantaski, partner of the poet and publisher Harold Monro, who, like Aldington, had recently been called up: H. D. tried to cultivate the friendship, but Alida made it clear she wanted to keep to herself, preferring the company of the insects she housed in a makeshift terrarium in her room. So H. D. largely spent her time in solitude. The French windows, which led to a balcony, were swathed in night-blue curtains and backed by thick shutters with iron bolts that she drew across during air raids. H. D. would later remember those curtains as a comforting seal of protection, forming a boundary which cocooned her from the dangerous world outside. Yet the curtains also gave her a marked feeling of claustrophobia, of being locked up in the room with her grief and tension, alone and trapped, unable to escape. The room, she wrote in *Bid Me to Live*, was "the frame to the picture": H. D. would come to see each contour and texture of the Mecklenburgh Square flat as inextricable from the emotional turmoil of this year.

On December 21, 1916, she wrote to Lowell, describing a scene familiar to women up and down the country: "I am waiting at Waterloo to say goodbye to R. He leaves England tonight." Alone, H. D. attempted to continue, in Mecklenburgh Square, the frenzied work she had been doing at Parracombe and Corfe. "All I want," she wrote, "is to keep the home-fires of divine poesy humming till the boys come home!" Yet after Aldington's departure for France, she found it difficult to concentrate. She was working on a translation of the choruses from Euripides's *Hippolytus*, focusing on the doomed queen Phaedra's misplaced passion for her stepson; she had also taken over Aldington's position as assistant editor of the *Egoist*, the magazine that claimed to "recognise no taboos," was a leading proponent of Imagism, and had recently serialized James Joyce's *Portrait of the Artist as a Young Man*. H. D. enjoyed the role, working alongside T. S. Eliot and publishing several of her own poems as well as reviews and pieces by her friends. But making art during wartime began to seem futile. In her long poem "The Tribute," published in the *Egoist* in November 1916, a city is overrun by a contemptuous demon, its people left bereft and helpless, with little language to describe their horror: "Squalor blights and makes hideous / our lives—it has smothered / the beat of our songs." H. D. oscillated between periods of intense productivity and episodes of self-destruction: writing from France, Aldington told Lowell that he had had to persuade H. D. not to burn work which she considered inadequate, and that she had already destroyed "some most poignant lyrics and a long poem of about 10,000 words." She told her friend

John Gould Fletcher that she felt "broken spiritually" in London; her creativity was choked by the undercurrent of death.

As the war continued, it was not surprising that H. D. began to lose sight of any future or purpose. She thought of the London sky as blotting paper, whose misery she absorbed daily. Zeppelin attacks were frequent, and Mecklenburgh Square, being close to the targets of Euston and King's Cross stations, stood at high risk from bomber planes, whose misfired debris regularly showered Bloomsbury. H. D., sitting on her balcony in the moonlight, grew accustomed to the sight of searchlight beams converging on a silvery airplane, the hoarse wails of bombs and shells piercing the atmosphere, antiaircraft guns bursting like firecrackers, then giving way to the all-clear bugles blown by enterprising Boy Scouts. Since the stillbirth, she had been hyperaware of the "imminent possibility of death"; walking through London, she felt she was traversing a graveyard, where "any stone might have been our tomb-stone." The constant air raids were a powerful psychological weapon which came to dominate the London imagination, threatening to wreak havoc when least expected. When the siren went, the residents of 44 Mecklenburgh Square would gather in the basement, where an atmosphere of false jollity was fueled by the landlady's hot and sugary "Zeppelin tea"; H. D. always refused to go, preferring to die alone in her room rather than socialize under such circumstances. During one attack, the house next door was struck. "We came home and simply waded through glass," she recalled, "while wind from now unshuttered windows made the house a barn, an unprotected dug-out. What does that sort of shock do to the mind, the imagination—not solely of myself, but of an epoch?"

Aldington asked Lowell to "write her cheerful lies to comfort her," and tasked Flint with taking H. D. to theatres and parties, even attempting to match the generosity with which H. D. had greeted his affair with Flo (or, perhaps, to clear his conscience): "For the Lord's sake don't interrupt H. D. if she is having a good time with anyone . . . if you can devise any sort of 'affaire' *pour passer le temps*, so much the better." In the meantime, in a poignant attempt to recover the warmth of their early marriage, he and H. D. communicated by an exchange of small chapbooks, made by a small press run out of an Ohio church by Charles Clinch Bubb, a reverend with a passion for printmaking. The delicate volumes explored their shared love of Greece, memories of their travels in Italy, their anger at the war which divided them, and the possibility that language can heal pain. Writing and receiving these private poems heartened H. D., and she wrote to Bubb to thank him for his commitment to the project. "You really can not imagine (though I have reiterated this so often) what courage they give us—what faith and courage to 'carry on' in another sphere than that of guns and slaughter." Writing cheerfully to Bubb, Aldington explained that he had met his wife when he was nineteen, and married her at twenty-one. "Everyone said I was ruining my life & that of a charming girl! I am happy to say these prophets of evil were entirely wrong and we have never quarrelled since our marriage although we often did before! You see, I was older at 21 than many men at 30; even now few people will believe I am only 24."

Over the early months of 1917, Aldington's battalion saw little military action. Stationed between Amiens and the Belgian border, far from the main front, his duties involved digging trenches, maintaining roads, and constructing wooden crosses to mark graves. In July—weeks before the Third Battle of Ypres would begin in earnest—he returned to England for officer training at a camp near Lichfield in Stafford-shire. H. D. joined him, taking rooms in the market square, where she worked peacefully and spent "delightfully lazy" weekends with Aldington.

A coincidence had enabled H. D. to sublet 44 Mecklenburgh Square during her absence. When he was living in Philadelphia, John Cournos had been wildly in love with a charismatic American woman named Dorothy Yorke, who preferred to be known more glamorously as Arabella. Possessed of a deep voice, flushed complexion, and copper-tinged hair, Arabella made her own clothes and experimented in abstract painting. She and Cournos had at one point been engaged, but after he followed Arabella to Paris in 1912, her mother, who disap-

proved of his poverty and Jewishness, had insisted the affair be termi-
nated. Two years later, when Arabella was back in America, the romance
had reignited through correspondence; thrilled, Cournos had worked
for months to raise the boat fare to visit her, but by the time he arrived
in New York, Arabella had changed her mind. Furious yet helpless, he
had returned to London, resolved never to cross an ocean for a woman
again.

In 1917, Cournos was working as an interpreter for the Wireless
Press on the Strand, translating government messages that came over
the Russian radio. Toward the end of the summer, he accepted a job in
St. Petersburg as a translator and journalist with the Anglo-Russian
Commission, organized by the British Foreign Office. One morning,
strolling down Southampton Row, he was surprised to encounter Arabella and her mother, looking into a shop window. He had parted from
her on bad terms, but in the Bloomsbury street cool civility gave way
to generosity: hearing that Arabella was staying on in London without
accommodation secured, Cournos suggested that she borrow the flat
below his, left empty while H. D. was away in Lichfield. Arrangements
were made on the spot. "A beautiful lady has my room," wrote H. D.
to Flint on August 30. Each evening, Cournos came down to Arabella's
sitting room; together they ate, talked, and finally confessed love. But
it was too late: he was set to depart for Russia in a matter of days. He
asked Arabella to wait for him; she said that she would.

When Aldington was sent back to France in September, Arabella
moved upstairs to Cournos's vacant room, and H. D. reclaimed the
bigger flat. Aldington returned at regular intervals on leave, shuttling
across the Channel on boats crowded with parties of nurses, reporters,
and fellow soldiers. The proximity of the front made separation all the
more unsettling on both sides: the noise of distant guns could be heard
at Dover, while soldiers could enjoy a leisurely breakfast in London
and be back in the rat-infested, sodden trenches by sunset, stung with
regret for all they were missing. Letters took between two and four
days to arrive from the front, so until Aldington walked through the
door, H. D. feared he might at any moment already be dead: even
when he was home on leave, she felt a strange sensation that she was in

the company of a ghost. When they embraced, she flinched as his reg-
ulation buttons pressed against her cheek; with his khaki tunic flung
over the back of an armchair, his service watch ticking away on the
table, its face barricaded by woven wire, H. D. felt the war closing in
on her, infiltrating her sanctuary.

H. D.'s discomfort at Aldington's new role was compounded by a
second, longer-lasting infidelity, which marked a definitive rupture in
the marriage. In the autumn of 1917, Aldington began sleeping with
Arabella Yorke. H. D. knew about the relationship from its beginning,
and acquiesced, if only because it relieved her of having to undergo the
trauma of sex, and because Aldington insisted it was merely a passing
passion: that he still loved H. D., but that—as H. D. later recalled—"as
he was certain to get killed whenever he returned to the Front he must
get every ounce of pleasure out of life while he had the chance." From
this point, when Aldington returned on leave, it was not only to see his
wife. Increasingly, he was spending nights upstairs in the tiny bedroom, while H. D. slept alone in the main flat, bitterly mourning the
transformation she saw in her husband. In her novel *Asphodel*, Jerrold
Darrington's affairs are multiple, casual, reckless: he seduces women at
parties and sleeps with them while Hermione lies awake on the other
side of the thin screen, feeling as if her body is split between the woman
with her husband and the woman lying silently alone. In *Bid Me to Live*,
the denouement is more specific: after a perilous air raid, Rafe and
Bella set off for the pub in Theobalds Road in search of restorative
brandy. Rafe returns alone, and Julia (the H. D. character) immediately senses something is wrong. "She flung her arms round me in the
Square," Rafe says dully, his eyes on the ground. He goes out, leaving
Julia standing among scattered books and broken glass. As if in a trance,
she tidies the room, knowing that nothing will be the same again.

From everything she later wrote about this period, it's clear that
Aldington's second affair affected H. D. far more deeply than the first
with Flo. In all her novels, this episode is marked by a surreal detachment, and a sense that the war has imposed roles—soldier, wife,
mistress—which everyone is playing out blindly, like characters in a
Greek tragedy, puppeteered by heartless gods. In public, H. D. acted

the accepted wartime part of the faithful wife, waiting at home like Odysseus's loyal Penelope; in private, she felt like Iphigenia, deceived by a soldier-husband with an appetite for destruction. H. D. had stayed in London hoping to live the life she had envisaged when she first arrived in England, surrounded by other writers and artists and working with a fellow Hellenist in their shared home. Instead, 44 Mecklenburgh Square was overcrowded and divided, each movement within the house now signaling new allegiances. The whole arrangement of the flat—the merged bedroom and living room making H. D.'s most private spaces vulnerable to scrutiny by any visitor—left H. D. feeling exposed and invaded: her room felt like a "stage-set": a fraught interchange of comings and goings, her own status unclear. This shared single room in a Bloomsbury boardinghouse was no longer a place of freedom from traditional domestic shackles, but a cruel distortion of the family home she might have shared with Aldington and their baby. She felt humiliated by the landlady's clear disapproval when Aldington and Arabella appeared in the downstairs drawing room in pajamas during a raid—and must have been aware that Katherine Mansfield and John Middleton Murry, living together unmarried, had recently been evicted from their boardinghouse on Gray's Inn Road, just behind Mecklenburgh Square, by a landlady determined to maintain propriety on her premises. H. D. shrank from the other tenants, with their inquisitive sidelong glances when they passed her on the stairs; she could hardly bear her private affairs to be the stuff of idle gossip among the residents of a Bloomsbury boardinghouse. But she did not feel strong enough to fight it. Eventually, in a final gesture toward self-obliteration, she offered Aldington and Arabella use of the main bedroom, and retreated up to Cournos's tiny garret, where she spent solitary evenings wrapped in the blanket she'd used when sitting out on deck during her first crossing to Europe. It seems another extraordinary concession, but by this point H. D. had thoroughly lost faith in herself. Number 44 Mecklenburgh Square now felt like "four walls about to crush her."

From the front, Aldington wrote plaintively to excuse his behavior, protesting that he had little to live for and never intended anyone to suffer. "The truth is," he wrote in a weak attempt at honesty, "I love you & I desire—*l'autre* (that is, Arabella)." His words reverberated with H. D. across the decades, and appear, exactly transcribed, in *Bid Me to Live*. There, Rafe claims to prefer his wife's company and conversation, but confesses he cannot any longer find her physically attractive, as he does Bella, who is more conventionally "feminine." "I would give her a mind, I would give you a body," he admits. Julia concludes that his stance reduces women to two types, neither of which allows any single woman to be whole. "I would be free," writes Julia, "if I could live in two dimensions." These unhappy circumstances produced the greatest insight of H. D.'s time in Mecklenburgh Square, and a thought echoed by every woman in this book: that real freedom entails the ability to live on one's own terms, not to allow one's identity to be proscribed or limited by anyone else. This was the realization that would eventually drive H. D. to leave Mecklenburgh Square, to seek analysis with Freud, to form new and experimental relationships, and to write the books that gave voice to her suffering. But it was not only her husband who posed a serious challenge to H. D.'s sense of herself during her time in Mecklenburgh Square. At the end of October 1917, an unexpected turn of events introduced several new characters to number 44, whose stay there would have consequences none of them could have predicted.

H. D.'s relationship with D. H. Lawrence is difficult to reconstruct, its texture long ago dissolved into fragments and fictions. He had been a member of the Imagist circle, though on its margins, being ensconced in his work and his marriage to Frieda von Richthofen, who had left her husband and children to be with him. After meeting in 1914 at the Berkeley Hotel, H. D. and Aldington had visited Lawrence several times in Hampstead, and were sympathetic to the financial troubles he suffered after his 1915 novel *The Rainbow* was removed from sale because of its open discussion of sexual desire. Lawrence, in turn, was sensitive to H. D.'s vulnerability: early in their acquaintance, he described her as "like a person walking a tightrope. You wonder if she'll get across." But he greatly admired her poetry, and considered H. D. the only one of the Imagists who was "worth anything"; to Edward Marsh he wrote, "Don't you think H. D.—Mrs. Aldington— writes some good poetry? I do—really very good." H. D. was thrilled at his attention, and stimulated by his support. Throughout the war years they sent each other works in progress for critique: early drafts of his novel *Women in Love*, and the new poem sequence she was writing, taking its voices from figures of Greek mythology.

At this time—sickened by the war, which he considered "a blasphemy against life itself"—Lawrence was evolving a project of escapist fantasy: to gather some like-minded souls, "sail away from this world of war and squalor," and build a new, utopian order elsewhere. He called it Rananim, a Hebrew word translated as "let us rejoice." H. D. wrote to John Gould Fletcher in excitement about the plans to find a ranch in the Andes, to "slough off Europe for some years, perhaps forever" and, on horseback, to "make for new kingdoms." Her letter expresses the same sense of sterility that Lawrence described, and her desire to leave the house where she now felt so constricted. "I myself can no longer breathe this dead air. It is really killing me—and driving my mind and spirit so far that I am becoming a sort of shadow," she told Gould Fletcher. The prospect of a life where creativity was prized over heroism, community over conflict, spoke deeply to her present anguish. But the proposal was little more than a fantasy: the Foreign Office had already confiscated Lawrence's passport.

Cornwall provided his alternative refuge. He and Frieda had found a cottage at Higher Tregerthen near the tiny village of Zennor, nestled beneath dramatic cliffs, where they lived "very quietly indeed, being far from the world." It was there that Lawrence met and befriended Cecil Gray, a young man who would play a brief but critical role in H. D.'s life. A cynical aesthete with little respect for received opinion, Gray had arrived in London from Edinburgh in 1915, determined to have nothing to do with the war but to spend his days composing music "of a wildness and audacity hitherto undreamt of in art." Aged twenty-one, Gray was wracked by compulsive self-doubt and fickle emotions: newfound passions would swiftly dissipate, leaving him dizzy at his own inconsistency. Living in Chelsea on a diet of baked beans and cheese, he was working on an orchestral score and a study of the relationship between Nietzsche and Wagner, spending long nights drinking with the circle of artists and bohemians that revolved around Fitzrovia's pubs and cafes.

Gray was introduced to Lawrence by his friend Philip Heseltine (the composer later known as Peter Warlock), who venerated Lawrence as "the greatest literary genius of his generation," and who had recently—in an attempt to counter what he perceived as Britain's unforgivable apathy toward genius and beauty—tried (and failed) to establish a publishing company specifically to distribute Lawrence's censored work. In spring 1917, Gray and Heseltine visited Higher Tregerthen, and Gray immediately fell in love with Cornwall. Like Lawrence, he savored the silence, the azure skies, the wildflowers carpeting the moors, and the sound of beating waves mingled with the cries of seagulls and swallows. The openness of the land—forty miles of the Atlantic visible from the cliffs—seemed somehow to disallow deception; Gray felt he had escaped to "a paradisal existence in which the War and everything connected with it had no place." On an impulse, he took a five-year lease on a seven-bedroom house three miles down the coast from Zennor, tucked behind the ruins of Bosigran Castle. Eager for a friendly neighbor, Lawrence attended furniture sales on Gray's behalf, painted the woodwork, and polished the floors, signing off detailed letters on the merits of different shapes of chairs and tables with the words "Remember the revolution."

Brought together as fellow exiles from "a hostile and unsympathetic world," Gray and the Lawrences were soon meeting every day. Gradually, rumors began to circulate among the locals, whose suspicions had already been aroused by Frieda's German accent: that the Lawrences' chimney, covered in tar to keep out the damp, was a signal to the enemy; that they held secret reserves of petrol buried within the cliff; that they were on a mission to carry food to the alien submarines that circled the coast. One day, officers followed the Lawrences back from the local shop and asked to inspect their groceries, seizing on a loaf of bread they mistook for a hidden camera. Another evening, at Gray's house, with the curtains drawn, Lawrence played the piano and Frieda led a resounding chorus of German folk songs. Suddenly there was a bang on the door and six men covered in mud (they had fallen into a ditch as they listened under the windows) marched in with loaded rifles, claiming they had seen lights flashing out to sea. Gray was fined a "vindictive" £20 under the Defense of the Realm Act for his alleged indiscretion; he later learned that their neighbors were so riled that an expedition armed with scythes and pitchforks had at one point set out for his house, its members losing nerve on the way and eventually turning back.

On October 12, officers arrived at the Lawrence house with an order from the military authorities that the Lawrences must leave Cornwall within three days. Frieda wept as the detectives rifled through the bread tin and tea caddy; Lawrence's remonstrations were met with impassivity. They were homeless, until a solution to their problem was found, which Lawrence outlines in his 1923 novel *Kangaroo:* "The American wife of an English friend, a poet serving in the army, offered her rooms in Mecklenburgh Square, and the third day after their arrival in London Somers and Harriet moved there: very grateful indeed to the American girl. They had no money. But the young woman tossed the rooms to them, and food and fuel, with a wild free hand. She was beautiful, reckless, one of the poetesses whose poetry Richard feared and wondered over."

Lawrence's return to London was fraught and painful. The city, he wrote to Gray, was a ghastly Inferno which "thinks and breathes and lives air raids, nothing else." He wandered along the foggy King's Cross Road, his shoes still caked with Cornish mud, longing to see the foxgloves around his cottage which would soon be in bloom; he asked Gray to send him a pound of Cornish butter, and wrote plaintive petitions to the War Office seeking a revocation of his exile. In his novel *Aaron's Rod*, he recalled nocturnal ramblings in Mecklenburgh Square:

> Beyond the tall shrubs and the high, heavy railings the wet
> street gleamed silently. The houses of the Square rose like a

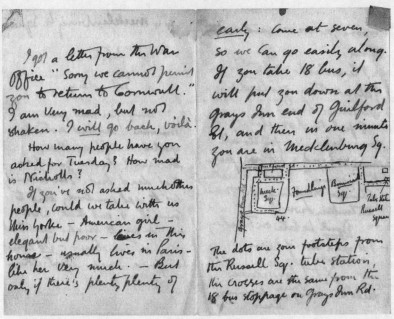

I got a letter from the War Office "Sorry we cannot permit you to return to Cornwall." I am very mad, but not shaken. I will go back, voilà.

How many people have you asked for Tuesday? How mad is Nicholls?

If you've not asked much other people, could we take with us Miss Yorke — American girl — elegant but poor — lives in this house — usually lives in Paris — like her very much. — But only if there's plenty plenty of

early: come at seven, so we can go easily along. If you take 18 bus, it will put you down at the Grays Inn end of Guilford St, and then in one minute you are in Mecklenburg Sq.

The dots are your footsteps from the Russell Sq. tube station, the crosses are the same from the 18 bus stoppage on Grays Inn Rd.

Letter from D. H. Lawrence to Lady Cynthia Asquith, November 17, 1917.

cliff on this inner dark sea, dimly lighted at occasional windows. Boughs swayed and sang. A taxi-cab swirled round a corner like a cat, and purred to a standstill.

There were happier moments: his friend Cynthia Asquith bicycled to Mecklenburgh Square for omelettes with sardines and pears, cooked by the fire in the "very handsome bed sitting-room"; they booked a box for Mozart's *Seraglio* in Covent Garden, offering a spare ticket to Arabella, whom Asquith described in her diary as "a chic poor American, like a drawing in *Vogue*." At the end of November, the Lawrences moved to stay with Gray's mother in a "bourgeois little flat" in Earl's Court, but returned regularly to spend evenings in Mecklenburgh Square, sitting round the fire playing charades with H. D., Arabella, and Aldington (who had a month's leave over Christmas), all laughing uproariously at Lawrence's talent for mimicry, while detectives skulked in the cold stairwell, hoping to catch Lawrence plotting further sedition. The Lawrences' relationship remained tempestuous, and H. D.

witnessed several violent shouting matches: from upstairs, Alida Klemantaski remembered seeing Frieda physically hurl her husband into the next-door flat, to the surprise of its occupant. But other evenings were merrier, despite the continual Zeppelin raids which on one occasion brought down the ceiling of Alida's bedroom. In a raucous pageant which the group devised in the flat one night, Lawrence paired them off: Cecil Gray (who was visiting) played an angel, with an umbrella as his flaming sword, while H. D. was a dancing Tree of Life. Aldington and Arabella were Adam and Eve (with chrysanthemums for fig leaves); Frieda was the serpent, writhing on the carpet. Lawrence, narrator and puppeteer, blithely cast himself as God Almighty. He wrote to Lowell that H. D. and Aldington "seem pretty happy, as far as it is possible under the circumstances. We have had some good hours with them in Mecklenburgh Square—really jolly, notwithstanding everything: remembering that evening at the Berkeley with you, when we all met for the first time, and laughing at ourselves. Oh my dear Amy, I do wish to heaven we could all meet again in peace and freedom, to laugh together and be decent and happy with each other. This is a more wintry winter of discontent than I had ever conceived."

Yet it was not Lawrence who rescued H. D. from her present despair, but his friend Cecil Gray. Later in life, H. D. rarely mentioned Gray, but in everything she wrote about this period his intervention is portrayed as having saved her from desperation. Recalling these events in 1938, she described how Gray was introduced to her by Lawrence, and took her out to dinner one evening while no one else was around. (In *Bid Me to Live*, Cyril Vane whisks Julia away in the middle of an air raid to a bustling restaurant, where they dine among officers on leave shouting across tables and ordering more wine in expensive obliteration.) Afterward, they returned to Mecklenburgh Square for coffee, where she opened up to him about her misery. He was immediately sympathetic and refreshingly straightforward, insisting that, whatever happened, she had to leave Aldington; it was clear to him that the situation was taking a terrible toll on her health, and that "it would be suicide for me to stay for another leave of my husband's under these circumstances." Across her fictional accounts of the period, Gray is presented with a consistency rarely afforded to other characters in this story: he is "someone not in khaki," someone who "did not talk of war." His hatred of militarism and his passion for music reminded her of the creative partner she now feared she had lost for good. Discussing art and beauty with Gray stirred in H. D. the memory of her prewar self; as they talked and laughed, she felt her identity as someone other than a soldier's wife seeping back into her.

Gray left London on March 11, 1918, and encouraged H. D. to follow him to Cornwall. At first, she was reluctant to leave Mecklenburgh Square and cement the break with her husband by abandoning their shared home. But as Aldington's next leave approached, she saw that Gray's invitation offered a chance to regain the solitude and privacy which the war had eroded—as well as a possible new romance. From Bosigran, Gray wrote to reiterate her welcome, offering a measured warning amid requests for her to bring sheets, towels, butter ration cards, and Flaubert's letters: "How I must have talked to you in London—about what I was going to do and how wonderful I was! I hope you did not take it too seriously." His words cannot have encouraged H. D., but they did not dissuade her. Before the end of March, she left Mecklenburgh Square and took the train to Cornwall. As she prepared to leave her home, H. D. received a letter from an old friend. It read:

> *Poor Dryad*
> *Buon Viaggio*
> *Ezra*

John Cournos's work in St. Petersburg was halted by the outbreak of the October Revolution; once the Brest-Litovsk peace was concluded on March 3, 1918, it seemed futile to stay in a volatile country where a civil war was brewing. On his journey home he spent three weeks in the Arctic port of Murmansk, stuck aboard a broken-down train, then sailed back to Dover on a perilously overcrowded vessel captured from the Germans. He arrived in London exhausted, expecting Arabella to greet him—though concerned that his regular letters and requests for chocolate had gone unanswered—only to discover that H. D. was in Cornwall, Aldington at a new training camp in Tunbridge Wells, and that Aldington and Arabella were apparently in love, their affair consummated in his own top-floor bedroom. He was furious, and blamed H. D. for failing to look after Arabella as she had promised. Remembering how she had condoned Aldington's fling with Flo, he immediately assumed that she had been complicit in this second affair: in his mind, not only had H. D. rejected him herself, but she had now allowed his fiancée to betray him too.

Aldington insisted that it was at Arabella's request that he had not disclosed their relationship to Cournos. "I am not ashamed of anything I have done; I regret nothing," he wrote, his letter veering between placatory and defiant. "What chiefly hurts you, I know, is that you feel I took advantage of your absence—but would your presence have altered things? I don't know; there are events which are stronger than we are; there seems a kind of fatality about it, a bitter irony . . . we fell in love with each other, that is all." H. D.'s letters were more contrite, begging for Cournos's continued friendship. "O, it was so terrible—you can't imagine," she wrote in April 1918. "I am not able to think of myself as a *person* now. I must move, act, & do as it is *moved* upon me to do & act . . . I am cut off from everyone in the old world." She told him that, as she had done in Devon, she was retreating into her work in the face of "curious mental and spiritual tangles," and suggested he do the same. "We will go mad with the general madness unless we 'build our house upon a rock.' Your rock (as mine) is creating & imaginative work . . . don't let the outside world hurt you."

Taking her advice, Cournos poured his anger into a vitriolic novel, incorporating many of H. D.'s letters verbatim. *Miranda Masters* shocked H. D. when she read it on publication in 1926 ("a most unseemly book about ME I think . . . a fool and an incompetent and suppressed nymphomaniac"). Cournos's novel offers a very different perspective on the Mecklenburgh Square episode: it is a sobering reminder that H. D.'s accounts, many and varied as they are, offer only her views of events which affected several other lives. The novel's acidity is directed entirely at Miranda, whom the *Spectator* reviewer denounced as "one of the most unpleasant, abnormal of women, even in current fiction"; while her husband's affairs are portrayed as the reasonable and inevitable result of his body's yearning for comfort, Miranda's crude flirtation with the central character, John Gombarov (a very lightly veiled version of Cournos himself), is represented as a sordid craving for male attention. The novel overflows with bitterness at the betrayal Cournos felt, abandoned as collateral damage in the Aldingtons' experimental marriage. He had looked to his friends' apparent happiness—"here were two poets," he wrote later, "man and woman, who were happy together and worked together"—as a model for the sort of marriage he had hoped to enjoy with Arabella; the revelations left him disillusioned and mistrustful, especially of women. Just as the period would remain with H. D. forever, so did these rejections sting Cournos in a way that would affect future relationships—particularly one forged two years later in the very same Mecklenburgh Square flat, with a young graduate named Dorothy L. Sayers.

In Cornwall, away from the ruins and misery of London, H. D. felt regenerated. Gray's house was beautiful and spacious, the walls lined with books, the housekeeper dignified and discreet. He gave H. D. her own room, where she wrote her celebrated poems "Leda," "Lethe," and "Song" gazing out through the window at the ocean and ancient rock formations, the timbers shaken not by air raids but by gales. She felt the Cornish landscape was bathed in a "cold healing mist, as if someone had breathed a cold, healing breath"; as it had to Lawrence, Cornwall felt to her like a fine substitute for Rananim, holding in it the promise of a new and vitalizing way of life. She continued to receive letters from her husband, pointedly addressed to Mrs. Richard Aldington, which she hid from Gray. No longer did Aldington try to shield H. D. from the reality of life at the front, to which he returned in April 1918. "Twice last week I tried to get killed," he wrote pitifully, "and was unlucky or lucky, whichever you like." In June, Aldington wrote frostily to Flint, who had heard rumors that he and H. D. had separated: "We are 'parted' to the extent that I am in France and she in Cornwall. But we are not 'parted' in any other sense . . . You—*et le monde*—are very blind if you think anything could ever part us two." He pleaded with her to accept money from him, and to keep her identity entwined with his: "I am so proud that you have my name—please, please won't you keep it, whatever happens, in memoriam as it were?" He wrote that John Cournos was "going about London . . . implying that I have committed some deed of revolting treachery," and that Arabella was trying to "enslave" him by pressuring him to divorce H. D. and marry her: "To you I have under-estimated my passion for A, to A I have under-estimated my tenacious devotion to you." His letters were insistent in their plea for forgiveness. "Out of this present utter darkness of mine, this confusion & complete lack of direction & interest, there is one thing that seems to matter—you."

At the end of July 1918, H. D. discovered she was pregnant. When she broke the news to her husband, Aldington was at first supportive, telling her to "cheer up and eat lots," and promising to accept the child as his if she wanted him to. But his feelings quickly changed: the attitude of casual acceptance he had cultivated toward her affair ("Damn it, Dooley," he had written, "I believe in women having all the lovers they want if they're in love with them") now vanished, and he reproached H. D. mournfully for her lack of caution. His letters were careful to imply that it was she who had broken the moral code of their permissive relationship, displaying an obtuse unawareness of the distress he had himself caused: "Gray becomes your husband & I merely your lover; because the emotions that bind lovers together are exquisite & sterile like poetry, but a child is a more ponderous link than any beauty . . . Oh, it is sad, bitter, biting sad, when our love was so deep, so untroubled really by our other love-affairs. But a child!" Yet the bond between H. D. and Cecil Gray was quickly to prove brittle. That same month, Gray—who had been rejected from military duty on four occasions owing to a childhood illness—was finally called up to the lowest category of service, which involved cleaning lavatories. He immediately vanished into hiding, judging that the war was too close to its end for the authorities to bother prosecuting him as a deserter. Sweeping H. D. to Cornwall had been a dramatic gesture, but he had no desire to take on the responsibility of fatherhood; he still aspired to a reckless life devoted to art, and convinced himself that the situation was a test of his resolve. While H. D. was wavering over whether or not to leave London, he had written to remonstrate with her for being "so elusive, so unapproachable": "You do not pretend to love me any more than you do," he wrote in wonder. But now it was he who drew their affair back to reality. His crumbling in the face of responsibility was certainly influenced by Philip Heseltine, who had recently become a father and wrote disdainfully to Gray about the financial drain and the incompatibility of domestic ties with making art. (He had refused to marry his child's mother, a model named Puma Channing whom Heseltine dismissed as a "vampire.") Gray's 1948 autobiography *Musical Chairs* (which does not mention H. D.) describes how he spent six months traveling Italy, "sick to death of the world and everything and everybody in it." She never saw him again.

H. D. was alone once more, abandoned unceremoniously by the man who had seemed to promise her escape. It was her second wartime pregnancy, and the memory of the stillbirth still traumatized her; furthermore, she was devastated at the news that her beloved brother Gilbert had been killed in France. Aldington was now adamant that their marriage was over—"fini, fini, fini"—but that they should remain friends and continue to correspond "on matters of art & literature & life." At the end of the summer, H. D. left Cornwall and stayed with her friend Amy Randall in Hampstead; she couldn't bear to return to Mecklenburgh Square, so she sublet her room for the rest of the lease. On November 1, Aldington informed H. D. that he was going "over the top," and sent her a blank check for use if he was killed. Ten days later, the war was over.

But just as she saw her newfound freedom beginning to dissipate, H. D. met someone who would offer her a new chance at the rebirth she had initially experienced in Cornwall. On July 17, 1918, H. D. had told Cournos—to whom she continued to write, despite his fury with her—that she had "begun really seriously on a novel." That same day, she met Bryher for the first time. Born Annie Winifred Ellerman, Bryher had changed her name to express the deep affiliation she felt with the Scilly Isles, and to escape ready identification with a single gender. She was the daughter of a shipping magnate said to be the richest man in England, but was determined never to write under her own name, to avoid any accusations that she was exploiting her father's influence. (Later in life, she would bestow her fortune liberally on struggling writers she met in Paris, and act as patron to numerous experimental presses, magazines, and film productions.) Bryher was eight years younger than H. D., whose collection *Sea Garden* she had learned by heart; she herself was desperate to write and learn ancient languages, and considered H. D. "a Greek come to life again." Bryher was staying in Cornwall, and when she heard that H. D. was nearby she resolved to visit her, walking to Bosigran through a storm. This meeting would mark the beginning of an open relationship which spanned forty years; in the various periods when they did not live together, they wrote to each other daily until H. D.'s death.

At first, stung by the betrayals and indignities of the last few years, H. D. was ambivalent about the prospect of taking on responsibility for another person's well-being. Bryher was volatile, and her devotion oppressive: "The worst thing is," H. D. wrote to Cournos, "the girl is in love with me, so madly that it is terrible. No man has ever cared for me like that. She seems possessed at times with a daemon or spirit outside herself . . . I must have my freedom first and if the strain becomes too great, I shall just chuck her." But Bryher's sensitivity and interventions proved indispensable over the first year of their acquaintance. Remembering the stillbirth, H. D. was listless throughout her pregnancy, almost in denial about the upheaval to come: she told a friend that "I feel it very wicked to worry yet about this one's life and future . . . I cannot talk about it, as I was so sad and ill the last time." Frances Perdita was born on March 31, 1919, in a nursing home in Ealing. "My only real criticism is that this is not my child," said Pound, who came to visit. Aldington—now released from the army, and experiencing deferred shell shock—brought bunches of daffodils. The birth and its aftermath were extremely traumatic for H. D., who was suffering from pneumonia resulting from the deadly influenza epidemic which spread across postwar Europe; her illness was so severe that her landlady, somewhat unsympathetically, suggested Bryher put up the money for H. D.'s burial in advance. Yet Bryher nursed H. D. loyally through this period and subsequent crises, and H. D. later acknowledged that "without her . . . I could not have gone on."

Bryher understood H. D.'s ambivalence about motherhood—her fear that caring duties would threaten her freedom and identity as an artist and confine her to the traditional role of "angel in the house." She was insistent that H. D.'s writing should not be interrupted. "I hope you will be sensible over Perdita," Bryher wrote to H. D. in April 1919, "and remember you were not given poetry to sit and worry over an infant in a solitary cottage. I am very jealous for your poetry and I will even fight Perdita about it." Early on in her pregnancy, when it seemed likely that she would be embarking on motherhood alone, H. D. had written to Bryher that she hoped to employ a nurse, recommended by Brigit Patmore, to "take, at times, entire charge, so that I may continue my work"—though she also wrote longingly of the "great adventures" she anticipated having with her daughter, when she was old enough. Bryher's support enabled an even more drastic solution: her money allowed Perdita to spend much of her first two years as a full-time resident at the renowned Norland Nursery in Kensington, where H. D.—still recovering from her illness—visited her daily. From 1921, Perdita lived with the two women and a revolving cast of nannies, friends, and devoted grandparents (Bryher's parents, and H. D.'s mother Helen, who came to Europe after her husband's death and often traveled with the group), an integral part of a loving ménage structured around H. D.'s work. Thinking back on the routines and rhythms of her childhood, Perdita remembered watching H. D. sharpen her yellow pencils and stack up her notebooks, before being

H. D. and Perdita.

whisked away by Bryher as the study door closed. Bryher's writing could be done while Perdita played under the table, but the child knew that her mother was not to be disturbed. For H. D., Bryher enabled a way of life where motherhood and creative work could be combined, if precariously: a life she had not felt possible. On July 17, H. D. would write to Bryher if they were not together: the message would read, "Every year I thank you for saving me and Pup."

During the 1920s, H. D. published several successful volumes of poetry, living at the center of a bohemian network of writers and artists that extended across Europe. But the creative crisis associated with her time in Mecklenburgh Square refused to abate. On her shelves lay the unfinished manuscripts she had drafted and abandoned over the years; she described the process as akin to weaving Penelope's web, constantly undoing work in a sterile cycle of destruction. By the early 1930s, her production had ground to a halt, and she felt trapped in a spiral of "repetitive thoughts and experiences," unable to move on. It was at this point that, with Bryher's encouragement, H. D. approached Sigmund Freud, whose radical theories on sexuality, the self, and the unconscious had shocked the medical establishment. Their relationship—in part one of teacher and pupil, as well as analyst and analysand—was mutually stimulating. Freud, whom she called "Papa" or "the Professor," was an unlikely mentor for H. D.: she was especially indignant when he told her that "women did not creatively amount to anything or amount to much, unless they had a male counterpart or a male companion from whom they drew their inspiration." Riled, she determined to prove to him that her artistic powers manifested through, not despite, her femininity. But Freud's provocative attitude and general demeanor reminded her disconcertingly of D. H. Lawrence. As their analysis progressed, she was surprised to find that memories of Lawrence kept swimming to the surface: a brief episode in Mecklenburgh Square, long suppressed, now took on greater significance than it had before.

After she left Mecklenburgh Square, H. D. never saw Lawrence again. But during her analysis—her memory pricked by the resemblance she saw in Freud—she asked Bryher to send to Vienna a copy of Lawrence's selected letters, edited by Aldous Huxley and published in 1932, two years after Lawrence's death from tuberculosis at the age of forty-four. Her interest piqued, she began to read various recent memoirs of Lawrence written by "fanatical" women—among them Catherine Carswell and Mabel Dodge Luhan—who seemed to have "found him some sort of guide or master." H. D. was irritated by this "cult," and the easy way Lawrence, in death, had begun to be idolized (in Virginia Woolf's words, he had acquired a posthumous reputation as "a prophet, the exponent of some mystical theory of sex"). But she found him more and more on her mind, even infiltrating her subconscious. In a dream where Lawrence appeared without a beard, he merged with an image of her father she remembered from a photograph: the connection seemed to symbolize a power he held over her, but also a vertiginous blurring of his identity with her own. Later, during a "dark, bomb-shattered night" of the Second World War, she dreamed again of "a fiery, golden Lawrence, it was nothing but a fleeting presence and the words 'Hilda, you are the only one of the whole crowd, who can really write.'"

But as well as his praise for her writing, which had meant so much, these visions reminded her of a certain discomfort she had always felt around Lawrence. H. D. had written to John Cournos in October 1916 that she was beginning to see people in relation to colors: Cournos the peaceful blue of lapis lazuli, Aldington a fiery wine red. "But there is another now," she confided. "There is a yellow flame, bright, hard, clear, terrible, cruel! There is the yellow that sees in me its *exact* complement. There is a power in this person to kill me . . . I do not mean physically—(though I do not expect to see him physically)—I mean in a more subtle way. I do not want to deny fate—but it is fate that I die or that I live!" She doesn't offer this person's name, and he isn't mentioned elsewhere in their correspondence, but in *Miranda Masters* Cournos gives his reaction to this letter, which is quoted almost verbatim, and reveals that he took her to be speaking of a poet "whose beautiful, passionate verses were shocking England by their frank pagan sensuality"—evidently a portrait of Lawrence. She didn't mention him to Cournos again, and this character doesn't recur in the novel, this episode left as an unexplained aside. But H. D.'s letter expresses a deep and complex emotion toward Lawrence. Even tenuous connections seemed, to her, imbued with portentous meaning: she had been struck by the fact that their birthdays were a year less a day apart, so that she and Lawrence were the same age for one day a year; their reversed initials also implied a twinship which felt to her significant. But her idea that Lawrence possessed a power to "kill me," though not "physically," suggests an anxiety that this sameness—the "*exact* complement"—bore within it a threat: a fear that he might wipe out her own creative powers, deprive her, somehow, of her voice.

Now, almost two decades later, that fear appeared to be realized. H. D. talked at length with Freud about Lawrence; she gradually became convinced that the Mecklenburgh Square years held the key to the unresolved problem which was curbing her ability to write. Above all, her sessions with Freud stirred up the memories of an artistic disagreement. Given confidence by Freud's encouragement, it was this argument with Lawrence which became the crux of the novel she now began to redraft, a markedly different version of the story she had written over and over again.

In all H. D.'s novels except for *Bid Me to Live*—mostly written in the early 1920s, and not intended for publication—the story ends with the H. D. character finding affirmation and freedom through partnership with another woman. In many ways, H. D.'s first attempts at writing about the Mecklenburgh Square period stand as a tribute to the new sort of family she, Perdita, and Bryher formed: a matriarchal clan focused on freedom and creativity, connected to one another not by law but by choice. In *Paint It Today* (a version composed around 1921, and the most explicitly lesbian of the novels), the Aldington character—married to appease and simultaneously escape overbearing parents—hardly figures, and the protagonist's marriage is presented as a brief interlude between two main affairs with female characters, based on Frances Gregg and Bryher. In *Palimpsest* (1926), a brutal version of the story set in a Roman army camp, which transposes the Aldingtons' marriage into a forced union between a lascivious soldier and a Greek slave, the Bryher character helps the protagonist return to writing poetry, reanimating the "sheer intoxicating intellect" which her marriage had suffocated. At the end of *Asphodel* (1921–22, and revised around 1926), pregnancy and childbirth—portrayed elsewhere in the novel as a source of violence done to women by men, and associated with war—become a form of creative expression. This version focuses on the happiness Hermione eventually finds with Beryl (Bryher), with whom she brings up her daughter, finally breaking the cycle of unsuitable relationships. No longer is Hermione terrified of pregnancy: having renounced heterosexuality, she is confident in her instinct for survival, able both to give birth and to write again.

Bid Me to Live is the only one of H. D.'s novels to focus entirely on heterosexual relationships: Gregg, Bryher, and her second pregnancy do not appear, and the novel's ending centers on Rico, a character absent from all the other manuscripts. Yet in 1949, H. D. wrote that this last novel was the first she was happy with: "I think I pay tribute in it, to that England, to that particularly Bloomsbury scene and those people . . . I never wrote anything of Lawrence, though I was asked to. I do think I have a very authentic Frederico, and that pleases me as I did not want to let all that go, without a sort of hail and farewell." This novel, unlike the earlier versions H. D. composed, is not about finding happiness in a new relationship or in motherhood. At its center is a different sort of self-assertion, one no less vital: H. D.'s assertion of herself as a writer.

Aside from the letter to Cournos, Lawrence is hardly mentioned in H. D.'s extant correspondence from the Mecklenburgh Square years: there's little evidence to suggest that they were especially important to each other personally, still less that they had any sort of romantic relationship. It was, therefore, a surprise to all when *Bid Me to Live* appeared to suggest a longstanding passion. In the novel, it's the support of Frederico (the character based on Lawrence) that sparks the very beginning of Julia's writing: H. D. attributes to Rico the words of Pound which famously launched her career, as if editing her own origin story.

"Don't you know, don't you realise that this is poetry?" said Frederico, edging her away toward the far end of the room. He held the pages that she had brought Mary Dowell for her anthology. "Don't you realise that this is poetry?"

In the novel, Julia's attraction to Rico begins to obsess her; she imagines herself and Rico projected into another dimension, outside of the room, the city, the war. The centerpiece of the novel takes place in the large sitting room, where Julia and Rico sit alone, at work, while the others are out shopping. For Julia, this moment has been deliberately engineered: "it was understood . . . she and Rico were to work something out between them." Rico opens a notebook and spreads it on his knee, looking to Julia like "the true artist working with no apparent self-consciousness." She moves to the window and gazes out on to the square, "where the plane-trees were swaying in the wind, their branches etched against the near sky." With a start she glances back into the room, and finds his eyes locked on her, his gaze marking a track through the air between them, filled with some peculiar magnetism. She gets up and edges her chair toward him; gently she touches his sleeve—and he winces sharply, recoiling from her touch with a shiver like a "hurt jaguar." Stunned, Julia retreats. Not a word is spoken between them before they hear voices at the door, and in sweep Elsa and Bella, laughing and teasing Rico about the landlady, who had inquired flirtatiously about him on the stairs. As the room is caught up in a call for teatime, Bella shoving things about proprietorially, Elsa flinging her bags on the floor, Julia notices that Rico has already started writing again.

When John Cournos and Arabella Yorke read *Bid Me to Live* on its publication in 1960, they were outraged at the depiction of the frisson between H. D. and Lawrence, which seemed to them a travesty. Both dismissed the idea that Lawrence could possibly have had romantic designs on H. D., and suggested that H. D. must have been duped by Lawrence into thinking his feelings were deeper than they were. But their interpretations of this scene—like that of the biographer who suggested that Lawrence was Perdita's father and H. D. the model for his Lady Chatterley—were too literal. Rico's importance, in the book, lies not in his status as love interest, but in the challenge he poses to

Julia's sense of self, and to her writing. When H. D. wrote about Lawrence in Mecklenburgh Square, it was not to reveal a romantic attachment, but to dissect the power his image had come to represent, and which she had spent her life trying to overcome. The exploration of sexual politics in *Bid Me to Live* is a response to H. D.'s wider, ongoing search for a way she could live "in two dimensions," as a writer and as a woman. The years of feeling stifled by men—a pain which went right back to her childhood, through her engagement to Pound and the breakdown of her marriage—now came to a head, as she connected her present inability to write with the control these men had always exerted over her. As she returned to the Mecklenburgh Square episode, the personal turmoil of those years manifested anew as an artistic crisis.

Lawrence himself had always remained reticent on the subject of H. D., though he wrote to Arabella's mother, Selina Yorke, in December 1918 (having learned of H. D.'s pregnancy): "Feeling sorry for her, one almost melts. But I *don't* trust her—other people's lives, indeed!" In 1926, writing to another friend, he expressed exasperation at H. D. ("a cat") for not divorcing Aldington and allowing him happiness with Arabella, "though she herself went off with Gray." Lawrence's most extensive discussion of the group is a brief section of his novel *Aaron's Rod*, begun in Mecklenburgh Square in November 1917 and published in 1922. It offers an account of H. D.'s behavior more nuanced but no less damning than John Cournos's. On his travels, the protagonist, Aaron Sisson, encounters a strange bohemian ménage engaged in a reckless display of domestic anarchy: bored of playing conventional parlor games, they are trying to fix candles and fireworks to trees in the forest outside. At their center is Julia (it is striking that, forty years later, H. D. chose the same name for her self-portrait), whose discomfort within the group is highlighted from the start. She is "a tall stag of a thing, but she sat hunched up like a witch"; she is wild-eyed, with long, twitchy fingers, prone to bouts of nervous high-pitched laughter. Lawrence has reversed the chronology of the two affairs, placing

H. D.'s before Aldington's—a galling distortion, given that the characters and situation would have been instantly recognizable to anyone familiar with the group. When we meet Julia, she is attempting—with increasingly overt coquettishness—to encourage her husband, Robert, "a fresh, stoutish young Englishman in khaki," to start an affair with a woman called Josephine: it soon transpires that she is longing to leave Robert for Cyril Scott, with whom she has established "a nervous kind of amour . . . based on soul sympathy and emotional excitement." Robert tells the others that he doesn't object to her affair at all, and Aaron deduces that Julia is trying to dramatize her dilemma in order to gain attention: that she really wants Robert to beg her to stay. The group's attitudes to Julia range from disgust to amusement to pity; for Aaron, she is manipulative and corrupt, her behavior confirming his fear that women are out to possess men, and to destroy men's freedom by asserting their own.

H. D., when she read the novel, found the characters "unrecognisable, as the characters of that war-time charade; least of all did I know myself, Julia . . . No doubt, I did not want to recognise her." She sounds resigned, but it must have been dispiriting beyond belief to see her suffering caricatured so cruelly—to see both Lawrence and Cournos condemn her from the safety of fiction, revealing the hypocrisy of their avowed commitment to individual freedom. The novel's central theme—that heterosexual love is "a battle in which each party strove for the mastery of the other's soul"—occupied Lawrence throughout his career, and also pervaded his own relationships. Friends, including Gray and Aldington, later wrote of Lawrence's possessiveness, the way he demanded total subservience and obedience from his friends, a sacrifice, wrote Gray, "which no one with any personality at all could make." This attitude was particularly entrenched in Lawrence's relationships with women. Gray later wrote that he grew "weary and skeptical" of Lawrence's attitude to the many women who admired him, and whose adoration he seemed to cultivate. And it's clear that even while he was in Mecklenburgh Square, Lawrence was alert to the power he held over H. D. Writing to Lawrence at 44 Mecklenburgh Square on November 7, 1917, Gray accused him of encouraging women to worship him as "a Jesus Christ to a regiment of Mary Mag-dalenes." In his reply—more amused than angry—Lawrence assured Gray that any woman who fell in love with him was seeking not physi-cal gratification but a spiritual awakening, which he was well placed to offer. He loftily argued that these women—"Hilda Aldington" included—represented to him "the threshold of a new world, or under-world, of knowledge and being"; a realm whose secrets he intended to reveal in his own writing. His letter is mysterious and allusive, but one part of its meaning is clear: women, to Lawrence, were not equals but muses; not artists in their own right, but simply material.

Almost forty years later, H. D. recalled Frieda warning her against her husband, in a rare private moment: "Lawrence does not really care for women. He only cares for men. Hilda, you have no idea of what he is like." Thinking back to that time, H. D. puzzled over something Lawrence had said in Mecklenburgh Square, as they sat around on the landlady's gilt-edged chairs: that "Frieda was there forever on his right hand, I was there forever—on his left." She was amused to think of Lawrence presenting himself as Jesus, with Frieda as John, the loyal disciple, and H. D. as Judas, the rival and potential betrayer. But the image was disquieting—whether good or bad, both women were no more than helpmeets to the prophetic male. She concluded that, like Aldington, he saw women only as either a body or a mind: while Frieda provided his emotional support, Hilda was there for intellectual stimu-lation, and neither was permitted to transgress into the other's terri-tory. In *Bid Me to Live*, Julia begins to sense that Rico's winning exterior is a mask: he suddenly appears the epitome of aggression, his red beard like a volcano, his teeth as he laughs ready "to tear, to devour." She suddenly realizes why Elsa, Rico's wife, has seemed to condone the potential affair: free of her husband, she will be able to pursue her own interests, while Julia will take over her role in offering support and inspiration for the great artist. Belatedly, Julia sees that in providing the conditions for Rico's freedom, she will be sacrificing her own: "She was to be used, a little heap of fire-wood, brushwood, to feed the flame of Rico."

One particular incident comes to represent Julia's fears. At a cru-

cial moment in the book, Rico responds angrily to a poem Julia has
sent him, an exploration of the doomed love of Orpheus and Eurydice.
"I don't like the second half of the Orpheus sequence as well as the
first," he tells her. "Stick to the woman speaking. How can you know
what Orpheus feels? It's your part to be woman, the woman vibration,
Eurydice should be enough. You can't deal with both." Rico's criticism
disturbs Julia, with its damning implication that she should curb her
ambitions and write only from personal experience, not try to say anything universal. Julia voices H. D.'s frustration at these double standards (made all the more egregious by the fact that in Mecklenburgh
Square, Lawrence had been correcting the proofs of his novel *Women
in Love*, which explores the inner lives of the Brangwen sisters): "This
man-, this woman-theory of Rico's was false, it creaked in the joints . . .
If he could enter, so diabolically, into the feelings of women, why
should not she enter into the feelings of men?"

H. D. did not allow Lawrence to silence her. Rather, she took up
and transformed his command to write "only" as a woman, by placing
women's voices and experiences at the center of her work. Her poem
"Eurydice," which Lawrence had critiqued, was printed in the *Egoist* in
May 1917. In the published version, Orpheus doesn't speak; if, as the
novel suggests, there was once a second section where he did, she evidently took Lawrence's advice and cut the verses. But the poem is a
striking riposte to the usual story in which Eurydice, condemned to
eternal silence by the carelessness of her poet husband, is pitied and
swiftly forgotten. Instead, H. D.'s Eurydice is powerful, independent,
and dangerous. She reproaches Orpheus for sending her back to hell;
finally, she claims the underworld as her own domain, a place where
she can find peace within herself at last, no longer drowned out by her
husband's stultifying song. H. D.'s time in Mecklenburgh Square was
painful for her personally, but it was a crucial juncture in her work: this
groundbreaking poetic monologue, longer than her previous works
and far more personal, marked her emergence out of the Imagist aesthetic toward a new voice that was distinctly her own. And its publication sparked a new, lifelong project for H. D. Over the next four
decades, her poetry moved away from the timeless, impersonal beauty

of *Sea Garden* to a more narrative style, centered around female figures drawn from mythology—Cassandra, Calypso, Demeter. Her work explored the inner lives of ancient heroines forging their own narratives, their own identities, outside of traditional legends where they were passive, ignored, or vilified; the project mirrored her concern, through her autobiographical writings, to interrogate her own past and renounce the "initiators" whom she had allowed to direct her. As

Richard Aldington (*front row, far right*) in 1918.

she wrote these women out of the myths they had been trapped in for centuries, H. D. began to write herself out of the situation that had overwhelmed her in Mecklenburgh Square.

Her major poetic sequence *Helen in Egypt* was published in 1961, the year after *Bid Me to Live,* and composed in tandem with it. In this work, H. D. counters the familiar myth in which Helen's infidelity is responsible for the Trojan War, favoring instead an alternative story, borrowed from Euripides's subversive drama *Helen.* H. D.'s Helen is not a capricious beauty indifferent to the slaughter unleashed in her name, but an innocent and bewildered woman, trapped in Egypt while a phantom double, created by the gods, wreaks havoc at Troy. For H. D., Helen is a mirror of Iphigenia, whose figure resonated for her during the First World War: both were sacrificed—in body or in reputation—to men's aggressive instincts, left voiceless while the tales of the men's martial exploits live on like Orpheus's songs. In *Helen in Egypt*, H. D.'s Helen embarks on a quest toward self-discovery, repairing her fractured psyche and stepping out of the fictional identities imposed on her (a famous beauty, a passive object, a contemptible adulteress) through a process of psychoanalysis, encounters with characters from her past, and beginning herself to write. Across her work, H. D. was seeking new ways to understand a simple fact: that women have always been shaped by expectations of how they should behave, and thus have been denied the freedom to discover and know themselves as they might want to be. H. D.'s triumph is to create a character who emerges as a complex whole, after whose discovery the passive, objectified Helen of tradition can never be read in the same way again.

The final chapter of *Bid Me to Live* takes the form of a letter from Julia to Rico. She answers back to his criticism of her poetry, to his insistence that women cannot write convincingly about men, that they should stick to subjects they know and not try to be "both." The letter is a firm retort to all those who, throughout her life, attempted to shape H. D. according to their chosen labels, and stands also as a wider statement about women's subordinate position in society. In Virginia

Woolf's novel *To the Lighthouse*, the artist Lily Briscoe seeks a form of creative expression that doesn't entail motherhood and domestic duty, ignoring the needling voices of men who insist, mockingly, that "women can't paint, women can't write." At the end of the book, her completed painting stands as a triumphant rejoinder to these taunts. In the same way, Julia's letter to Rico—also coming at the end of a poetic and complex novel—rejects the suggestion that being a woman is incompatible with being an artist. Her words affirm her desire to be a writer, not a muse; a person ready to transcend the confines of contemporary womanhood through her radical art.

Freud had told H. D. she was the "perfect bisexual," and during her analysis she wrote to Bryher that she realized she had, apparently unusually, never identified with one parent over the other: "I have tried to be man or woman," she wrote, "but I have to be both." In *A Room of One's Own*, published five years before H. D.'s analysis, Woolf famously argued, following Coleridge, that "a great mind is androgynous . . . it is fatal to be a man or woman pure and simple." Instead, she calls for women writers to be "woman-manly or man-womanly," and to refuse to limit their scope or ambition in deference to conventional gender roles. H. D. had the book in her library, and it's tempting to suppose that Woolf's phrasing may have influenced Julia's closing words. Speaking of the many dangers women face across their lives—the "biological catch" of accidental pregnancy, boredom as an "affable hausfrau," the invisibility of an "old maid"—Julia suggests that creative work may offer women a chance at "true fulfillment":

> There was one loophole, one might be an artist. Then the danger met the danger, the woman was man-woman, the man was woman-man. But Frederico, for all his acceptance of her verses, had shouted his man-is-man, his woman-is-woman at her; his shrill peacock-cry sounded a love-cry, death-cry for their generation.

At the end, Julia achieves what H. D. calls *"gloire"*: a modern version of the ancient Greek *kleos*, the undying glory afforded to those whose achievements live on after death, a concept most commonly associated with war heroes, but also with poets. No longer will Julia allow Rico to play God, as Lawrence did in the game of charades: no longer shall he dictate the parameters within which she may write. *"Gloire,"* for H. D., becomes a fluid creative power, possessed by men and women alike.

> Perhaps you would say I was trespassing, couldn't see both sides, as you said of my Orpheus. I could be Eurydice in character, you said, but woman-is-woman and I couldn't be both. The *gloire* is both.
>
> No, that spoils it; it is both and neither. It is simply myself sitting here, this time propped up in bed, scribbling in a notebook, with a candle at my elbow.

H. D. remembered writing the book's ending in a strange Swiss hotel where "the room grew colder as 'it' compelled my pencil." After she added her last corrections and typed out the text afresh, she found herself suddenly contented: reading the pages out loud, she "realised that at last, the War I story had 'written itself.'" In 1953, she told Aldington that writing *Bid Me to Live* had played an essential role in helping her feel free at last. "You must not think I minimise your output and your years of hard work. I just had to do my own work and was from the first, even with Ezra, in danger of being negated by other people's work. I speak of this in regard to DHL in the book." In her seventies, H. D. looked back on Lawrence's injunction, carelessly thrown out in Mecklenburgh Square while he was criticizing her poetry, to "kick over your tiresome house of life." She reflected on her long and satisfying career, her happy relationships and many friends, her four grandchildren, and the success of her final novel. "This is my House of Life," she wrote, "but it is not tiresome."

DOROTHY L. SAYERS

(1893–1957)

44 Mecklenburgh Square
December 1920–December 1921

I should try the garden in Mecklenburgh Square. A thing
might lie quite a long time under those bushes.
—DOROTHY L. SAYERS, *Strong Poison* (1930)

O n October 14, 1920, the autumn sun pouring through the windows, the University of Oxford's first women graduates were presented in the Sheldonian Theatre. As the south doors swung open to reveal the principals of the women's colleges, resplendent in caps and gowns after decades of campaigning for the honor of degrees, the theatre—containing the largest-ever assembly congregated at the university—rang out in spontaneous applause. Among the celebrants that day was twenty-seven-year-old Dorothy Leigh Sayers, receiving a first-class degree in modern languages from Somerville College five years after she had completed her studies. She had written to the university especially to request a place in this ceremony, ostensibly because she was on the brink of leaving the country—"but really, of course," she wrote to her mother in August, "because I want so much to be in the first batch. It will be so much more amusing." That evening the Somerville graduates—including the writers Vera Brittain and Winifred Holtby—celebrated with a jubilant dinner, where a special toast was drunk to Emily Penrose, principal of the college, and where

Professor Gilbert Murray presided as guest of honor. "I gnash my teeth when I think of all yr Somerville young women preening in cap & gown," wrote Murray's friend Jane Harrison from Cambridge, where proposals to admit women to full membership of the university—for which she had been petitioning since 1895—were rejected that December for the second time. "So like Oxford & so low to start after us & get in first!"

The first women graduates, October 1920.

"Of those Somerville students in the years immediately preceding the First War," wrote Vera Brittain, "Dorothy L. Sayers made the most lasting impression both on her contemporaries and on the outside world." Brittain was writing in 1960, when Sayers was firmly established as a doyenne of detective fiction, whose flamboyantly monocled detective Lord Peter Wimsey was a household name, as widely beloved as Hercule Poirot, Father Brown, or Sherlock Holmes. But in 1920, with few concrete plans beyond a staunch refusal to settle as a teacher and a yearning to achieve success through her writing, Sayers's future prospects were beginning to cause consternation to her long-suffering parents, and—though she did her best to hide it—to herself. It's easy to read the year Sayers spent in Mecklenburgh Square, writing her first novel, as her apprenticeship, the starting point in her inevitable rise to fame and commercial vindication. Yet at this point, success was far from assured for Sayers. Like H. D., she faced scorn from male contemporaries who dismissed her work just as she was finding her voice, while her sense of independence was shaken by an unsatisfying relationship which forced her to examine whether any form of partnership was compatible with her commitment to her work. This was the year in which Sayers's life could have taken any of various directions: she might have agreed to marry an unsuitable man for the sake of security, or accepted the entreaties of her parents to take a respectable permanent teaching job and keep her writing as a pleasant hobby. It was due to her own imagination and determination that her life would follow a very different path.

Dorothy L. Sayers was born in 1893 in Oxford, where her father was headmaster of the Christ Church Cathedral School. She grew up—an only child—in Bluntisham, a small farming village in Cambridgeshire, where Reverend Sayers had been appointed rector. Religion was a constant presence in her childhood, but not the mysterious spirituality of H. D.'s Moravian heritage; she later described her first years as "hedged about . . . with moral restrictions," and remembered an early sense of frustration that religious life at the rectory was not conducted with the critical rigor to which other aspects of thought and study were subjected. Nonetheless, Dorothy's intellectual development was a priority for the whole household. Her father started her on Latin at the age of six, and across her teens encouraged her many literary projects, which included a dramatic version of *Little Women*, a narrative poem concerning a suicidal prisoner of war, and a self-conscious piece entitled *Such is Fame* about a "very young authoress" who finds trouble when her aunts realize they have been pilloried in her latest bestseller. Among her most extended pieces was a work in cantos called *The Comediad*, in which the spirited heroine breaks off her engagement to a stolid gentleman whose wits have disappointed her. "Dear me!" wrote the teenage Sayers, expressing an attitude that she would hold on to throughout her twenties: "At nineteen, a woman expects to enjoy life, and not to be tied to a 'good husband'!"

Reflecting two decades later on the start of her writing career, Sayers contrasted her prospects with those of her aunts, "brought up without education or training, thrown, at my grandfather's death, into a world that had no use for them." One became a nun, another a " 'companion' to various old cats, saving halfpence and cadging trifles, aimlessly doing what when done was of little value to God or man." Sayers's own mother was a keen letter-writer, who taught her daughter to read before she was four; much later, Sayers described her as "a woman of exceptional intellect, which, unfortunately, never got the education which it deserved." It was thanks to her parents that Sayers's did. Though not especially well off, Henry and Helen Sayers were fascinated and delighted by their daughter's precocious talents, and made sure that her curiosity and interests were nurtured; their attitude would prove instrumental in giving her the time and confidence to develop as a scholar over the coming years. H. D.'s astronomer father had tutored her in math and science, his own passions, but forbade art school; Virginia Woolf had been encouraged to read widely by a father who nonetheless didn't consider that he had any duty to train his daughter for a profession. But Sayers, after years of rigorous homeschooling, was sent in 1909 to board at the Godolphin School in Salisbury. In 1912 she entered Oxford's Somerville College on a Gilchrist Scholarship, having topped the whole country in the Cambridge Higher Local Examination—a nationwide school-leaving test—the previous spring.

Having up to now taken her education for granted, Sayers arrived at the ancient university at a time when the position of women there was the subject of fierce debate. Over the latter half of the nineteenth century, campaigners had pressed for universities to allow girls to continue their education beyond school on equal terms with men. This upheaval of the status quo stirred virulent opposition among commentators: some medical detractors argued that education would disrupt menstruation and cause dysfunction of the reproductive system; others feared that educated women would be introduced to sexual licentiousness through classical literature, that spinster teachers might peddle "oblique and distorted conceptions of love," or that women's widespread employment might presage an apocalyptic war between the sexes, culminating in the ultimate extinction of the race. In 1873, two Oxford colleges offered a scholarship to the school student who obtained the highest results in the "Cambridge Locals," only to withdraw the prize in embarrassment when that pupil's name was revealed to be Annie Rogers. Rogers (who was awarded a set of books as a consolation prize) became the symbol of women's fight for education, specifically in Oxford, where that year a series of "Lectures for Ladies" was established in borrowed buildings and attended by the daughters, sisters, and wives of sympathetic dons. In 1879, Somerville opened as a residential hall for women, where twelve pupils lived and devoted their time to study.

In subsequent years, Somerville became the first of the women's halls to adopt an entrance examination and call itself a college, as well as the first Oxford college to be nondenominational. This secular stance attracted Sayers, by now fed up with the "sentimental" and overly dutiful Christianity practiced at home and school. When she arrived at Somerville, the college was tentatively established within the university: women were allowed to sit all classes and examinations, though were not considered "full" students, nor was their work acknowledged with the award of a degree at the end. But women's increasing freedom was marked by several new buildings, as the university began to carve out new spaces to accommodate its female students. Somervillians no longer had to share the single bathroom, which had once doubled up as a servant's bedroom; the college now boasted a magnificent library, and a grand dining hall was under construction in a new quadrangle appended to the original house. The renovations were designed to make it feel less like a family home—which the original arrangement had tried to emulate—and more like a real college, a place where students could focus on their professional work. Nonetheless, Sayers's contemporaries remembered tepid water, unpleasant food, and a general atmosphere of restriction, since their academic and social behavior was under constant scrutiny from opponents eager to cite the slightest misdemeanor as ammunition to demand a revocation of women's place at Oxford. A female student recalled a don who began his classes "Gentlemen—and others who attend my lectures," and another who insisted that the women sit behind him so he didn't have to see them as he declaimed. Articles in the press constantly feigned concern that women were overworking, and that their minds and constitutions were not geared to such intensive toil.

But this didn't prevent Sayers from having fun. She threw on the fire a letter from an elderly cousin attempting to recruit her for the Christian Social Union, and flung herself into artistic activity: she sang in the Bach Choir (and was reprimanded by the college dean for rehearsing in the bath), attended lectures by G. K. Chesterton (after whom she named the overstuffed armchair in her bedroom), and frequented Gilbert and Sullivan operas and university debates (including one in which her friend Charis Barnett—later a pioneer of birth control—proposed the motion "That the reluctance of the modern woman to marry is a benefit to Society"). While the dons fretted that girls in tight skirts were distracting male examiners, and urged their charges to maintain decorum in public, Sayers and her peers enjoyed giving chaperones the slip to meet male friends in Oxford's tearooms, hosting late-night cocoa parties amid swirls of cigarette smoke, and testing the limits of their seniors' outrage. Sayers was well known to her friends for her penchant for "extravagant indoor headgear" and her long earrings featuring a parrot perched in a gilded cage. Later in life, Sayers would ride a motorbike and dress in masculine attire ("If the trousers do not attract you," she insisted in an essay, "so much the worse; for the moment I do not want to attract you. I want to enjoy myself as a human being."). Even at this age, when others at Somerville were more interested in meeting husbands than in scholarship, she was eager to rebel against the norms of femininity, aware that conformity might curtail her creative ambition.

At Somerville, Sayers found new audiences for her writing, previously restricted to indulgent aunts and reluctant schoolfriends. With Barnett and several others, including Muriel Jaeger, Muriel St. Clare Byrne, and Dorothy Rowe, she founded the Mutual Admiration Society for the open critique of members' literary efforts. (If the group didn't take the name themselves, she noted sardonically, others would surely bestow it on them.) The unwavering support of this group of

Dorothy L. Sayers as Sir Hugh Allen in the Going-Down Play of 1915.

women was a spur to Sayers's self-belief as a developing writer, and provided her first taste of a literary circle, each participant committed to improving their own and each other's work. Several members went on to publish novels, plays, and poems, and remained friends and regular collaborators; throughout her life, Sayers would share works in progress with her old group, who wrote back with rigorous analysis as well as generous praise. Twenty-five years later, Sayers knew some of the Inklings, a far more famous Oxford writing group. But while these men—C. S. Lewis, Charles Williams, J. R. R. Tolkien—were established writers in and outside the university, the MAS offered a subversive community within an institution where women were constantly reminded that their talents were not wholly welcome.

Sayers's offerings to their weekly meetings were mainly in verse, which, she later wrote, she considered "the best medium in which to form one's style": "I write prose uncommonly badly, and can't get ideas," she told a friend. Yet although her poetry mainly employed conventional forms and a serious, austere tone, at college she participated with gusto in ribald storytelling sessions and ongoing battles of wit. At one point, she wrote home that Somerville was in the grip of "quite a ghost craze," with everyone telling "psychic stories": her own contribution to this trend involved a dead millionaire giving an account of his life to the Devil to establish how many years his soul should spend in purgatory. But at the end of her second year, the outbreak of war rendered fictional horrors obsolete.

Sayers spent the beginning of the First World War on holiday in France, having blithely disregarded her family's concerns; with no close friends in immediate danger, and removed from the despair of those like H. D. left behind on the home front, she found the situation "immensely exciting." The following summer, living at Oriel College since Somerville had been transformed into a military hospital, she completed her degree, specializing in medieval French, and began to contemplate her future. She toyed with the idea of staying on at Somerville, but soon changed her mind: "Do you know," she wrote to her parents, "it is dreadful, but the longer I stay in Oxford, the more certain I am that I was never cut out for an academic career—I was really meant to be sociable." Many Somerville students took on war work, for the British Red Cross or St. John Ambulance Brigade, serving as radiographers in military hospitals, as chemists and War Office administrators, or, like Vera Brittain, as nurses in France. Sayers considered similar pathways, keen to do "something real for the first time in my life," but decided against it, wary of "hard labour and horrors," and in January 1916 she accepted a position as modern languages mistress at a girls' school in Hull, deciding it "wouldn't do any harm" to try teaching for a year.

It wasn't long before she felt her brain "growing rusty," and in April 1917 she returned to Oxford to work as apprentice to the publisher and bookseller Basil Blackwell, an early supporter of her writing. (One of her earliest poems had appeared in his anthology *Oxford Poetry* in December 1915, alongside "Goblin Feet," the first published poem by J. R. R. Tolkien; in December 1916, Blackwell had published her debut collection, the appropriately titled *Op. I.*) "There is no future in teaching," she insisted to her father, "and I think that I might really make something of publishing." She enjoyed the work, which combined her literary acumen with a pleasing emphasis on practicality. But in the summer of 1919, keen once more for "a thorough change," she left Blackwell's for Normandy.

Sayers had an ulterior motive for accepting a secretarial position at L'École des Roches in the French village of Verneuil, a school for boys founded on the model of the English public school system. It would involve working alongside Eric Whelpton, an Oxford friend with whom Sayers had fallen in love. Unfortunately, Whelpton (so he later claimed) had failed to notice Sayers's attraction to him—which was obvious to their friends—due to post-traumatic stress from his time in the army, as well as his consuming dalliance with "an intelligent semi-Austrian countess." Before she left, Sayers's father summoned Whelpton to dinner at the family home, where Whelpton—awkwardly attired in a formal suit—later remembered assuring him that "my affections were already engaged, that I had no romantic intentions whatsoever with regard to Dorothy, that she would be lodged in a different house and I should see very little of her outside office hours."

Regrettably for Sayers, his promises proved true. In July 1920, Whelpton suddenly declared his intention to move to Florence with a divorced woman whom he had met at the theatre and tracked down via an advertisement in the personal column of *The Times*. "The whole thing would be most heroic and pathetic if one didn't see the comic side of it," wrote Sayers in wry acceptance of the situation. Whelpton suggested she stay on at the school and take over his job, but she decided against it, though she had enjoyed the casual atmosphere, the company of the lively boys, and the good food: she wanted new excitements, and a home of her own, where she could devote herself to work that truly interested her. "I really want to get to London if possible," she told her parents. In August, on the back of some paper headed with the address of Whelpton's new employer, she jotted down her hopes for the future. "Certainly no more teaching—I have had my share of that . . . Settling down is as unsettling as being unsettled—however I suppose I shall get used to it." At the end of September 1920, she arrived in London, with no job and nowhere to live. The news that the University of Oxford had, on May 11, passed a statute allowing women to take degrees (except in theology) under the same conditions as men was a brief triumph in a period of gloom. As she stood in the Sheldonian in her new cap and gown, Dorothy L. Sayers faced an uncertain future.

London, in the years immediately after the First World War, was a dismal place, the streets haunted by an air of gloom and decay. "Our generation is daily scourged by the bloody war," noted Virginia Woolf, who grew used to passing veterans with "stiff legs, single legs, sticks shod with rubber, and empty sleeves" on the streets. "People in a century will say how terrible it all was." It was widely accepted that the cohort "lost" in the war was, as J. B. Priestley put it, "a great generation, marvelous in its promise," and the country fell into a prolonged national display of mourning. In November 1920, the corpse of an unknown soldier was brought from France by boat in a coffin carved from Hampton Court oak and given a state burial in Westminster Abbey, attended by King George V. But behind the pomp of Armistice Day lingered the shadow of everyday, unspoken suffering. While the peace agreement signed in Paris in 1919 had professed to herald a new era for international relations, founded on the harmonious cooperation of countries under the League of Nations, its announcement of harsh reparation terms for Germany led many to suspect that the courage and idealism of the generation who had fought to end war had been betrayed. In 1922 the War Office Committee of Enquiry into "Shell-Shock" submitted a bland and unsympathetic report to parliament, equating the condition to cowardice and suggesting that only "a real effort of will" was required to surmount it; many seriously ill men were diagnosed insane and left to fester in their trauma. Within a few months of the Armistice, thousands of ex-soldiers were sleeping destitute in Hyde Park. During Sayers's first month in London, major demonstrations against unemployment were held in the city, where men charged Whitehall and were beaten back by police.

These events are largely absent from her letters home at the time, as she concentrated on her own predicaments, though they came to shape her later fiction. But in 1920, London signified possibility to Sayers. She was introduced to a film producer who told her that screenwriting was "a frightfully paying business if one had the knack" and encouraged her to try drafting a scenario from Vicente Blasco Ibáñez's 1908 novel *Blood and Sand*, a romantic drama about a Spanish matador. Sayers poured research from the book and from contemporary cinema into her proposal for a silent film, written in turquoise ink on the back of adverts for L'École des Roches. The commission came to nothing—it soon became clear that the producer had neglected to confirm that the rights were actually available—but this setback was a thrill in its own way: it signaled that she was a professional, learning to take the rough with the smooth, and allowed her to hope that next time might be different. "There seem to be plenty of opportunities going about, anyhow," she wrote to her parents; her father enclosed a five-pound note with his sympathetic reply. "More than ever, though, I realise the paramount necessity of always being on the spot—I feel as if I hardly dared leave London for a second."

Her determination to pursue the London literary life only renewed, Sayers's thoughts now turned to accommodation. A plan to share a flat with her friend Muriel Jaeger ("I think we could manage without quarrelling, on a strictly independent basis of course") fell through, but on October 26 she told her parents she had "fixed up to take a very nice unfurnished room at the top of a sort of Ladies' Club in St. George's Square, S. W.," where she slept on "an excellent camp bed, slightly damaged." But this turned out to be a short-lived home: the landlady having proved impossible ("her rents are too high, and she won't try to be amiable"), Sayers gave notice on December 3 and began, with some urgency, to seek alternative digs. A friend of Muriel's alerted her to a "rather beautiful room" she had considered for herself. On December 7, 1920, Sayers wrote to her parents in improved spirits: "Dearest People—The die is cast and I am departing on Thursday to 44 Mecklenburgh Square W.C.1, where I think I shall be much happier." She hired a local greengrocer to move her belongings, and was relieved to be free of the Pimlico landlady's "diabolical" temper. She hoped that Mecklenburgh Square—and, by extension, her life there—would prove "very different, and a success":

> It is the room Mrs. McKillop saw and liked so much—a lovely Georgian room, with three great windows—alas! would that I could afford curtains to them!—perhaps I shall in time—and a balcony looking onto the square. There is an open fireplace, and the last tenant has thoughtfully left some coal behind, which I can take over at a valuation—and there is a gas-ring. The only drawback is, no electric light, but I shall get a little oil-lamp, which will look very nice. It is a beautiful big room, far larger than the one I am in now, and costs less money. The landlady is a curious, eccentric-looking person with short hair—the opposite of Miss Latch in every way—and thoroughly understands that one wants to be quite independent. That is really all I want—to be left alone, and I can't think why people won't leave me!

It was the very room which H. D. had left in 1918. (The night-blue curtains, no longer required for blackout purposes, had evidently disappeared.) Sayers's landlady, Elinor James, was the same woman H. D. described in *Bid Me to Live* as a "valiant militant suffragette" always swathed in Venetian shawls and clutching a glass of Chianti, who filled her house with young bohemians. As Cournos put it in *Miranda Masters*, "She would rather see her rooms empty than fill them with bourgeois undesirables. She looked askance on married couples and gave preference to couples unmarried, living in the bliss of informal union." This eccentric environment suited Sayers well. "I am installed in my new quarters," she told her parents on December 9, "and think I shall like them very much, though I and my little belongings look rather lost in this vast space at present." She asked Basil Blackwell to send her a print of Botticelli's *Birth of Venus* ("to adorn my chimney-piece") and told her parents, "I do very much hope I shall be able to stay here. I'm going to try hard."

Instantly, Sayers felt at home in Mecklenburgh Square—far more so than H. D. had ever felt in the same room. The house, she wrote, was (as before) "full from attic to basement," and was presided over by Miss James, no longer the stern host of dreaded Zeppelin teas: "very nice—one never sees her. Only occasionally, just as one is hurrying away to an appointment, she wanders out and engages one in a discussion of art, literature or domestic economy." H. D. had felt oppressed by Miss James, had sensed her presence as a silent judgment on her domestic upheaval. Sayers, by contrast, saw the landlady as an amusing neighbor and potential confidante, and enjoyed rubbing along efficiently with transient neighbors: after boarding school and college, the lack of privacy, to her, felt companionable rather than uncomfortable. Both women projected on to the house their own feelings about their life there. To H. D., more insecure and anxious by nature, the boardinghouse had signified the dissolution of all domestic structures, mirroring the collapse of her marriage; to Sayers, happily unmarried, it meant independence.

Another "very nice" woman did the cleaning and washing-up "for a moderate stipend," leaving Sayers to enjoy her newfound freedom. She embraced domesticity, beginning to make jumpers from old remnants, and planning ahead to "delightful underclothing, all over little purple parrots!" Living alone involved learning some lessons which had evaded her at Somerville and L'École des Roches, where meals were provided in halls. "I have discovered," she wrote cheerfully, "that the one really vital necessity for living in unfurnished digs is a frying-pan. I bought one the other day, and have just been illustrating my favourite theory—the superiority of the trained mind, no matter what its training has been. Although I can't remember ever having had a frying-pan in my hand before, there was nothing wrong with the eggs I had this evening—or at least, if there was, it was only a sort of urban flavour which wasn't my fault. Of course, if it was ever possible to send new-laid rustic eggs by post—but there!" Her parents were sympathetic to their daughter's travails—and on January 22, 1921, Sayers wrote to thank her mother for "the lovely eggs, which are a great joy." Nonetheless, her new home's proximity to the restaurants of Fitzrovia and the West End offered temptations hard to resist. "Don't ever think I'm not feeding myself well," she wrote. "Food is my most sinful extravagance. I am just going out to get a huge dinner in Soho for two shillings and threepence (beer extra)!"

When later asked to describe her aspirations upon leaving university, Sayers replied that she must have "felt that I was cut out by nature to be the world's greatest something-or-other, but that all I was likely to achieve was an educational job of some kind." Teaching—considered a respectable extension of women's nurturing role—was where 80 percent of women graduates from Oxford and Cambridge found employment until they married, which legally ended their contracts until the marriage bar was lifted in 1935. Moving to Bloomsbury, where literary women were congregating in the cheap boardinghouses around the British Museum, was a brave announcement that Sayers was serious about a different way of life. "It's immoral," she wrote sternly to Muriel Jaeger, "to take up a job solely for the amount of time one can spend away from it, which is what most of us do with teaching." But she was acutely aware that an alternative path would be precarious and came with no guarantee of success. With reluctance, but to prove to her parents that she was pragmatic as well as ambitious, Sayers accepted a temporary teaching post at Clapham High School for the first months of 1921. She was remembered by a former pupil as "looking rather ungainly, pale-faced, hair crimped back into a bun, pince-nez dangling round her neck, wearing a shapeless black dress down which it looked as if she had dropped half her breakfast." Cultivating an air of eccentricity betraying the fact that she didn't really want to be there, she would teach supine, lying on a bench, and once employed a sword with which to gesticulate at the blackboard.

This was not her only employment: she was pleased to find, through a contact of her father's, "a little gold-mine" in providing French translations for "some unspecified Polish organisation," which paid a shilling a page and enabled her to buy a bedcover "of a sort of futurist pattern in orange, black and violet." The agency was erratic in paying on time, but when she mentioned this to Miss James, the landlady (perhaps sympathetic to Sayers's anguished desire both to pay her own way and to pursue her writing seriously) offered to lend her money and delay her rent payments. "She really seems a model sort of landlady," Sayers wrote. And the money earned by this hackwork allowed her to continue with her own poetry. A translation from the Old French of the twelfth-century *Tristan* by Thomas of Britain—whom she admired 'as a master of the psychological novel, and as a lyric poet"—had been published in the *Modern Languages* journal in June and August 1920, and she was delighted to report on December 14 that her poem "Obsequies for Music" had been accepted by J. C. Squire, editor of the *London Mercury*, "a particularly swell sort of monthly, run by tip-top people." The following week, she apologized to her father and aunt for misleading them into supposing she was in actual debt; they had both sent large checks, alarmed by her cheerful claims of destitution. In fact, Sayers was proud of her Bloomsbury independence, contrasting her tenacity favorably with that of Muriel Jaeger, who had quit a job as a subeditor at the feminist weekly *Time and Tide* to return to her family home. "She really isn't as good at roughing it in rooms as I am. She really likes comfort and needs it, of course, being much more delicate than I am—but she doesn't know in the least how to make herself comfortable."

Life in London soon revolved around work. "I don't seem to have any news," she wrote to her parents. "I read and write at the British Museum and have my meals and go to bed!" She went to see Marlowe's *Edward II* at Birkbeck College, "and came to the conclusion that Elizabethan tragedy was rather over-rated"; she visited the National Gallery, and attended "a meeting of 'Faithists'—an obscure sect at Balham, where the minister is 'controlled' by a spirit—THE Spirit, he says—and hurls fearful inspired speeches at one in the dark." But Sayers's greatest pleasure during the year—which would inspire a significant new project—was the season of Grand Guignol plays at the Little Theatre on John Adam Street, a seedy alleyway just off the Strand. The lease of the tiny theatre, its entrance announced by revolving red lights, had been taken over by the director Jose Levy in homage to the Theatre du Grand Guignol in the Montmartre district of Paris, where so many visitors fainted during performances that a resident doctor was employed. The productions were known for their heady combination of the violent and the erotic, and reveled in breaking taboos and disquieting audiences with a blend of titillation and horror. The first London season opened in September 1920 and closed in June 1922 after numerous run-ins with the censors, who balked at the nudity, adultery, poisonings, blood, and occasional eye-gouging. One poster advertisement—featuring a cartoon of a terrified audience in states of collapse or rushing away from the theatre—was deemed so frightening that it was banned on the London Underground.

The plays courted plenty of controversy, but their high-caliber writers (Noël Coward was among Levy's roster) and celebrity actors (such as Sybil Thorndike, whose bloodcurdling scream was notorious) enticed devoted audiences, including, on at least one occasion, Virginia Woolf. Sayers adored the experience and attended several times with various friends—"I hear that this new series of plays surpasses everything else in grisliness," she wrote. This initiation into the macabre infiltrated her latest projects, revealed on January 22, 1921 in a letter to her mother. "I'm in a great hurry, because I'm doing the Clapham work and the Poles, and of course have chosen this moment to be visited with ideas for a detective story and a Grand Guignol play, neither of which will certainly ever get written . . . My detective story begins brightly with a fat lady found dead in her bath with nothing on but her pince-nez. Now, why did she wear pince-nez in her bath? If you can guess, you will be in a position to lay hands upon the murderer, but he's a very cool and cunning fellow. The Grand Guignol play ends with a poisoned kiss!"

In Sayers's 1934 novel *The Nine Tailors*, a young character named Hilary Thorpe is asked whether she plans to become a poet. "Well, perhaps," she replies. "But I don't suppose that pays very well. I'll write novels. Best-sellers. The sort that everybody goes potty over." Now that Sayers was living independently, paying her own rent and bills, she was happy to adjust her literary aspirations to the commercial realities of attempting to live by her pen. Sayers's early poetry was expressive and lyrical, her subject matter gesturing to the melancholic but never to the morbid. But the prose with which she had begun to experiment while in France, and then in Mecklenburgh Square, displayed a distinct relish for the gruesome. In a film script titled *Bonds of Egypt*, a jealous professor chloroforms a love rival and substitutes him, barely breathing, for an ancient Egyptian mummy on show in a regional museum; the unfortunate man's plight is discovered at the last minute when the caretaker notices ice crystals, produced by his desperate gasps, on the inside of the glass case. Another early story, "The Priest's Chamber," introduces a tormented medieval priest who has an affair with the wife of a baron, and is so terrified of public disgrace that he crucifies her in his chamber, the ghastly cross lit by six flaring altar candles. The second part of the story, dated 1919, sees a young woman, visiting a friend in her castle, discover that the house remains haunted by vestiges of the long-ago crime.

But Sayers's main enthusiasm was for stories where chilling misdeeds were followed not by rescues or exorcisms but by logical, immediate investigation. Before she left for France, Sayers had attempted to enroll some university friends into a detective-writing syndicate, and was disappointed that Eric Whelpton—whom she had earmarked as a collaborator—scorned her passion for the genre, considering it beneath their intellectual interests. He later remembered that on her bedside table at Verneuil were "the works of Eugène Sue, the memoirs of various French police officers, and masses of what we used to call penny dreadfuls"; doubtless she also kept close volumes by Edgar Allan Poe, whom she credited with writing the first modern detective story; books by her heroes Wilkie Collins and Sheridan Le Fanu; and the works of G. K. Chesterton, which she later told his wife were "more a part of my mental makeup than those of any writer you could name." At Somerville, she and Muriel Jaeger had pored over the saga of Sexton Blake, a Baker Street–dwelling detective created by Harry Blyth in 1893 ("the Holmes tradition . . . crossed with the Buffalo Bill adventure type"). After Blyth's death, others took over his characters (Blake's assistant Tinker, bloodhound Pedro, and rotund housekeeper Mrs. Bardell), and Sexton Blake's exploits continued to appear in a dedicated magazine, in silent films, on the radio and stage, and even on a set of playing cards, as his character evolved from Victorian gentleman to full-blown action hero.

Sayers adored Blake, and considered the series "the nearest modern approach to a national folk-lore." Unlike Whelpton, she had no pretensions to exclusively highbrow tastes, and saw no reason to differentiate her reading according to a preconceived hierarchy of quality; she devoured both medieval poetry and lurid crime paperbacks with the same imaginative verve and critical rigor. A decade later, Sayers could report that detective fiction "is no longer read [only] in back kitchens" but rather "in Downing Street, and in Bloomsbury studios, in bishops' palaces, and in the libraries of eminent scientists": for now, however, she was delighted to challenge anyone who sneered at her reading matter, pulling them up robustly for their snobbery. In an unpublished essay, written while she was living in Mecklenburgh Square, Sayers addresses a "Miss Dryasdust, MA"—perhaps a version of Whelpton—who "disapproves of my fondness for detective stories of the more popular kind." While her interlocutor begrudgingly accepts Sherlock Holmes "as we put up with the Albert Memorial," she dismisses works by less famous practitioners as "vulgar" and written "by office-boys for office-boys." This "undemocratic contempt," writes Sayers with customary animation, masks the fact that this literature holds in the contemporary imagination the position once occupied by the myths and legends of Arthur and Robin Hood, or the heroic epics of Scandinavia and ancient Greece: the detective, she argued, "is really the last of the great heroes who have stood up for civilisation against disorder and invasion. Roland fought the Saracens; Beowulf fought the dragon; Sexton Blake fights crime." In March 1920, she had asked Muriel to dispatch to Verneuil "all the Sexton Blakes you can lay hands on . . . in discreet packages of about two at a time so that they go as letters and don't get stopped in the Customs." Her letters to Muriel from France abound with lively debate on the comparative merits of different Blake writers, and elaborate theories tracing Blake's origins to solar mythology, the mystery cults of Osiris, and biblical legend of sacrifice and resurrection ("Sexton Blake = Christus").

At Verneuil, recovering from an attack of mumps, Sayers had begun her own attempt at a Sexton Blake story. She never completed "The Adventure of the Piccadilly Flat," which survives only as five chapters and a synopsis. But this effort marks something more than a crucial moment in her development from reader of detective stories to writer of them. The work is particularly notable for the fact that the body (of a French politician) is found, mysteriously, in the bachelor flat of one Lord Peter Wimsey, a character whose charismatic potential was so strong that she would spend the next year writing him into his own novel. For the unfinished story, Sayers had planned a rollicking fantasia involving mutually distrusting British and French agents, an airplane pursuit, and a dramatic unmasking at Westminster Cathedral, as Blake and Wimsey work together to reclaim a stolen code book. The criminal's disguise is uncovered, in an ingenious twist, when the men notice a figure in women's clothes speaking angrily to French officials at a train station, forgetfully referring to "her" self using a masculine adjective. Already Sayers's story departed from the tradi-tional Blake formula, which prioritized action over deduction, speed over sagacity, and hair-raising journeys to outlandish locations over subtle analysis of the evidence: this is an outline for a sophisticated plot bolstered by characteristically highbrow detail.

Over the next months, Sayers experimented with her character, testing him out in dashed-off fragments of stories and sketches for plays. Lord Peter Wimsey soon acquired a monocle and a rare-book collection, and a cheerful ability to unravel apparently preposterous solutions without doffing his slippers. Later in life, though he never finished any of Sayers's books, Eric Whelpton would encourage the rumor that the affable aristocrat was based on him, with characteristics borrowed from other members of L'École des Roches staff. During Sayers's tenure at the school, Whelpton was asked to appoint a new teacher, and rejected the application of "a shy Irishman named James Joyce" in favor of an unqualified Old Etonian named Charles Crichton, "a very handsome man of forty-five who quite frankly said that women were his hobby." Sayers had little patience for tales of Crichton's Casanova exploits, and scorned Whelpton's willingness to listen to him boast about his club, his gentleman servant, his country house, and his flat in Mayfair's Jermyn Street—yet she retained some of these details when constructing Lord Peter Wimsey's London life. But Lord Peter is not primarily a biographical creation. Rather, his character—his ready wit, acute emotional intelligence, and elegant accoutrements—is testament to Sayers's imagination and immersion in the canon of detective fiction.

In January 1921, in the first-floor room at Mecklenburgh Square, gazing out of her window on to the tennis players in the square's garden below, Sayers began to draft a novel in earnest. Lord Peter Wimsey, on his way out to a rare-book auction, receives a call from his mother, the Dowager Duchess of Denver, informing him of "such a quaint thing": the architect repairing the church roof has arrived home to find an unrecognized body in his bathtub, naked, closely shaven and with a pair of pince-nez perched mockingly on his nose. Sensing an invaluable opportunity to indulge "his hobby of criminal investigation," Lord Peter delightedly hotfoots to Battersea. It's soon discovered that a financier named Sir Reuben Levy has disappeared, after dining with friends at the Ritz, on the very day he had arranged to complete a deal worth millions—but Wimsey realizes that the connections between Levy and the body in the bathtub are not what they might logically seem.

The novel—which she called *Whose Body?*—brims with exuberance: although the murder is one of Sayers's most grisly, Wimsey's enthusiasm for his task is irresistible, his attitude to murder playful and intuitive. While his overly pedantic rival Inspector Sugg officiously arrests all the wrong people, Wimsey inveigles the owner of the flat into showing him the corpse, and manages to make a full inspection— "with the air of the late Joseph Chamberlain approving a rare orchid"— while distracting his host with punning patter about soot and servants. He's smart enough to notice everything Sugg doesn't—that the corpse smells of Parma violet, its hair is recently cut, and its fingernails neatly trimmed, but that the hands are calloused, teeth decayed, toenails filthy, and the torso is pocked with flea bites. (In the original manuscript, he also noticed that the body was uncircumcised and therefore could not be the Jewish businessman—but Sayers's publisher insisted this reference be removed.) "Uncommon good incident for a detective story" is Wimsey's objective analysis. "We're up against a criminal— the criminal—the real artist and blighter with imagination—real, artistic, finished stuff."

When Sayers reread *Whose Body?* in 1937, she considered it "conventional to the last degree, and no more like a novel than I to Hercules. This is not really surprising, because one cannot write a novel unless one has something to say about life, and I had nothing to say about it, because I knew nothing." But as well as presenting a remarkably assured hero, *Whose Body?* already displays Sayers's determination to explore and expand the possibilities of the genre she knew and loved. Golden Age detective fiction, which promised order restored satisfactorily from chaos, justice delivered by a detective of apparent omniscience and transgression punished, is often seen as a symptom of the postwar British yearning for escapism, exemplified by the popularity in the 1920s of football pools, crossword puzzles, and light entertainment (such as the musical comedy *Chu Chin Chow*, which premiered in London in August 1916 and ran for five years straight). "It may be," Sayers later wrote, perhaps thinking of her own motivations for immersing herself in both the reading and the writing of detective stories, "that in them [one] finds a sort of catharsis or purging of [one's] fears and self-questionings."

DOROTHY L. SAYERS
AUTHOR OF
WHOSE BODY?
PUBLISHED BY BONI & LIVERIGHT $1.75

Advertising material for *Whose Body?*

But Sayers's work is exceptional because, for her, such questions were never so easily resolved. Even in this first outing, Lord Peter displays a complexity of character and a relationship with the consequences of his work that was unusual in fictional detectives. "I took it up when the bottom of things was rather knocked out for me, because it was so damned exciting," says Wimsey (a war veteran) of his detection habit, during a frank conversation with his policeman friend Charles Parker. "If it was all on paper I'd enjoy every bit of it. I love the beginning of a job—when one doesn't know any of the people and it's just exciting and amusing. But if it comes to really running down a live person and getting him hanged . . . there don't seem as if there was any excuse for me buttin' in." When Wimsey realizes who the murderer must be—a person so unexpected that at first he feels "as if I'd libelled the Archbishop of Canterbury"—he finds himself shaking, plunged into memories of the war: his teeth chatter, he hears the crackle of gunfire and is convinced he's in the trenches under attack. In her very first novel, Dorothy L. Sayers laid the groundwork for a new sort of moral detective; in Mecklenburgh Square, she fed all her current influences into the creation not only of a fresh plot but also of a long-lasting character whose depths and delights would provide her with enough material for several further novels.

"You don't know what it means to be stuck for money," the culprit in *Murder Must Advertise* (1933) tells Wimsey. But his creator certainly did. When Sayers looked back on her year in Mecklenburgh Square, her retrospective pleasure at the eventual success of *Whose Body?* was tinged with the memory of her fluctuating moods as she wondered whether writing would ever be a profitable path. Her letters to her parents—always remarkably open about her everyday routines and her feelings about work, but less so about her darker emotional states—give some indication of her frustrations, though she shielded them from the full extent of her worry. "Things have been very up-and-down and tiresome and pleasant, and I've never known from one minute to another whether I was in high spirits or the depth of gloom," she told them. "One reason why I am so keen about Lord Peter is that writing him keeps my mind thoroughly occupied, and prevents me from wanting too badly the kind of life I do want, and see no chance of getting." Later, she recalled the despondency that dampened her excitement at her newfound independence, her determination to write plagued by a painful awareness that the longer she spent on her novel, the greater the desolation she set herself up for—emotionally and financially—if nothing came of it. Much like H. D., it was only with hindsight that Sayers would acknowledge quite how much resilience she had employed throughout this crucial year. In Mecklenburgh Square, she imagined her way to a life of splendid elegance, distracting herself from occasional fits of melancholy by granting her character all the riches she wished her writing might earn for her. "Lord Peter's large income (the source of which by the way I have never investigated) . . . I deliberately gave him," she wrote years later. "After all it cost me nothing and at that time I was particularly hard up and it gave me pleasure to spend his fortune for him. When I was dissatisfied with my single unfurnished room I took a luxurious flat for him in Piccadilly. When my cheap rug got a hole in it, I ordered him an Aubusson carpet. When I had no money to pay my bus fare I presented him with a Daimler double-six, upholstered in a style of sober magnificence, and when I felt dull I let him drive it. I can heartily recommend this inexpensive way of furnishing to all who are discontented with their incomes. It relieves the mind and does no harm to anybody."

Through 1921, these dreams spurred Sayers on. As long as she kept up the rent on Mecklenburgh Square, she told herself, the literary success she longed for remained a possibility. In the back of her mind always was the sobering prospect of having to devote herself full-time to teaching or, worse, return to the rectory and forgo her independence: "I simply must hang on in London if I possibly can," she wrote. "It's the only place, and I love it in spite of everything." It was not so much the glamour of a literary life that compelled her, or the anticipation of great wealth or fame, but the firm desire to spend her time on work which she truly enjoyed and knew she was good at. She spent Saturdays in the British Museum, reading the *Notable British Trials* series for reports on the case of George Joseph Smith, hanged in 1915 for the murder of three women whose bodies were found in bathtubs, and William Hare and William Burke, who committed a series of murders and sold the corpses to an unsuspecting anatomy professor for dissection. (Aspects of these cases—both referred to by Wimsey as examples of serial murderers who never would have been uncovered had they not grown overconfident—are evident in the plot of *Whose Body?*.) On weekdays, when not at the school, she sat where H. D. had sat three years earlier, a large notebook open on her desk and a telephone directory to hand, to scour for inspiration when naming minor characters.

She was cheered in March when another tranche of freelance work came in from the Polish organization: "I'm just going on and not worrying," she wrote. "I'm a great believer in things 'turning up.'" She advertised her writing services in *The Times*, and cultivated a passing acquaintance who had hinted she might need some French translations done. In July, Sayers insisted that her money worries had not dampened her social life, which involved "lots of parties—theatre and a night-club (!!) last week, teas and things this week, lunch at the Ritz next week." But soon even London's charms were exhausted, and she was fed up that her friend Dorothy Rowe hadn't invited her to visit her in Bournemouth. "I can't get the work I want, nor the money I want, nor (consequently) the clothes I want, nor the holiday I want, nor the man I want!!"

Writing to her parents on July 27 about coming home for the summer, she mentioned this man for the first time: "I'm inviting a friend for the end of September, but ten to one he won't be able to come." Later in the letter she added with apparent nonchalance: "He'll be no trouble if he does come, being used to living under pretty uncomfortable conditions and asking nothing but kind treatment . . . He is *not* the young man who entertains me at the Ritz, and will not expect Ritz standards." It was John Cournos.

After Cournos returned from St. Petersburg to discover Arabella Yorke's and Richard Aldington's treachery, he had left Mecklenburgh

Square and thrown himself into work both political and literary. It's unclear how he was first introduced to Sayers—and whether their meeting was connected to their shared association with 44 Mecklenburgh Square—but it seems likely to have occurred at a Bloomsbury party such as one Sayers describes in her novel *Strong Poison*, with sausages sizzling on the stove, the samovar boiling over, and shouted discussion above avant-garde piano music of "free love, D. H. Lawrence, the prurience of prudery, and the immoral significance of long skirts." In 1921, Cournos was living in Oxford and working intensely on *Babel*, the third novel in his trilogy after *The Mask* and *The Wall* (heavily autobiographical fictions, admired by Yeats and Ford Madox Ford, about his childhood in Ukraine and American adolescence). This installment covered his move from Philadelphia to London and his immersion in the world of the Imagists. "Just now I am living for this alone," he wrote.

Cournos—who was twelve years older than Sayers—never did visit her parents, despite her entreaties. "Perhaps I could get hold of him at Christmas, but he is really devoted to his work and finds it hard to get away," she wrote, her disappointment barely disguised by her casual tone. Throughout this year Cournos was writing regularly to John Gould Fletcher—whose friendship, he noted, "has consoled me for many betrayals." Both were distressed at the dissolution of their prewar circle—Pound was about to leave London for Paris, Eliot's health was deteriorating, H. D. and Bryher were living in Switzerland, and others, such as Henri Gaudier-Brzeska, had died during the war. Cournos liked to imagine himself and Gould Fletcher as "prisoners of life, trying to paint the walls of our prison with beautiful designs"; their letters to each other contain—alongside plenty of mutual reassurance, and anxiety about their own limitations—ever more virulent diatribes against philistine British readers, against their publicists and agents for not sufficiently promoting their books, and against fellow writers ("these cliques and gangs of misbegotten charlatans who infest London") whose hostility rendered them "literary outcasts." In all these pages of personal correspondence, Cournos never once mentions Dorothy.

Cournos's seeming indifference, throughout their year-long relationship, saddened and bewildered Sayers at a time when she was vulnerable. It was clear to her that she was less important to him than his book, which he hinted dramatically was driving him to unprecedented contortions of the soul; his desire to keep her separate from his literary friends must also have disappointed her, as it cut off a potential entry to the world she longed to join. And she was chastened by his apparent belief that a writing life was incompatible with personal attachments. Her own romantic experience was limited—apart from Eric Whelpton, she had entertained fleeting, unrequited passions for various actors and Dr. Hugh Allen, the eccentric conductor of the Oxford Bach Choir—and this was the first relationship for which she had seriously contemplated a future. Despite her matter-of-fact demeanor and her firm belief in women's intellectual equality to men, the life Sayers had begun to envisage was not so distant from the ideal of marriage and children propounded in her vicarage upbringing: she was determined to devote her energies to work, but—unlike H. D.—didn't necessarily aspire to unconventionality in other areas of life, and there were limits to how far she would allow her disregard for social norms to go.

In 1919 she had, on request, sent a poem—a lightly erotic elegy for a lost love—to *The Quorum*, a magazine founded by members of the radical British Society for the Study of Sex Psychology and the Order of Chaeronea, a society for gay men which aimed to challenge puritanical ideas about family and relationships. But despite this intriguing and incongruous contribution (she was the only female writer to feature in the magazine, which closed after a single issue), she was at pains to insist in her letter to the editor that her own inclinations were heterosexual: "Few friendships among women will stand the strain of being romantically considered . . . I avoid them like the plague." She was always, however, adamant that she would not settle for any man who placed her on a pedestal, like the Victorian "angel in the house": she was too comfortable in her Mecklenburgh Square boardinghouse, despite its disadvantages, to be in any hurry to preside over a traditional family home. In 1917, at a dinner party in Oxford, she had been shocked to receive a flustered proposal from an acquaintance, the Reverend Leonard Hodgson ("a man I wouldn't have touched with the tongs"), while their hosts were making coffee in the kitchen. "Don't get agitated!" she wrote to her parents. "I'll never marry a man I don't care for." Later, when Hodgson attempted to renew his suit, she elaborated. "To have somebody devoted to me arouses all my worst feelings. I loathe being deferred to. I abominate being waited on. It infuriates me to feel that my words are numbered and my actions watched. I want somebody to fight with!"

But her idea of a partnership of equals, fueled by spirited arguments and easy-going affection, was not to be found with Cournos. His experiences with H. D. and Arabella had left him suspicious of women and wary of attachment; he preferred to spend his time on the work that gave him purpose and wouldn't deceive him. His abiding air of gloom dampened Sayers's natural enthusiasm, but she was compelled, she later realized, by a "sort of abject hero-worship" to try to please him, miserable though it made her. And she hated that her desire for him to love her forced her into a submissive role; that competing for his attention made her feel she was compromising her independence. With hindsight, Sayers acknowledged that Cournos was "a rotten companion for a poor girl," who never appreciated her wit but "drilled and sermonised the poor thing out of existence." "How stupid you are!" she wrote to him later, admonishing him for his lack of patience with music halls, crossword puzzles, or the "grimlies" at the Little Theatre. (She recalled "having tramped half London with a bad blister on my heel" before he could find a cinema showing a film he would "condescend to see.") "It wasn't that I wanted to dance—I wanted somebody to think I was worth teaching to dance. I'd never been treated as a woman—only as a kind of literary freak." It's a poignant and revealing statement. In public, Sayers was the first to insist that men should treat women as fellow humans, that any gallant concession to femininity was condescending and unnecessary—which made it hard to articulate her disappointment at Cournos's lack of chivalry, though it was clear his behavior was not the product of any respect for women. H. D. had been devastated when Aldington told her he was attracted to her mind but not her body, that he saw her as an intellectual companion but not as a lover. But Sayers's situation was even worse: not only did Cournos show no appetite for romance, he also cared nothing for her writing.

Sayers shared Cournos's absolute dedication to work, but not his supercilious conviction that his books' obscurity was due to an undiscerning public. ("You can't be both a 'best seller' and a great man," he loftily wrote after receiving a royalty statement printed with a damning "No Sales.") Sayers encouraged her parents to read his novels, brushing aside his enigmatic hints that they would be shocked by his ideas: "Personally, I think *The Wall* is not nearly so alarming as John thinks it is. Why do men love to make themselves out such wonderful devils when they aren't anything of the sort? John imagines he's a terrible person!" But Cournos—whether or not he even read it—dismissed Sayers's writing as lowbrow nonsense. "I fear he has no sympathy with Lord Peter, being the kind of man who takes his writing seriously and spells Art with a capital A," she wrote, her bullishness disguising a touching vulnerability. Unlike H. D., she wasn't part of an established literary circle with whom she could exchange ideas as equals; her Somerville friends remained supportive and kind by letter, but she was far away now from the bedrooms where the Mutual Admiration Society had gathered over toasted marshmallows, roast chestnuts, and cocoa. It probably didn't cross her mind that Cournos's lack of interest in her work was a symptom of his insecurity about his own. Later, vindicated by sales and prestige, she could laugh at his scornful attitude toward the work she took so seriously. But at the time, the sneering of this older, experienced writer must have significantly shaken her already faltering self-belief. But Sayers was cheered by a quotation she had read in the newspaper from the essayist Philip Guedalla, suggesting that "the detective story is the normal recreation of noble minds": "It makes me feel ever so noble," she wrote proudly to her parents. She was not about to give up on Lord Peter Wimsey for John Cournos.

While Cournos remained in Oxford, rarely tempted down to London, Sayers finished writing *Whose Body?* at the rectory in the summer of

1921. She had sublet her room in Mecklenburgh Square to an Oxford friend, Egerton Clarke, who left the cupboards "full of mouldy sandwiches." By November 8, Lord Peter was at the typist's ("I expect he'll cost about £7, curse him!"). But doubts, exacerbated by Cournos's condescension, were setting in. "I've been promised introductions to various publishers," she wrote, "but I don't suppose anything will ever come of it. I really haven't the least confidence in the stuff, which is a pity, because I really enjoy turning it out." She built up the courage to send the manuscript to a literary agent, who promptly died: "I think of advertising him as 'the book that killed an agent.'" Nonetheless, she began straightaway on her second Wimsey novel, *Clouds of Witness*. "I spend all my time reading or writing crimes in the Museum! Nice life, isn't it? I've done the coroner's direction to the jury today, and I feel quite exhausted."

Toward the end of November 1921, Sayers received bad news: she was no longer able to live in the first place where she had felt at home. Miss James was leaving Mecklenburgh Square, and asked her tenants to vacate their rooms by December 5. "I shall either have to find somewhere else to live—without either money or job! Or else give up beloved London and return ignominiously home." The latter, she insisted, was hardly an option. "I shall really want to be in town just now to try if there really is the smallest chance of getting Lord Peter published." Her parents gently suggested, for the first time, that her writing might be better kept as a hobby rather than relied on for subsistence, but Sayers's determination to be professional did not waver, and she defended her choices staunchly, offering to sell her violin rather than apply for extra teaching. "I'm afraid he could never be 'only a jolly extra,' because as a matter of fact, it takes all one's time and energy to invent even bad, sensational stories." She acknowledged, however, that her parents' anxiety was understandable: "Nobody can feel more acutely than I do the unsatisfactoriness of my financial position," she wrote. "I wish I could get a reasonable job, or that I could know one way or another whether I shall be able to make money by writing . . . If you like, I'll make a sporting offer—that if you can manage to help me to keep going till next summer, then, if Lord Peter is still unsold, I will chuck the whole thing, confess myself beaten, and take a permanent teaching job." Her exhaustion is palpable, but, keen to demonstrate that her intentions to live a Bloomsbury life had not faltered, she took a flat at 24 Great James Street, just a couple of minutes' walk south from Mecklenburgh Square, and resolutely continued to work, hoping against hope that this time her luck would be in.

And in the spring of 1922, just when Sayers was at her lowest ebb, her fortunes began to change. In May she was offered work as a copywriter with the Holborn-based advertising firm of S. H. Benson; she was paid a salary of £4 a week, and found herself at last "actually settled in a job, and quite a nice job with prospects, too." Writing jingles allowed her to use her talent for wordplay, and her parents enjoyed reading her witty promotions for Guinness and Colman's Mustard in the newspapers and adorning billboards across the country. She found the work "full of energy and rush" and was delighted when her manager told her she "showed signs of eventually turning into a first-class copywriter. It really does seem to be the right job for me at last!" Humbled and greatly relieved, she wrote to her parents: "I want to thank you again and again ever so much for the wonderful patience with which you've stood by while everything was so unsatisfactory— never cursed me or told me I was a failure, and have forked out such a lot of money and been altogether ripping to me." And moreover, the publication of her debut novel was looking increasingly likely. That April, a friend had introduced Sayers to a literary agent, Andrew Dakers ("he has a strong sense of humor, and likes a spicy story"), who pronounced himself "very confident" about Lord Peter's prospects and was "certain of selling him, though it may take a little time." In July 1922, to Sayers's delight, the publishers Boni & Liveright in America offered her an advance of $250 for *Whose Body?* Dakers came to Great James Street for a celebratory dinner, charming her by turning up in evening dress and engaging her in "a lively discussion of many things— werewolves, religion, marriage, fashions in dress and the mechanicalness of the present civilisation." By April 1923, the book had been sold in the UK to Fisher Unwin, and Lord Peter Wimsey was launched.

. . .

But while her career was taking off at last, John Cournos showed no signs of offering Sayers—who was "passionately wanting to be loved and to be faithful"—the sort of partnership she hoped for. Whenever she raised the subject of commitment, Cournos closed her down with "talk about being free to live and love naturally": though he had dreamed of marriage to Arabella, he now insisted that he had no desire to take on the responsibility of a wife or potential child, conditions which, to Sayers, "stripped love down to the merest and most brutal physical contact." On January 18, 1922, she wrote to her parents that Cournos had "turned up the other day and was all right, though deeply buried in *Babel*. He and I have had a difference, though, on a point of practical Christianity (to which he strongly objects) and I may hear no more of him." He visited Great James Street for dinner on a few more occasions, which sent Sayers, still eager to impress, into fits of culinary frenzy ("I had 5 courses, and they were all thoroughly successful, and none of them came out of tins—except the jelly mixture, of course"). But that October, Cournos abruptly left England and sailed to New York. On November 28, she wrote ruefully that "John hasn't so much as sent me a post-card since he went."

The "point of practical Christianity" which shook their relationship related to the use of contraception—an issue at the heart of contemporary debates about women's economic freedom, sex, and the modern family. On March 17, 1921, around the time Sayers must have met Cournos, Marie Stopes had opened the British Empire's first free birth-control clinic at a house in Holloway, not far north of Mecklenburgh Square. Trained nurses and midwives dispensed advice to queues of women, to the distress of conservative commentators, who condemned Stopes for lowering the nation's moral standards and enacting irreversible damage to the sanctity of matrimony. Stopes saw her mission as to make birth control respectable, and firmly directed her advice toward "the married and the about-to-marry." (She also advocated the sterilization of those she deemed unfit to reproduce.) But after her 1918 book *Married Love* became a bestseller—despite being published privately, since no publishing house would take the risk—Stopes received hundreds of letters from young women, caught between their Victorian upbringings and a new, more permissive status quo, who were terrified that early motherhood would limit their careers but in anguish about what the Anglican Church, in July 1920, denounced as the "grave physical, moral and spiritual perils incurred by the use of contraceptives."

Cournos didn't want to marry Sayers, and told her as much; but he let it be known that he wanted to have sex, using protection. Sayers had qualms, not so much about the contraceptives themselves, but about what their use represented, and denied. Sex for itself—aided by "every dirty trick invented by civilisation to avoid the natural result"—did not attract her: she was not moved, as Cournos was, by "animal passion." She wanted to sleep with Cournos, but in the context of a loving partnership, not one which deliberately "excluded frankness and friendship and children." Yet Cournos saw her reluctance merely as hypocrisy, a disappointing limitation on her professed desire for freedom. From the Algonquin Hotel in central Manhattan, Cournos hinted to Gould Fletcher at the source of the frustrations that had sent him away. "Everywhere, in the hotels, men meet women for the first time, look into each other's eyes, and say 'Yes, let's!' And the same night they go to bed together! This, too, is love! This, too, is life! Dear John, do not regret 'not living.'"

Sayers's despondency at Cournos's departure did not last long. "Don't faint," she wrote to her parents on December 18, 1922. "I am coming home for Xmas on Saturday with a man and a motor-cycle, with request that you will kindly give same a kind welcome and a few words of friendly cheer." Bill White was a bankrupt former clerk now trying his luck in the motor trade, who had arrived in London that autumn in search of work and taken a temporary room above Sayers's. She felt sorry for the "poor devil," who—so she was led to believe—possessed "not a red cent or a roof," and had begun to cook meals for him ("I'm getting more and more ingenious in the cookery line!"). Her concern came from sympathy for his suffering, now that her own situation was more stable: "I've been lonely and poor enough alone in London to know what it feels like," she told her parents, "and I know you'll have a fellow-feeling for the jobless." White was cheerful, roguish, and fun, everything Cournos was not: he took her dancing to jazz at the Hammersmith Palais, polished her sitting-room floor, and taught her to ride a motorbike. "Intellect isn't exactly his strong point," wrote Sayers, tactfully. "In fact he's the last person you'd ever expect me to bring home, but he's really quite amiable." Their liaison was always far more casual than her fraught affair with Cournos; perhaps for this reason—or simply because he was more attractive, and made the prospect sound far more appealing—she did embark on a sexual relationship with White, using contraceptives. But in a cruel stroke of luck, in spring 1923, Sayers discovered she was pregnant.

At this point, White—now living in "a revolting slum off Theobalds Road"—admitted he was married, with a wife and seven-year-old daughter living in Dorset. The revelation was a terrible shock to both women, but—Bill himself now sullen, reneging all responsibility—the situation brought them together in unlikely solidarity. Beatrice White, braced to deal with the consequences of her husband's deception, came to London to meet Sayers. Learning that she was not seeking to marry Bill, but conversely was desperate—somehow—to keep the pregnancy hidden from her family and employer, Beatrice took charge and invited Sayers to give birth in her own hometown of Southbourne. In an act of exceptional unselfishness, she arranged a room for Sayers in a local guesthouse, and asked her brother, a doctor, to oversee the birth at a local nursing home, without mentioning that he would be helping to deliver his brother-in-law's illegitimate child.

The day Sayers left London she bumped into John Cournos on Southampton Row, in what must have been almost the same spot where he had encountered Arabella in 1917; she did not tell him she was pregnant and he didn't guess. Meanwhile, Beatrice and her daughter Valerie stayed at Great James Street, feeding Sayers's cat Agag and forwarding her letters to her parents with a London postmark. In November, seven months pregnant, Sayers had told them that she would not be returning home for Christmas, as she wanted to get her accounts straight and send her new book to press. "I'm awfully rushed and rather bothered," she had written. "Don't come up till the Spring." Her managers at Benson's were told she was ill with exhaustion, and signed her off on leave without suspecting. On 3 January 1924, Sayers gave birth to a son. Cournos must have remained on her mind, for she named the boy John Anthony.

Beatrice White kept the secret until her death. Sayers thanked her, tacitly, by giving her maiden name (Beatrice Wilson) to a minor but admirable character in her 1935 novel *Gaudy Night*, a young girl who declares that she's going to become a mechanic, despite her mother's insistence that she'll never get a husband ("I don't want one . . . I'd rather have a motor-cycle"). Just as Bryher had stepped in to help H. D. when pregnant and alone, Beatrice's practical kindness fortified Sayers immeasurably after being let down by Bill's departure, which was no less swift than Cecil Gray's. (White had moved on to another woman before his child was born, which didn't bother Sayers unduly: "I never meant him to be more than what he wanted to be—an episode," she insisted.) Beatrice's behavior toward her husband's mistress was certainly unconventional but not self-consciously so, unlike H. D.'s tortured acceptance of Flo Fallas or Arabella Yorke. Her generosity to Sayers was not born out of any desire to live outside society's moral structures, but rather to remain within them: probably thinking of her young daughter, Valerie, and the stigma that attached to the child of divorced parents (and aware that Bill was unlikely to support Valerie financially after a separation), Beatrice did what she could to make the best of the terrible situation in which she found herself— perhaps with a glimmer of sympathy for a woman who, like her, had been deceived by the smooth talk of a charming man. Sayers later wrote that "of all motives for crime, respectability—the least emphasized in fiction—is one of the most powerful in fact, and is the root cause of a long series of irregularities, ranging from murder itself to the queerest and most eccentric misdemeanors." Respectability drove Beatrice to her actions, distressing as they must have been for her to take; respectability was also at the forefront of Sayers's own private anguish as she made her excuses to Benson's and to her parents and began to ponder her child's future, and her own.

Her friends only discovered that Sayers had a son after her sudden death in 1957—though she did, just once, impulsively confide in a stranger on a train, a woman recently divorced with a ten-year-old child who had opened up to Sayers about her own troubles. Since Sayers told so few people about her pregnancy, there's little evidence from which to reconstruct her thoughts at this chaotic time: whether she ever considered an abortion (illegal, but not difficult to procure if one had the means), or why she was so sure that her loving parents, who had always stood by her, should not know about their grandson ("it would grieve them quite unnecessarily," she insisted, without further explanation). Her religious upbringing may well account for either or both of these decisions, but the subterfuge of a hidden pregnancy must have taken an enormous toll on Sayers's mental and physical health. And still the question remained of where and how the child would live.

Two days before she gave birth, Sayers wrote to her cousin Ivy Shrimpton in Oxford, who made a living fostering children, telling her of "an infant I'm very anxious you should have the charge of . . . At present everything depends on the girl's not losing her job." Ivy accepted the commission, and on January 27, Sayers wrote again: "Everything I told you about the boy is absolutely true—only I didn't tell you he was my own!" We don't know whether Ivy's response was admonitory or reassuring, but she seems to have accepted her cousin's insistences that the child's identity should remain hidden from their family, and took in John Anthony at one month old. Sayers brought him to Oxford in a Moses basket, returning to London that same evening, whereupon she found she had locked her keys inside the house and had to sit alone in a cinema for hours waiting for the charlady to arrive with a spare set. On February 1, mere days after stopping breastfeeding, she returned to work, having been off for exactly eight weeks. She wrote regularly and anxiously to Ivy seeking details of her son's eating and crying, and forwarded her £3 a month plus extra for doctors' bills, though was reluctant to visit too often. She told her cousin she wanted the child brought up with "affection rather than pomp"; "I hope he doesn't intend to be musical or artistic," she warned Ivy, probably thinking of Cournos. "I'm so bored with writers and people like that."

Her letters to Ivy at this time remained upbeat and pragmatic, but the conflicts they masked must have been extraordinarily painful. Everything had been arranged meticulously—Sayers's experience cracking and composing detective plots had given her excellent grounding to cover her tracks—but the distraction of logistical planning could not displace emotion forever. This was far from the situation she had imagined for her first child, and for herself, when she had planned out a future with Cournos. But she knew that being a single mother to an illegitimate child—possibly cut off by her ashamed parents, with little state support and extra difficulty earning her own living—would render impossible the life she had wanted so deeply and finally saw the chance of having: one of independence, professional success, and intellectual freedom, which she had moved to Mecklenburgh Square in the hope of finding. Her situation is strikingly similar to that in which H. D. found herself after leaving the square; but without a Bryher to provide emotional and financial support, the idea of disregarding the safety of a nuclear family structure seemed, to Sayers, not an act of bravery but a pathway too fraught and shameful to countenance. She still wanted nothing more than to write, and couldn't imagine a way of combining the focus required of her work with the self-sacrifice expected of a mother. At this point, it seemed inconceivable that she could have both domestic and professional happiness. With her freedom in the balance, Sayers made her choice.

Apart from the Whites, Ivy, and the man she later married, only one other person knew about the existence of John Anthony in Sayers's lifetime: John Cournos. Soon after arriving in New York, Cournos had—despite his alleged opposition to marriage and fatherhood—become engaged to a woman named Helen Kestner, who had been married twice before, had two children, and wrote romances and detective novels under a variety of pseudonyms. On New Year's Day 1924—just as Dorothy was preparing to give birth—they married at the Strand Palace Hotel in London. That August, Sayers wrote to him in faux-nonchalant tones that do little to disguise her pain. The correspondence reveals a vulnerability strikingly absent from the capable persona she constructed for her parents:

> Dear John,
> I've heard you're married—I hope you are very very happy, with someone you can really love.
>
> I went over the rocks. As you know, I was going there rapidly, but I preferred it shouldn't be with you, but with somebody I didn't really care twopence for. I couldn't have stood a catastrophe with you. It was a worse catastrophe than I intended, because I went and had a young son (thank God, it wasn't a daughter!) and the man's affection couldn't stand that strain and he chucked me and went off with someone else! So I don't quite know what I'm going to do with the infant, but he's a very nice one!
>
> Both of us did what we swore we'd never do, you see—I hope your experiment turned out better than mine. You needn't bother about answering this unless you like, but somehow I've always felt I should like you to know. I hope you're ever so happy —
> Dorothy

When Cournos replied, mournfully admonishing her for apparent double standards in having sex with White and not him, she was quick to bolster her sense of integrity: "The one thing worse than bearing the child of a man you hate," she informed him, "would be being condemned to be childless by the man you loved." He suggested meeting, but Sayers shot him down: "Last time we met, you told me with brutal frankness that you had no use for my conversation. Do you think my misfortunes will have added new lustre to my wit? Or am I to provide you with material for a new chapter of John Gombarov's philosophy? If I saw you, I should probably only cry—and I've been crying for about 3 years now and am heartily weary of the exercise." She boasted to him of her efficiency in dealing with the situation, and preventing anyone at Benson's from suspecting the reason for her absence: "You can put that in a book if you like; no one will believe it."

He took her at her word. In subsequent years, just as he had with H. D., Cournos turned his relationship with Sayers into bitter fiction—his cruelty aggravated by the fact that he left her identity open to recognition by anyone familiar with their circumstances, thus compromising the secrecy of her arrangements for John Anthony. In 1927, he published a short story entitled "The Generous Gesture" in the anthology *Americana Esoterica*, which provided the basis for a similar episode in an immensely long, rambling novel published in 1932, *The Devil Is an English Gentleman*. In details, both closely correspond with the portrait of the relationship discernible from Sayers's letters: each involves a bohemian man, who denounces marriage and believes in new ideas, frustrated by a woman who insists on a promise of commitment before she will consent to sex. In the novel, the unfortunate woman (a lively Cambridge graduate with unattractive ankles, who "insisted on talking, on being heard, and indulged in an excess of badinage") tearfully gives in, whereupon the man storms out, furious that she perceives sex as a sacrifice, not as the "generous gesture" given freely and unstintingly which would, on his terms, have affirmed her love—but on hers would have only confirmed his power over her.

Sayers's letters to Cournos in 1924 and 1925, when both their lives had changed dramatically, reveal her delicate negotiation of intimacy and individual freedom as she was working it out: she could only be happy within a situation of utter mutual trust, where neither partner had to compromise their desires, their ambitions, or their values. In this way only, she insisted, could love be "free and careless": "I have become impatient of the beastly restrictions which 'free love' imposes," she wrote. What to Cournos was a flamboyant riposte to conservative morals, to Sayers meant risking exactly the sort of miserable situation she had found herself in with White. His position as an artist was never at stake in their tussle, while she knew hers was liable to combust in a moment's carelessness. Sayers's experiences with Cournos and White had left her painfully aware that women's independence was precarious in a way men's was not. But in these two failed relationships, Sayers came to clarify her own priorities. In Sayers's vision, a free woman does not "make her man's interests her own," as the protagonist of *The Devil Is an English Gentleman* suggests she should, but pursues her own intellectual freedom within the framework of a supporting and nurturing alliance, with someone whose "interests are my interests, his home my home, his time my time." She would explore this idea, rooted in her Mecklenburgh Square year, over the rest of her career, through polemical essays and religious plays, and in her detective novels, through the new character of Harriet Vane.

John Cournos was not the only one capable of transmuting fact into fiction, and Sayers—having published three further Wimsey novels and a collection of stories since *Whose Body?*—turned to the unlikely form of the detective novel when she chose to address their relationship herself. Her fifth novel, *Strong Poison* (1930), opens in a law court, where a judge "so old he seemed to have outlived time and change and death" haltingly addresses the jury as reporters scribble. The defendant, Harriet Vane, is a detective novelist, "a young woman of great ability, brought up on strictly religious principles" who has, by the age of twenty-nine, "made herself independent in a legitimate way, owing nothing to anybody and accepting help from no one." She is on trial accused of poisoning her former lover, Philip Boyes, a writer of "immoral or seditious" treatises on anarchy, atheism, and free love (which were, to his great chagrin, far less commercially successful than Harriet's novels). Boyes, the judge stiffly explains, was "conscientiously opposed to any formal marriage," but had pressured Harriet to "live on terms of intimacy with him" outside that bond; some time later, neighbors heard Harriet packing her bags and leaving, claiming only that she had been "painfully deceived." The cause of the argument was not, to their surprise, unfaithfulness or cruelty, but the fact that Boyes had, in spite of his alleged principles, offered legal marriage to Harriet. Harriet was furious at Boyes's hypocrisy in making her compromise for no good reason. "I quite thought he was honest when he said he didn't believe in marriage," she tells Lord Peter Wimsey from her prison cell. "And then it turned out that it was a test, to see whether my devotion was abject enough. Well, it wasn't. I didn't like having matrimony offered as a bad-conduct prize."

The courtroom embodies all the tensions between Victorian and modern mores, and it's clear that the ancient judge considers Harriet "a person of unstable moral character." The charge she faces is serious, since Sayers took no mercy on Cournos's fictional avatar: after visiting Harriet one evening for a cup of coffee, Philip Boyes collapsed and died "in great pain" following several days of vomiting and diarrhea. The case is really a trial of Harriet's lifestyle; the judge's implication is that an educated and highly successful working woman who rejects conformity in her living arrangements (Harriet lives in "a small flat of her own" in Bloomsbury's Doughty Street, a milieu assumed to be unregulated by established morals) is likely to be willing to undermine social order to the extent of murdering her ex-lover. "Genius must be served, not argued with," sniffs an associate of Boyes's, insisting that Harriet poisoned her lover out of jealousy at his superior intellect. A friend of Harriet's puts it differently, summing up the attitude a successful woman writer had to contend with: "She ought to have been ministering to his work, not making money for them both with her own independent trash." Harriet knows her own worth, and refuses to spare Boyes's ego by diminishing her own achievements. Yet her situation is a stark reminder of the dangers women faced: Harriet's choices have not resulted in pregnancy, as they did for Sayers, but they have left her vulnerable to a nightmare of public shame and punishment, on the verge of losing her freedom forever in the most definitive of ways, at the gallows.

Wimsey, hopelessly in love with the prisoner, has a month to prove her innocence—which he does with panache, thanks to the valiant efforts of a determined cast of spinster spies, from Miss Murchison, who masquerades as an error-prone secretary to insinuate herself into the office of a scurrilous solicitor, to Miss Climpson, who extracts information from a spiritually inclined paid companion via a Ouija board of her own devising. By the end of the novel, Harriet is vindicated and declared free. Although the ignominy of the case threatens to haunt her indefinitely, she receives a full apology from the court, and her books sell like wildfire. Sayers's revenge on Cournos was complete. But she was not finished with Harriet Vane. Writing about this brave, clever woman, resilient in the face of grave challenges to her independence and integrity, who found solace in her work and the support of a devoted troupe of female friends, had been a cathartic experience. As Sayers reflected on the achievements and regrets of her own life, she began to wonder whether she could help her fictional creation achieve that elusive balance between public success and private happiness.

Sayers had at first intended to end *Strong Poison* with Harriet and Peter becoming engaged. Although she was loath to subject Wimsey to the fate of Sherlock Holmes—thrown to certain death at the Reichenbach Falls (though subsequently resuscitated by a sheepish Conan Doyle)—she had grown fed up with her "puppet," who remained essentially static, triumph after triumph, solving mysteries with ever-gallant bravado and mind-boggling flourishes of logic. Wearied of Wimsey's "everlasting breeziness," she began *Strong Poison* "with the infanticidal intention of doing away with Peter; that is, of marrying him off and getting rid of him." And so she planned a case in which Wimsey would, "in the conventional Perseus manner," rescue a young woman falsely accused of murder, and crown his achievement with marriage, thus drawing his career to a neat and respectable "happily ever after" conclusion.

Sayers's dissatisfaction with her hero was largely due to the feeling—which had pricked her since *Whose Body?*—that the genre was preventing her from addressing the moral questions in which she was increasingly interested. In her wide-ranging introduction to the anthology of detective stories that she edited for Gollancz in 1928, Sayers argued that the gradual progression from sensational Victorian thrillers to the logical puzzles of the Edwardian era meant that, for her generation, detective writing was essentially a matter of technical craft, not of style or art. Sayers derided novels of the sort which G. K. Chesterton called "a drama of masks and not of faces," where the excitement is purely on the surface, the murder apparently committed only to provide a corpse, and nothing more serious at stake than the detective's reputation. Rather, she insisted, detective novels should—like any "literary" fiction—contain atmosphere, character, human truth and a driving force beyond the mechanics of plot. Only then, she suggested, could an author "persuade us that violence really hurts."

Dorothy L. Sayers at the Detection Club in 1939.

Sayers had found models for the sort of detective novel she wanted to write in Wilkie Collins's *The Moonstone* (1868) and E. C. Bentley's *Trent's Last Case*, a "revelation" to Sayers on its publication in 1913 (and a novel for which Virginia Woolf admitted "a passion"). Bentley had set out "to write a detective story of a new sort," and explore what happens when the detective's logical powers are swayed by human fallibility. Sayers praised Bentley's characters as "breathing and moving with abounding vitality" and his love story—the detective falls for the main suspect, compromising his investigation most awkwardly—as "moving, credible and integral to the plot." The influence of *Trent's Last Case* is easily discernible in *Whose Body?*, and it shaped Sayers's direction for her later novels, too, in its ambition and scope, and its willingness to subvert convention with an ending in which the detective's deductions are revealed to have been entirely wrong. It was Bentley's example that made Sayers believe Lord Peter could be salvaged. But it was her own circumstances that gave her the idea of not only sparing her hero from death, but also saving his bride from a potentially stultifying marriage.

As *Strong Poison* unfolded, Sayers increasingly felt that simply to marry off her characters under the circumstances outlined in the novel would be "in every respect false and degrading." Having invented Harriet Vane—the "Bloomsbury bluestocking" with a distinct resemblance to herself—Sayers realized that to relegate her character to the passive role of Wimsey's love interest would undermine her own creation: there was no way that this ambitious woman, previously hurt in love, could quietly marry the man who had saved her from the gallows "without loss of self-respect." "Notwithstanding the usual practice of heroines rescued from humiliating positions," wrote Sayers five years later, "it soon became clear to me that no good could ever come of a marriage founded on gratitude and an inferiority complex." After the disappointments of Cournos and White, and the pain of giving up her child, Sayers had found her greatest satisfaction in her career and wanted to afford her character the same freedom—yet hesitated to deprive Harriet of a chance at the productive relationship of equals, and possibly the happy motherhood, that had eluded her author.

Nonetheless, at the end of the novel, when Wimsey has secured her release from prison, Harriet rejects his proposal. "The best remedy for a bruised heart," wrote Sayers in her next Harriet Vane novel, *Have His Carcase* (1932), "is not, as so many people seem to think, repose upon a manly bosom. Much more efficacious are honest work, physical activity, and the sudden acquisition of wealth." It was a lesson Sayers had learned herself. Rather than luxuriating in a life of leisure on the Denver estate, Harriet goes traveling around Europe with a woman friend, gathering material for novels and selling travel articles. When she returns, she moves into a new, superior, one-bed flat in Mecklenburgh Square. Her address represents the self-sufficiency Harriet prizes so dearly: a decade after Sayers had left the square, it remained a byword in her mind for a life devoted to intellectual endeavor. From her new home, Harriet continues to write detective fiction which, thanks to the publicity of the court case, is making her a tidy income of her own.

If Lord Peter were to become a suitable husband for Harriet, Sayers decided, his character would require "a major operation": his psychology had to be deepened, his moral compass steadied, all "squared somehow or other with such random attributes as I had bestowed upon him over a series of years in accordance with the requirements of various detective plots." Fortunately, right from *Whose Body?* Sayers had given Wimsey the depth that would enable this metamorphosis: the work she had done in Mecklenburgh Square, creating a detective who was already unusual in his sensitivity to ethics and attention to the real-world ramifications of his entertainment, now enabled her to make a further leap toward a new kind of detective novel. *Strong Poison* is the first Wimsey book in which Lord Peter's investment in the case over-reaches the pure intellectual challenge: for the first time, dead ends leave him not titillated but helpless, terrified that he will fail and be unable to "save the woman he imperiously wanted from a sordid death by hanging." In *Have His Carcase*, Harriet discovers a corpse on a beach and once again finds herself under suspicion. Wimsey is called to investigate and the pair work together, not entirely comfortably: Harriet keeps him at a distance, unwilling to weaken her position by acknowledging the "detestable burden of gratitude" she owes him. It doesn't help that Wimsey has instigated a regular pattern of proposals, on April 1 each year. (One is delivered simply as a telegram containing the single Latin particle "Num?"—as Sayers's father would have taught her, the prefix to a question expecting the answer "No"—which occasions Harriet to rummage in her grammar book for "polite negatives.") But she strives to keep her relationship with Wimsey strictly professional, determined to investigate the case alongside him not as wife or Watson but on equal terms as partners.

Sayers ruminated on the question of Harriet Vane's future for several years. Like H. D., she could not expunge the pain of her time in and after Mecklenburgh Square until she had worked out how to write about it. She had learned, from that period, not to depend on others for her own sense of worth: throughout her life, she would extol the importance of vocation, convinced that it was only in "good work, well done" that a person could find real "spiritual, mental and bodily satisfaction." Sayers's insistence on the value of work was inextricable from her firm belief that women must be treated "as human beings, whose activities are not all and always comprised within their sexual function."

In her essay "The Human-Not-Quite-Human" (published in her 1946 collection *Unpopular Opinions*) she describes the brain as "that great and sole true Androgyne," echoing Virginia Woolf's phrasing in *A Room of One's Own*, which H. D. also picked up in *Bid Me to Live*: "in each of us two powers preside, one male, one female . . . The normal and comfortable state of being is that when the two live in harmony together, spiritually cooperating." The absurdity of women's exclusion from intellectual activities was apparent to Sayers, as it was to Woolf, and to H. D. too. All these women were absorbed, in their life and their work, in finding ways to live in a society which still refused to allow those powers to reconcile—which still believed women's needs and desires must be quite different from men's, and imposed expectations accordingly. Responding in another essay to the question "What on earth do women want?," Sayers wrote that she was not sure "that women, *as* women, want anything in particular, but as human beings they want, my good men, exactly what you want yourselves: interesting occupation, reasonable freedom for their pleasures, and a sufficient emotional outlet." It's difficult to think of two writers and personalities more different than Dorothy L. Sayers and H. D.—but they are linked on a level far deeper than that of their shared address, and their shared acquaintance with John Cournos. When Sayers pointed out that society had made little provision for women "who are cursed with both hearts and brains," she was expressing the same thought as H. D. when Julia in *Bid Me to Live* describes her urge to live "in two dimensions." As they tried to assert themselves as writers, both of these women had to negotiate the double standards that threatened to split them into pieces and diminish their sense of self. As she contemplated what to do with Harriet Vane, Sayers was also seeking an answer to the question that had occupied both her and H. D. since their time in Mecklenburgh Square: how a woman can live without having to compromise between intellectual and emotional fulfillment, between a desire to write and the bounds of accepted femininity.

On June 13, 1934—her forty-first birthday—Dorothy L. Sayers returned to Somerville for a celebration in honor of her old French tutor Mildred Pope. Asked to propose a toast to the University of Oxford, Sayers meditated on the preparation for life the university had given her, not as "a passport to wealth and position," but in teaching her the value of knowledge for its own sake. (There was, she noted darkly, "perhaps never a time in the world's history when scholarship was so bitterly needed.") At the reunion, she recognized that the Oxford women's college offered her a route toward solving her fictional problem: how to effect the marriage of Lord Peter Wimsey and Harriet Vane without loss of dignity to either party. Her time at Somerville had given her the confidence to pursue a writing career; while she did not regret leaving the college and striking out alone, she was reminded of how grateful she'd been for the support she had received from its community of women, among whom her talents were appreciated and nurtured and her scholarship never deemed incompatible with her gender. In this setting, where (uniquely for women) intellectual achievement was prized above emotional commitments, Harriet could at last stand "free and equal with Peter." And, wrote Sayers, thinking back on Cournos's insistence that she compromise her beliefs, "By choosing a plot that should exhibit intellectual integrity as the one great permanent value in an emotionally unstable world I should be saying the thing that, in a confused way, I had been wanting to say all my life."

At the time, Sayers was working sporadically on an idea for a "straight" novel about "an Oxford woman graduate who found, in middle life, and after a reasonably satisfactory experience of marriage and motherhood, that her real vocation and emotional fulfillment were to be found in the creative life of the intellect." This autobiographical work, provisionally titled *Cat O'Mary*, grew out of some reminiscences she had started drafting under the title "My Edwardian Childhood." In its new form, the first-person narrator morphs into the fictional heroine Katherine Lammas—a refraction of Dorothy L. Sayers, and also of Harriet Vane—whom the novel follows through her childhood in rural Cambridgeshire. The manuscript breaks off just before Katherine goes up to Somerville, but a short series of fragmented vignettes—and a notebook with further jottings and notes—continue the story into Katherine's later life. Now married to a city worker whose career takes precedence over her own, Katherine is trapped as a leisured upper-class wife, overcome by domestic concerns, bored, and pregnant. In the next section, she has divorced her husband after his affair with a young secretary, and plans to return to academic work, to his fury: "I suppose you want to go and turn into a sort of Bloomsbury frump with all your Museum friends," he sneers. His words recall Sayers's early fears of being dismissed as a "literary freak"—yet now, given a different slant, this insult is merely comical. A life of Bloomsbury independence, surrounded by like-minded friends and ignored by judgmental men, is exactly what Katherine wants, and she's no longer ashamed to admit it. In the final scene, Katherine is interviewed by a professor, who asks her why she has been wasting so much time on domestic pursuits, since she has "the mind of a scholar." The happy ending comes not with Katherine finding a new partner but with her discovering a purpose, not as somebody's wife or mother, but as herself.

It's hard not to imagine that her trajectory reflects Sayers's own feelings. By this point, Sayers herself was married, not entirely happily. After her relationship with Bill White ended, Sayers had told Cournos that she was "learning to cope with loneliness," and had decided to forgo romance because "it interferes with one's work"—though she admitted that she would welcome "a man that's human and careless and loves life, and one who can enjoy the rough-and-tumble of passion." In the autumn of 1925 she met Mac Fleming, a divorced *News of the World* journalist who reported largely on crime and motor cars. Little is known of their courtship, but they married, quietly, the following April; she only informed her parents via an extremely casual letter five days before the ceremony, aware that they would be distressed to learn that the marriage could not take place in a church. Mac had recently moved away from his wife and two daughters and was no longer supporting them financially, but Sayers was glad to report to Ivy that he seemed "quite satisfied to throw the eye of affection and responsibility over John Anthony in the future." She had initially suggested to her cousin that Anthony (as he came to be known) might come to live with her later on, when his care would be less consuming and her parents "too old, if they are still alive, to worry much about anything." But this never transpired, despite Mac nominally adopting him in 1935: the child was content with Ivy, and though Sayers wrote to Anthony diligently, if somewhat formally, through her life, neither Sayers nor Mac was eager to give up work to care for him full-time. (He had been brought up to believe Sayers was his cousin, and discovered their true relationship—which he had already suspected—by accident when applying for a passport.)

At first, Sayers was happy in this egalitarian domestic partnership: Mac did most of the cooking (his 1933 cookbook, *The Gourmet's Book of Food and Drink*, was dedicated to "my wife, who can make an omelette"), and enjoyed "looking after" Sayers, who in turn liked knitting him socks and joining him at race meetings. Snapshots of their early relationship from her letters suggest an easy-going, teasing camaraderie, founded on a sense of fun, an enjoyment of cinema and theatre, and a shared bent to independence. But Mac was deeply affected by his time serving as a major in the war, and was increasingly ill, distant, and resentful of Sayers's success. Their relationship became semi-detached after they bought a house in Witham in Essex, where Mac spent most of his time while Sayers retained Great James Street as her private sanctuary, a useful base for her busy professional life in London, and a reminder of her early days of independence at Mecklenburgh Square. In a way, marriage settled her domestic affairs and left her free to focus her energies on work; while it ultimately brought her little satisfaction, she took solace from the fact that her career was thriving—with high sales, glowing reviews, a devoted readership, and new, prestigious commissions. But Sayers wanted something more for her character Harriet, something she had not herself achieved: a relationship which would not force a choice between private happiness and intellectual independence, but would instead provide the conditions for both. In her next Harriet Vane novel, Sayers sketched out the ideal solution to the emotional difficulties she had not been able to reconcile.

Gaudy Night (1935) opens with Harriet Vane sitting at her writing table, absentmindedly gazing at the tulips and the tennis players in the Mecklenburgh Square garden, just as Sayers had done fifteen years earlier. Yet before long, Harriet is tempted out of the square by an invitation to a reunion (known in Oxford-speak as a gaudy) at her old college. Back at Shrewsbury—a fictional college standing on the cricket grounds of Wimsey's alma mater, Balliol—Harriet finds herself wishing she hadn't come. She is saddened to meet her old friend Mary, previously a lively personality heading for a first, who since leaving college "had married and scarcely been heard of," and now seems dull and directionless, with a "haggard face and look of defeat." Mary serves as an example of what might have happened to Harriet had she married Philip Boyes, or Sayers had she married John Cournos—a point made wickedly clear by the fact that Mary's name is listed in the gaudy program as Mrs. H. Attwood, the official name of Cournos's wife,

Helen, who had previously been married to a Harry Attwood. Seeing Mary, Harriet thinks, "What damned waste," and reaffirms her own desire never to allow marriage to erase her identity or foil her ambitions. "To be true to one's calling, whatever follies one might commit in one's emotional life, that was the way to spiritual peace."

Soon after the gaudy, Shrewsbury is "victimised by a cross between a Poltergeist and a Poison-Pen," who is scattering across the buildings notes containing threats and misogynist insults. Suspects are confined to the college—the students, the dons, and the servants—and all are under scrutiny. As newspaper reports begin to hint at an apparent outbreak of insanity in a closed environment of educated single women, Harriet sees at once that this scandal risks doing considerable damage to the ongoing fight for women's education: " 'Soured virginity'—'unnatural life'—'semi-demented spinsters'—'starved appetites and suppressed impulses'—'unwholesome atmosphere'—she could think of whole sets of epithets, ready-minted for circulation." Encouraged to use her novelist's experience in the service of a real investigation, Harriet returns to Shrewsbury, by day working peacefully on a study of Sheridan Le Fanu, by night snooping the corridors and patroling the grounds, and avoiding London with its incessant reminders of her turbulent past.

Lord Peter Wimsey's absence for most of the novel is atoned for by a cast of some of Sayers's most brightly drawn characters, from a black-mailing former porter to a reckless band of male undergraduates, determined to scale the college walls for nocturnal liaisons with their cloistered counterparts. And the lack of an actual murder is compensated amply by a series of increasingly chilling incidents, from spiteful letters slipped into gown pockets to a full-blown midnight chase through the college, the "poltergeist" rushing madly through the quadrangles blowing fuse boxes, hurling ink bottles at portraits, and chucking books through windows.

But this premeditated attack on an institution of women's education also serves to dramatize Harriet's private dilemma, as she wonders whether to accept Lord Peter's suit. At Shrewsbury, the dons have dedicated themselves to their work at the expense of family life (making them exemplify, to detractors, a monstrous perversion of woman's natural instincts). Among the characters Harriet encounters are the proudly unmarried Miss Hillyard, who displays a suspiciously acute interest in the technical aspects of historic crimes by women against men, and the austere economic historian Miss de Vine, who left her fiancé when she realized that "I simply wasn't taking as much trouble with him as I should have done over a disputed reading." Yet it is de Vine who shows Harriet, during a discussion of "the difficulty of combining intellectual and emotional interests," that there may be a way to avoid the sort of choice Sayers had felt she had to make in the early 1920s. Harriet wonders aloud whether one should marry anyone if one is not prepared to make them one's full-time job. "Probably not," the don replies, "though there are a few rare people, I believe, who don't look on themselves as jobs but as fellow-creatures . . . If you ever find a person who likes you in spite of [your detachment]—and still more, because of it—that liking has very great value, because it is perfectly sincere, and because with that person, you will never need to be anything but sincere yourself."

When Harriet is in London, she enjoys from time to time the company of Lord Peter Wimsey, who entertains her gallantly in country inns and Soho restaurants. On one occasion, after a journey home spent "babbling pleasantly about the Georgian architecture of London," he tentatively proposes to her as the taxi turns into Mecklenburgh Square from Guilford Street, accepting with grace her customary refusal. Yet Harriet is struck by the realization that Wimsey is, despite his persistence, commendably sensitive to her resistance: her feelings begin to turn when she realizes that he understands instinctively the importance to her of a room of one's own. He never, she notices, "violated the seclusion of Mecklenburgh Square. Two or three times, courtesy had moved her to invite him in; but he had always made some excuse, and she understood that he was determined to leave her that place, at least, free from any awkward associations." Resolved to block out all thoughts of softening, she tries to focus on her work: this, she admits to Peter, is "the only side of life I haven't betrayed and made a mess of." But as the danger at Shrewsbury deepens, Harriet finds herself perplexed by the case, and also struggling, unusually, with the novel she's writing. She has trapped five suspects in a watermill, all with suitable motives and alibis for a crime, but finds that their attitudes and relationships are beginning to become formulaic, divorced from the messy unpredictability of human problems. It is Peter who encourages her to take the leap Sayers herself made in the writing of this novel: to "abandon the jigsaw kind of story and write a book about human beings for a change." When Harriet admits that she's afraid of the self-exposure, he replies that only taking risks will produce a book which lives up to her potential. At this point, she realizes that unlike Philip Boyes, who found her success unbearable and who (like John Cournos) encouraged her only to take personal risks which were to his benefit, Peter truly cares about her work, and wants her to succeed on her own terms.

Without spoilers, it's hard to convey the joy of *Gaudy Night*—it has one of the most moving and thrilling denouements Sayers ever wrote, featuring chess sets, dog collars, and a fateful river picnic—but by the end, a series of dramatic events leaves Harriet in no doubt that Peter not only understands how impossible it would be for her to enter a marriage on unequal terms, but also has stylishly worked out exactly how to ensure that Harriet can accept his suit "as a free agent." Toward the end of the novel, Peter and Harriet attend a performance of Bach's double violin concerto in D minor, where they admire the way the two parallel melodies set each other off beautifully without either subsuming the other. Here, finally, is a model for partnership that will not degrade Harriet or curtail her freedom, but rather provide the conditions under which her writing will flourish. When Peter proposes for the last time, he uses the words of the Oxford graduation ceremony—"Placetne, magistra?" This time the Latin construction expects the answer "Yes."

Sayers never expected *Gaudy Night* to achieve commercial success. "Whether you advertise it as a love-story, or as educational propaganda, or as a lunatic freak, I leave to you," wrote Sayers to her publisher, Victor Gollancz. But despite its length and the fact that, as Sayers freely admitted, it is "not really a detective story at all, but a novel with a mild detective interest of an almost entirely psychological kind," it achieved instant popular and critical acclaim: the *Times Literary Supplement* admired it as "a discussion from every standpoint of the problem of Woman and the Intellectual Life," and insisted that *"Gaudy Night* stands out even among Miss Sayers's novels. And Miss Sayers has long stood in a class by herself." It remains her most popular book today, widely acclaimed as "the first feminist detective novel." In *Gaudy Night*'s celebration of education, independence, and intellectual freedom, Sayers finally addressed the existential questions that had possessed her since her year in Mecklenburgh Square. In the book, Harriet thinks back to "that hot unhappy year when she had tried to believe that there was happiness in surrender . . . to subdue one's self to other people's ends was dust and ashes." Cournos's affections and respect were conditional on his principles dominating and obliterating hers: now, like H. D., Sayers had successfully written back to her detractor. Through her writing, Sayers constructed a blueprint for modern relationships which held intellectual and personal integrity at their core.

Aged forty-three, Sayers was asked by an interviewer whether she would like to be twenty-one again. Her response was a resounding "No." "For no bribe," she insisted, "would we again have endured the fumbling experience, the emotional miseries, the self-conscious humiliations of youth." Furthermore, she argued, advice on how to stay young smacks of a "period of social history when women were expected to do no thinking, but only feeling": it would, she suggested, "be more sensible to tell them how to grow up." Her time in Mecklenburgh Square had taught her to grow up: it had also cemented her resolve to live a fulfilling and varied life. "One thing I think ought always to be said to young people, and it is this," wrote Sayers to a correspondent in 1944. "Youth is an unsatisfactory period, full of errors, uncertainties and distress. You will grow out of it. What's more, you were meant to grow out of it, into something more mature and satisfactory. Don't let middle-aged people get away with the story that this is the best time of your life and that after it there is nothing to look forward to . . . Go on doing the thing you think you ought, or want, to be doing at the moment, and at about 40 you may discover that you actually are doing it and settle down to enjoy it."

JANE ELLEN HARRISON
(1850–1928)

11 Mecklenburgh Street
May 1926–April 1928

I think the Jane–Hope liaison interests me most. Win their confidences. I am sure they are a fascinating couple.
—Dora Carrington to Lytton Strachey, August 27, 1923

One summer's day in 1909, a strange entourage arrived in Grantchester, outside Cambridge, and set up camp in a field. The caravan was parked and the carthorse tethered; washing lines were erected and straw laid down for children's bedding. Augustus John, the charismatic Fitzrovia artist, had come to Newnham College to paint a portrait of Jane Ellen Harrison, the famous classics don. "John is encamped with two wives and ten naked children. I saw him in the street today—an extraordinary spectacle for these parts," wrote John Maynard Keynes, who was engrossed in work on probability theory at King's College. "All the talk here is about John," he told Duncan Grant. "According to Rupert [Brooke] he spends most of his time in Cambridge public houses, and has had a drunken brawl in the streets smashing in the face of his opponent."

Yet if John caused consternation among most whose paths he crossed that month, he won the affection of his subject. To the art critic D. S. MacColl, who had recommended John for the commission, Harrison described the notorious artist as "delightful": "I felt spiritually at home with him from the first moment he came into the room." Though they made an unlikely pair, the admiration was mutual: John was kept well entertained by Harrison, a slight woman in her late fifties with wiry grey hair and unusual grey-blue eyes which she attributed to Viking ancestors. He painted her in black lace, reclining on a sofa while chain-smoking cigarettes and chuckling with her close friend and fellow classicist Gilbert Murray. Harrison was delighted with the result. Writing to her friend Ruth Darwin, Harrison concluded that John "seems to me to have a real vision of 'the beauty of ugliness'. . . character, I suppose it would ordinarily be called, that comes into all faces however 'plain' that belong to people who have lived hard, and that in the nature of things is found in scarcely any young face." John later described her as "a very charming person tho' a puzzle to paint": his portrait is the first of many people's attempts to solve the enigma of Jane Harrison's life, or to capture its ambiguities.

Jane Ellen Harrison by Augustus John, 1909.

Dorothy L. Sayers and H. D. came to Mecklenburgh Square as young women, hoping that long and exciting careers lay ahead of them. But Jane Harrison arrived there aged seventy-five, having renounced her comfortable life as a Cambridge don and destroyed all traces of her previous existence: she was not beginning her life in the square, but enacting a rebirth no less urgent for coming so late. She died, aged seventy-seven, in her home at 11 Mecklenburgh Street—just off the main square—on April 15, 1928. The guest list for her memorial service, held four days later at St. Marylebone Cemetery in Finchley, is testament to the rich variety of Harrison's friendships, and especially those of her final years: professors of Greek mingled warily with mournful Russian poets; publishers and Bloomsburyites with distant Yorkshire relatives; eminent European philosophers with the doctors and nurses who had tended her devotedly through her long illness. But as an insight into the life being celebrated, the ceremony left guests deflated, feeling as though their friend had become more unknown to them than ever before. Gilbert Murray found the funeral—planned by Hope Mirrlees, who had spent the past decade living with Harrison— "odd & disappointing," and sensed that "one somehow felt as if she was deserted." Leonard and Virginia Woolf arrived late, shuffling into the chapel just as the readings ended. In her diary, Virginia recorded her bemusement at the choices, feeling that the service belied the complexity of Harrison's own thinking about religion. "Who is 'God' & what the Grace of Christ? & what did they mean to Jane?"

Hope Mirrlees spent the remaining months of her tenure in the house they had shared on Mecklenburgh Street attempting to control the way Harrison's memory would be preserved. Over the next three decades she worked on a biography, which never materialized: whether this was a loyal act of discretion, or a severe case of writer's block, is impossible to know for sure. "The problem of what to say and what to leave out is a very difficult one," she wrote apologetically to Jessie Stewart, another former pupil of Harrison's, who had reproached her for her reticence. "Jane was extremely reserved about her own past. She had weathered a great many storms, and I think wanted them to be forgotten—in fact, I feel almost certain that she did. And yet if one omits them, the life loses what she would have called its 'pattern.'" Yet Harrison's life had no single "pattern": those who knew her in separate periods each remembered, and felt possessive of, a very different character, which they wholeheartedly believed to be the "true" Jane. In March 1950, Gilbert Murray wrote to Stewart about a lecture given by the Russian writer Prince Dmitry Petrovich Svyatopolk-Mirsky, who had known Harrison well at the end of her life. "I thought it very clever but, to speak frankly, I did not really like it. I do not like to have Jane mixed up with Freud and Joyce, nor even with Communism . . . Of course Mirsky knew a side of her which I perhaps did not but I think he runs his own ideas too hard." Murray had been very close to Harrison in the years she spent teaching classics at Newnham between 1898 and 1922. His anxiety to decry Mirsky's version of Harrison—as a true radical and a distinctly modern thinker—betrays a certain bewilderment at how deliberately her interests and way of life had shifted when she left Cambridge, aged seventy-two, to spend the last five years of her life among a community of Russian political exiles in Paris and Bloomsbury, burning all her papers, including Murray's letters to her, before she went. "I never understood what happened at the end of her life," wrote Murray to Stewart. "Did Newnham refuse to continue her Fellowship, and was she greatly hurt? Or did she, for other reasons, determine to leave Cambridge and Greek and her old associations? And what part did Hope play in it?"

Jane Harrison's brief, charming, artful autobiography represents her own contribution to the myth-making that has always surrounded her. *Reminiscences of a Student's Life* was published in 1925 by Leonard and Virginia Woolf's Hogarth Press; thanks to her significant public stature, it was serialized in the popular weekly the *Nation and Athenaeum*. "I send you a very small book on a still smaller subject," she wrote with characteristic self-deprecation to Murray. "And so my tale must end." But the main narrative of the memoir ends in 1916, nine years before the time of writing: Harrison refuses to reveal anything of times "too present, too intimate," hinting only that recent years have been

enlivened by her passion for the Russian language and the companionship of a "ghostly daughter, dearer than any child after the flesh."

The publication of a memoir often signals that a life is drawing to
an end, that the writer is assessing the past with the synthesizing gaze of
one whose work is done. But Jane Harrison went on living, in strikingly
new circumstances. Having defied expectations throughout her career,
she refused to settle down to a decorous retirement and stop outraging
the establishment with her cheery disregard for traditions and received
truths. Though she studied the ancient past, she was always looking to
the future. One of the main figures in her research was the "eniautos
daimon," or Year Spirit, an ancient deity of seasonal regeneration,
whose regular death and rebirth allowed the community to grow and
flourish. His ability to shift form and constantly reinvent himself mirrored Harrison's ever-eager curiosity and her regular interrogation of
herself as well as of others, always alert to the possibility of doing things
differently. Jane Harrison was so fervently committed to her own freedom that she was willing to make significant changes and sacrifices,
even in her seventies, in order to create the best conditions for her
work. Her story shows that the question of "how to live" is not restricted
to a single answer; when one environment ceased to provide what she
needed, Harrison did not hesitate to reexamine her situation.

Reminiscences of a Student's Life offers the narrative most often
invoked in relation to Jane Harrison: the tale of one Yorkshirewoman's
determination to find an education and fulfill her potential, which
made her such an appealing model for Virginia Woolf. Harrison's
mother had died from puerperal fever shortly after Jane's birth in 1850,
and like Mary Shelley, whose mother Mary Wollstonecraft died from
the same disease, Jane grew up with a painful sense of responsibility for
the breakdown of an idealized family and the unfortunate creation of
another. A beloved aunt, who had taken on the children's upbringing,
left the family abruptly for an unexpected marriage, and within six
months Jane's father had proposed to the governess he had employed
to replace her. Her brothers (like Woolf's) were sent to public school,
but Jane—whose mackintosh had to be trimmed with fringe, at her
stepmother's insistence, to make it appear feminine—was taught at

home along the standard Victorian girls' curriculum of needlework, deportment, etiquette, and committing Bible verses to memory—"miscellaneous rubbish," as Harrison summarized it. One "ignorant but willing" teacher, keen to learn alongside her inquisitive pupil, helped Jane pick up the rudiments of German, Latin, Greek, and Hebrew, but this educational experiment was brief: "Alas! My kind governess was shortly removed to a lunatic asylum. What share I may have had in her mental downfall I do not care to inquire."

Eventually, in "dire disgrace" after a misplaced flirtation with a curate (which began when Jane waylaid him for advice on a mistranslation in the Greek Testament), she was sent to Cheltenham Ladies' College, a school founded to provide middle-class girls with an education on a par with that of their brothers. Her father and stepmother saw education as a disagreeable but worthwhile investment to fit Jane for the job of staying at home and educating her younger siblings before an expected marriage. But a satisfying piece of good planning enabled Jane to reject their narrow plans for her future and strike out alone. From 1871, when she was twenty-one, she began to receive an annuity of £300 (a very significant sum) from her mother's will. Her father, who disliked the idea of women earning money, and who was already disgruntled that his father-in-law had arranged for Jane's mother and aunts to receive their inheritances independently of their husbands, was powerless to stop his daughter's path to financial freedom. In 1874, having won a scholarship as the best-performing candidate in the University of Cambridge's General Examination for Women, Harrison arrived at Newnham College to study classics as one of the college's first twenty boarders, with a reputation as "the cleverest woman in England."

Newnham had opened in 1871, to provide accommodation for women eager to attend Cambridge's new series of "Lectures for Ladies." Its first principal, Anne Jemima Clough, impressed on potential donors the importance of surroundings conducive to study, arguing—as Woolf would do later—that women can work far more effectively "where all the arrangements of the house are made to suit the hours of study, where she can have undisturbed possession of one

room, and where she can have access to any books that she may need."
It was a radical notion, but Clough insisted that each of her students be
furnished with a private room of their own—all the more essential
since women were barred from the university library. Harrison decorated her bedsitter in "the newest thing in dolorous Morris papers"
(which George Eliot, on a visit to the college, particularly admired),
and relished the unfamiliar freedom of college life. Now she could set
her sights on an academic career, developing her interests and ambitions in supportive surroundings.

Harrison left Newnham in 1879: to her disappointment, her unofficial result placed her only in the second class, and she was not invited
to stay on as a tutor. Instead, she made her way to London and looked
for work. Though it was back at Newnham that Harrison wrote her
most famous books, she did not return to the college until she was
forty-eight years old. Those later years, on which her legacy is founded,
comprise only a small portion of her life: narratives which focus on her
success tend to gloss over the long decades she spent uncertain that her
talents would ever achieve recognition. Later, Harrison and Gilbert
Murray—lifelong friends, collaborators, and lively correspondents—
would be considered the two foremost classicists of their era, both
public intellectuals commanding respect within and beyond their field.
But the contrast in their routes to that position is sobering. After leaving Oxford, Murray—at the age of twenty-three—was appointed Professor of Greek at the University of Glasgow and provided with
comfortable accommodation and a generous annual income of £1,300,
thanks to his tutor informing the electors that this was the most distinguished undergraduate he had ever encountered. Jane Harrison, in
contrast, spent the greater part of her youth and early middle age living cheaply in London boardinghouses, experiencing the frustration of
being constantly passed over for prestigious posts, while building up
her reputation outside academia through the undervalued labor of lecturing in schools, museums, and working men's clubs across Britain.

After brief spells teaching girls at Oxford High School and Not-
ting Hill High School, she was introduced to Sir Charles Newton,
keeper of Greek and Roman antiquities at the British Museum, who

was impressed by her vivacity and invited her to guide parties of elderly ladies around the antiquities rooms. Soon, Harrison was making a living through her "perambulating lectures": over the next decade she traveled the country delivering almost theatrical performances, designed to bring alive the spirit of ancient festivals, dances, and sacrifices. She would dress in spangled satin gowns, strings of Egyptian beads, and a glittering shawl, which she shrugged off her shoulders at moments of high drama; she would dim the lights to simulate nocturnal mystic worship, launch into peals of fluent Greek, and on one occasion placed two collaborators at the back of the auditorium to swing "bull-roarers'" in the manner of Orphic initiations, so the audience could experience the eerie sound emanating from an unseen place. In 1891, the *Pall Mall Gazette* described Harrison as "the lady to whose lectures during the last ten years the revival of popular interest in Greece is almost solely due."

Yet popular acclaim was not mirrored by institutional support. In an interview with the *Women's Penny Paper* in 1889, when asked whether being a woman had hampered her in launching her career, Harrison—who never wanted to be pitied—insisted it had not: "A woman was a novelty in this field, and my being one was in my favour with regard to professional popularity." But the previous year, Harrison had applied to succeed Newton as the Yates Chair of Classical Archeology at University College London, and was rejected at the final stage. Despite the recommendation of a long list of referees—including a roster of international archeologists, museum directors, and academics—two of the committee signed a document stating that it was "undesirable that any teaching in University College should be conducted by a woman." In 1896, she tried again for the post; this time the board refused her, with no hint of irony, on the grounds that despite her Newnham education she "had not enjoyed the same opportunities for a thorough scholarly grounding in the details of the various branches." A quiet word from a committee member in favor of his former student, Ernest Gardner, confirmed Harrison's exclusion. In her novel *Jacob's Room*, Woolf describes a female student staring at the ceiling of the British Museum Reading Room while she waits for her books, noticing not a single

Jane Ellen Harrison as Alcestis, Oxford, 1887.

woman among the names engraved on the dome: the library's very architecture implies that only men have been and will ever be scholars. Aged nearly fifty, with honorary degrees from Aberdeen and Durham to her name yet no university appointment, Jane Harrison must have felt the same sinking conviction that the world was skewed against her.

She knew, as Woolf did, that time, space, and money were required in order to produce a significant work of scholarship; it appeared inevitable that Harrison was destined to remain a perpetual outsider, despite her efforts and obvious ability.

But just as her mother's legacy had secured her university education against her father's wishes, it was the help of women, and the support of a female institution, that changed Harrison's fortunes. In 1898, she was invited to return to Newnham College as the first recipient of a new three-year fellowship created especially for the benefit of former pupils. Harrison accepted with delight, determined, now she had the chance, to create an environment in which she could dedicate her life to work. In London, Harrison's freelance income had been precarious, her concentration disrupted by lecturing engagements all over the country, her housemates difficult, and her shared rooms cramped. But now, she had a regular salary and her own private study once more; the calm of the college's large garden provided a welcome sanctuary for ideas to form, while she was surrounded by an energetic community of women scholars, many of whom—including Pernel Strachey, Mary Paley Marshall, and Eleanor Sidgwick—became lifelong friends. From the start, eager to make up for lost time, Harrison insisted that her position should involve only research, forgoing teaching duties along with the administrative and pastoral responsibilities that such roles usually entail. After negotiations, it was agreed that she would give one lecture a week in exchange for the freedom to travel, read, and write. Within college, Harrison's commitment to pure scholarship was admired: she gained the respect of her colleagues (though several resented having to perform the drudgery she had circumvented) and quickly became a favorite among the students, who would flock to her rooms after dinner to share cigarettes and whiskey, lounging in her sunken armchairs and rifling through the prints of Greek vases scattered across the floor. An enthusiastic profile of Harrison in the feminist weekly *Time and Tide* praised her as "one woman who did not allow herself to be limited by what anyone expected of a University woman lecturer: who in that capacity dressed as she liked, theorised as she liked and taught as she liked."

When she had first arrived at Newnham as a student, Harrison's grasp of Greek grammar lagged behind that of her male counterparts who had been studying the subject since childhood, and she never felt entirely confident in philology. But on her return as a fellow, she made a virtue of that outsider status by smashing through the existing boundaries of the discipline. Within five years, Harrison had published her groundbreaking *Prolegomena to the Study of Greek Religion*, a sprawling, conversational work which she referred to gleefully as "the fat and comely one." It was the product of decades of research, finally come to fruition at Newnham, where the recognition of an institution at last gave her the confidence to write at length and with authority. Over the next two decades, the support of the women's college was repaid with a series of triumphant works of scholarship which wrote women back into history, and opened up creative possibilities for historians, poets, and novelists alike.

Jane Harrison had entered academia at a time when the field of classical scholarship was focused narrowly on the detailed editing of canonical texts. But over the last decades of the nineteenth century, archeological digs sprang up across Europe and the Middle East, and a host of dramatic discoveries made the ancient world feel suddenly alive, close, and human. Heinrich Schliemann, an eccentric former businessman with an eye for drama, made international headlines for his excavations at Hisarlik in Turkey, which he insisted offered historical proof for the battle described in Homer's *Iliad*. "I have gazed upon the face of Agamemnon," he is supposed to have declared, emerging from a tomb, while newspapers printed photographs of his glamorous wife, Sophia, bedecked in the jewels of Helen of Troy. Harrison traveled the continent with the archeologists' retinues, gathering fresh material for her books and lectures: to Athens, where she smoked a pipe on the steps of the Parthenon, to Corinth, where her party mounted the Acrocorinth on mules, and to Bassae, where she slept out on the hillside under the remains of Apollo's temple. She visited Knossos, a newly discovered palace on the island of Crete, in the first year of Arthur Evans's famous excavation there, and discovered something which captured her imagination: a seal impression of a bull-headed

Minotaur, seated on a throne with a worshipper bent before him. "Zeus is nowhere," she wrote in triumph to Murray. "I always knew he was a tiresome parvenu & I have been doing my best to discredit him for years, he is so showy and omnipotent . . . What a dear delight it is to 'put down the mighty from their seat.'"

The ongoing excavations offered a material parallel to Jane Harrison's major scholarly fascination: digging down beneath the "layers of cult" to retrieve a lost history of ancient Greek worship. Harrison was frustrated that her contemporaries, taking Homer's epics as the starting point of Western literature, tended to assume that these poems also represented the earliest theology. Instead, she argued, the articulate, anthropomorphic Olympian gods of Homer and Greek tragedy—the warring and capricious family of deities dominated by the almighty, adulterous Zeus—provide no evidence of true popular religion, but are "the products of art and literature," divested of their mystical and monstrous attributes and merely "posing as divinities." Among her favorites of the finds she was allowed to examine at Knossos was a clay seal which she read as "a veritable little manual of primitive Cretan faith and ritual." Clearly discernible was the figure of a woman sitting atop a mountain, flanked by lions, a subject bowed down in ecstasy before her. In this image, Harrison identified an ancient ritual of mother-worship, long since hidden from history. Her discovery would shake the foundations of classical scholarship.

Harrison was not the first scholar to search for alternative cults to the Olympian pantheon. Friedrich Nietzsche's 1872 work *The Birth of Tragedy* (which Harrison called "real genius") had already questioned whether the apparent monopoly, as presented in literature, of the Olympian gods had any basis in the reality of ancient religious practice, while Sir James George Frazer, in his immensely popular and influential comparative study *The Golden Bough* (1890), had set out to show that ancient religions revolved around the worship and sacrifice of a mystic king who died at harvest and was reborn in the spring—a cycle he considered central to almost all mythology. But while both men's work focused on male deities and archetypes, Harrison now suggested that the origins of the well-known myths lay in a much older worship, anchored in emotion and community spirit, centered around rituals designed to ward off evil and celebrate the changing seasons, and which placed the greatest importance on women.

Harrison's major works, *Prolegomena to the Study of Greek Religion* (1903) and *Themis* (1912), drew on cutting-edge material evidence from the archeological digs she'd personally witnessed, and revealed an array of powerful goddesses who once reigned alone over cult shrines—Hera at Argos, Athena at Athens, Demeter and Persephone at Eleusis, Gaia at Delphi—but whose ancient worship had silently been replaced by later cults to Zeus, their temples renamed, their powers reattributed and their legends altered to accommodate the rationalized Olympian pantheon. These new gods, Harrison insisted, reflected not only human form but also man-made hierarchies: their rise was testament to the gradual erosion of women's importance in Greek society. When ideology wanted to confine women to the domestic sphere, these powerful, public goddesses appeared a threat to state order: the "outrageous" myth of the birth of the goddess Athena from Zeus's head, Harrison argued, is the "religious representation . . . of a patrilinear social structure" designed to erase the mother. Dionysus, Harrison suggested, was originally worshipped alongside his mother, Semele, an ancient Thracian earth goddess, but as society began to record lineage through a paternal line, Semele was gradually effaced and Dionysus became known as Son of Zeus.

But in early local cults, Harrison found evidence of a different world order, where descent was traced through the mother's family, where women's activities formed the heart of community life, and where "matriarchal, husbandless goddesses" were not mocked or feared but reverently worshipped. Not only were women central to early Greek religion as objects of worship, wrote Harrison, but as active participants in religious practice too. In *Prolegomena* she insisted that the frenetic band of maenads who attend Dionysus in Euripides's *Bacchae* were not invented mythical figures, but rather a literary portrait of real worshippers, whose seasonal assembly at women-only festivals was seen as central to the survival of the community at large. It was clear to her readers that Harrison was writing a version of history with serious repercussions on the present day, which mounted a force-ful challenge to women's current subordination. "We are so possessed by a set of conceptions based on Periclean Athens, by ideas of law and order and reason and limit," wrote Harrison, "that we are apt to dis-miss as 'mythological' whatever does not fit into our stereotyped pic-ture. The husbands and brothers of the women of historical days would not, we are told, have allowed their women to rave upon the moun-tains." Writing from a women's community, long shut out from insti-tutions run by men, Harrison saw things differently. In fact, she notes an overlooked source citing a group of female Dionysus-worshippers in Macedonia who frightened their husbands "out of their senses" by their "rites of possession and ecstasy." The men, writes Harrison, were too in awe of the evident power at work to put a stop to such practices, and with good reason: "The women were possessed, magical, and dan-gerous to handle."

To modernist writers, Harrison's efforts to reread history through the lens of gender and power offered fertile encouragement to their own experimentation with radical new forms. "Few books are more fasci-nating," wrote T. S. Eliot, who cited her work in a graduate paper at Harvard University, "than those of Miss Harrison . . . when they bur-row in the origins of Greek myths and rites"; her influence can be seen permeating *The Waste Land* (1922), with its pungent descriptions of seasonal ritual and divination. Harrison's insistence that art must derive from "a keen emotion" sounded a clarion call to writers, including Pound and the Imagists, who were seeking ways to express feeling directly, communicate truths, and "make it new." Her legends of pow-erful, creative, and vengeful women—and her compelling evidence of the way women have been systematically devalued by centuries of patriarchy—inspired others, over subsequent decades, in their creation of female characters, from E. M. Forster's Schlegel sisters to James Joyce's Molly Bloom, Virginia Woolf's Mrs. Ramsay, and D. H. Law-rence's Brangwen women. (Lawrence read Harrison's *Ancient Art and Ritual* a few months before he first met H. D., and told a friend that "it just fascinates me to see art coming out of religious yearning," though he supposed it to have been written by "a school marmy woman.") In turn, Harrison keenly followed the work of her younger contemporaries, eager to learn from them too: though she couldn't make much sense of *Ulysses,* she admired the way Joyce was "trying to make audible, make conscious the subconscious. He is dredging the great deeps of personality. That is his tremendous contribution."

For emerging women writers—H. D. and Virginia Woolf among them—Harrison's work opened up exciting new artistic possibilities. As a young woman, H. D. had studied Greek on her own, translating Euripides with the help of French and English versions. She never refers to Harrison directly, but might well have read the articles praising her work in the *New Freewoman* in 1913; she also devoured Gilbert Murray's studies of Greek religion, in which he summarized many of Harrison's theories. During a Hellenic cruise in 1932, on which the Reverend Wigram, Canon of Malta, delivered lectures largely paraphrasing *Prolegomena* and *Themis,* H. D. wrote to Bryher in amazement that "there were *mother*-cults under *all* the Zeus cults, from Dodona, down the coast!" The revelation was highly suggestive to H. D., who since her Mecklenburgh Square days had always been drawn to the collective female voices of Greek choruses, rather than heroic soliloquies. Her later poetry exudes a fascination with powerful mother-figures who represent creativity and love rather than war and destruction: her long-term project giving voice to ancient heroines found a parallel in Harrison's recovery of goddesses subsumed into legends not their own.

For Woolf, too, Jane Harrison was a major influence and inspiration. Virginia and her sister Vanessa, marked out for a genteel routine of domestic duty and self-sacrifice, were not sent to school with their brothers; determined nonetheless to learn and create, they spent their days upright in their shared room, Vanessa standing at her easel, Virginia at her tall writing desk, where she worked on her Greek, which she doggedly studied at home with tutors through her teenage years. In October 1904, while Virginia was staying with her aunt in Cambridge to convalesce from her second suicide attempt, her cousin Florence Maitland took her to Newnham to meet Jane Harrison "and all the other learned ladies"; it's perhaps not too far-fetched to imagine that this experience solidified Woolf's resolve, when she moved to Gordon Square later that year, to begin writing her first articles and reviews and to strike out on a public life of her own. Harrison's work gave Woolf a new, subversive model of history which informed all her subsequent novels and essays: one whose revelations offered powerful "mothers" for women to "think back through," and which revealed as man-made—and flimsy—the constructs on which patriarchal society rests. Woolf always felt set apart from the male Bloomsbury set— Lytton Strachey, John Maynard Keynes, E. M. Forster—who had met at Cambridge and been part of an elite, exclusively male Apostles circle under the mentorship of the philosopher G. E. Moore; even in the drawing room of Gordon Square, where men and women talked freely together, the men would occasionally congregate in a corner and chuckle over a Latin joke Virginia did not understand, leaving her with a sharp pang of exclusion. (Roger Fry once said that Harrison had "a really Apostolic mind," a high compliment delivered apparently without irony.) Jane Harrison offered Woolf an alternative lineage in which she could see herself reflected: a different Cambridge, a different Bloomsbury, a different approach to history, and the possibility of a different future.

Over the years she spent at Newnham, Harrison's work flourished within a small community founded on liberal values and a firm belief in women's intellectual equality to men. Yet her public presentation, so at odds with the sympathetic image of the deferential, motherly woman teacher, soon made her enemies across the conservative Cambridge classics faculty, where rumors flew that she was advocating "free love" among Newnham women by teaching them Sappho. Grumblings were heard all over town when Harrison came out with new theories: her books were roundly attacked for extrapolating liberally from scant evidence, for their bagginess and emotive language, for an alleged feminist agenda leading to overemphasis on women's roles, and for her "florid" style, often condemned as displaying "an excess of sympathy" and being "subjective" or "propagandistic." Critics, desperate to discredit her conclusions, linked her work with the "corybantic Helle-nism" of the ballerina Isadora Duncan, dismissing Harrison as a creative artist working in the modernist tradition, not as a serious his-torian dealing in the realm of material fact. As her time in Cambridge wore on, colleagues outside Newnham grew more virulent in their criticism. When in 1916 she postulated that the traditional Russian puppet show and the legend of the Head of John the Baptist might share an origin in ritual dance, Sir William Ridgeway (a distinguished archeologist from Gonville & Caius, and an arch-conservative, active in the National League for Opposing Woman Suffrage) wrote to M. R. James, the provost of King's and a very influential figure in the univer-sity, to condemn "such an audacious, shameless avowal of charlatan-ism, debauching young minds wholesale." James, in turn, published a vituperative condemnation of Harrison's article, accusing her of every scholarly sin from a poor understanding of Latin idiom to a blasphe-mous attack on Christianity. But Harrison—who openly set herself against the hegemony of what she called "sound scholars"—was satis-fied by her contemporaries' flustered reactions, which proved that her bold theories had made an impact. Reflecting later on *Themis*, from her home in Mecklenburgh Street, she wrote: "To the orthodox among my contemporaries, and to the younger reactionaries, *Themis* has appeared dangerous. Their fear is justified. A hand was laid upon their ark."

Jane Harrison's presence in the Cambridge classics faculty was a challenge to the status quo, whereby women's access to knowledge remained a source of discomfort. In the nineteenth and early twentieth centuries, the study of ancient Greek was a marker of social status, taught in public schools to boys who were expected to go on to hold positions of power and influence. As such, the classics came to signify an intellectual territory unassailable for women and the working classes, an emblem of their exclusion from systems of power. "I'd give ten years of my life to know Greek," muses Clarissa Dalloway, the upper-class wife who wants for nothing except an education, in Vir-ginia Woolf's debut novel, *The Voyage Out*. For women, "knowing Greek" meant far more than a good memory for grammar and vocabulary; as girls' education became increasingly formalized, learning an ancient language provided not only a challenge and a pleasure, but also a way for women to assert their intellectual standing.

In her essay "Scientiae Sacra Fames," Harrison wrote of the "delight of learning for learning's sake a 'dead' language for sheer love of the beauty of its words and the delicacy of its syntactical relations . . . the rapture of reconstructing for the first time in imagination a bit of the historical past." Women's education had so long been constructed around its practical application to the life of a wife and mother that choosing a subject for pure stimulation felt like an act of delicious daring. Harrison considered "freedom to know" to be the "birthright of every human being"; she was furious when it was implied that any realm of knowledge should be considered "unwomanly." The memory of a Greek grammar book being confiscated by an aunt—who tartly reminded Jane she would have no use for it when she had a "home of her own"—rankled for the rest of her life: "She was a little girl, and thereby damned to eternal domesticity; she heard the gates of the temple of Learning clang as they closed." These clanging gates find an echo in *A Room of One's Own*, where the doors of the Cambridge library slam shut on Woolf as the officious beadle confiscates the key. In her essay, Woolf transforms the cloying servility of that "home"—where women's interests are sidelined—into a vision of a new living space, and by extension a new society, where such scholarly interests can be celebrated and nurtured. Harrison's example made that transformation seem possible to Woolf, writing in 1928. But two decades earlier, as the voices of Harrison's detractors grew ever louder, she began to question her position at the university.

Harrison was well aware that the backlash against her—her works dismissed for flawed logic and an overflow of emotion—employed many of the same arguments that were still being used to deny women any education at all. In an increasingly impassioned series of essays written between 1909 and 1914, published as *Alpha and Omega*, Harrison demanded that we must "free women" from the idea that "man" connotes humanity and "woman" does not; over and over she insisted that it was dangerous to the whole of society to "confine man or woman within the limits of sex." "We must free women before we know what they are fit for intellectually and morally," she insisted. "We women may have all to go back into the harem tomorrow for the good of the race. If so, back we must go in the name of science. But, again in the name of science, we are *not* going till the experiment has been tried." Like Dorothy L. Sayers, Harrison was always swift to contradict any suggestion that men's and women's brains were suited to different sorts of knowledge or work: in a thought that may have influenced Woolf's idea of the androgynous brain, she praised the ancient worshippers of Orpheus, who "made their god in the image of neither male nor female, but a thing bisexed, immaculate, winged, and—this is the interesting thing for us—looking out on the world *four-eyed.*" Harrison's convictions revolved around ideas of power; bolstered by the archeological evidence for women's importance to ancient community life, she argued that the virtues commonly considered "womanly" are "the outcome, not of sex, but of status," and wrote that "to be set in authority over a fellow human being, as man has been set over woman, is a serious spiritual danger." As 1914 approached, she began, like Woolf and H. D., to connect the tyrannies of patriarchy explicitly with the militarism now threatening to destroy society.

Like H. D., Harrison was deeply depressed by the outbreak of the First World War, the alacrity with which many of her colleagues joined up and wrote in its support, and the patriotic fervor that swept Britain: "With every fibre of body and mind, I stand for Peace," she wrote. Harrison's simple belief that women should be accepted as human soon became a denunciation of dominion in all its forms, founded on the conviction that "freedom for ourselves must involve freedom for others"—of any race or nation. Now her ongoing spat with Sir William Ridgeway turned personal. When Harrison delivered a rousing speech arguing for Bertrand Russell—expelled from his lectureship at Trinity College for his anti-conscription activism—to have his punishment revoked, Ridgeway publicly condemned Newnham as "a notorious centre of Pro-German agitation" and refused one of Harrison's students entry to his class because she was a member of the pacifist Union of Democratic Control.

But Harrison was unswerving in the face of such challenges from the conservative establishment: "To be a heretic today," she wrote, "is almost a human obligation." She saw "the rejection of traditional faiths and customs" as a prerequisite for intellectual freedom, not possible in a conservative society in thrall to the past and to power. War, to her, represented the natural result of a "herd" society where blind faith and homogeneity are prized over reason, where a dominant class, unchallenged in their "power to compel," can lead their subordinates into dangerous actions with unconscionable consequences. Hatred of arbitrary authority lay at the heart of all Jane Harrison's work, from her critique of the Olympian gods to her dislike of institutional religion. But her convictions stood starkly at odds with everything that, outside of its women's colleges, Cambridge represented: a university with ecclesiastical foundations, a bastion of elite male privilege for generations, with unchecked power—the university could elect its own MP, voted for by alumni, while its vice chancellor could overrule local jurisdiction—built into its constitution.

Harrison's unladylike penchant for free thinking disturbed the establishment. To reactionaries such as Ridgeway and James, she stood for the threats to religion, the British Empire, and male supremacy which they associated with unwelcome modernity. Increasingly, she began to feel cloistered at Newnham, ground down by the constant reminders that its members were not equal. She was especially frustrated by Cambridge's ongoing refusal to grant women degrees, even after Oxford changed its rules in 1920. "Sometimes I feel that the virtue fostered among us is conformity," she wrote wearily to Murray, outlining the continued pressure on Newnham staff and students to prove their worth to men. "I don't suppose you realise how convention and all the conservative virtues are canonised in a women's college . . . I don't think it is quite our own fault that our virtues are mainly those of slaves but they *are*—nice well-educated slaves but still slaves." A first motion on women's degrees had failed in 1897, the year before Harrison returned to Newnham, when truculent alumni and an army of country parsons (who retained voting rights based on an ancient university statute) were shepherded in to cast their votes against. In October 1921, a watered-down proposal to offer honorary degrees to women students was once again rejected. Following the vote, a jeering mob of male undergraduates marched on Newnham, vandalizing the college gates.

Harrison was furious at Cambridge's intransigence, and could put up with it no longer. She decided that her intellectual interests should henceforth be pursued outside the university, where "much of our ingenuity & energy goes in cringing": rather than remain at Cambridge as a second-class citizen, Harrison began to imagine a new life, in a place where traditions could be challenged and assumptions interrogated. Since the war, her focus had shifted from ancient religion toward a wider fascination for the human mind—for Freudian psychology and Russian literature, the philosophy of language and contemporary art. In *Reminiscences*, she admitted that she felt she had "lived too long the strait Academic life with my mind intently focused on the solution of a few problems" and that she "wanted before the end came to see things more freely and more widely." But leaving Cambridge, aged seventy-two, represented more than a desire to learn and travel: it was a determination to establish a way of life where her refusal to conform would be valued. Not many people in their seventies would consider such a dramatic change, let alone go through with it, but Harrison was convinced that life had more to offer her—and that she had more to give. It was time to abandon the staid academy and start afresh in an international metropolis, where politics and art were thriving, and where new ideas were welcomed with delight. In 1922, Harrison departed for Paris, where she would spend three years before settling, finally, in London at 11 Mecklenburgh Street. Before she left, she burned all her papers—obliterating all traces of her former life. We can't know whether the bonfire was impetuous or premeditated, but this dramatic act of destruction ensured that when Harrison set out to reshape her life, she did so free from any physical reminders of the past. Her friends sent her off with a fund of £325 and a cheerful note congratulating Harrison on her triumphant rebirth. Of all her colleagues, only Ridgeway refused to contribute to her farewell present.

· · ·

Her departure from Cambridge, as well as signaling new intellectual opportunity, offered a chance for Harrison to reflect on how she wanted to live her private life, and with whom she wanted to share it. Over the years, Harrison had experienced various romantic disappointments: while an undergraduate, she had been led to expect a proposal from her supervisor, Henry Butcher, who had omitted to mention he was already engaged to someone else; later, she had tentatively agreed to marry the classical scholar R. A. Neil, who died suddenly of appendicitis in 1901. In time, she played down these setbacks, explaining that she had ultimately chosen "to live in the things of the mind and to find my great joy and peace there." Unlike H. D. and Sayers, who were a generation younger, Harrison didn't agonize over finding a partnership of equals; by this point she was steadfast in her conviction that marriage, experimental or otherwise, was not for her. Just as Harriet Vane in *Gaudy Night* muses that perhaps "one oughtn't to marry anybody, unless one's prepared to make him a full-time job," Harrison valued her hard-won independence too highly to risk it. "Marriage, for a woman at least," she wrote in *Reminiscences*, "hampers the two things that made life to me glorious—friendship and learning . . . The role of wife and mother is no easy one; with my head full of other things I might have dismally failed."

Nonetheless, Harrison maintained a series of extraordinarily intense relationships across her life, with men and women who shared her scholarly passions. During her time in Cambridge, she was especially close to her younger colleague Francis Cornford, but their intimacy cooled in 1909, when he announced his engagement to Frances Darwin. After Cornford's marriage, Harrison never spoke of her feelings for him, and her friends knew to avoid the subject; in Harrison's archive, the story can be reconstructed in outline through various dark allusions to "beautiful happiness" in their shared work, uncomfortable gossip at Newnham, and her dismay, when he wrote formally to thank her for helping him find his path, at realizing she was considered merely a motherly mentor figure.

It's been generally assumed that Harrison's disappointment lay in deep-seated hopes of marrying Cornford herself. But all other indica-

Jane Harrison with H. F. Stewart, Gilbert Murray, and Francis Cornford, circa 1909.

tions of her attitudes to marriage suggest that this was not the case. Later, Cornford complained to his wife that Harrison had treated him "as if he were a lover who had abandoned her." But to Harrison, the betrayal was something more complex. She didn't want to sign herself over to a husband (it's hard to imagine this self-proclaimed heretic promising to obey anyone at an altar), but she had grown reliant on

Cornford for their comfortable "sort of unmarried-married life," both independent, yet utterly committed to their shared work, a purpose each considered higher than themselves. Now, she was saddened and frustrated that his marriage not only drew a boundary around their friendship, but also spelled an end to their close working partnership. Distracted by domestic bliss—including the birth, in quick succession, of five children—Cornford no longer had unlimited time to pore over hieroglyphs and cuneiform late into the night, or accompany Harrison on a whim to archeological excursions or to seaside rest cures when her health failed. When he joined the army in 1914, revealing a longstanding enthusiasm for musketry, his renunciation of their intellectual camaraderie was complete. Writing to Frances Darwin at the time of the engagement, Harrison admitted that she was "just now faced by the blank unalterable fact that for more than 6 months Francis has not cared & could not care at all for the work that has been for years our joint life & friendship." Yet Harrison was able to recognize that she expected too much of a colleague, gently adding that she bore Frances no ill-feeling: "you could as yet not understand, nor can he, how—late in life—work & friendship come to be the whole of life."

Harrison thrived on the company of a committed sparring partner; being without one sent her into spirals of depression. But over her last years at Newnham, she found someone who was willing to devote herself wholeheartedly to the relationship, and whose fidelity would be the mainstay of Harrison's new life away from Cambridge. The major relationship of Jane Harrison's later life offered her a radical alternative to marriage, an intellectual stimulus, and a fresh energy for new collaborations. This was with Hope Mirrlees, a Newnham pupil thirty-seven years her junior, with whom Harrison lived, worked, and traveled from around 1915 until her death in 1928 in their shared home on Mecklenburgh Street.

Hope Mirrlees, wrote Virginia Woolf (who knew her through Karin Costelloe, who was married to Woolf's brother Adrian Stephen and was Hope's closest friend from college), came from "a typical English family, devoted, entirely uncultured, owning motor cars." Descended on one side from aristocrats and on the other from sugar entrepreneurs,

Mirrlees had arrived at Newnham in 1910, having quit a drama course at the Royal Academy of Dramatic Art. She was engaged at the time to the illustrator Henry Justice Ford, a stout and awkward friend of the family who was fifty to her twenty-three; when the arrangement was dissolved, Jane Harrison wrote politely to advise her that the following term's text would be *The Odyssey*. "Thank you for writing to tell me about your engagement," she added. "I *am* relieved it is ended—for tho 'pedestrian love' is a good & great thing it is not quite enough I think . . . Anyhow I am truly glad we shall have you at Newnham next autumn." Later that year, she admitted to Hope's mother (who, to be near her daughter, had taken a house in Cambridge, where Harrison visited the family for dinner) that she was sad her lessons with Hope were over, but that "that is only the end of one chapter I hope. In some ways when the relation of teacher & taught is past, it is easier to get to know one another." This marked the start of the relationship which would lead Harrison to refer to Mirrlees, in her autobiography, as a "ghostly daughter"—a phrase that not only highlights their close bond, but also suggests something otherworldly about Mirrlees, hinting at the complex layers to a relationship which cannot easily be defined.

Jane Harrison's Cambridge friends were always deeply suspicious of Mirrlees, whom they blamed for the bonfire Harrison made of her papers when the pair left Cambridge together in 1922, and whose stubborn gatekeeping during Harrison's last illness left them feeling excluded and perplexed. Their desire to minimize her significance in Harrison's life has influenced later assessments of their intimacy: biographers have suggested that Mirrlees sought fame by association with Harrison, used her company as cover to persuade her anxious parents to let her travel abroad, or merely served as Harrison's assistant and companion in old age, managing her affairs and controlling her movements. Mirrlees has been portrayed in turn as predator and victim, as manipulator and as parasite, just as Bryher's significant career as a writer and publisher has often been downplayed in narratives that see her merely as a silent midwife to H. D.'s dominant talent. Not only do such accounts underestimate Mirrlees—an accomplished poet and novelist in her own right, whose long poem *Paris* has recently been hailed as a lost modernist masterpiece—but they also diminish the deep affection and intellectual compatibility which made this partnership the foundation for the variety of exciting new projects on which Harrison embarked in the 1920s.

Their closeness, despite the significant age difference, was certainly unusual. Virginia Woolf airily told a friend that Mirrlees "has a passion for Jane Harrison, the scholar: indeed they practically live together," and having read Mirrlees's 1919 novel *Madeleine*—about a precocious seventeen-year-old girl who enters the glamorous entourage of the famed seventeenth-century Parisian hostess Mademoiselle de Scudéry, with whom she falls in love—Woolf took the book as straight autobiography: "It's all Sapphism so far as I've got—Jane and herself." Unlike Harrison, Mirrlees (her youthful betrothal notwithstanding) never showed any romantic interest in men, and her early work in particular shows a deep engagement with ideas around sexuality and same-sex desire. In the early twentieth century, female sexuality was increasingly scrutinized by sexologists, psychoanalysts, and lawyers; by 1921 the subject was seen as dangerous enough for parliament to debate making lesbianism (associated with over-education, prostitution, alcohol, nightclubs, divorce, and vampires) a criminal offense like male homosexuality, but the question was shelved on the basis that women might not have considered the concept and it was preferable not to put ideas into their heads.

Until the latter half of the century, language for lesbian desire remained, for the large part, either coy and euphemistic or clinical, even medical. In public, women tended to present their relationships vaguely: Virginia Woolf's affair with Vita Sackville-West existed, sometimes uneasily, alongside their respective marriages; H. D. and Bryher referred to each other publicly as cousins, and masked their partnership—which Bryher's parents never accepted—behind Bryher's two marriages, first to the American writer Robert McAlmon, then to the bisexual novelist and filmmaker Kenneth Macpherson, who was at the time H. D.'s lover. If same-sex desire was depicted in popular media, it was through the stereotype of the "mannish lesbian": the bicycle-riding, trouser-wearing New Woman mocked with relish in

Punch cartoons, whose alarming attitudes were assumed to extend to sexual depravity. There was little language for women whose "transgressions" were less public, who enjoyed relationships with women which could not so easily be mapped on to the template of a heterosexual marriage—relationships, like Jane and Hope's, which may or may not have been sexual (and there's rarely the evidence to be sure either way) but which offered a subversive intimacy outside a nuclear family setup. When Hope or Jane spoke of their relationship, it was always in coded, allusive terms, acknowledging that others might not understand, but not requiring outside approval: Hope's 1923 novel *The Counterplot* is dedicated to Jane Harrison with a quote in Greek from *The Odyssey*—"Nothing is greater than when two people keep house together, man and wife, a great grief to enemies and joy to friends."

Woolf spent a good deal more time in her diaries and letters analyzing Mirrlees's character, not in an entirely positive way. She certainly admired Mirrlees's literary talents, and was eager to support her career: she gave *Madeleine* a positive review in the *Times Literary Supplement* (though both she and Katherine Mansfield admitted privately that they found it pretentious and heavy-going), and in 1920 the Hogarth Press published *Paris*, typeset by Woolf, who made several mistakes and had to make corrections by hand in most of the 175 copies. But Woolf's private descriptions of Mirrlees indicate a grudging respect tinged by jealousy, not only of her writing but also, significantly, of her intimacy with Harrison. In 1919, listing in her diary her friends, among whom she counts Mirrlees "latest of all," Woolf dismisses her as a "spoiled prodigy": "over-dressed, over-elaborate, scented, extravagant" with a "greed, like a greed for almond paste, for fame." But that August, Woolf described Mirrlees to a friend as one who "knows Greek and Russian better than I do French; is Jane Harrison's favourite pupil, and has written a very obscure, indecent and brilliant poem, which we are going to print. It's a shame that all this should be possible to the younger generation; still I feel that *something* must be lacking, don't you?" Woolf, who had always wanted a female mentor, and who herself had entered ambivalently into marriage, immediately saw the liberating potential of Jane and Hope's partnership, founded on a deep affection and intellectual compatibility. Just as her life with Bryher offered H. D. a release from constricting gender norms and a new energy for writing, with Bryher as facilitator and collaborator, their relationship gave Harrison and Mirrlees a fresh stimulation and freedom. Unlike Cornford, Mirrlees was utterly committed to Harrison and to her writing: she looked after Jane, encouraged her, and poured her own energies into shared projects. Later, Hope wrote that "influence was hardly the word of her effect on me. It was, rather, re-creation." Yet she also recalled, to her pleasure, Harrison's telling her "that she had learned a great deal from me," too; after Harrison's death, when Mirrlees's output had dwindled and her reputation declined, this glancing memory—and a few small books featuring both their names—would be the lasting reminder of these years, probably the happiest and most vital of both women's lives. And in Paris and Bloomsbury their life together, begun at Newnham over pots of coffee and ancient Greek texts, flourished around a new, highly modern passion: for the Russian language and culture.

Jane Harrison had first taken up Russian in Cambridge during the First World War, seeking a new interest to distract her from the horrors being reported, and from the breakup of her intellectual cohort as friends and colleagues began to enlist. She told Gilbert Murray that learning the language had made her weep for joy: it was palpably clear, she wrote, that Russia "cares more than any other nation for things of the spirit." Her choice of language was somewhat subversive in the circumstances. The signing of the Anglo-Russian Convention in 1907 had made Britain and Russia uneasy allies, but at the outbreak of war in 1914, the British press debated suspiciously whether Russia (still an autocracy rather than a democracy) should be considered Western or Eastern, civilized or barbaric. That August, while Zeppelins droned overhead, Harrison wrote to Mirrlees (who was back at her family home at Chislehurst in Kent), telling her she was learning Russian "for our new allies" and urging Hope to learn it too. Whether out of her own interest or a desire to humor Harrison's enthusiasm, Mirrlees accepted the challenge. In the spring vacation of 1915, the pair traveled together to Paris and joined a second-year Russian class ("grammar and the Brothers Karamasoff") at the École des Langues Orientales, where fellow students included a priest, some pawnbrokers, a French suffragette, and a man "so fat he can scarcely speak." "It is too fascinating," wrote Harrison to Murray. "I have always meant to devote my dotage to languages and now it is coming on."

In a lecture given back at Cambridge that autumn, Harrison described her days as "growing richer every moment" with the study of Russian, which had offered her "a new birth and a new life." She was not attracted by the prospect of access to works of literature (the products of individual minds), but to the language itself, which she saw as offering a rare insight into another group's unconscious. Around this time, the idea of a common European language had begun to gain currency as a way of forging connections between nations, but Harrison disliked the proposal: "If Esperanto alone were spoken throughout the world, think of the desolation of it! To most of us life would be barely worth the living . . . When we take the trouble to learn a people's language, it is then we draw near and touch their innermost, unconscious souls." Specifically, Harrison was fascinated by Russian grammar, especially the "far famed, much dreaded" imperfective aspect—a voice which captures a sense of ongoing action and expresses a collective memory of a past beyond that of the individual—which she believed to be of "profound psychological significance."

Harrison was deeply influenced by the work of Henri Bergson, whose lectures in Paris, London, and New York packed out halls, occasioned traffic jams, and prompted his blacklisting from the Catholic Church. Bergson argued that Western thought went wrong in its determination to see time as a succession of events, one after the other; he preferred to consider time as an ongoing, endless process, a series of changes "which melt into and permeate one another, without precise outlines." He called this *la durée*. Harrison was immediately riveted by the concept, which she saw reflected in the Russian imperfective aspect. *Durée*, she wrote, implies that we are something far greater than just ourselves, that we contain within us both the present and the past at once, and are somehow part of one another: "Each of us is a snowball growing bigger every moment, and in which all *our* past, and also the past out of which we sprang, all the generations behind us, is rolled up, involved." For modernist writers including Woolf, Joyce, and Proust, Bergson's theories opened up the opportunity to reimagine linear plots and to play with representations of consciousness, perspective, and memory, while his existential call for humans to situate themselves in a time beyond the immediate present resonated with the generation seeking to rebuild society after the First World War. For Harrison, the realization that an understanding of *la durée* was built into the Russian language made her feel a deep empathy with the Russian people: inherent to their self-expression was a sense of kinship that disregarded borders or national identity.

Harrison and Mirrlees arrived back in Paris in October 1922, excited by the possibilities of the city and ready to immerse themselves in the study of Russian. They took rooms at the American University Women's Club, a residence for postgraduate students recommended by Harrison's old friend Alys Pearsall Smith, on the rue de Chevreuse in Montparnasse (Hope was delighted that ice cream was served daily, and the extensive library contained "all the recent detective stories"). After so many years in Cambridge, Harrison felt her world expanding, as if she had been launched into a technicolor future. Paris in the 1920s, wrote Gertrude Stein, "was where the twentieth century was." The cafés of the Left Bank hummed with conversation about art, philosophy, and literature, while its nightclubs pulsated with the euphoric rhythms of jazz. Montparnasse—known simply as "The Quarter"—was home to an international community of artists, composers, poets, and novelists who had gathered in pursuit of freedom and inspiration. Sylvia Beach's and Adrienne Monnier's bookshops on the rue de l'Odéon, in the sixth arrondissement, sponsored readings and offered convivial places for the avant-garde to meet informally in a semi-private space; James Joyce and Jean Cocteau struck poses for Man Ray at his studio; while Stein and Natalie Barney—both influential women who wrote and spoke openly of lesbian desire—hosted regular salons and cocktail parties in their homes, all within a short stroll of Jane and Hope's lodgings. Angela Lavelli, an Italian-Russian friend of Roger Fry, took them to see the latest works by Picasso and Derain at contemporary galleries on the rue La Boétie ("Cubism is now a back number & the stunt now is to be 'savant,' i.e. Eclectic," wrote Hope excitedly), and persuaded the reclusive dealer Auguste Pellerin to show them his famous personal display of works by Cézanne ("owing to Pellerin's churlishness, his collection is almost inaccessible & so for most people Cézanne is an invisible source of inspiration—rather like God"). Hope purchased an embroidered blue frock coat of the latest style, a velvet cape, and a grey felt hat "to wear with my coats & skirts in that holy place of ritual purity & reticence—LA RUE," in between spurts of work on a novel. Virginia Woolf visited Paris in April 1923, and wrote home of their "Sapphic flat," where she enjoyed seeing the two women "billing and cooing together." But Jane and Hope's Paris was not the elegant milieu of Paris Lesbos or America Abroad, but rather a community of Russian exiles, living on the margins of French society.

Like many others in British literary and socialist circles, who saw in it a romance and sense of liberation akin to the French Revolution, Harrison had greeted with delight the February Revolution of 1917, during which the Tsarist establishment was overthrown by a mass uprising of soldiers and workers demanding liberty, justice, and equality. "I feel that our chiefest hope for the future is Russia," wrote D. H. Lawrence that May, echoing the language with which he was describing his dreams of Rananim to H. D. and others around the same time. But in October 1917, Vladimir Lenin's Bolshevik Party had ousted the provisional government, imprisoned (and later executed) Tsar Nicholas and his family, and seized control of the country. From that point, the triumphant insurrection turned into a chaotic civil war between the Bolsheviks and the counter-revolutionary White Army, forcing millions to flee the country and creating fledgling diasporas in cities across Europe. In the early 1920s, Paris became the cultural and political center of Russia Abroad, its sixteenth arrondissement especially popular with émigrés.

Unlike the American expatriates—Ernest Hemingway, F. Scott

Fitzgerald, Gertrude Stein—who lived abroad by choice, enjoying Parisian café culture and its attendant freedoms, Russian émigrés arrived as refugees resigned to long-term exile. In a speech given in Paris in February 1924, Ivan Bunin—who in 1933 would become the first Russian to be awarded the Nobel Prize in Literature—proclaimed that "we are not in exile, we are on a mission": to preserve Russian culture and heritage in their new homes and to transmit it to the wider world, recreating a version of national identity which could survive without territory or borders. Harrison's sympathy was piqued immediately by the exiles' predicament; her natural compassion for outsiders and underdogs made her determined to do what she could to help the displaced. She and Mirrlees attended all the performances given by the Moscow Art Theatre when it visited Paris in late 1922, as part of an ongoing European tour; Harrison was overwhelmed with emotion when several émigrés appeared on stage at the end of a Christmas Eve show and declared that the performance had given them hope for Russia's continued survival. "All along it has been such a mixed joy," she wrote, "the wonder of their art and the pity and the shame that this amazingly gifted people were starving in thousands—it was almost unbearable."

Harrison's personal relationship with Paris's Russian community began the following year. In the summer of 1923, in recognition of her reputation as a preeminent thinker, she was invited to participate in the annual colloquia convened by Paul Desjardins at a twelfth-century Cistercian abbey at Pontigny in Burgundy. These "*entretiens*" were ten-day sessions of intellectual exchange—interspersed with walks, concerts, and swims in the river—to which select scholars were invited. They aimed to counter the spirit of nationalism that had arisen since the First World War, forge collaborations which might form a model for a modern global society, and extend conversations across European borders. Among the representatives invited in the postwar years were Edith Wharton, André Gide, Lytton Strachey, Jacques Raverat, Vernon Lee, and Roger Fry (though never Virginia Woolf, to her annoyance). At Pontigny, Harrison took her place among a distinguished assembly of philosophers, writers, and historians, including, to her delight, various members of the displaced Russian intelligentsia.

During the first week, at which the main question under discussion was whether there is something intangibly national in poetry that cannot be translated into another language, Harrison was placed at dinner next to the existential philosopher Lev Shestov. That evening, they discussed the plight of Russian intellectuals, and Shestov told Harrison the story of a writer friend of his, Alexei Mikhailovich Remizov. Exiled by the Russian state after multiple arrests for his subversive politics, Remizov was currently struggling in Berlin, where postwar hyperinflation was diminishing living standards and the government was starting to clamp down on immigration. His friends and admirers, among them the writer Thomas Mann and the painter Nicholas Roerich, were raising funds to bring him to France: affected by Shestov's account of his desperation, Harrison promised £5 and agreed to promote Remizov's cause among her English friends. In November 1923, Remizov and his wife, Seraphima, arrived in Paris, and the following February, Shestov introduced him to Jane and Hope. Their shared passions, and unlikely friendship, would bring Harrison and Remizov together on two important projects of cross-cultural relations.

Extremely short, with wide-rimmed horn glasses, Alexei Remizov spoke in a whisper, but friends primarily remembered his mischievous grin. Occasionally he wore a wizard's hat he had fashioned himself, and he was known to leave the house with a monkey's tail protruding from a slit in his jacket. Harrison was instantly charmed by Alexei's eccentricity and the kindness of Seraphima—a fellow radical socialist and a specialist on ancient Russian scripts—and above all, she was fascinated by his work. Harrison had first come across Remizov's name some years earlier, when learning Russian at the École des Langues Orientales. She had been taken by his stories about the lives of Russian saints and the legends of Russia's ancient, pre-Christian past, which struck her as sharing an affinity with the pre-Olympian Greek rituals she had studied. But she had soon given up struggling through his texts, de-

ciding he "uses too many hard words" for her rudimentary grasp of
the language. Fortunately, his work was just beginning to appear in
English translation, thanks to the assiduous efforts of none other than
John Cournos. While in Devon with H. D. in 1916, Cournos had written an extensive essay about Remizov which was published in the *Egoist*
that year, arguing that he "must be classed among those artists who
say an old thing in a new way"; in 1924, Chatto & Windus published
Remizov's novel *The Clock* in a translation by Cournos, which he had
begun while living in Mecklenburgh Square and continued to work on
throughout his relationship with Dorothy L. Sayers. During his stint
in St. Petersburg in 1917, Cournos had met Remizov, then living in
great poverty, toiling in a dark room, his windows draped in black fab-
ric, and tall candles lighting the old icons arranged before him on his
writing desk. Seven years later Remizov still remembered with gratitude a bottle of concentrated bouillon Cournos had given him, which
had lasted him through several meager winters.

Harrison's association with Remizov—and the encouragement of
another Russian friend, D. S. Mirsky—prompted her first foray
into Russian translation. In the spring of 1924, she became intrigued
by a seventeenth-century memoir—considered the earliest Russian
autobiography—written from prison by the archpriest Avvakum. Born
around 1620, Avvakum led a rebellion against adjustments to the rites
of the Russian Orthodox Church, which would have suppressed ancient
customs in favor of modernized liturgy; he spent the last fourteen years
of his life imprisoned in a pit at Pustozyorsk, an icy wilderness in Russia's polar region, where he was finally burned at the stake. Harrison's
sympathy with Avvakum was born out of her fascination with popular
rituals and her dislike of imposed dogma: she admired his commitment
to preserving a religion based on genuine folk practice, rather than a
sanitized orthodoxy divorced from what communities actually believed.
Though Dostoevsky had famously declared the book untranslatable,
Mirsky, whose relatives had been exiled in 1664 for their support of
Avvakum, suggested that Harrison and Mirrlees attempt an English
translation—their first creative collaboration, and a significant linguis-
tic challenge.

Remizov offered to lend the women his own copy of the text, and to assist them with any difficulties deciphering the language. Throughout the summer of 1924, Jane and Hope enjoyed Monday reading parties at the Remizovs' apartment on avenue Mozart. Over mugs of strong tea—and, for particularly knotty sections, tumblers of ice-cold vodka—they progressed haltingly, Alexei and Seraphima patiently explaining the Old Russian, and other friends occasionally interpreting when the Remizovs' idiosyncratic English proved a barrier. In August, Harrison and Mirrlees returned to Pontigny, where they revised the manuscript a final time. On August 20, 1924, they wrote to the Remizovs, in faltering Russian: "We have finished Avvakum. There were many mistakes!"

The translation was published in October 1924 by Leonard and Virginia Woolf's Hogarth Press, the press's forty-first publication and ninth translation from Russian. Both Woolfs had long been fascinated by Russia: Leonard had founded the 1917 Club, a political salon for socialists in Soho's Gerrard Street named for the February Revolution, while Virginia—who had read *Crime and Punishment* in French on her honeymoon and immediately declared Dostoevsky "the greatest writer ever born"—had begun to learn the language in order to read and translate from the original. And their passion was enthusiastically shared, both in and beyond their circle. In the early decades of the twentieth century, British interest in Russian literature, dance, music, and politics was a widely remarked-on national frenzy. The "savage-joyful panther-leaping" of Sergei Diaghilev's Ballets Russes took Covent Garden by storm in 1911; that year also saw the first London productions of Chekhov's plays, while the following autumn Roger Fry included a section of Russian art in his acclaimed *Second Post-Impressionist Exhibition*, curated by the St. Petersburg-born mosaicist Boris Anrep, whose Byzantine-inspired designs adorned the homes of many of the artist's Bloomsbury friends.

But above all, Britain was captivated by its discovery of Russian literature. In 1912, Constance Garnett's translation of *The Brothers Karamazov* introduced Dostoevsky to an English-speaking readership. A former student at Newnham—where, according to her son, she had admired Jane Harrison, "whose short curls and freedom from the trammels of her sex aroused as much awe as envy"—Constance had worked as a librarian and a social activist in East London until her marriage in 1889 to the editor Edward Garnett. She had come to Russian through the political exile Feliks Volkhovsky, who, while she was pregnant and bored in the summer of 1891, had given her a Russian grammar and dictionary and suggested she learn the language. Over the subsequent decades, Garnett translated into English almost the entire canon of nineteenth-century Russian literature: most of Tolstoy, all Dostoevsky's novels, Chekhov's plays and stories, and the works of Turgenev and Gogol. Her prolific labor meant that the nineteenth-century Russian greats were felt as contemporaries by their twentieth-century British counterparts, their releases as hotly anticipated as the latest bestseller. Virginia Woolf wrote that Garnett's translations shattered the conventions of Victorian realist fiction by offering something grander and more profound. For D. S. Mirsky, Dostoevsky's lack of emotional inhibition meant that, "together with Freud," the publication of his work in English was "the most powerful single influence to give the death-blow to the Victorian mental order."

The Woolfs were "immensely impressed" by Harrison and Mirrlees's translation, and delighted to add *Avvakum* to their list. Mirsky sent parcels of the book to the Russian press hoping for reviews, but the packages were returned "non-admis." "Oh dear!" wrote Harrison, "will intolerance never cease to breed intolerance?" Hogarth's publication of *Avvakum*, in the same year as Freud's *Psychoanalytic Library*, demonstrated the Woolfs' commitment to modern, internationalist publishing. It also marked a definitive new chapter in Jane Harrison's work. Her entry into Russian translation made her a mediator between Russians in exile and the fashionable circles of Bloomsbury, and set her at the heart of an influential contemporary cultural movement. And the role formed a contrast to the closeted world of academia which she had left behind: no longer did she look inward to her position within an institution, but instead responded in her own way to events in the outside world. Harrison had always hated the idea that anyone should "draw your inspiration from your local soil, from the very chairs and

Hope Mirrlees and Jane Harrison in Paris, 1915.

tables and clocks and mirrors of your ancestral home"; her endless curiosity for languages (she learned eleven living and five dead) was born of a deep empathy and fascination for other cultures. When the First World War broke out, she had been perplexed to see how a perceived "bond of a common fellowship" could drive men to sign up to fight against other nations; that a love of one's country could so easily turn into an urge to force others to obey its laws, adopt its language and customs, and envelop the world in a "deadly uniformity." This sort of patriotism seemed to Harrison a repression of all humanity. For thinkers in her mold, she wrote, patriotism "was not an inspiring word. It spelled narrowness—limitations. We aspired to be citizens of the world." Now, working in metropolitan centers among friends from all over the globe, translating and promoting other languages, cultures, and histories, Harrison was living in harmony with her principles. And in 1926 she returned to Bloomsbury, to continue her work.

By 1925, Jane and Hope were ready to establish a more permanent home after three exhilarating years in Paris. "Yes, our delightful Club at last 'hoofs us out' & we go back to London in September to hunt for a flat," wrote Harrison to Mirsky in May. "I shall be sad to leave Paris but my roots are deep in England." Her main regret was forsaking the Remizovs, who had baked a cake "the size of a small mountain" with which to send them off. Having traveled around the South of France, the pair moved back to London in the spring of 1926. Mirrlees was working hard on her novel *Lud-in-the-Mist*, a charming work of fantasy set in a bourgeois, law-abiding state which is thrown into disarray when fairy fruit begins to be smuggled across the border. Harrison, meanwhile, turned her mind to household arrangements. "We hope to get into our queer little house at the beginning of May," she told Mirsky, "& then I shall cease to think of nothing but corbels and chairs—how dreadful all the machinery of life is."

That "queer little house" was 11 Mecklenburgh Street, an extension of the square's east side toward Heathcote Street in the north. Unlike H. D. and Sayers, Jane and Hope didn't take rooms in a boardinghouse, but rather set themselves up independently. "We have taken a tiny mousetrap of a house and are at last installed," Harrison wrote to Gilbert Murray. "Will you come and inspect it? . . . We should like your blessing on our new cave." Number 11 Mecklenburgh Street was

Harrison's first private home in almost thirty years. Before her return to Newnham, she had shared rooms with other single women, in friendly (though occasionally fraught) setups of mutual support. But she had much preferred living in college, where women could combine independence with companionship in a congenial atmosphere, and where her desire for personal freedom and deep need for company could both be satisfied. In *Reminiscences*, Harrison wrote that she had "a natural gift for community life," which seemed to her "sane and civilised and economically right": had she been rich, she added, she would have "founded a learned community for women, with vows of consecration and a beautiful rule and habit; as it is, I am content to have lived many years of my life in a college." If Harrison's utopia was modeled on a nunnery, it was one united not by belief in a god, but by a sincere conviction that this form of living—communal, celibate, scholarly—was best suited to allowing her talents to prosper.

College life, with its retinue of staff employed to cook and clean, had allowed Harrison to devote her time to work without the distractions of domestic duty, like the spinster dons of Sayers's *Gaudy Night*. The American University Women's Club, where they were provided with complimentary breakfasts, access to a huge garden, and "baths galore," had also represented a community where Harrison could flourish as one among many, and where she could live without having to worry about material comforts. As soon as they arrived in Mecklenburgh Street, they employed a housekeeper: Hope told her mother that she and Jane had realized in Paris that "a servant is indispensable to our permanent comfort." This alleviated any anxiety that household management would interrupt their scholarly pursuits, but given Harrison's aversion to domesticity it wouldn't be surprising if she arrived in London somewhat trepidatious about these new arrangements.

But Bloomsbury proved an accommodating home. Harrison already knew several members of the Bloomsbury set, whose disregard for authority and tradition—whether in the form of war tribunals, literary censors, or set dinnertimes—matched her own; many of them also rejected conventional family dynamics, living with friends and lovers as often as husbands or wives. The pair saw plenty of Virginia

and Leonard Woolf, Desmond and Molly MacCarthy, John Maynard
Keynes and his Russian wife, the ballerina Lydia Lopokova, Ottoline
Morrell, Roger Fry, and Lytton Strachey, who were delighted to allow
Harrison to hold court and welcomed Mirrlees warmly into their circle. Harrison, wrote Leonard Woolf, "was one of the most civilised
persons I have ever known. She was also the most charming, humor-
ous, witty, individual human being. When I knew her she was old and
frail physically, but she had a mind which remained eternally young."
This generation looked to her as a wise but irreverent elder, admiring
her idiosyncratic humor, her fresh and unpredictable perspectives on
all manner of intellectual or personal matters, and her unfailing interest in their ideas and endeavors.

In their new home, the pair worked together on a new, even more
ambitious translation project, for which the idea had come about during those mirthful sessions with the Remizovs. "Knowing my totemis-
tic tendencies," Harrison wrote to Mirsky, "you will not be surprised
that we are writing a small book for children or persons in their dotage—to be called *The Book of the Bear.*" This was to be a collection of
Russian folktales about bears, chosen and translated by Harrison and
Mirrlees. The idea had arisen from the success of *Avvakum* and from a
desire to delve further into Russia's culture and history, but also from
Harrison's longstanding fascination with the human psyche. For years,
she had been gathering evidence which suggested that early cultures
saw human life reflected in plants or animals. In *Themis*, she had identified the earliest stage of religion with a time when ritual practice
celebrated the essential codependence of human and nonhuman, with
worshippers rallying around a symbol of unity—often an animal figure—in a collective dance. This totemism, Harrison argued, was not a
form of worship but a state of mind; a stage of epistemology where
humans did not see themselves as individuals, set against the outside
world, but as part of an expansive and porous species, inseparable from
the rest of existence. For Harrison, the eventual separation of human
from animal was "pure loss," and emblematic of man's fateful desire to
assert dominance over the world around him—to express identity in
terms of difference and hierarchy, rather than of kinship. She consid-

ered this arrogance an affliction which doomed modern society; in *Themis* she warned that still "there are few things uglier than a lack of reverence for animals."

Jane Harrison's scholarly interest in totemism was matched by her own deep love for bears of all forms, an affection recalled, often with some bemusement, by many who knew her. Frances Partridge, a student at Newnham, remembered Harrison's rooms being "full of them—pictures of bears, wooden bears, silver bears. 'I *love* bears,' I hear her say in her deep voice." Harrison's personal "bear cult" (which Mirsky called "the emotional residue of her anthropological studies") began with their association with Greece and female independence: she had written animatedly about the coming-of-age rituals celebrated at the sanctuary of Artemis at Brauron, where young girls would mark their transition to womanhood by dancing for the goddess in imitation of she-bears. But as her interests shifted to Russia, Harrison saw great significance in the fact that the bear was something of a national mascot, often used in cartoons to personify the country. Though a somewhat crude stereotype, the figure of the Russian bear, Mirsky later wrote, was "one of the psychological starting points of her love for Russia."

One particular bear also held special status for Jane and Hope, as a symbol and mediator of their relationship. A group of Newnham students had given Harrison a bespectacled teddy bear, which she called Herr Professor, or the Old One, or the "authentic plaything," and kept in pride of place on her mantelpiece. Jane and Hope developed an elaborate private world surrounding "the Bear," in which they were his Elder and Younger Wife, united in common fidelity to the venerable male. He provided a ritual outlet for their intimacy, a shared surrogate husband to whom they could address their feelings for each other at one remove. Through his medium they communicated emotions in notes—"the OO commands me to send a wave of his paw"—and expressed sentiments: "I know the Bear is happy, he always feels in his great heart when any one really cares for him as you do." Together they composed a whole mythology around the bear, charted by Hope in a small blue notebook under the heading "Him"; a "sound scholar," an anti-suffragist, a stickler for tradition, he was in many ways a foil to both of them, whose foibles allowed them teasingly to conspire against him. Later, Hope would end her published books with an image of the constellation of Ursa Major (with which they often signed off notes), in subtle dedication to Jane. In this private language, they found an expression for their affection, not easily understood by outsiders, but which embodied the devotion—and humor—which characterized their relationship.

Their game with the Bear was performative, tongue-in-cheek, and playful, yet also (it's clear from the extensive correspondence) serious and of genuine emotional significance to them both. Their love of bears endeared them to Alexei Remizov, whose study was adorned with a collection of "grotesque toys": wooden birds, plush elephants, bones and branches, and rag dolls dressed as witches, which he considered protective spirits (and which Jane and Hope liked to imagine him privately animating in "fantastic dramas"). Like theirs, Remizov's behavior with his animals had an element of the surreal and the spectacular. But also like them, he considered games and jokes valuable repositories of human truth, where the usual codes of society are upended, and where received opinion can be daringly ignored. In *Themis*, Harrison argued that it was children who still feel the strongest affinity to animals, their minds not yet having been shaped by the rational impulses which put an end to totemism and to the openness and tolerance she associated with it. And she was thrilled to discover that the worship of bears was inscribed in the most ancient Russian legend—that this rich culture held within it an empathy for animals which she felt had long been lost in the British imagination.

With Remizov's and Mirsky's help, she began collecting tales for her and Mirrlees to translate, excavating sources including Krylov, Pushkin, Tolstoy, scriptures, and the anonymous *skazki* or wonder-tales from the store of Russian national folklore. *The Book of the Bear* also contained four stories by Remizov, the only living contributor to the collection: "Since Aesop," wrote Harrison, "nobody has written more deliciously about beasts (especially about bears) than Remizov." Three of these, translated by Mirrlees, came from his 1907 collection *Posolon*, a surreal reworking of material from old folktales, riddles, spells, and lullabies. *Posolon* took its cue from the lost seasonal rituals that existed in Russia before the arrival of Christian missionaries led to widespread conversion and liturgical reform. Remizov believed that, when these ancient pagan gods were banished, their rituals became dances or children's games, actions divested of their purpose or religious meaning. Harrison found his work immensely suggestive, and noted parallels with the shifts in Greek religion she had explored in her historical work. In the introduction to *The Book of the Bear*, she identified the forced Christianization of Russia with the end of totemism, which survived only in legends of the sort she and Remizov collected. Harrison saw in Remizov's stories—as she had in *Avvakum*—a moving attempt to preserve Russian identity at a time of national crisis, through revitalizing the rituals which had brought its communities together in earliest times.

In her letters to Gilbert Murray (who was bewildered by the turn her interests had taken), Harrison played down *The Book of the Bear*, insisting that it was an indulgence undertaken in her old age, a piece of children's entertainment, not a consequential work. But Jane Harrison's games are always to be taken seriously. In their introduction, Harrison and Mirrlees wrote that the bear stories were intended to "hold the mirror up to human nature": in its subtle way, the book was Harrison's homage to totemism, her plea to a world ruptured by war to think of a time when humans saw animals as companions to be respected rather than enemies to be subdued, feared, or hunted. If, in the past, even the boundaries between human and nonhuman were flexible, asked Harrison, then how could it be that so recently, mere difference of nationality was considered significant enough to justify unmediated slaughter? Though she claimed, self-deprecatingly, that she had no more aptitude for politics than for plumbing, all her works, in their different ways, call for a society opposed to violence and domination, where creativity and cooperation are prized above war and individual heroism. *The Book of the Bear* is her poignant warning that only by celebrating difference can a lasting peace be won.

• • •

"We chose this neighborhood," wrote Harrison from Mecklenburgh Street to Murray, "because it is close to the Nonesuch Press at which we are publishing a work of capital importance—*The Book of the Bear*. You will not receive a copy of it," she warned him slyly, "for your tone on that great subject is not all I could wish." The publishing house—a chaotic but successful venture begun in the basement of a Soho bookshop—was run by David Garnett, the affable Bloomsburyite always known as Bunny, and the son of Constance and Edward Garnett; Lytton Strachey had introduced him to Harrison in Paris. In 1925, his press had moved to a purple-and-emerald-paneled room at 16 Great James Street, the road where the *Nation and Athenaeum* (with Leonard Woolf as literary editor) had offices at number 38, and where Dorothy L. Sayers was living at number 24, preparing her second Wimsey novel, *Clouds of Witness*, for publication. From Mecklenburgh Street, Jane and Hope could walk in a couple of minutes to Bunny's office to discuss matters of print run, paper quality, and the illustrations commissioned from his then wife Ray Garnett, sweet drawings of chubby children leading amiable bears, which Harrison disliked ("The Bear never rises to his real majesty," she complained to Jessie Stewart). From their new home, Jane and Hope dispatched regular updates on the book's progress to Alexei and Seraphima Remizov, signing off with their Russian nicknames—Elena Karlovna and Nadezhda Vasilevna. They were deeply anxious about their friends, whose financial difficulties persisted: Mirrlees wrote a long essay in praise of Remizov's work, and when *The Book of the Bear* was published at Christmas 1926, Harrison sent Remizov a check in advance of royalties, urging him to take a seaside holiday.

Harrison's desire to help Remizov was shared by D. S. Mirsky, a regular visitor to 11 Mecklenburgh Street. A former White Army soldier, Mirsky had arrived in London, disillusioned and impoverished, just as the Soviet government began to strip all civil rights from those who had fought against it. Living in Bloomsbury, first at 15 Torrington Square then at 17 Gower Street (though he spent half the year in Paris), Mirsky taught at the School of Slavonic Studies, then based at 24 Gordon Square, where he became Britain's first full-time specialist in Russian literature, writing regularly on the subject for mainstream publications and traveling the country on lecture tours. Since she had first met him in 1924, Harrison had delighted in Mirsky's company, enjoying spirited debates on the finer points of Russian grammar, Bolshevism, and contemporary literature. "I have lost my aged heart to a Bear Prince," she wrote to Murray: "why did I not meet him 50 years ago when I cld have clamored to be his Princess?" Their friendship was not only a fruitful personal connection, but also gave each of them a way into the other's world: while he introduced her to Russian writers like Marina Tsvetaeva and Sergei Efron, Harrison brought Mirsky into the circle of the Woolfs and literary London, and secured him an invitation to Pontigny. The international coterie they created in London and Paris, bringing together friends from across the world, offered Harrison the community she had left Cambridge to find.

Mirsky was deeply frustrated that the British appreciation of Russian culture appeared to be founded on a romanticized conception of the "Slav soul," as extrapolated from Dostoevsky novels—impenetrable, mystical, and melancholy—which he felt betrayed a superficial engagement with the literature. Mirsky's annoyance at British readers was compounded by the fact that they appeared only interested in the classic novelists, and ignored modern writers, who were often struggling—like Remizov—in poverty-stricken exile. What made this even more egregious, to him, was that the work of these contemporaries tended to expose and interrogate the widespread brutality of Russia's contemporary political climate, of which many British Russophiles remained blissfully unaware. Harrison was sympathetic to his complaints, and eager to use her influence to help his efforts in whatever way she could. She helped edit Mirsky's books *A History of Russian Literature* and *Contemporary Russian Literature 1881–1925*, which included chapters on Remizov and Shestov. ("I had a book dedicated to me by a Russian Bear—isn't that elating," wrote Harrison to Murray.) Around the time Harrison and Mirrlees moved to Mecklenburgh Street, Mirsky was developing a new project, born out of his frustrations: to found, in Bloomsbury, a Russian-language literary journal, which would be free from political control, would preserve and promote Russian literary culture in exile, and would unite within its pages writers living both in and outside Russia.

Since the revolution, publishing in Russia had practically ceased, especially for those who did not hold the same political opinions as the regime: Alexander Blok died of cancer accelerated by malnourishment; Anna Akhmatova's work was banned and her flat kept under constant surveillance. Across other European countries, Russian-language publishers began to print books and newspapers, many deliberately avoiding the new spelling system and neologisms introduced by the Soviet government. These publications allowed émigrés a way to voice their concerns about the future of their homeland, or express their sense of disorientation, but they tended to be politically partisan and were reluctant to publish those—like Remizov and Marina Tsvetaeva, whom Mirsky considered the most significant writers outside Russia—whose work was not explicitly anti-Soviet in its themes. Mirsky's journal was called Вёрсты (*Versty*), or *Milestones*, named after an Old Russian measurement unit which corresponded to the posts marking distances along main roads. Containing poetry, prose, literary criticism, and historical documents, as well as articles on philosophy, art, and linguistics, it sought to interrogate "today's Russia and Russianness" from an international standpoint. Each volume, to Harrison's delight, included new work by Remizov; a supplement to the first issue contained the complete text of *Avvakum*, which Remizov had specially edited and transcribed. Harrison called the scheme "deeply interesting," and zealously helped Mirsky with his fundraising efforts (on the proviso that Remizov was not appointed business manager—"you might as well elect a squirrel"). She personally sent him a check for £50, wishing she could provide the whole £200 he needed to underwrite the endeavor: "What fun it would be to be a millionaire & finance things really worth doing. It is intolerable that men like Remizov shld be dependent on the whims & silly politics of their inferiors."

Harrison turned her mind to connecting Mirsky with people who might help him, eager to ensure that *Versty* would be a significant project of Anglo-Russian cooperation. She advised him first to take counsel with Leonard and Virginia Woolf—"Not that they cld give money they are poor as rats but he is so experienced in journalism & has such a good business head also he is always interested in an adventure in thought"—and to request an introduction to John Maynard Keynes: "a first-rate man of business & it is a sort of hobby of his to finance intellectual experiments that don't and can't pay." Moreover, she insisted, Keynes being married to a Russian ballerina, "Russia has for him a special glamour (is it really true that Russian has no word for glamour—what a language) . . . if you had Maynard at yr back you would be safe." Mirsky did write to Keynes, who donated £20, and to Leonard Woolf, who recommended E. M. Forster for a piece Mirsky hoped to commission on contemporary English fiction. The resulting essay, an early version of his *Aspects of the Novel*, appeared in Russian translation in *Versty*'s second issue, alongside a rave review by Mirsky of T. S. Eliot's poetry ("he is no doubt the best poet in England and is perhaps the greatest of post-war Europe"). Harrison was gratified by the success of her machinations, and thrilled to help a true collaboration emerge between exiled Russians and Bloomsbury literati. From her small house in Mecklenburgh Street, she was helping to forge projects which would reach audiences far beyond the square.

Versty was a short-lived endeavor: its third issue (by which time the paper quality had noticeably diminished) would be its last, as its editorial board—Mirsky, the poet Sergei Efron, and the musicologist Peter Suvchinsky—succumbed to arguments and in-fighting. But that final issue, published in 1928, included a substantial appraisal, by Mirsky, of the work of Jane Harrison and Hope Mirrlees: "prominent friends of Russia . . . and notable luminaries of contemporary English culture." In his essay, Mirsky argued that Harrison's eclectic passions were united by their insistence on "the destruction of the 'Victorian' world view and the liberation of thought from puritan restrictions." After Harrison's death, he picked up this theme in a memorial lecture, arguing that Harrison's work played a significant role—alongside the birth of Freudian psychoanalysis and the work of Dostoevsky—in the intellectual revolution of the early twentieth century. "The way walked by her from the study of Greek vases through that of primitive religion to Freud and to Tolstoy," he concluded, "will be recognised as one of the most illuminating expressions of the intellectual evolution of the English mind at the turn of two historical epochs."

After the First World War, Harrison claimed, she didn't open a Greek book for ten years. In her new homes she had created work very different from her classical studies—experimental collaborations and translations, the products not of solitary research but of friendships and circumstance. But in Mecklenburgh Street she returned to *Themis*, writing a new preface and adding an introduction by Gilbert Murray for a fresh edition. She also began learning Icelandic, in order to read the Eddas, and continued the Persian lessons she had started in 1921 ("the richest civilisation I have touched yet—in some ways") with the Islamic scholar Guy Le Strange. Her appetite for new ideas was undimmed, and the chance discovery—gleaned from an unusual coincidence she noticed in her reading—that the ancient cult of Orpheus and the work of Dante might share roots in early Iranian tradition set her mind whirring with links between ritual and language, literature and history. She acquired a commentary on the Qur'an, convinced that she was on the trail of an etymological echo across cultures and religious traditions which would "upset the whole eschatological, orthodox, Orphic apple-cart." Just as decades earlier she had enjoyed confounding the establishment with evidence for early matriarchal societies, now she relished the chance to suggest that both a classic work of Western literature and the ritual practice of the ancient Greeks—the basis for Athenian democracy, still idealized as the epitome of rational order and enlightened thought—originated from an entirely other, Eastern religious tradition. It would be a provocative undertaking of just the sort she most enjoyed. But as her scholarly interest returned to myths of regeneration, Harrison's own health began to decline. "Bother my vile body," she wrote, "I must wait a month before I plunge in." By September 1926 she was gleefully making plans "to re-write the mysteries." But her illness precluded concentration, and a postcard sent that year to Jessie Stewart showed two donkeys resting in the sand, labelled in fountain pen J. E. H. and H. M., the caption "Nothing Doing."

Jane Harrison's time in Mecklenburgh Street was marked by difficulties with her blood pressure; she took to lying in the square's garden on a chaise longue, wrapped in a green rug, where she would dictate her letters to Hope, who remembered "a stream of suave sentences, punctuated by my giggles and her grimaces." In June 1927, during a visit to a friend's house at Camber, Harrison was taken ill with phlebitis and had to be brought back to London in an ambulance; at the end of August, she reported to Murray with some relish, she "went right down to the Gates of Hades & there she stayed fluttering to and fro, & it seemed that the gates must clang behind her." A team of doctors and nurses (one living in Mecklenburgh Square, another deputized from Harley Street), including "a lusty masseur of Herculean build," nursed her back to health, but her movement was now diminished. On January 16, 1928, she attended Thomas Hardy's funeral at Westminster Abbey; otherwise, most of her time was spent in bed, in the tiny back drawing room of the Mecklenburgh Street house, where Hope read letters to her and regularly rebuffed visitors at the door. Harrison's older friends, who already suspected Hope of trying to wean Jane away from her former life, grumbled to one another that she was "ungracious" and "overwrought"—but admitted she was clearly "very anxious and *very* devoted." Virginia Woolf visited several times from Tavistock Square, in the midst of writing *A Room of One's Own*.

Jane Harrison died in Mecklenburgh Street on April 15, 1928. While the immediate cause of death was bronchial pneumonia, it was discovered in her final weeks that Harrison suffered from lymphatic leukemia, which was somehow fitting, Hope wrote to Seraphima Remizov, since it was a disease "which as a rule only attacks *young* people." Seraphima replied: "Dear N. V., I thank you for having written to me about the last days of our E. K., whom I shall always love . . . E. K. died on the first day of our Easter. According to an old belief, those who die on the first day of Easter—their soul goes straight to Paradise."

On April 17, 1928, Virginia Woolf recorded in her diary a poignant encounter in St. George's Gardens, the old graveyard behind Mecklenburgh Square:

> crossing the graveyard in the bitter windy rain, we saw Hope & a dark cultivated woman. But on they went past us, with the waver of an eye. Next moment I heard Virginia, & turned & there was Hope coming back—"Jane died yesterday" she murmured, half asleep, talking distraught, "out of herself." We kissed by Cromwell's daughter's grave, where Shelley used to walk, for Jane's death. She lay dead outside the graveyard in that back room where we saw her lately raised on her pillows, like a very old person, whom life has tossed up, & left; exalted, satisfied, exhausted.

Later, Hope received from Woolf a note which she would never forget. "It was only one line," Hope told her friend Valerie Eliot in 1965, consoling her on the death of her husband T. S. Eliot, "but it was more comforting than all my other letters put together: 'But remember what you have had.'"

A former Newnham student recalled Jane Harrison, at dinner, throwing out a theory that everyone has a time of life at which they are most fully themselves: some never surpass the promise of youth, some mellow and flourish in middle age, while others might suffer disappointments but end life happy as "delightful old ladies." In Mecklenburgh Street, reflecting on her long life, Jane Harrison might well have concluded that her seventies were her time. When people asked if she'd like to be young again, Harrison pointed out that this was a silly question: "You cannot be—you that are—young again. You cannot unroll that snowball which is you: There is no 'you' except your life—lived." There's an echo here of Dorothy L. Sayers's insistence that youth is overrated. Both these women felt anxious and awkward in their twenties, when the pressure to be feminine and beautiful—and to marry—was at its greatest, and before their decisions to live unconventional lives could be validated by achievement and success. But later in life, each came to value most highly her accumulation of knowledge and experience, which had molded her into the person she was.

When Augustus John described Harrison, in 1909, as a "puzzle to paint," he recognized that she was still a work in progress: that he was capturing only one moment in a long, varied, and complex life. Harrison's illness thwarted work which might have made her time in Mecklenburgh Street even more central to her legacy. But in her final years, living and working independently in Bloomsbury alongside intellectuals and revolutionaries, still learning new languages and developing fresh ideas, Harrison was as fulfilled as she had ever been. It's fitting that her lasting memorial should be in *A Room of One's Own*, as an example of intellectual inquiry, a woman who was determined to interrogate assumptions in spite of society's censure, and who was committed to finding a way to live that suited her own interests and accommodated her devotion to her work. In this way, as many of her friends suggested, she always remained young. "I had not realised that she was quite as old as 77," wrote Lytton Strachey to Roger Fry, when he heard of Jane Harrison's death. "What a wretched waste it seems that all that richness of experience and personality should be completely abolished! Why, one wonders, shouldn't it have gone on and on? Well! there will never be anyone at all like her again."

EILEEN POWER
(1889–1940)

20 Mecklenburgh Square
January 1922–August 1940

I don't really think I feel like a don.
I want to write books. Oh dear, Oh dear!
—Eileen Power to Margery Spring Rice, May 17, 1911

Eileen Power was in Madras when she received the letter that would determine the course of her life. A thirty-one-year-old lecturer in medieval history at Girton College, Cambridge, Power was traveling as the first woman to receive the Albert Kahn Traveling Fellowship, a grant which funded scholars for a year's global exploration in the hope that "by the study and comparison of national manners and customs and of the political, social, religious and economic institutions of foreign countries," they might return "better qualified to take part in the instruction and education of their fellow countrymen." Kahn was an eccentric philanthropist whose major project, *The Archives of the Planet*, sent photographers to every continent in an attempt to document people's everyday lives in color; Power described her benefactor as "an enlightened French banker who gave you £1,000 and sent you round the world with instructions to widen your narrow academic mind." The award came as a surprise to Power: her interviewer had commented suspiciously that she "might 'defeat the objects of the trust' [sic] by subsequently committing matrimony," and she had resigned herself to being passed over in favor of a man, in whom the same crime might be excused. Yet in September 1920 she left Cambridge and embarked, alone, on her first voyage outside Europe: an intrepid journey encompassing Egypt, India, China, Japan, Canada, and North America.

Power was entranced by Alexandria's bazaars and open workshops, where she watched merchants at the roadside welding fine gold chains or weaving delicate tassels for vibrantly colored scarves. In India she was entertained at dinners by politicians, journalists, and reformers—regularly the only woman present—and noted in her University of Cambridge pocket diary that she "enjoyed the novel experience of hearing problems of government discussed in terms of 'I.'" It was a fascinating time to be immersed in the country's political life, as activists campaigned to overhaul British colonial rule and reclaim a national identity: Power was eager to learn all she could about the methods and motivations of the new independence movement, which had launched that summer to huge popular support. On December 21, she refused an invitation from a genteel colonial administrator to a dance at his club ("I would not be a lady of leisure in India in *worlds*," she insisted to a friend) and instead dodged through the heaving crowds to take a seat at the Nagpur Congress. There, she became one of only six Europeans present to witness the assembly vow to adopt the wholesale policy of noncooperation, as urged by Mahatma Gandhi, the "saintly" figure whom she was delighted—as a committed pacifist and member of the Labour Party—to meet briefly in Delhi, where they sat on the floor and discussed the futures of their countries. On leaving the city, Power traveled north to the Khyber Pass—a key part of the ancient Silk Road which connected Europe with the great markets of India and China—only to find that its passageway was, under a British bylaw, closed to ladies. Her hosts received an angry letter from border officials when it was discovered that Power, undeterred, had made the crossing in male disguise.

"I found myself deeply interested in and charmed with all these countries," wrote Power in her eventual report to the fellowship trust, "but my heart is irrevocably given to China." Power spent two months in China, at a moment of fundamental social and political change. Industry and education were fast transforming, a new phonetic script was facilitating a revolution in contemporary literature, and young women were agitating for the vote "more stridently than ever did the suffragettes." Visiting the British colonies there and in India, speaking to locals and to government representatives, Power began to grasp for the first time the human impact of the British Empire, as a complicated reality beyond "the historical textbook or the debating society." At first hand, she observed the fact that "gigantic Western rivalries are creating more & more problems in the East"; despite this, she left the country convinced "that China can become a great modern power, should she seriously desire to do so." Power's travels furnished her with a spirit of curiosity and empathy that would inform all her subsequent work, and a determination to write history which would reach far beyond her immediate surroundings. "The A. K. fellowship has been my ruin," she wrote to her fellow medievalist George Gordon Coulton, "for my heart will stray outside its clime & period. I think I shall have to compromise by working at the trade between Europe and the East in the Middle Ages."

The letter Power received on December 4, 1920, having discovered three weeks' mail waiting for her at the Thomas Cook office in Madras, was from the London School of Economics, where she had spent two years as a student. It contained the offer of a lectureship in economic history, to start the following autumn. Power had read in the *Times of India* the "perfectly disgusting" news that Cambridge had rejected a proposal to follow Oxford in granting women full membership of the university and, like Jane Harrison, felt disillusioned and betrayed by the institution where she had spent a decade studying and teaching. "I never felt so bitter in my life," she wrote to Lilian Knowles, professor of economic history at the LSE. "Oxford only got degrees and women only got votes because these measures sailed through on the crest of the wave of sentiment over women's war work. We let that moment pass, and now the wave has broken and people see the obvious truth that women are worth what they always were worth and no more. We think that covers and has always covered degrees and votes, but male public opinion at bottom doesn't." On Christmas Eve, she replied tentatively to the LSE, expressing her hope—just as Harrison had insisted to Newnham—that her time would not be entirely swallowed by teaching, but that the position would entail plenty of time for pure research ("the thing which I *really* care about"). She received assurances, and on March 6, from a boat passing between Rangoon and Shanghai, she wrote formally to accept the job. Sailing later from Japan to Canada—where she was accompanied by Bertrand Russell and his pregnant partner, Dora Black, their animated discussion of politics, literature, and feminism interrupted by the flashes from a bevy of journalists trying to photograph Russell—she wrote to her friend Margery Spring Rice to remonstrate on the difficulty of making such an important decision so far away from home.

"I thought it was time for me to change my way of life, so when they wrote & offered me the job (I didn't apply for it) I said yes," Power explained. "I hesitated a lot, because it would mean a lot more teaching than I've done before & the screw is only £500—but I want to be in London for a bit . . . So I shall go into digs for a term or so & look for someone nice to share a flat with. I'd rather live alone, but don't think I can afford it: I've got so many books that I couldn't fit into too wee a flat. So if you can think of anyone who would do for me or hear of a nice flat in Bloomsbury, let me know . . . I have got some lovely furniture & hangings in China." To William Beveridge, principal of the school, she wrote that she looked forward to starting this fresh phase of life, with new students and colleagues, and a chance to employ some insights from her travels. "You need not be afraid lest I should not throw myself into the work," she assured him, "because I invariably become violently interested in the things which I am doing!"

Power ended her journey by traveling through Boston, where she had arranged to meet H. D.'s friend Amy Lowell, whose work she greatly admired. ("I rather begrudge every moment when you are not writing poetry," wrote Power, demurring to take up too much of her heroine's time.) In September 1921, she returned to London via New

York, starting her new job just ten days later. She took a temporary room in Belgravia, but toward the end of the year her thoughts turned to a more permanent home. On January 30, 1922, she wrote to Coulton of her delight at finding a "quite perfect" place to live with a teacher friend, Marion Gertrude Beard, which seemed to hold within it the promise of an exciting new independence:

> I am extremely jubilant at present, because I have, after much travail & tribulation, found a charming half-house in Mecklenburgh Square, looking on to an enormous garden of trees, & I hope to move in at the end of term. I have found a convenient friend to share it, of the sort who is never there except on weekends, when I am often away. My idea of life is to have enormous quantities of friends, but to live alone. And I do not know whether Girton or the study of medieval nunneries did more to convince me that I was not born to live in a community!

We don't know a lot about Eileen Power, the private woman. After her sudden death in 1940, at the age of just fifty-one, her sisters burned most of her personal papers, leaving little more material for biographers than Jane Harrison did; though both these women were dedicated to recovering forgotten histories, and lived bold and fascinating lives, they allowed their own pasts to be expunged, for reasons unknown. At any rate, after she joined the LSE and became a public figure of international reputation, Power's long, witty, matter-of-fact outpourings to Margery died out, and in her archive at Girton the thick folders packed with closely filled pages of handwriting are replaced by thin portfolios of short, professional correspondence, interspersed with reams of notes and plans for lectures, seminars, articles, broadcasts, and books. Tantalizing fragments of personality glimmer through others' memories: that she loved jazz, but instantly resigned membership of Soho's Gargoyle Club when it didn't let her enter with her friend Paul Robeson, the African American actor (who starred in the avant-garde 1930 film *Borderline* alongside H. D. and

Bryher); that she was asked to contribute a short biography to *Who's Who*, where she listed her interests as "travelling and dancing"; that she spent her earnings on modern jewelry and beautiful dresses from Parisian salons, to the bafflement of the less sartorially inclined Girton dons ("I certainly feel there is something radically wrong with my clothes from an academic point of view," she told Margery). But these personal details provide less a revelation of an inner life than an insight into the ways she wanted others to see her. Power's public presentation was always carefully constructed: she sought to position herself simultaneously as a woman and a serious scholar, negotiating—as others had done before her, and continue to do—the bind which ensured that "feminine" appearance and preoccupations would, to the wider world, diminish the respect she commanded as a professional at the forefront of her field.

The obituaries—mostly by male historians—comment approvingly on how "lightly carried" her knowledge was, how admirably she "made no parade of her learning." The eminent economic historian John Harold Clapham wrote, as if this was a surprising achievement from a distinguished faculty member, that Power could "hold her own in conversation with any tableful of men," though hastened to add that she "hardly looked, or usually talked, the professor." The historian and diplomat Charles Webster remembered "an audible gasp of surprise" when Power, radiant in a glamorous evening gown, arrived late to a dinner in her honor at Harvard, and the table of hoary scholars realized "that this enchanting creature was the learned lady whom they had come to meet." G. G. Coulton recalled first meeting Power when she accosted him in the street and asked for advice on sources for the lives of medieval women; he openly admitted that, noticing her stylish clothes and easy charm, he "took it for granted that this was one more fashionable girl with a momentary enthusiasm for 'research.'" It was two years later, when he read her seven-hundred-page study of medieval nunneries and found it "incomparably better in quality than anything of the kind that has been done on this subject before or since in any European language," that he realized the error of his initial assumption. Power saw no reason why an interest in clothes and a sense of humor could not be

Eileen Power lecturing at Girton, circa 1915.

combined with professional rigor. But it's sobering to wonder how many more "fashionable girls" may have abandoned their "enthusiasms" on recognizing that pursuing an academic career would require them to justify themselves at every juncture.

These men were Power's friends and collaborators; in life, they loved and supported her. Yet their words reveal that Eileen Power was an anomaly to them; an honorary member of their group, accepted graciously once she had proven herself, but only then by dint of how truly exceptional they considered her scholarship and personality. To some extent, she seems to have reveled in such presumptions, playing up her femininity with confidence that her wit and academic prowess would make a fool of anyone who underestimated her. Yet her sense of frustration remains palpable. Power was aware that she was consistently paid less than her male contemporaries: that while she was invited on international lecture tours and offered honorary degrees from respected universities, she had to ask for raises and promotions. Even when appointed professor, a position with international prestige and further administrative burdens, her salary rose only in small increments not commensurate with the long hours she devoted to her work. The vacancy to which Power was appointed in 1921 had been originally intended as a readership commanding a salary of £800; when Power was approached she was offered, instead, the position of lecturer at £500 a year. When she accepted the job, she expressed her hope that this offer was only the beginning, "because I can't possibly continue for long making only that in a non-resident post in London. I do not really think it is good enough for the amount of work." Her determination to extend education outside the academy, producing public lectures, broadcasts, children's books, and popular articles, kept her scholarly output lower than might be expected; she had little interest in turning out dry tomes written only for other academics "like the community in the political economy book," as she wrote in an article, "who earned a precarious livelihood by taking in one another's washing." Much of her work survives only in the form of notes or unpublished lectures; a large and important facet of her legacy is intangible, residing in the form of impressions made on children in their formative years.

Power was very conscious that, as Jane Harrison put it in 1914, "the virtues supposed to be womanly are in the main the virtues generated by subordinate social position." Like Dorothy L. Sayers, who wrote in her caustic 1938 essay "Are Women Human?" that it was "repugnant . . . to be reckoned always as a member of a class and not as an individual person," Power railed against the social system which "is so anxious for people to be correct that it effectually prevents them from being true." In an early essay entitled "Women at Cambridge," Power recalled being asked to provide a "woman's perspective" on a problem, and argued, in terms strikingly similar to those Sayers often used, that "a woman's outlook on art and science has nothing specifically womanly about it, it is the outlook of a PERSON . . . The difference is between good books and bad books, straight-thinking books and sentimental books, not between male books and female books." Eileen Power's life is the story of her attempt to forge a new image for a woman intellectual, and create a way of living for which there was little precedent: not as the stereotype of a dowdy bluestocking, but as a professional who could entertain an international reputation while also enjoying fashion and frivolity, whose public status was defined not by her family but by her work. Just as H. D. wanted to find a universal voice unmarked by gender, or as Sayers pondered a suitable balance for women "cursed with both hearts and brains," Eileen Power sought the freedom to be contradictory and yet whole, to live richly and excitingly, "extracting all I can from life."

Throughout her eighteen years in Mecklenburgh Square, Power balanced her desire to live untrammeled by social expectations with a wider commitment that the same privilege be extended to people of all races, nations, and classes. And the strength of her ideals was not unnoticed by those around her, who looked to her as a role model. Judith de Márffy-Mantuano was a student at the LSE from 1926 to 1929, having arrived alone from Hungary and looked up the school in the telephone book; her parents, though extremely wealthy, had given her no allowance for her studies, considering them a waste of time, so Power (her tutor) took her in when she couldn't afford a flat of her own. "At her house in 20 Mecklenburgh Square," Judith wrote later, "I began to make out—like a skyline breaking through a lifting fog—the shape of another world . . . It was a world in which men and women did not belong to classes, but were individuals, and succeeded each according to his merit. Eileen Power herself exemplified for me the possibilities open to women."

In 1908, as an undergraduate at Cambridge, Eileen Power wrote a spoof fairy tale called "The Intractable Princess," which she dedicated to her director of studies, and illustrated with deft cartoons of a cheerful, bucktoothed damsel. A king and queen ruled over "the red city of Girton." All the goddesses came to the christening of their daughter Eileen, bringing with them their blessings, except for Bellona, goddess of war, who was fighting battles in a far-flung land; her absence ensured "that the Princess Eileen grew up a pacifist." When the princess refuses the suitor to whom her parents have betrothed her, they lock her in a tower. She's rescued by the Girton shopkeeper, who expects her to marry him, as "any self-respecting heroine would do," in exchange for this "enormous amount of trouble." But Princess Eileen refuses. She hails a passing Zeppelin and asks for a lift; the bemused pilot asks her if she's sure she wants to travel with a Hun, but she blithely replies, "We're internationalists!" They escape to China, and live "happily unmarried ever after."

As a form of autobiography, the sketch provides a neat illustration of Power's lifelong political values as well as her sharp humor: her abiding feminism, pacifism, and internationalism are all present, as is her commitment to her own independence. Born in 1889, Eileen Power's upbringing—in Altrincham, near Manchester—was overshadowed by a scandal which sundered her family when she was three, and left a sense of shame and disillusionment with patriarchal authority. Her stockbroker father was caught forging clients' signatures to raise loans to himself totaling £28,000 (the equivalent of £3.5 million today). He was declared bankrupt and imprisoned for fraud. Eileen's mother, Mabel Grindley Clegg, facing destitution, moved with her daughters to Bournemouth. Out of loyalty to her mother, or her own anger, Eileen never saw her father again and rarely spoke of him to friends, though she later mentioned offhand to Margery the residual fear of finding him "pirouetting in the daily press at any moment." When

Eileen was fourteen, her mother died of tuberculosis, leaving instructions that her daughters should receive the best education possible. Eileen and her younger sisters, Rhoda and Beryl, moved to Oxford to live with their aunts and grandfather. Determined to ensure their wards' future independence—and perhaps aware that the disgrace made advantageous marriage unlikely—these relations stretched their own finances to send the girls to Oxford High School, an academically rigorous institution with a strong record of sending pupils to university (and where, coincidentally, Jane Harrison had taught for a term in 1880). In 1907, their foresight was rewarded: Eileen received a scholarship to Girton College, Cambridge, where she ended three years' study with an unofficial first class in history.

At Girton, Power was introduced to her first mentors, who raised her consciousness of the political struggle faced by women outside of the college's closeted, supportive community. She was taught by the formidable Ellen McArthur, a pioneering economic historian and committed suffragist. And McArthur's example was supplemented by the encouragement of Alys Pearsall Smith, who was then wife of Bertrand Russell, a close friend of Jane Harrison, and the aunt of Power's university friend Karin Costelloe, with whom Eileen spent several summer vacations. Alys swept Eileen along to her first suffrage meeting, alarming her by thrusting her onto the platform. Sensing a potential protégée, she then enlisted Eileen in campaigning alongside her nieces (Karin and Ray, who as Ray Strachey would go on to write the celebrated history of the women's movement, *The Cause*). Power was entranced by life at Alys's home, Court Place in Iffley, which was only a few miles from her aunts' austere house on Oxford's Woodstock Road, yet represented a completely different world. It showed her a casually luxurious life of parties, motor car expeditions, open discussion of marriage, philosophy, and politics, and an implicit conviction that one's own activities, public and private, could have a real bearing on society. The daring conversation stunned Eileen to silence: "I feel stupid," she told Margery, "because I've been associating with such brilliant people." There, she met Hope Mirrlees, another great friend of Karin's, who impressed Eileen with her effortless sophistication and her ability to pull off "an elopement or two & several disappearances" during an evening dance, even under the watchful eye of several elderly chaperones. "I'm quite in love with the Mirrlees girl," wrote an awe-struck Eileen to Margery.

She appears not to have kept in touch with Hope, but was thrilled when Alys announced that she was determined to "push" her, "in order to try & save me from the fate of high school teaching." Much like Dorothy L. Sayers at the same age, Power felt wary of "stumbling along the dull path of dondom," but was unsure what route to pursue instead; nonetheless, thanks to Alys, her sense of righteous indignation at women's position was now ignited. Back at Girton, she became an officer of the college branch of the National Union of Women's Suf-frage Societies, and spoke twice at meetings alongside Millicent Gar-rett Fawcett. She began to expound at length in letters about the "monstrous" social system "which divides the world into male men and female women and cannot conceive of the existence of human per-sons"; she entered fierce arguments with her uncles, "exasperating them by ultra radical motions, just as they are descanting upon the merits of tariff reform and the House of Lords," and broke into furious French in a pub, attacking a Frenchman who had "asserted that woman's object in life was to be a wife and mother" while man's province was "reason, brain, intellect." "I don't think I have ever been so angry," Power told Margery. Yet triumph was hers: "I tore him into tiny little bits and scattered them on the floor and danced on them."

Power's own determination to trespass into the "male province" was never in doubt. After leaving Girton in 1910, she took up a schol-arship at the Sorbonne in Paris ("living la vie Boheme in an atmo-sphere of much cigarette smoke, conversation and respectability"). There, she wrote a thesis on Queen Isabella of France, the wife of Edward II and "the most disreputable woman of her day," whose life, as Power saw it, was "a perfect hotchpotch of lovers and murders & plots." Power enjoyed her time in Paris, where she spent days soaking up medieval art in the Louvre and the Cluny, and wrote in anguish to Margery about the poverty of her French teacher, a single mother who lived among "feminists, radicals and poets" and supported herself by sewing: "Imagine, Margie, that brilliantly intellectual little thing tied down to slaving all day with her needle (which she loathes) for a wretched little pittance." Though it was a stimulating experience, she decided not to stay on in Paris for a doctorate—but in the summer of 1911 an enticing new opportunity arose. As was the case for Jane Harrison, it was a woman-led initiative that gave Power her break as a historian. Power was invited to join the London School of Economics as a Shaw Research Student, on a generous fellowship established in 1904 by Charlotte Payne Townshend Shaw, a prominent feminist and the wife of George Bernard Shaw. When her scholarship was awarded to a man for the fifth consecutive year, Charlotte stipulated that it should henceforth be reserved for women only, and given specifically to support research into women's lives, in the hope that the monographs produced by fellows would form a much-needed canon of women's history.

It was an exciting time and place for Power to launch her research career. Since its foundation by the Fabian socialists Sidney and Beatrice Webb, George Bernard Shaw, and Graham Wallas, the London School of Economics had stood at the center of London's left-wing activities. In 1894, a lawyer and Fabian Society donor named Henry Hunt Hutchinson had committed suicide and appointed Sidney Webb his executor, specifying that a legacy of £20,000 was to go toward advancing the socialist cause, which the Fabians considered the only viable response to pervasive inequality in Britain. To this end, the Webbs decided to found a school in London, inspired by Paris's École Libre des Sciences Politiques, where students of economics would be supported in their research by professors and activists wholly dedicated to social reform, with an emphasis on vocational training and on the application of economic theory to practical problems. Coeducational from its inception, by 1904 the LSE had over fourteen hundred students, many studying for the new degrees of B.Sc. (Econ) and D.Sc. (Econ), the country's first university degrees devoted to the social sciences. Classes held in the day were repeated in the evenings for working students, many sent by railway companies, insurance offices, and the civil service. In the narrow side streets between Kingsway and High Holborn, their tall buildings stained with London smog, the school bustled round the clock with learning and discussion. Nearby, the Webbs—Beatrice towering over Sidney—worked on their anti–Poor Law campaign from the Fabian Society office in Clement's Inn Passage, while next door was the headquarters of the Women's Social and Political Union, packed with determined women at work making placards, typing pamphlets, and occasionally hiding from the police.

At the LSE—though the idea was surely conceived during her time in a Cambridge women's college—Eileen Power began her study of medieval nunneries, which would become her first full-length published book. In the early years of the twentieth century, the fight for equal suffrage had sparked a growing interest in women's and working-class history. Frustrated at their political disenfranchisement, women looked to the past for models and alternatives, eager to establish a historical framework from which to agitate for change. Many turned to historians such as Jane Harrison, whose work offered fertile proof that women's subordination was carefully constructed over time, and not based on any "natural" order. Power and her friends—among them the historians Alice Clark, Vera Anstey, and Ivy Pinchbeck—pored eagerly over Olive Schreiner's new book, *Woman and Labour*, which argued that capitalism had systematically eroded women's productive labor and thus their independence (and which, wrote Vera Brittain twenty years later, "sounded to the world of 1911 as insistent and inspiring as a trumpet-call summoning the faithful to a vital crusade"). When Power returned to Girton in 1913, to take up a position as director of studies, she began making notes for short biographical studies of medieval women, a project which would occupy her sporadically across her career.

Power's imagination was not captured by the idealized ladies of chivalric romances, nor the writings of the Church or the aristocracy, which could afford to "regard its women as an ornamental asset." Instead, she scoured records of daily life for traces of independent, working women, and found a "practical equality" prevailing among the villeins and cotters who administered their own holdings, the enterprising widows who traded as "femes soles," and the poor women who worked in fields and at benches to support their families, then went to church on Sunday, where "preachers told them in one breath that woman was the gate of hell and that Mary was Queen of heaven." "Certainly," she wrote, "the middle ages would not have understood the Victorian relegation of women to the purely domestic job of running the home." It was the stories of these women that Power wanted to uncover—the duties and preoccupations of their everyday lives, their relations with their husbands and children and the world around them—as she began to make her own way as an independent woman in a world run by men.

But Power's interest was not just personal: it was piqued, like Harrison's, by a strong desire to change the common conception of history as "the biographies of great men," and to shatter the assumption that "to speak of ordinary people [was] beneath the dignity of history." Power's upbringing, though fractured, was middle-class, but she had been fascinated by both the aristocratic glamour of Court Place and the poverty she had seen in Paris, and had been struck by her ability to move freely between divergent worlds. In Paris, a longstanding railway strike had left her feeling "wildly socialistic and revolutionary," furious that the division of society into "capitalists and workers" stacked the balance of power so firmly against the poor. Now, spurred by the longer view she had developed at the LSE, she wanted to interrogate the class system that offered people such variable prospects from birth. Study of the medieval period had long been dominated by nationalists and constitutional experts, who wrote to explain and preserve prevailing systems of power, focusing on wars, dynasties, and kings, and on records which indicated deep-rooted national character. Instead, Power wanted a living history which probed "the obscure lives and activities of the great mass of humanity" and took into account the things that affected them: the introduction of the turnip to England in 1645—providing enough food to stoke the Industrial Revolution—rather than the beheading of Charles I four years later; the gradual evolution of a banking and credit system rather than the building of a single cathedral; the daily misery of war rather than the significance of territorial gains.

And above all, she wanted to write in a way that would be accessible. During her years back at Girton she poured her research into her next book, *Medieval People* (1924), a revelation and a surprise bestseller (republished in paperback in 1937 as one of the first Pelican books, and advertised as "a classic of social history"). Populated with prioresses, pilgrims, clothworkers, and wool traders, it was original in its focus on ordinary people whose lives were "if less spectacular, certainly not less interesting" than those of the aristocrats, criminals, or otherwise exceptional figures—predominantly men—whose voices have survived in the records. Addressed explicitly to the "general reader," Power's intimate style is novelistic, her focus not on manor houses but on "the kitchens of history." Through nuanced speculation and vivid detail she fleshed out her subjects—to whom she refers as "our ancestors"—into sympathetic, complex characters, sensitive to their mundane yet defining concerns: the practical pressures of rent, diet, childcare arrangements, and travel expenses; the joy of songs or games. The book stands as her manifesto for what history can be: illuminating, personal, entertaining, and political. Virginia Woolf knew Power's work well, and it's likely that she had its message in mind when she called, in *A Room of One's Own*, for "Anon" to be returned to her rightful place in history. "We still praise famous men," Power wrote, "for he would be a poor historian who could spare one of the great figures who have shed glory or romance upon the page of history; but we praise them with due recognition of the fact that not only great individuals, but people as a whole, unnamed and undistinguished masses of people, now sleeping in unknown graves, have also been concerned in the story."

When Eileen Power joined the LSE as a student, she was scathing about its social life, finding the school full of "dew-dabblers, pretentious socialists & frothy Fabians & unconscionably earnest young people generally!" But when she returned as a lecturer in the autumn of

1921, she joined a faculty full of radicals, whose company and collaboration would be integral to many of her future projects. In 1919, William Beveridge had taken over as director, and the LSE had undergone a swift expansion, transforming from a cramped and casual evening institution to a leading modern university at the forefront of developments in sociology. A generous yet egotistical character utterly devoted to his work, Beveridge quintupled the school's annual income, securing lucrative grants from the government, the Rockefeller Foundation, and the business world. His schemes for advancement were unpredictable, directed by his enthusiasms and sped on by his fundraising verve: at one point a rumor arose that cages of chimps were going to be installed at the school so that students could study their mating habits.

In 1921, the university was a building site: classes took place in converted army huts approached by leapfrogging over puddles, while lecturers fought to be heard above the noise of drills. That year, the school enrolled almost three thousand students from more than thirty countries, while the Senior Common Room buzzed with discussion of the rapidly changing political climate. In the 1920s and 1930s, the LSE was the epicenter for what Beatrice Webb described as a "circle of rebellious spirits and idealist intellectuals," many of whom invested their hopes for social reform in the fledgling Labour Party. Established in 1900 out of the trade union movement, the party briefly took power in 1924 as a minority government under Ramsay MacDonald, but collapsed after nine months and did not return to government until 1929, being ousted again in 1931. Through the interwar years, LSE economists and historians were hard at work establishing a democratic platform on which socialism could be brought to Britain, focused on confronting the practical issues of policy that hampered Labour during its stints in power over the decades; their programs for an overhaul of the economic system would form the basis of the post-1945 Labour administration. Members of the economics department, including Lionel Robbins and Friedrich Hayek, regularly traded blows with Cambridge's John Maynard Keynes over market reform, while Charles Webster—who lived at 38 Mecklenburgh Square—

arrived straight from the Foreign Office to become Stevenson Chair of International History. The Polish-born anthropologist Bronisław Malinowski (who lived on Guilford Street) worked alongside the future prime minister Clement Attlee, who had begun his career as Beatrice Webb's secretary. At the center of most of the Common Room's controversies was the Marxist political scientist Harold Laski, whose outspoken lectures led one Conservative MP to denounce the LSE publicly as a "hotbed of communist teaching," forcing Beveridge to ban the school's Marx Society from meeting on LSE premises and to placate business-world investors anxious about the ends to which their money was being put.

But its staff's intimate involvement in politics, both British and international, proved the LSE's greatest strength. On Monday afternoons, staff and students would convene for "grand seminars" where issues of the day were discussed without hierarchy and with a sense of urgent practical purpose. As soon as she arrived, Power was delighted by the intellectual stimulus of conversations in the Common Room, at clubs and cafés in Soho and Fitzrovia, during lively country weekends at Passfield Corner in Hampshire with the Webbs and their guests, or over long dinners in Mecklenburgh Square. Just as she had hoped, the LSE offered a way of life utterly different from the one she had led in Cambridge. While Girton had given Power a friendly community to which she always felt loyal, she had "often chafed at being cooped up" there, and when she accepted the LSE job, she admitted to Margery that she was "tired of community life," which had begun to constrain her. Just like Jane Harrison, she was painfully aware that the women's colleges (particularly Girton, which stood well outside the town center) remained separate and subordinate within the wider university: she felt the same ambivalence Harriet Vane outlines in *Gaudy Night*, glad that the women dons can support each other in dedication to their work yet frustrated at their apparent unworldliness and lack of a public voice. Like Harrison, Power felt an overwhelming urge to strike out from Cambridge as her interests became more political and she began to envisage a wider audience for her writing. And arriving in London gave her a taste of the freedom she wanted.

At the LSE, women students and lecturers were not segregated, but worked alongside their male counterparts as equals; Power took her place in a modern, metropolitan university established on egalitarian principles, and joined a ready-made circle of progressive thinkers eager to include her in their plans. Power entered London social life with gusto, frequenting restaurants and jazz clubs, attending clandestine political confabulations in hotel basements and rallies in the parks. Her regular "kitchen dances" at 20 Mecklenburgh Square were attended by economists, politicians, and novelists, including Virginia Woolf, who recalled sharing a packet of chocolate creams there with the civil servant Humbert Wolfe. "I like people to be all different kinds," Power wrote to her friend Helen Cam in 1938, explaining why she had chosen not to apply for a job back in Cambridge; her letter gives a joyful snapshot of London life. "I like dining with H. G. Wells one night, & a friend from the Foreign Office another, and a publisher a third & a professor a fourth; and I like seeing all the people who pass through London and putting some of them up in my prophet's chamber."

Power, who was always sensitive to the emotional effects of her environment, was determined that her London home should allow her work to prosper. When she had stayed with a great-aunt back in Altrincham in 1910, she had written disparagingly to Margery about the "cabbage wallpapers and horsehair sofas," which expressed "concentrated essence of mid-Victorianism, after the Victorians had ceased to be interesting." The old-fashioned furniture had been compounded by a claustrophobic expectation that Power would be "girlish and sweet," and "a deferential *jeune fille.*" "If I lived here for more than a fortnight I should die," she had insisted. Number 20 Mecklenburgh Square was arranged on very different lines. Power shared its two floors casually with friends—Marion Beard stayed until 1937, while Power's sister Rhoda joined the pair in 1929. Power set up a desk by the window, where neighbors often saw her working late at night, and decorated her quarters lavishly with the ornaments she'd bought in China and knickknacks found in Parisian "curiosity shops." Her bookshelves reflected her eclectic tastes—J. H. Clapham recalled that she had "scores

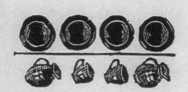

EILEEN POWER

invites you to a

Party

on

~~~~~~~~~~~~~

from 8.30 to 12 p.m.

Dancing in the kitchen : morning dress

~~~~~~~~~~~~~

R.S.V.P. *20 Mecklenburgh Square*

London W.C.1

Invitation to a kitchen dance.

of books of poetry to one *Principles of Economics*"—and each room was decked with fresh flowers and throws in Jacobean patterns. "I never realised before how one's material surroundings could affect one's spirits," she wrote, "and what a difference to one's state of mind could be made by a merrily served meal."

Merrily served, for Power was reluctant to curtail her newfound freedom by taking on the burden of domestic chores. When she took 20 Mecklenburgh Square in January 1922, she "snatched back" Jessie, the "admired and much-loved" woman who had kept house for Eileen and Karin Costelloe when they shared a flat in Victoria while Power was a student at the LSE. Jessie, wrote Power, "looked after me like a mother"; she was devastated when Jessie died, after a short illness, in August 1923. "We had been friends for 15 years," she told Coulton. "I cannot imagine what I shall do without her. She was the old type of family servant & a real friend." At this point Power hired Mrs. Saville, by all accounts an extremely devoted housekeeper, who remained with her at Mecklenburgh Square for the rest of Power's life. Mrs. Saville catered Power's dinner parties, which were renowned for exquisite food and choice wines. (Power herself once refused to host a friend on the grounds that "I've lent my housekeeper to my next-door neighbour for a dinner party that night & if *I* cooked I should poison you.") It's poignant that these women became mother-figures to Power, who had lost her own mother at such a formative age; it's also interesting that, despite the evident imbalance of power, she considered them genuine friends, an integral part of the supportive community of women she gathered around her in her home. Power was conscious that their work enabled hers, and was certainly grateful for it, though it's tempting to wonder whether she felt uncomfortable, as a socialist, that her intellectual freedom depended on the labor of other women. Lilian Knowles, Power's predecessor at the LSE and the first woman in Britain to work as a full-time teacher of economic history, once told a student that "any woman can have a career if she has A, a good husband, and B, a good housekeeper"; as trailblazers in an academic world heavily dominated by men, both these women knew that they needed a reliable support system if they were to exceed expectations of what women could do.

At the LSE, Power found one particular colleague—and a neighbor in Mecklenburgh Square—whose commitment to historical research as a form of activism helped her recognize the political potential of her own work. Richard Henry Tawney (known as Harry)—whom Beatrice Webb called "a scholar, a saint and a social reformer" and Virginia Woolf "an idealist with black teeth"—disguised his radical socialism behind the veneer of a scruffy, absentminded Victorian gentleman, sporting creased clothes with permanently ink-stained fin-

gers and spectacles liable to tip over the back of his head. He had
arrived at the LSE in 1913 as the first director of the Ratan Tata Foundation—a school of social studies established to endow research into
the causes of poverty—following years spent at the Workers' Educational Association, teaching tutorial classes across Britain to educate
workers in the economic history of the eighteenth century. Tawney
believed in the nationalization of industry and free universal schooling,
and wanted "to abolish all advantages and disabilities which have their
source . . . in disparities of wealth, opportunity, social position and
economic power." His influential 1931 manifesto, *Equality*, his high-
profile work as a trade union representative on the Coal Mining Commission, his advocacy for adult education, and his involvement in the
Labour Party made Tawney a household name in the interwar period,
regularly courted by government commissions for his advice.

For Tawney, economic history was "the study, not of a series of past
events, but of the life of society." (As if in proof that history was living,
he used to absentmindedly head his letters with dates from the seven-
teenth century.) At other universities, especially Oxford and Cambridge, history was studied as scholarship for its own sake, independent
of practical applications. But at the LSE, where across the corridor
sociologists and anthropologists pioneered comparative methods of
study, where the Webbs compiled detailed histories of government
alongside their work on policy, and where her colleagues in the history
department were also delegates to international peace conferences,
Power began to see how her historical research could be applied to the
problems facing contemporary society. Suddenly, the medieval period
revealed intriguing parallels to the economics of Soviet Russia, to rising
capitalism in Asia, to nationalism in Europe. "The main business of the
historian whose work lies in a school of social studies," she wrote in a
lecture delivered at the LSE in 1933, "is to contribute his data and the
assistance of his method to the general purpose of elucidating the present." Her feminism had already been awoken in the Cambridge wom-
en's college, but at Mecklenburgh Square, Power's internationalism
began to flourish. At the LSE, her historical research took an overtly

political turn, as her early interest in gender equality extended to a wider struggle for class freedom and world peace.

Power began research on the medieval cloth industry, developing a history of international trade in tandem with Tawney's work on the origins of capitalism. Their shared vision manifested in the joint courses they soon established, which explored the rise of modern industry from sixteenth-century agrarian law, through the Industrial Revolution, to the Factory Acts of the nineteenth century and on into the trade union movement and the evolution of Labour—and the future politics which members of the School staff were actively shaping. Power and Tawney coedited a book, *Tudor Economic Documents*, its three volumes published between 1924 and 1927, and in 1926 they became founding members of the Economic History Society, an international alliance of scholars. Power's work for this society—particularly her editorship of its journal, the *Economic History Review*— placed her at the forefront of her discipline, and led her into fruitful collaborations with economic historians across the world. And her strong friendship with Tawney outside of the LSE made Mecklenburgh Square the vibrant center of an alternative Bloomsbury set, its activities focused not on abstract discussions of art or philosophy but on practical policies designed to change society for the better.

When Power's friend Karin Costelloe became engaged to Virginia Woolf's brother Adrian Stephen in 1914, Power wrote to Margery to complain that she considered "all those Bloomsberries as unsatisfactory folk w. whom to have permanent relationships." She eventually came round to Adrian—and dined with his sister on at least two occasions—but Power was always determined to define herself in opposition to what she thought of as stereotypical "Bloomsbury." Likewise, Tawney's wife, Jeanette (the sister of William Beveridge), insisted that on moving to Mecklenburgh Square they had "hankered after the geographical Bloomsbury, not the mental attitude"; Tawney, more bluntly, called the Bloomsbury set "a mental disease." These judgments were, at least in part, made for rhetorical effect—Leonard Woolf collaborated with Tawney on a petition for miners' rights after the General Strike of 1926, when Mecklenburgh Square became an unofficial distribution ground of the Labour strike paper *The British Worker*, while the Tawneys knew that the Hogarth Press had demonstrated a commitment to working-class and socialist writing. But Power was never interested in artistic bohemianism for its own sake; she was impatient with philosophical posturing or self-indulgent introspection of the sort the Bloomsbury Group's famous Memoir Club went in for, and preferred her gatherings to center on action, not aesthetics. The activities of her Bloomsbury group were focused on concrete solutions to social injustice; here, discussions ranged from nationalism to nationalization, with occasional excursions into Freudian psychoanalysis, modern painting, and the novels of D. H. Lawrence.

Tawney rented four different houses in Mecklenburgh Square over the decades, but during the time Power knew him he was living at number 44, the former home of H. D. and Dorothy L. Sayers. In contrast to Power's elegant decoration, Tawney's tables were invisible beneath piles of books, tobacco residue, and old cheese sandwiches, while he worked hunched over his desk or supine on his window seat, wrapped in his moth-eaten sergeant's tunic from the First World War. To his chaotic study—once described by an *Observer* interviewer as "a compost-heap"—came a regular trail of visitors, from LSE students to miners, Cabinet ministers to cotton workers, all hounded on entry by Jeanette's band of lame dogs and Harry's rival troupe of cats. This was a time when close relationships existed between political leaders, journalists, theorists, and writers, when gatherings in kitchens and drawing rooms could hope to change society as effectively as debates in the House of Commons. Power and Tawney were determined to make Mecklenburgh Square a place where their students could join them for open discussions of urgent economic questions, putting their studies into action.

Their gatherings were eagerly attended by one particular student, who had joined the LSE at the same time as Power. Michael Moissey Postan—known to his friends as Munia—had been born in Russia in 1899, and had studied at the universities of Odessa, Kiev, and St. Petersburg. A socialist activist, thoroughly grounded in Marx's writings, but a staunch anti-communist, he had left the country after the revolution and traveled around Central Europe, like Mirsky and Remizov, in search of a sympathetic home. In the autumn of 1921, he had enrolled at the LSE as an undergraduate, becoming one of Power's first pupils. He left to undertake postgraduate study in economic history at University College London, but Power, sympathetic to his background and alert to his potential, helped him procure the funding to return to the LSE as her personal research assistant in July 1924 ("he really is quite outstanding . . . We really need Postan very badly for all our schemes," she wrote to the board). He began by checking her references in archives and books, then joined a project she was leading on wool merchants; thereafter she proposed him for a lectureship at the LSE and invited him to co-run her famous medieval economic history seminar. In Postan, Power found first a protégé whose talent she identified and nurtured, then a collaborator from whom she could learn as well as teach ("you are continually having to give me advice & help in work for which I get the credit," she told him guiltily). Their relationship would, over the years, deepen and develop into something else; at this stage, he and Tawney were her closest friends at the LSE, firm allies on projects both historical and contemporary.

Postan lived on Taviton Street, not far from Mecklenburgh Square; he was part of a young, international gang of historians, economists, anthropologists, and artists who lived around Bloomsbury and frequented the 1917 Club and the Hambone (a cabaret in Soho's Ham Yard famous for its whiskey and saxophones), the Russian ballet and Soho's Indian restaurants. Through Postan, Power met Hugh Dalton, Evan Durbin, and Hugh Gaitskell (all University of London economists, tipped to be future stars of the Labour Party), who became regular fixtures at the various dining tables in Mecklenburgh Square, once Power had in turn introduced them to Tawney. Sharing a zeal for democratic socialism and a sympathy for the disenfranchised, they formed a group to discuss the historical and sociological implications of current economic problems and to debate the ideology and policy of a future Labour government. From these informal meetings, throughout the 1930s, the group developed a detailed economic program setting out a blueprint for socialist policy that took in plans for industry, banking, employment, and social justice. It was an exciting moment to be invited to Mecklenburgh Square—and an even more exciting time to live there. When Vera Brittain and Winifred Holtby (Dorothy L. Sayers's contemporaries at Somerville) left the top-floor flat they shared in Doughty Street, a horrified friend asked them, "Why are you leaving the neighborhood of Tawney and Eileen Power for a place called Maida Vale?"

Power was not only concerned with an overhaul of domestic policy. Her trip to the Far East in 1920 had expanded her horizons at a time when Europe was in deep aporia about its own survival. The First World War—"the war to end all wars"—had ended two years before Power set sail from Dover, but the Paris Peace Conference at Versailles had left national boundaries in disarray and pacifists distraught over the punitive measures meted out to Germany. Most on the left believed that the treaty would weaken Germany so disastrously that a second war—fueled by newly developed destructive weapons—would be inevitable; hopes now rested on the prospect of a new, transparent system of world government, which could override the divisions entrenched by the sanctions, promote a common system of law, and settle future disputes without recourse to arms.

At Girton, Power had volunteered as treasurer of the Cambridge branch of the Union of Democratic Control, a pacifist organization also supported by Jane Harrison. Along with her friend Margery— later a founding member of the National Birth Control Association and author of the pioneering social study *Working-Class Wives: Their Health and Conditions*—she also joined the League of Nations Society, established in 1915 following a report, commissioned by Sidney Webb for the Fabian Society and written by Leonard Woolf, which argued that the first step toward a peaceful future must be the creation of "an international authority to prevent war," based on cooperation, moral pressure, and shared values. Power organized informal meetings in Cambridge to discuss the society's work, and made copious notes analyzing the possible difficulties such a league might face in practice. She lectured on its platform about the Congress of Vienna of 1814–15—a meeting of European ambassadors to negotiate a peace plan for Europe following the French Revolution and the Napoleonic Wars—and the subsequent, flawed attempt at government by a European confederation. "The parallel with the present is simply amazing," she wrote. "It is exceedingly important as propaganda because it broke down for reasons which will wreck the League of Nations after the Congress at the end of this war, if its mistakes aren't avoided."

The Peace Conference of 1919 resulted in the foundation of the League of Nations, the first international organization with the declared aim of maintaining world peace. The previous October, the League of Nations Society had merged with the League of Free Nations Association, chaired by Jane Harrison's friend Gilbert Murray, to form the League of Nations Union (LNU), a campaign group designed to promote public understanding of the work of the League. Over the interwar period, the LNU would be the most influential organ of the peace movement in Britain, with local branches up and down the country organizing meetings, writing letters, and hosting parties and study circles. Leaflets proclaiming the League "the greatest ideal that the world has seen since the founding of Christendom" were distributed to homes all over Britain, positing it as the savior of war-torn civilization and the harbinger of a new modern age for democracy. "The hope of the world is the League of Nations," wrote H. G. Wells in 1917. "Let us insist upon that. Not only German imperialism, but English Toryism and every class and clique, every antiquated institution, every cant of loyalty and every organised prejudice, must be sacrificed and offered up to that great idea of World Peace and a unified mankind."

Power was a friend of Wells, and a regular visitor at his Essex home, Easton Glebe. After the First World War, he turned his energies—previously invested in Fabian socialism—to the promotion of a "world vision." Wells was fascinated by the idea of "salvation by history": that the ways in which we understand the past could directly affect the way we conceive of the future. From his conviction that "there can be no common peace and prosperity without common historical ideas" sprang his book *The Outline of History*, which structured its narrative not around the rise of individual, competing nation states, but around humanity's shared endeavors. Power admired the book immensely, both for its use of history as an intervention into politics and for its mass-market potential. She especially appreciated its emphasis on what people have in common across time and place, the subject which had occupied her since her Kahn Fellowship. While commentators fearful of a second war were darkly warning politicians to learn the

Eileen Power and H. G. Wells, 1930s.

lessons of history, Power knew that the content of such lessons—and their usefulness—would depend on the perspective of the historians writing. "The only way," she wrote, "to cure the evils which have arisen out of purely national history (and to a lesser extent out of purely class solidarity) is to promote a strong sense of the solidarity of mankind as such; and how can this be better begun than by the teaching of a common history, the heritage alike of all races and all classes?"

Wells was not the only writer at this time who looked to the past as a means of interpreting—and coming to terms with—the present political instability. In the years following the Armistice, a gradual stream of publications exposed the betrayal of the heroic ideals for which soldiers had thought they were fighting. Novels such as Richard Aldington's *Death of a Hero*, memoirs including Vera Brittain's *Testament of Youth* and Robert Graves's *Goodbye to All That*, and R. C. Sherriff's hugely popular trench drama *Journey's End* emphasized the incongruity in encouraging enmity along national lines, and the meaninglessness of patriotic sacrifice. The Victorian certainty that Western civilization was progressing toward a pinnacle of invincibility now seemed catastrophically misjudged. As peace movements looked to the future, historians looked to the past, for roots, messages, and warnings. While Oswald Spengler's 1918 history *The Decline of the West* argued gloomily that all civilizations follow predetermined patterns and that the West was now on the precipice of its own inevitable decline, Arnold Toynbee's bestselling *A Study of History* (1934) proposed that historical destiny lay in individuals' moral choices, and suggested that a new international order, based on collective security, could prevent the downfall Spengler had predicted. Toynbee, like Wells, was a friend of Power's, and she followed his work closely; she too wanted to offer new narratives about the past, but ones which would draw connections between splintered nations and forge consolation and friendship. After *Medieval People*, her thinking took a distinctly pacifist stance, shifting from social history dwelling on personalities toward comparative, international history exemplifying the values that propelled the new League of Nations, and which seemed the world's best hope for preventing the horror of another war.

"If the League of Nations is ever to become real," wrote Power, "children must leave school with some idea of the community to which they belong—mankind." Education was a crucial aspect of the LNU's work; its council agreed that a single, coherent body of knowledge shared between children of different nations, emphasizing cultural similarities and "peaceful interdependence," could combat the climate of suspicion and mistrust that had led to the First World War. The LNU's efforts to change the school curriculum were among its most successful ventures: members lobbied the Board of Education for the revision of textbooks along internationalist lines, drew up proposals to ban physical drills in schools alongside their campaigns for disarmament, and dispatched children to international summer schools at the League's headquarters in Geneva. Power, too, considered it "no less imperative a duty to awaken a sense of international solidarity" in children as in adults. She personally fought for the annual celebration of Empire Day—a holiday that had been marked in British schools since 1904, with parades and dressing-up—to be complemented by a "Humanity Day," which she envisioned as a festival teaching children about achievements in science and culture instead of in war. She joined H. G. Wells in protest against "the teaching of patriotic histories that sustain and carry on the poisonous war-making tradition of the past," and proposed that teachers should focus not on kings, wars, and political skirmishes, which present other countries as enemy or ally, but on the many activities which have connected nations, such as trade, travel, literature, agriculture, and religion. Her aim—which she reiterated in numerous articles and speeches throughout her career—was to teach history "so as to widen instead of to narrow sympathies," instilling in students an essential sense of community beyond their own class or nation. Around this time, several of Power's male friends—Gaitskell, Dalton, Tawney—were standing for office, seeking political influence as a means to changing minds. Power was no less ambitious, but took a different approach—more self-effacing, less likely to lead to fame and fortune, but grounded in firm principles. History, she insisted, "is one of the most powerful cements known in welding the solidarity of any social group . . . If we can enlarge the sense of group solidarity and use history to show the child that humanity in general has a common story, and that everyone is a member of two countries, his own and the world, we shall be educating him for world citizenship."

Power's determination to disseminate her message as widely as possible found a productive outlet in modern technology. In 1924, the

BBC established a series of educational radio broadcasts, enabling expert voices and fresh perspectives to be transmitted directly into living rooms and classrooms across the country. By 1927, three thousand schools were making use of the daily programs. That same year its director, Lord Reith, hired Power's good friend Hilda Matheson to become the BBC's first Director of Talks. Matheson (formerly political secretary to Nancy Astor, the first woman in Britain to take a seat in Parliament) expressed an "active desire to promote the international spirit" through her platform; she commissioned speakers including Virginia Woolf, E. M. Forster, John Maynard Keynes, Rebecca West, and Vita Sackville-West (with whom she had a long affair, sending Woolf into fits of jealousy) to speak on topics which regularly outraged the right-wing press. In 1929, Matheson confessed to Power her desire to secure an appearance from H. G. Wells, who had refused invitations to broadcast due to the BBC's initial censorship of talks on politically sensitive subjects. Power accepted the challenge with glee. That June, Matheson, Wells, and Bertrand Russell were guests at a specially convened tea party at 20 Mecklenburgh Square, where—in a twist beyond contrivance—Wells accidentally left with Matheson's purse, and Russell had to lend her money for her bus fare home. In the ensuing correspondence, Matheson charmed Wells into submission ("It is fun to address twelve million or so British Islanders and some dozens of millions of Europeans all in one breath—I do assure you it is"). On July 10—after a celebratory dinner at the Savoy Grill attended by Power and the Woolfs, among others—he delivered an impassioned address (which prompted several letters of complaint), denouncing nationalism and calling for world peace, and urging the cessation of patriotic teaching in schools. "I'm so pleased you snared H. G.," wrote Power to Matheson in triumph.

But Power's own involvement with the BBC was preceded by that of her younger sister. Eileen had always felt responsible for her sisters, Beryl, a highly respected civil servant in the Ministry of Labour, and Rhoda, another intrepid traveler with a passion for children's education; in part, it was the duty she felt to provide financially for their futures that drove her commitment to her work, taking on extra lecturing and research jobs throughout her years at Girton and the LSE. The Power sisters were a close and formidable trio, and Rhoda's story is no less fascinating than Eileen's. After studying history at the University of St. Andrews, she had traveled to Russia as a governess, where she witnessed the October Revolution—spending seven weeks hiding from soldiers in a cattle shed—then lived for two years in Palestine, editing a newspaper printed in Arabic, Hebrew, and English. When she returned to England, she came to join Eileen at 20 Mecklenburgh Square. There, the sisters collaborated on a series of history books for children, starting with *Boys and Girls of History* (1926), a sort of children's equivalent to *Medieval People*, and began to put together a world history textbook which they hoped would be taken up by schools. In 1927, Rhoda was invited to present a series of BBC broadcasts on "Boys and Girls of Other Days." Helped by Eileen, who checked her scripts for historical accuracy, Rhoda came up with a novel presentation style, enhancing her talks with period music, interludes of dramatized dialogue, and varied sound effects. The exceptionally vivid, immersive format—focused on conveying the human interest of her subject—proved instantly success-

Recording one of Rhoda Power's history lessons, 1931.

ful with children and adults alike. She began touring the country to address teachers on pedagogical technique, and her employment at the BBC was soon extended to a staff position. Her fame was such that her face appeared (unauthorized) on a cigarette card, to the amusement of her sisters. A director from America's National Broadcasting Company, based in New York's Rockefeller Plaza, wrote to congratulate Rhoda on creating "one of the most effective means of education which has yet come to my attention."

Eileen Power made her first broadcast in 1928, on "Europe Throughout the Ages." Across the 1930s she broadcast regularly to schoolchildren aged thirteen and over. (She refused to adapt her work for younger children as she wanted to be sure that "some definite lessons could be absorbed from it.") Together she and Rhoda presented a World History series, planning the episodes late at night around the dining table in Mecklenburgh Square, after days spent shuttling between the house and the British Museum Reading Room. Eileen would prepare the lessons while Rhoda arranged the dramatic interludes; in partnership they produced a pamphlet with exercises and suggestions for the teacher to follow up, blackboard notes and bibliographies, and accompanying articles for the *Radio Times* and the *Listener*. Power's own courses covered international history, from ancient times—Babylon, Egypt, Rome—to the present day, with the First World War and the Russian Revolution, and ending on the establishment and work of the League of Nations. Her broadcasts were her form of peace activism, and the political import of her messages was never diluted for her young audiences, nor did she ever compromise on her political convictions. She wrote in fury to Mary Somerville of the Schools Broadcasting department over the insertion of a picture entitled "Bolivar and his Generals discussing the Campaign of the Andes" in a World History pamphlet: "It is, as you know, entirely against my principles to concentrate attention on wars in the World History course." She refused to broadcast on British history in isolation: "It seems to me an essential purpose of history teaching in schools to explain his wider as well as his narrower environment to the child, who is a future citizen of the world as well as of Britain." Her words recall Jane Harrison, who wrote in

1914 that she and like-minded people "aspired to be citizens . . . of the world," convinced that any other mindset would lead to schism and war. Instead, Power proposed a course on the history of China, with an emphasis on "the common contribution of all peoples to world civilisation, and the increasing interaction of East and West from the beginning."

These stances were characteristic of Power's commitment to a new sort of history. And at the LSE, her academic work developed in a similar direction. She began to research the rise of sovereign states at the end of the fifteenth century, examining the development of nationalism in the context of a contemporary Europe increasingly rife with aggression. After the Wall Street Crash of 1929 plunged the world into an international economic crisis, panic swept Europe: in Britain, Oswald Mosley's Blackshirts prowled past hunger marches and dole queues, while across the continent arose factions promoting a bloodthirsty military impulse and mounting enthusiasm for another war. In January 1933, Adolf Hitler assumed office as chancellor of Germany, and withdrew the country from the League of Nations. Over subsequent months, bars, clubs, and meeting places closed, and books were burned in front of the Berlin State Opera to loudspeakers of Joseph Goebbels's voice calling for a purely national literature. William Beveridge and Lionel Robbins were in Vienna that April, and saw in the evening paper the news that Nazis had ordered the dismissal of several Jewish academics from their universities—the beginning of an extended expulsion of Jewish scholars from Germany. On his return to the LSE, Beveridge called a staff meeting to discuss this "serious attack upon the whole principles of academic and scientific freedom of thought." At once, seeing a chance to transform empathy into action, Power proposed a motion to establish an initiative at the college to make it "financially possible for university teachers who have lost their posts for reasons of race, religion, or political opinion, to continue their scientific work." Within a fortnight, the Academic Freedom Committee had invited displaced scholars to the LSE as visiting lecturers, funded by grants to which LSE staff donated a percentage of their salaries. That October, Beveridge spoke alongside Albert Einstein, himself a refugee from Germany, at a fundraising gala at the Albert Hall, broad-cast live on the BBC. Einstein's speech was a stirring call for thinkers to unite across borders and speak up against fascism: "If we want to resist the powers which threaten to suppress intellectual and individual freedom we must keep clearly before us what is at stake, and what we owe to that freedom which our ancestors have won for us after hard struggles . . . It is only men who are free who create the inventions and intellectual works which to us moderns make life worthwhile."

But the rise of nationalist aggression—and its threat to the League of Nations's vision of world unity—was not restricted to European power politics. In September 1931, Japanese forces invaded Manchuria, a region of northeastern China. By March 1932 they controlled Man-churia and Shanghai under a puppet government, renaming the area Manchukuo. Eileen Power, along with Harold Laski, R. H. Tawney, and Leonard Woolf, signed a letter in the *Spectator* urging Britain to defend international order and ensure that the Covenant of the League of Nations be upheld: "If, in the case of a really serious issue between two Great Powers, this system fails, the peace of the world will be imperilled, and belief in the validity of collective treaties will have been undermined." But Japan refused to hand back the territory, and on March 27, 1933, it gave formal notice of its withdrawal from the League of Nations.

Eileen Power's fascination with China and its culture remained undimmed since the two months she had spent there in the spring of 1921. She dressed regularly in traditional embroidered gowns she had bought on her travels, and she focused much of her own research—as she had predicted at the end of her Kahn Fellowship—on the ancient trade routes between China and Europe, seeking out examples of col-laboration, religious tolerance, and shared scholarship. Her work derived in part from an abiding dislike of the British Empire, and by extension of the Western imperial impulse, feelings which had only intensified since her fellowship. She had been irate at the way the Ver-sailles Treaty calmly apportioned Muslim countries to dominant European powers, and was certain that this attempt to keep the East in subjection would lead to deep resentment and future conflict. She saw this attitude reflected in conventional narratives of history, and dedicated much energy to exposing the dangers of writing without an awareness of perspective and context. In an excoriating review (entitled "The Story of Half Mankind") of Hendrik van Loon's 1921 book *The Story of Mankind*, which left out the Mughals in favor of the Tudors, and included a diagram showing the "centre of civilisation" moving westward, Power set out the principles behind her own conception of world history. Picking up on the tendency in textbooks to provide "an adequate account of the ancient empires of the Middle East, after which they subside into a history of Western civilisation," Power argued that portraying the modern East "merely as a barbaric force, which the West was obliged from time to time to hurl back" is "not only false to history, but dangerous. In the world into which his young readers are born, one of the most pressing problems is that of the relations of East and West . . . Only by a mutual understanding can the heirs of the great civilisations which were born in India, China and the Mediterranean basin live together today, for only the mutual respect born of knowledge and understanding can save a clash, in which all may perish."

Power's enduring interest in China stood against the fear of "Yellow Peril" which had swept Britain since the Opium Wars of the nineteenth century: the belief that China and the Chinese presented a danger to Western supremacy. In popular discourse, China was exotic and backward, seductive yet dangerous; Kipling's dictum that "East is East and West is West and never the twain shall meet" was regularly, lazily quoted to characterize a fundamental social gulf. Large Chinese communities existed in London, particularly congregated in crowded boardinghouses in Limehouse, but their presence was met with disdain and, regularly, violence: twice in the 1920s the Home Office sent immigration inspectors to all Chinese homes in Britain, in the clear hope of making evictions, while the press regularly accused Chinese-owned shops, laundries, and restaurants of drug-trafficking. In the late 1920s, a public hysteria around mixed-race relationships—"White girls hypnotised by yellow men," screamed one tabloid headline—left the Chinese immigrant community vulnerable to abuse by commentators who associated them with a sexual threat and the collapse of imperial hierarchy.

Among artistic circles there flourished a wide-ranging—if often just as exoticizing—appreciation of chinoiserie. Ezra Pound, calling on the modern artist to "make it new," was creatively translating classical Chinese poetry, while in 1912 the British Museum had established its first Department of Oriental Prints and Drawings, run by Laurence Binyon, a close friend of H. D. and Aldington. Over the course of the 1930s, horror at Japan's ongoing military occupation of China prompted new British interest in Chinese culture. In November 1934, Power lent her embroidered costumes to the Little Theatre (where Dorothy L. Sayers had enjoyed the Grand Guignol a decade earlier) for a production of the play *Lady Precious Stream*, by Hsiung Shih-I, a friend of George Bernard Shaw. The play ran for one thousand nights, transferred to the West End and Broadway, and was attended by royalty, celebrities, and several prime ministers. In 1935, the Royal Academy held the largest exhibition of Chinese art ever before shown, attended by over four hundred thousand visitors. (Virginia Woolf went twice.) Almost a thousand objects—bronze, jade, lacquer carvings, porcelain, and paintings, many of which had been in storage since the outbreak of war with Japan—were loaned from museums and collections in China, and shipped to Britain by the Royal Navy. The Chinese government hoped the exhibition would draw attention to China's situation, and garner appreciation for its culture and history; Power was eager to support such initiatives of cultural collaboration, aware that public support was essential to alleviating China's present plight.

But Power's interest in China was personal as well as political. Her first visit there as a Kahn Fellow had set the course for her history work; it had also heralded a significant development in her private life. In 1921, during a walking tour in the Western Hills, she had spent a weekend at the home of Reginald Johnston, an eccentric Scottish civil servant, practicing Confucian, and philosopher, who had arrived in China on Christmas Day 1898, aged twenty-four, serving initially in

Hong Kong, then at the British territory of Weihaiwei. In 1919, he was appointed tutor to thirteen-year-old Puyi, the last emperor of China. Since he had been forced to abdicate in 1912, aged six, after the Qing dynasty was overthrown, Puyi held no power outside the palace walls, but his courtly life in Beijing's Forbidden City continued in traditional pomp; he dined every night in the height of luxury, and was attended wherever he went by a throng of deferential eunuchs. The Foreign Office encouraged Johnston to take the post, hoping that his influence would come in useful should the boy be restored to the throne, and instructed him to teach Puyi English and constitutional history, in order to prepare his charge for modern governance. But Johnston was reluctant to instill Western values in Puyi, preferring to shape a ruler who would guide China forward with respect for the traditions which might otherwise be lost in the ferment of revolution. Together they studied world history, philosophy, and cinema alongside Chinese folklore, history, and religion, while Johnston encouraged his student to write poetry, ride a bicycle, and cut down on waste in the Forbidden City.

Most British expatriates in China were missionaries and businessmen who kept themselves isolated from the Chinese; Johnston, though politically conservative, traveled the country, learned the language, and immersed himself in Chinese art, literature, and landscape. In 1920, having found a plot of land in the Western Hills, Johnston built Cherry Glen, a small oasis at the end of a rough mountain track bordered by fruit trees, with a panoramic vista of the valley below. There, he erected shrines to gods and poets in the winding paths, and built a temple where he slept in summer. Power was entranced by the solitude and spirituality of the place, and the life Johnston led there: she loved drinking rose-infused wine and scented tea from handleless cups on the veranda at twilight, waving to the children who crowded to watch Johnston at his work, and meeting the monks and scholars who came to discuss poetry or philosophy with their learned friend. Two years later, Johnston's impression remained in her mind: "I remember him with pleasure," she wrote to Coulton, "because he was soaked in Chinese things & because he was so amusing & because he lent me a horse."

During her Kahn Fellowship, Power had written longingly to Margery of her determination to return to China and live there on "journalism and odd-jobs"; it was, she insisted, the one place to which she would "never be happy unless I can return." In October 1929, Power did go back to China, now traveling as an established public intellectual with an international reputation. She had been invited to attend a conference in Kyoto organized by the Institute of Pacific Relations to discuss questions such as the economic position of Japan, the changing nature of rural life, and the benefits of industrialization. After the conference, she traveled through Manchuria with Arnold Toynbee, a fellow delegate, visiting the Great Wall, Peking, Shanghai, and Nanjing. He was working on *A Study of History*, while she was researching the Europeans who had traveled to China under the Mongol Empire. At Christmas, she stayed for two weeks at Cherry Glen with Johnston, who was fifteen years her senior. Their relationship remains shadowy, scarcely attested in material form; letters and diaries shed tantalizingly little light on the events that led up to the end of the fortnight, when she and Johnston became engaged.

There is no evidence to suggest that Power, now aged forty, had previously expressed any interest in marriage or children. We can only speculate whether the engagement was serious or merely experimental, its suddenness born of passion or a realization of mutual convenience. In any case, thousands of miles from her usual intimates, Power confided her news to Toynbee. The next morning, a flustered Toynbee declared his own love for her, despite being married to Gilbert Murray's daughter Rosalind and never before having shown any signs of romantic interest. Stunned, Power rebuffed him, and later wrote to offer a somewhat exasperated apology: "You gave me a sudden and violent shock, for which I was totally unprepared, and what really animated me was a frantic and quite irrational desire to stop you from putting into words what I didn't want to hear."

Power refused to let these personal events distract her from her professional engagements, and her time with Johnston as a newly engaged couple was short-lived. In January 1930, she sailed alone from Shanghai to San Francisco, spending the journey cutting out paper dolls for a group of Chinese children and completing crosswords with a wisecracking British financier. From there she traveled to New York, to take up a post as visiting lecturer at Barnard College; she told Toynbee—who had written to apologize for the "irrational and most devastating association of ideas in my mind"—that she was "dashing all over New York and Massachusetts and even down to Virginia talking to women's colleges" and had addressed the Federation of University Women at Rochester and the Medieval Academy in Cambridge, Massachusetts, where she was delighted to meet "everyone whose work I had ever known." (She cheerfully informed the college's dean, Virginia Gildersleeve, that in a month she hadn't dined a single night at home.) Johnston, meanwhile, attended the ceremony in which Weihaiwei became the first British colony to be returned to China, reading out the agreement in Chinese and English as the Union Jack was lowered.

At the end of November 1930, after thirty-two years in China, Johnston returned to London to take up a professorship at the School of Oriental Studies—though he took a house in Richmond, and Mecklenburgh Square remained Power's private domain. That same month, Power wrote to Gildersleeve, thanking her for an invitation of a permanent professorship in New York. Power regretfully turned down the post ("the difficulty is that I am also very fond of my work at the London School of Economics & have now got a wide circle of friends in London"). But she refused to "say no definitely," asking whether she might reconsider the offer—a rare and prestigious opportunity—"say in a couple of years' time": "New work always interests me," wrote Power, "and it is possible that I might feel it easier to take the plunge then than I do now, and the professorship and the generous terms which you suggest are certainly very attractive." Her reluctance to close off this possible path may suggest an ambivalence about her future with Johnston, who himself was in constant touch with friends in China, intimating that his own presence in London might not be permanent.

Their engagement was announced publicly in December. But by the summer, the arrangement appears to have been called off. (Johnston remained in London until 1937, when he retired peacefully to his own tiny Scottish island.) It's not clear quite what caused this decision, but in July 1931, Power accepted the highly coveted post of chair of economic history at the LSE, awarded on the grounds of "her contributions by research to the advancement of social and economic history, her known powers as a teacher, her high standing as a social and economic historian." To her satisfaction, her annual salary was raised to £1,000. She was only the second woman (after her former tutor Lilian Knowles) to be appointed to this position, and she took seriously her responsibility to serve as a role model to the next generation of scholars. Demands on her time, already substantial, only intensified. That December, she was invited to join the Committee of Experts on School Textbooks by the International Institute of Intellectual Cooperation, a Paris-based organization which aimed to promote exchange between scholars. The following year, she was called on to address the annual conference of the International Federation of University Women, a body with close links to the League of Nations, which served as a sort of travel agency for female scholars across the world: Power appreciated her ties to this community, and told the congregation that she could conceive of "no more powerful means of binding nations together than by the infinite multiplication of these tiny invisible threads of personal contact and mutual understanding." And in 1933, she received an honorary degree from the University of Manchester. It may be that she simply didn't have the time or inclination to take on a domestic role that might compete with the position she had, at long last, achieved: a public scholar of recognized reputation.

In the winter of 1937, reports reached Britain of the Japanese capture of Nanjing, and attendant atrocities: widespread looting and rape, and the dropping of aerial bombs indiscriminately on civilian territories. While the British government offered ineffectual concessions in a weak attempt to persuade Japan to withdraw its troops, antiwar councils and pacifist groups organized mass protests calling for action to uphold the Covenant of the League of Nations and to condemn Britain's apparent accommodation of Japanese imperialism. Power was one of many academics who signed a telegram in solidarity with the Ministry of Education at Nanjing, expressing their horror at the destruction of schools and colleges there. That year, she was involved in the foundation of the China Campaign Committee, which head-quartered on Bloomsbury's Gower Street; its president was Lord Listowel (later a Labour peer), its chairman Dorothy L. Sayers's publisher, Victor Gollancz, and the vice presidents included Power, Tawney, and Laski. Its policy statement condemned Japan's war on China as "a threat to world peace and the whole system of world security," and urged Britain "to stand firm by the Chinese people, believing that theirs is a struggle for real democracy." Power helped organize the dispatch of medical supplies by plane and ship, and lobbied for a boy-cott of Japanese goods. At Christmas 1938, the committee organized a protest at Selfridges on Oxford Street against the sale of silk, one of Japan's major exports. That same year, Power contributed a whimsical essay about Cherry Glen to *China: Body and Soul*, a collection intro-duced by Gilbert Murray which also contained—among essays on symbolism, calligraphy, religion, and narcotics—a piece by Roger Fry on Chinese art and architecture, and another by Harold Laski on China and democracy. The proceeds went to the relief of distress in China: a "stupendous tragedy," wrote Murray, "to which we must reso-lutely refuse to become accustomed if any humanity is to remain in the human race."

Eileen Power recognized that China's problem was the world's problem. She instantly saw that the Manchurian crisis was no private quarrel between far-off, uncivilized lands, but an act of imperial aggres-sion, a militarist effort to stifle a nascent democracy, in direct contra-vention of the League of Nations and its cooperative vision for world peace. She saw, as too many others did not, that standing in solidarity with China's democracy was an essential act of resistance against fas-cism. Power watched the outpouring of sympathy for the Spanish Republicans in 1937, when socialists across Europe united to oppose

Franco and fight for liberty in a crisis many saw as an ominous prelude to a bigger war; students demonstrated in the streets, poets conscripted to fight with the International Brigade, and crowds rallied around Picasso's painting *Guernica*, which was exhibited at London's Whitechapel Gallery in 1938. But the fact that the Chinese cause did not attract the same attention was, to Power, a failure of the expansive vision that she had spent the decades promulgating, and one for which the world would suffer. Neville Chamberlain had recently delivered a rousing speech in the House of Commons, denouncing Germany for its barbaric attempts to starve Europe into submission by cutting off supplies from overseas and attacking civilians. The first lady of China, Madame Chiang Kai-shek, wrote to the China Campaign Committee to point out that she had been broadcasting for years using the very same words and phrases to condemn the Japanese activities in China, and had been ignored. She blamed these double standards on a blinkered worldview that prioritized European suffering and failed to understand that pain far away required a robust response not only because it could presage similar atrocity at home, but also for its own sake. It was a concrete example of real-world damage caused by the very attitudes and perspectives which Power had identified and sought to alter through her writing and her work for schools. And now it seemed to be too late.

Throughout the 1930s, world events made clear that the League of Nations policy of collective security was failing to deter aggressors. In 1934 the LNU held its famous Peace Ballot, polling Britain to assess support for the League; its results—that the country voted overwhelmingly in favor of continued membership of the League—were announced in an invigorating public rally. But the ballot was little more than an empty PR stunt. The LNU's membership—which peaked in 1931 at over four hundred thousand registered subscribers—was fast declining in a country increasingly pessimistic that collective security could stand up to the capacities of those determined to undermine it. "War seems inevitable," wrote Virginia Woolf in her diary in

1935. That October, Italy invaded Ethiopia and subjected it to military occupation. In his essay "The Doctrine of Fascism," Mussolini had made clear his disdain for the League, which Italy quit in 1937, dismissing the dream of international cooperation with his famous words "nothing outside the state." In Germany, Hitler adopted compulsory military service and, in 1936, reoccupied the Rhineland, directly contravening the Treaty of Versailles and effectively declaring his intention to govern with force rather than negotiation. That year, H. G. Wells told a friend to "forget about the League of Nations . . . a blind alley, in which a vast wealth of hope and good intentions has been wasted"; it had, he argued, "almost as much reality in it as a vegetarian league of wolves."

In the spring of 1936, amid the light relief of the rumors swirling around King Edward VIII's affair with the American divorcee Wallis Simpson, debate intensified among pacifists on the efficacy of the League approach. The Peace Pledge Union—founded by the Anglican clergyman and former army chaplain Dick Sheppard as a humanitarian rejection of militarism—gathered one hundred and twenty thousand members in its first year of existence, all pledging to renounce war. But many others began to turn toward reluctantly supporting war as the only way to stand up to fascism and achieve peace in the long term. The chancellor of the exchequer, Neville Chamberlain, accelerated Britain's rearmament with a military expansion program that would triple the country's expenditure over the next four years. Yet after becoming prime minister in May 1937, Chamberlain remained hesitant to commit to war, instead attempting diplomacy with dramatic eleventh-hour flights to the continent for meetings with Hitler and Mussolini. On March 12, 1938, German troops crossed into Austria. In September, Chamberlain signed the Munich Agreement, allowing Nazi Germany to dismember Czechoslovakia. That year air-raid practices began in every large city in Britain, while volunteers began to be conscripted for the war that now seemed certain.

Power was shocked at Chamberlain's concessions to Hitler, and his refusal to denounce the violence being perpetrated on Jews in Germany. She joined an antiappeasement movement and signed a letter in the *Manchester Guardian* entitled "A Manifesto by Leading Education-alists," calling for states to surrender their arms and establish a settlement to "lay the foundations of lasting peace." Over the summer of 1938, Power found herself compulsively reading books about the fall of the Roman Empire, struck by discomfiting parallels with the present. She dropped all her teaching to write a lecture, "The Eve of the Dark Ages: a tract for the times," delivered to the Cambridge History Club in November. Her handwritten draft has "Munich" penciled over its title. In the lecture, Power portrayed Rome in the fifth and sixth centuries A.D.—a time, she suggested, when "the lights were going out all over Europe"—as a melting pot of cultures, directly refuting the Nazis' promotion of themselves as a "new world empire" in Rome's image. Her focus, characteristically, was on the human suffering of this period. "Why did they not realise the magnitude of the disaster that was befalling them?" she asked, conjuring an image of Romans complacent in the superiority of their way of life, blithely dismissing the danger of invasion between games of tennis and siestas and baths. With the advantage of hindsight, she argued, it's easy to criticize those who simply couldn't believe that their culture would ever disappear. Taking Gaul as a case study, she isolated two points of blame, both resonating with her contemporary concerns: first, the "policy of appeasement" which allowed the Goths a sphere of influence within Europe; second, the flawed education system. "The things they learned in their schools," she argued, "had no relation to the things that were going on in the world outside and bred in them the fatal illusion that tomorrow would be as yesterday, that everything was the same, whereas everything was different." It will have been clear to her audience that this lecture on ancient history was really Power's manifesto for the present.

Power saw her hopes of international unity fading away in favor of the nationalist, militarist fervor she knew as a force for destruction across time and place. But she kept working, determined to communicate history's lessons to future generations if not to her own. While others, including Wells, had given up on it, she continued to believe in the League of Nations, and attended its 1939 assembly in Geneva, where delegates mingled with detectives hired to guard the event from protesters. That January, she also became the first woman to deliver the prestigious Ford Lectures at Oxford, an annual series given by a distinguished scholar to huge audiences. Her subject, the wool trade in English medieval history, represented the culmination of decades of work on international economic history. She began by eviscerating the view of the Middle Ages in Western Europe as a period of small, self-contained communities, positing it instead as a time of "large-scale international trade." Hers was not the usual patriotic story of English domination of the wool trade, but one of trade routes, migration, cooperation, told in her characteristically lucid style, with emphasis on personality and feeling. For Eileen Power, the greatest horror of war lay in its negation of personal bonds: its infringement on private freedoms and its disdain for the human values of empathy and tolerance. As a historian, she wanted to mobilize against fascism and nationalism, and to affirm, through her writing, the value of a cultural tradition that transcends borders and rejects parochialism. The Ford Lectures, delivered as the world waited for war, were her rallying call to the future.

The lecture series was significant to Power for another reason. Her thinking had evolved over two decades of collaboration with Munia Postan, whose company had been a constant throughout her years in Mecklenburgh Square. After he returned to LSE as her research assistant, they began to write not only in the same room but even poring over the same manuscripts, sharing their ideas and taking cues from each other's interests; he soon became a confidant in matters personal as well as professional. At some point—probably in 1933—they became lovers. Years later, during a wartime separation, Power wrote longingly of the excitement of these early days "in your little flat in Hampstead, passing a white night in lovemaking and breaking off to talk about medieval history between them; and in the morning drinking our coffee in your narrow bed, running out to buy ices and lunching at the little table for two." While Johnston had been significantly older than Power, staid and serious, Postan was young, charismatic, and freethinking; if Power had hesitated to alter the dynamic of their close working relationship, she relaxed her guard on realizing that the intellectual spark which drew them together translated into a deeply satisfying emotional connection.

Their affair, remembered Postan's friend Raymond Firth, was "rigorously concealed" from LSE colleagues; Power was reluctant to cause "a sensation at the school," and knew that being the subject of gossip—a professor of some standing, intimate outside the bonds of marriage with a lecturer ten years her junior!—would inevitably diminish her reputation in and outside the school. Mecklenburgh Square remained a place of professional decorum, where Power worked and hosted friends in her public persona: her relationship was conducted in Postan's flat at 6C Willow Road in Hampstead (the next street to Christchurch Place, where H. D. and Aldington had lived in the first years of their marriage) and in what Postan called a "funk-hole" in the Cotswolds, rented for clandestine weekend getaways. But at the end of 1937, they decided to eliminate all need for secrecy. On December 11, when Power was forty-eight and Postan thirty-nine, they very quietly married at the St. Pancras Registry Office, with two friends and Power's sisters in attendance, before returning together to 20 Mecklenburgh Square. "He and I have been working together in one way and another for fifteen years now and getting steadily fonder of each other and it seemed a good idea to continue the partnership," she wrote, almost apologetically, to Toynbee. She told few people about the wedding, writing casually after the event to most of her friends, anxious only to dispel any concerns that her new status would alter her commitment to her work. (When her bank automatically transferred her accounts to her married name, she immediately instructed it to change them back, having checked with a solicitor it was quite legal for her to continue to use her maiden name.) "I am not giving up my job (it will, I'm afraid, be rather a semi-detached marriage)," she told Lionel Robbins. Her letter ended on a note of professional, rather than domestic, triumph, a sensation of the sort she did court: "Did you know that I had been invited to give the Ford lectures next year? This almost drove my marriage out of my head!"

Power had long been doubtful about marriage as an institution, and—much like Jane Harrison—concerned that its domestic binds were incompatible with a woman's public ambitions. In her twenties, she grew "furious and miserable" with her old friends who were announcing engagements one by one; as she signed congratulatory cards and dispatched begrudgingly embroidered babies' frocks, she lamented the widespread assumption "that the ideal wife should endeavor to model herself upon a judicious mixture of a cow, a muffler, a shadow, a mirror. A lump of plasticine, a doormat and a vacuum, and algebraically indicated by a negative." Should her friend Margery follow the example of several peers who had lost "their old interests and their old individuality and their old friendships" upon their marriages, Power insisted with mock seriousness that she would never speak to her again: "The abstract cause which I care for more than anything else is the cause of women and it seems to me that until women learn to keep their individuality after marriage and to recognise that love is not the only thing in the world and its satisfaction, with all that that entails, their only function, we shall never get anywhere or be anything." When in 1936 Margery separated from her husband, Dominick Spring Rice, Power was unfazed at the scandal, and wrote solicitously to Margery, urging her to keep up her political work and offering refuge in Mecklenburgh Square. There's a slight relish in her letter, perhaps a certain satisfaction that her own resolute opposition to marriage had proved the safer course in the long term.

Like all the women in this book, Power found very meaningful stimulation and intimacy in her friendships with like-minded women, where she could simply be herself—"I do think that absolutely straight, equal, free and sympathetic intercourse is the best thing in the world," she wrote to Margery, describing a long day with her friend Mary Gwladys Jones spent "talking history all afternoon and ourselves all evening"—and had never seen male company as an essential for a fulfilling emotional life. Having worked so hard to carve out a place for herself in a male-dominated world, marriage threatened to disrupt that delicate balance between femininity and professionalism which she always had to negotiate with the utmost care. Most of the men who displayed an interest in her were much older than she was (such as Johnston) or more established in their field (Toynbee); like Virginia Woolf, who wrote to Leonard before their engagement that she refused to "look upon marriage as a profession," Power was reluctant to jeopardize her independence, and (like Sayers and Harrison) was conscious that she would be deeply unhappy in any relationship where her interests were expected to be subsidiary to another's.

But with Munia, things were different. After years of close collaboration, their academic interests were so closely entwined as to be almost indistinguishable: while Power had clearly begun as the senior partner, she had found that Postan's stimulation shaped and deepened her own thought without, crucially, overpowering it. "One of the greatest joys I have had has been to work with you," she wrote to Postan later, describing the "unperishable happiness" of their years together. "I owe my whole intellectual development of the last ten years to you." They came to take pleasure in each other's personal passions, too: Power was delighted to share her love of Chinese art (over the years, Postan amassed a considerable collection of Chinese ceramics which augmented her own), while she gamely embraced his enthusiasm for mountain-climbing (though she had always claimed to be deficient in physical courage "to the extent of fearing dreadfully anything of the genus cow"). Together they climbed from the Rudolfshütte in Austria, from Capel Curig in Snowdonia, and from Chamonix at the base of Mont Blanc: far from confining her to domestic duty, Power's marriage sent her up mountains, testing her physical limits safe in the knowledge that Munia was by her side. "We have had in common everything that two people can have in common," she wrote to him later, "and all I grudge is the years in which we did not have each other." It was clear to her friends that this marriage was that rare thing: an eminently viable partnership, a satisfactory balance of head and heart. When she broke the news to their mutual friend and colleague J. H. Clapham, his daughters immediately proposed a most suitable toast: to "Harriet Vane and Lord Peter Wimsey."

As the British public gathered around their wirelesses waiting for the news that war had been officially declared, Power was working hard on one last effort of international cooperation: a new volume of the

Cambridge Economic History of Europe, which she had conceived with Clapham and worked on throughout the 1930s. The encyclopedia was to provide a modern, comparative canon of world history, with entries sent in from historians all over the world, including contributions from the Hebrew University of Jerusalem, the Lycée Henri-IV, the Sorbonne, and the universities of Ghent, Helsinki, Vienna, Lund, and Zurich. In his introduction to the first volume, Clapham admitted that the project had been difficult to coordinate. A Finnish scholar, he lamented, "had occasion to write from 'somewhere in Finland' in November 1939 that he hoped to get back to economic history but that 'it was a small thing compared with the independence of his country.' We have not heard from him since. Our Spanish contributor sadly threw up his task because he was a refugee in Santander and his notes were in Seville. There has been no later news of him either . . . Of Professor Rutkowski all that we know with certainty is that he cannot be at his University of Poznan; we believe that Professor Ganshof, an officer of the reserve, is alive in Belgium; and that Professor Marc Bloch, after serving with the armies, is safe in America."

In her 1938 book *Three Guineas*, Virginia Woolf asks how to formulate a feminist response to war. She argues that, since women have historically had little, if any, stake in their country—deprived of education, employment, and political influence—the forces of patriotism which spur men to fight mean little to women. Woolf, like Power and Harrison, saw pacifism—like feminism—as a struggle without borders, which aimed to give voice to the disenfranchised and to overthrow their oppressors, whether these took the form of tyrannical fathers, societal structures, or fascist leaders. "As a woman," she writes, "I have no country. As a woman I want no country. As a woman my country is the whole world."

Eileen Power's life-work stands as a firm riposte to the narratives of nationalism that Woolf denounced as symptoms of an unequal society, but also takes Woolf's statement further. While Woolf suggested that women should form a "Society of Outsiders," rejecting the structures of a world not built for them, Power's response to militarist patriarchy took the form of direct action, through her valiant efforts to reshape the narratives that uphold those systems of exclusion. During her Kahn Fellowship, Power saw how entrenched stereotypes and unchallenged assumptions of cultural superiority lead to misguided, ignorant, violent politics. Her history displays a loyalty not to her country, but to the world she wanted to see in the future. where women and the lower classes would be given voice, where East would be afforded the same respect as West, and where military threats would be replaced by international cooperation in the service of peace. In her extensive notes on the League of Nations, to which she added throughout her life, Power wrote that she wanted to inspire through her work a sense of "international patriotism," cultivating the same mix of reason and emotion that drives people to fight for their country, but funneling it toward a commitment to world citizenship: the belief that, "in spite of national antagonisms and divergent interests, mankind as a whole is what the League of Nations presupposes it to be: a community with common aims and a common history." It was a bold and hopeful ideal. But in the autumn of 1939—just as Virginia Woolf was moving into Mecklenburgh Square—Power's vision appeared to be crumbling.

VIRGINIA WOOLF

(1882–1941)

37 Mecklenburgh Square
August 1939–October 1940

Up & down—up & down.
—VIRGINIA WOOLF, diary, June 13, 1940

When Virginia and Leonard Woolf arrived in Mecklenburgh Square on August 17, 1939, they found the entrance to their new home obstructed by sandbags, laid by the band of Irish laborers digging an air-raid shelter in the square's garden. Six days later, news came that Germany and Russia had signed a nonaggression pact; Hitler consequently invaded Poland, an act to which the British government had pledged to respond by entering into war. The following day, as parliament was recalled, the Woolfs came up from their Sussex home, Monk's House, to oversee the move of their personal possessions from 52 Tavistock Square to 37 Mecklenburgh Square. The journey was somber and silent: the train was nearly empty, and as they walked from the station they found London eerily indifferent, the British Museum shut, "no stir in the streets." Their removals man had just received his call-up notice, and informed the Woolfs that he wouldn't be there tomorrow. "It's fate, the foreman said," wrote Woolf in her diary that evening. "What can you do against fate? Complete chaos at 37."

The Woolfs' tenure at Mecklenburgh Square began—and continued—in a state of tension and unease, the immediate political crisis echoing the domestic disruption of the move. They had signed a lease on 37 Mecklenburgh Square "rather rashly" in May, after the noise from building works on the Royal Hotel on Tavistock Square rendered their home there almost impossible to live in. That summer, Virginia had lain dozing on her bed, her head "a tight wound ball of string," while Leonard and their solicitors negotiated in vain with the Bedford Estate to annul their current lease. "I long for 37 Mecklenburgh Sq," wrote Woolf: "a large seeming & oh so quiet house, where I could sleep anywhere." But unlike Sayers or Power, who arrived at Mecklenburgh Square excited to make a new start, the process of undoing and reassembling her life reminded Woolf uncomfortably of her mortality, forcing her to confront a future which seemed increasingly futile.

The move was the culmination of a difficult year for the Woolfs, as personal tragedies accentuated the deepening political danger. On June 23, their friend Mark Gertler had committed suicide, only a fortnight after dining with the Woolfs and discussing, among other subjects, his fear at Hitler's treatment of Jews. The following week, Leonard's elderly mother, already suffering from a protracted illness, had broken two ribs in a fall, and died soon afterward. Visiting Leonard's mother had always convinced Woolf of "the horror of family life," but her loss left them both feeling strangely unmoored. The fresh promise of the new house dissolved into a dull anxiety that they had made a terrible mistake in leaving Tavistock Square, where they had spent fifteen largely happy years. As they went through the Mecklenburgh Square house that July, fitting electric lights and planning how to arrange their furniture, "a grim thought struck me: wh. of these rooms shall I die in?"

On September 3, 1939, Chamberlain announced to the waiting nation that Britain was at war with Germany. Woolf spent hours sewing blackout curtains while listening for sirens, finding herself "too tired, emotionally, to read a page." Number 37 Mecklenburgh Square seemed uncomfortable and hostile—"The kitchen very small. Everything too large. Stairs bad. No carpets." The external uncertainty dampened the Woolfs' enthusiasm for domestic comfort: a week after they had moved in, the hallway remained blocked with boxes, and even in November, Woolf informed a friend that there was "a chamber pot in the sitting-room, and a bed in the dining-room." Gradually, uneasily, they unpacked and settled in, Woolf and their servant Mabel Haskins emptying cases and laying carpets. As before, the house was divided, with the Hogarth Press lodged in the basement, while the solicitors Dolman & Pritchard—who had sublet part of Tavistock Square since 1924—occupied the ground and first floors, and the Woolfs "perched" on the upper two stories. "I've two nice rooms at the top," Virginia wrote to Vita Sackville-West. "I like them—there you'll come—one side is chimneys on a hill, I suppose Islington—t'other all green fields and the Foundlings playing."

"How to go on, through war? thats the question," wrote Virginia ten days after moving into the square. That dilemma occupied Woolf throughout her tenure in Mecklenburgh Square, infiltrating every aspect of her writing and daily life. During the First World War many of the Woolfs' friends had been conscientious objectors, but now most of their circle was resolved that fascism had to be countered, through militarism if necessary, since the League of Nations's policy of collective security seemed to have failed. David Garnett—who had worked as a fruit farmer throughout the First World War—now joined the RAF; E. M. Forster broadcast in defense of war; Leonard published *The War for Peace*, which argued that Britain's participation in a military defense of democracy could no longer be avoided. Virginia's own determined inclination to nonresistance left her feeling isolated and helpless. "She is for Peace, Leonard for the war," wrote Rose Macaulay after bumping into Virginia at the London Library. Since 1915, Virginia had, like Jane Harrison and Eileen Power, considered patriotism "a base emotion," which she associated with an uncritical acceptance of tradition and an arrogant sense of superiority: in her 1938 essay *Three Guineas*, she had urged her readers "to take no share in patriotic demonstrations; to assent to no form of national self-praise." But now, much like H. D. in 1916, Woolf felt out of step with the national mood.

Leonard and Virginia Woolf photographed by Gisèle Freund in 1939.

The "preposterous masculine fiction" of war haunts Woolf's writ-ing, from the futile death of Jacob Flanders in *Jacob's Room* (1922) to the "insidious . . . fingers of the European War" that claw at the shell-shocked and suicidal Septimus Smith in *Mrs. Dalloway* (1925). Her novels often represent the First World War as a gap, an absence; it is portrayed in *To the Lighthouse* (1927) by a short section entitled "Time Passes," and in *The Years* (1937) by a "complete break" after which no character can remember what they were saying before. For Woolf herself, that war was connected with a dark period of mental illness which confined her to bed and forced her to leave Bloomsbury for the comparative peace of Richmond. Now, Woolf felt herself plunged into another blank. The political consequences of a second war blended, for her, with its devastating repercussions for her last decades of writing and a peaceful old age: defeat, she wrote, would signal "the complete ruin not only of civilisation, in Europe, but of our last lap." She was terrified that her beloved nephew Quentin Bell would be conscripted—she knew this would be unbearable for her sister Vanessa, already traumatized by the death of her son Julian in the Spanish Civil War—and that she would never again settle to writing another book. When a woman in a Bloomsbury coffee shop cheerfully assured her that Britain would win the war, Woolf replied: "But what's the point of winning?"

Now, she called the declaration of war "the worst of all my life's experiences." The Woolfs knew that the Gestapo had drawn up a 350-page blacklist which included the names of "Leonhard Woolf, *Schriftsteller*" and "Virginia Woolf, *Schriftstellerin*"; after a "sensible, rather matter-of-fact talk" they agreed that, in the event of defeat, they would gas themselves at home rather than await capture. But Virginia refused to contemplate this fate. "No, I dont want the garage to see the end of me. Ive a wish for 10 years more, & to write my book wh. as usual darts into my brain." Throughout her year in Mecklenburgh Square, Woolf galvanized energies for an astonishing variety of projects: she completed, with relief, a biography of her old friend Roger Fry, she wrote a novel, *Between the Acts*, and she began sketching her own memoirs, as well as making notes for a new study of English literature. Her diaries and correspondence mix the constant "rumors of war" with accounts of dinners, parties, commissions for stories and journalism, and changes in her Sussex garden. To read them is to experience a dizzyingly intimate insight on a time of turbulence and transition, both in European politics and in Woolf's own life. Often, in her diary, she jots quick,

distracted lists, amalgamating public and private fears in her characteristic, penetrating shorthand: "Over all hangs war of course. A kind of
perceptible but anonymous friction. Dantzig. The Poles vibrating in
my room. Everything uncertain. We have got into the habit however.
Work, work, I tell myself." The work Woolf undertook during this
year formed responses to ideas she had long explored: the nature of the
self, the impossibility of knowing others, the effects of culture on people, the violence of patriarchy, the relationship between art (and the
artist) and society, and a concept of community founded not on patriotism but on a shared sense of history.

The Woolfs soon established an uneasy "betwixt and between" routine, spending four days of every fortnight at Mecklenburgh Square
and the rest of the time writing uninterruptedly at Monk's House in
Rodmell ("our village—which must be typical of all villages"), a
sixteenth-century cottage which they had bought at auction in 1919.
This arrangement was designed to help Virginia negotiate "the usual
fight between solitude & society," her delicate balance of public and
private life which the war threatened to shatter. But the constant back
and forth, by car or train, soon began to aggravate. "We lead a distracted life—one week in London, the next here," she wrote to her
friend, the composer Ethel Smyth. "As you can imagine I leave there
what I want here, and t'other way about."

London—"this doomed and devastated but at the same time mor-
bidly fascinating town"—became the site for the Woolfs' sociability,
while at Rodmell she enjoyed being able to "take my brain out, & fill it
with books, as a sponge with water." They crammed their days in the
square with engagements: Leonard would hurry to the House of Commons to carry out his duties as secretary of the Labour Party Advisory
Committee, then return to discuss with Kingsley Martin whether the
New Statesman should declare in favor of peace ("all in the know say we
are beaten"). The Russian translator S. S. Koteliansky visited to rage
against fascism with a vehemence that took Virginia aback ("He gets
up at 6 to listen to the BBC at 7, is obsessed—brooding alone at Acacia

Road"). Over dinners in Mecklenburgh Square she and her guests darted easily between contemporary gossip (the death of Sigmund Freud, whom Woolf had met earlier in 1939, on which occasion he had given her a narcissus; her niece Angelica Bell's scandalous affair with David Garnett, the one time lover of her father, Duncan Grant, who himself had just sold a painting to the queen) and animated discussions about Joseph Conrad's servants, Thackeray's prostitutes, and Dickens's mistresses, "all spoken of as if they were old friends." One evening, T. S. Eliot, Clive Bell, and Saxon Sydney-Turner came over to debate whether "this war means that the barbarian will gradually freeze out culture," before wandering out in the early hours, leaving the door ajar. Virginia strolled with Elizabeth Bowen from Mecklenburgh Square through Temple and along the river to the Tower of London, then rode back again on the top of a bus, talking away about house moves, writing, and the escalating tensions between Britain and Ireland. "A good idea; talking in many changing scenes," wrote Woolf, happily, that evening: "it changes topics & moods." But despite these glimmers of the old pleasures of London life, she could not long be distracted from the encroaching threat.

Woolf admired the stoic bustle of the city, full of people "all set on getting the day's work done," but was unsettled by the "sense of siege being normal" which was coming to replace the initial terror. Barrage balloons floated above the waving plane trees in the square's garden; on the streets, pairs of soldiers in helmets and khaki greatcoats listlessly patrolled. Shops shut early and people dashed quickly between destinations, glancing anxiously around for any sign of emergency—which still didn't come. Soon, disgruntled commentators were referring to the period—which lasted until the spring of 1940—as the "Phony War." Many Londoners had rushed to volunteer for war service when the announcement was made, but now found themselves bored as the threatened invasion failed to materialize. One night, Virginia roused the whole house, having in her heightened state of anxiety mistaken the buzzing of two wasps in a jam jar for the urgent hum of planes overhead.

Driving up to London, passing posters proclaiming "Hitler says,

Now it's on," Virginia felt they were "driving open eyed into a trap."
News was scarce: the Woolfs relied on gossip from a neighbor's nephew
who worked at the War Office and on the "few facts" that came nightly
from the wireless. As Hitler made no move, a heated exchange of letters in the *New Statesman* debated whether Britain should simply
ignore the war, leaving the Russians and Germans to come to terms.
John Maynard Keynes argued that the left had been vociferous in
demanding that Nazi aggression must be resisted at all costs, and was
now being defeatist in not supporting an attack; George Bernard Shaw
countered that it was folly to enter a war without knowing what one is
fighting for. That Christmas, radio broadcasts expressed the tentative
hope that the new year would bring peace. "Yes, its an empty meaningless world now," wrote Woolf soon after the declaration of war. "It
seems entirely meaningless—a perfunctory slaughter, like taking a jar
in one hand, a hammer in the other. Why must this be smashed?
Nobody knows."

"This idea struck me," Woolf mused in her diary, "the army is the
body: I am the brain. Thinking is my fighting." It's a somewhat preposterous statement—showing little concern for the brains among the
armed forces—but work, for Woolf, provided comfort and consistency
amid the uncertainty of the Phony War. In the mornings she would
write, sitting in a low armchair in the Monk's House living room. On
her knees rested a large notebook of plain paper, laid on a plywood
board with an inkstand glued to it. Strewn around her on the table and
floor was an array of old nibs, used matches, crumpled envelopes, and
ink bottles. In the afternoons, she would type out what she had written
that morning, revising as she went; long walks across the water meadows would provide intense periods of solitary rumination. She found
herself able to focus on work as never before, the numbness of the first
days of war giving way to a whirl of ideas—for stories, articles, and
books—which forced her to organize and work fast, carefully balanc-
ing the demands on her time. The Woolfs' Sussex housekeeper, Louie
Everest, recalled often hearing Virginia reciting the previous day's sentences in her morning bath, and when she brought in the breakfast
tray, she would notice pencils and scraps of paper—several with the

same sentence written over and over—lying around Woolf's bed, remnants of the previous night's work.

Immediately after moving into Mecklenburgh Square, Woolf wrote to Raymond Mortimer, then literary editor of the *New Statesman*, to propose some books for review: "It's best to have a job, & I don't think I can stand aloof with comfort at the moment." Woolf was drawn to "the frying pan of journalism" as a way of remaining engaged with the outside world, though public work brought with it the fear of negative reception, and she lamented the loss of "my old age of independence" in favor of the grind of "1,500 words by Wednesday." But both Woolfs saw journalism as an essential means of shoring up financially. Although they benefited from substantial capital investments as well as the money they made from their own work, they still had to pay for Tavistock Square, which remained unlet, as well as even higher rent on Mecklenburgh Square. The war had driven up prices, and the Woolfs began to ration their paper, sugar, and butter, and to count up the logs they had amassed from an elm tree that fell ("This will see us through 2 winters. They say the war will last 3 years"). On October 1, 1939, Virginia told her niece Angelica that they might have to reduce the allowance they sent her: "Leonard says we shall be a good deal poorer, owing to taxes, not having let 52, the Press not paying etc . . . What a damnable curse the war is."

Their financial difficulties were exacerbated by the increasing pressures placed on the Hogarth Press, a longstanding and important source of income for the Woolfs. They had begun the press in 1917 in Richmond, where they had moved to provide calm for Virginia. She had experienced nervous breakdowns in 1895, 1904, 1913, and 1915, each one preceding a suicide attempt. Doctors were bewildered by her symptoms, which included headaches, racing thoughts, hallucinations, refusal to eat, and fainting; any strain was a risk, and if an episode intensified, it might take weeks to dissipate. Seeking a form of manual therapy—Virginia found that repetitive tasks like typing or gardening helped her in convalescence—she and Leonard had spent £38 on type and a small printing machine which could stand on their dining table, and taught themselves to use it. "You can't think how exciting, soothing, ennobling and satisfying it is," wrote Virginia in delight. Following a successful series of hand-bound pamphlets (starting with a volume containing a story by each of them), they quickly grew more professional and began to send their books to commercial printers—though the editorial and design work was always done in the house. By 1923, they were publishing over a dozen titles each year, including Virginia's own books, beginning with her third novel, *Jacob's Room*. From this point, relieved no longer to have to shape her work to the taste of outside editors, she considered herself "the only woman in England free to write what I like." The Woolfs worked together on the press, editing, commissioning, typesetting, and packing up books to be sent to reviewers and customers; Leonard kept assiduous notes of their profits, from which each of them took an allowance at the end of the year, to be spent entirely on themselves.

The success of the Hogarth Press is testament to the strength of the Woolfs' partnership, a marriage founded—like that of Power and Postan, or Wimsey and Vane—on a mutual commitment to freedom and to work. Though she loved her nephews and nieces, Virginia had long shied away from domestic life, seeing it as a potential threat to the intensive solitude she required for writing: aged twenty-five, she insisted that she was content to spend her life "a virgin, an Aunt, an authoress." When Leonard—whom she had met through her brother Thoby—first proposed marriage in April 1912, Virginia was ambivalent. "As I told you brutally the other day," she wrote to him, "I feel no physical attraction in you. There are moments—when you kissed me the other day was one—when I feel no more than a rock. And yet your caring for me as you do almost overwhelms me. It is so real, and so strange." She was insistent that she could only possibly consider a new sort of marriage (of the type to which H. D., Sayers, and Power all aspired, and that Harrison, a generation earlier, simply couldn't conceive): "If you can still go on, as before, letting me find my own way, that is what would please me best; and then we must both take the risks. But you have made me very happy too. We both of us want a marriage that is a tremendous living thing, always alive, always hot, not dead and easy in parts as most marriages are. We ask a great deal of life, don't we? Perhaps we shall get it; then, how splendid!" Woolf's articulation shows a fierce commitment to her freedom, even when she was aware of the challenges this unconventional marriage would present: nonetheless, she knew she could not live outside her principles—and Leonard was willing to experiment.

The marriage went through difficulties. During an early illness Virginia refused to see Leonard for some months; she resented his insistence on rest during the time they lived in Richmond, where she felt trapped and scrutinized, while her relationship with Vita Sackville West—which Leonard tacitly condoned—provided a flurry of erotic excitement which the marriage did not have. Yet Woolf never considered leaving Leonard; he anchored her, and offered routine and safety in times of turbulence. During her affair with Vita, she wrote movingly of the comforting "dailiness" of their marriage, the small joys of a shared life, and the contentment of their complete trust in one another. And the dynamics of their relationship were echoed in the Hogarth Press which turned their marital home into an egalitarian workplace, where Virginia wrote her books surrounded by the printing paraphernalia that would bring them to the public, and the secretaries and managers the Woolfs had hired to support them. When others recalled their relationship, they mainly spoke of Leonard's steady devotion to Virginia, and his determination to protect her from anything that could disrupt the fragile equilibrium she required to write. By 1939, their relationship had mellowed into an affectionate codependency that reassured them both: "their bonds were very close indeed," wrote John Lehmann, their neighbor in Mecklenburgh Square and partner in the Hogarth Press, "as anyone who had observed them together would testify."

Lehmann had joined the press as manager in 1931, aged twenty-four. A university friend of Virginia's nephew Julian Bell, Lehmann brought Hogarth in touch with a new generation of poets—among them Stephen Spender, Louis MacNeice, Cecil Day Lewis, and W. H. Auden—lambasting the futile devastation of war, the economic violence of the precarious peace, and the hypocrisy of social convention. In 1932, frustrated with Leonard's controlling attitude to the business,

John Lehmann and Leonard Woolf at the Hogarth Press.

he walked out ("That egotistical young man with all his jealousies & vanities & ambitions," raged Virginia) but in January 1938 he returned and bought a half-share in the press for £3,000, becoming managing editor alongside Leonard, while Virginia retired to a position on the advisory board in order to spend more time on her writing. Lehmann was more entrepreneurial than the Woolfs, and was keen for their publishing program to engage meaningfully with contemporary politics, to publish a wider range of international voices (building on its Russian connections), and to establish Mecklenburgh Square as a bastion of culture in a beleaguered world. From his second-floor back room at number 45—which he had decorated with maps of the old Austro-Hungarian Empire—Lehmann worked on his magazine, *New Writing*, which he had founded in 1936 to "create a laboratory where the writers of the future may experiment," and to set writing by his own generation, who had come of age after the First World War, alongside international luminaries such as Boris Pasternak and Bertolt Brecht.

In the first days of the war, the doorways to London bookshops were blocked up by sandbags, and sales plummeted. After a few weeks,

Leonard sent Lehmann on a tour of the country to gauge the mood among booksellers, who proved optimistic about Christmas trade, forecasting a renewed enthusiasm for reading while other entertainments ceased in the blackout. But in March 1940, the government implemented Paper Control, limiting publishers' paper consumption to 60 percent of the previous year's usage. After urgent confabulations in Mecklenburgh Square, the press decided to use its allotted stocks to keep steady sellers in print—Virginia's novels, the poetry of Rilke, the complete works of Freud, which Hogarth had been the first to bring into English translation—and retain enough paper for the eventuality of a surprise bestseller, and also for new books by existing authors, to avoid losing them to bigger publishers. The first novel Hogarth published from its Mecklenburgh Square address was Henry Green's *Party Going*, a portrait of Bright Young Things stranded at Victoria station when a thick fog halts all transport; their nervous imprisonment conjures something of the uneasy limbo of the wait for war. But Virginia Woolf had stepped back from the operations of Hogarth, and the works of the press were a diverting backdrop to her London life: in her upstairs room, while Leonard and Lehmann debated downstairs about the future of European literature and politics, she was thinking back over her past.

Woolf's fiction is populated by characters whose sense of self is uncertain, their inner lives at odds with the personae they present to the outside world. Many of her characters feel isolated from those around them, unable to see beneath the surface of others' behavior or reveal their own thoughts: in *Night and Day*, Katharine Hilbery is struck, looking at her fiancé, by "the infinite loneliness of human beings"; Rhoda in *The Waves* feels "alone in a hostile world"; Lily Briscoe in *To the Lighthouse* wonders "how . . . did one know one thing or another thing about people, sealed as they were?" and resigns herself to understanding others by "the outline, not the detail." Woolf loved to watch and analyze the people around her, both strangers and friends.

("Observe perpetually," she enjoined in one of her last diary entries, quoting Henry James.) Yet she was always aware that perceptions can be unreliable.

Throughout her life, Woolf engaged in an examination of the problems and potentials of biography. Like H. D., she turned parts of her own life into fiction, with episodes from her diary and letters recurring, in various forms, in her novels. She kept a diary on and off from the age of fourteen until her death, ripe with caustic portraits of her friends and acquaintances (regularly jotted down the minute guests had left), though often reticent on significant aspects of her private life, such as her illnesses. As she grew older, she was increasingly aware that her diary might be mined by future biographers for juicy revelations about herself and her eminent contemporaries ("Which of our friends will interest posterity most? Maynard?" she asked in January 1940), and spent a good deal of time reading other diarists—Francis Kilvert, André Gide, Augustus Hare—and pondering how to order her reflections. She published spoof biographies of Elizabeth Barrett Browning's dog Flush and of the fictional, slippery Orlando, whose personality and gender shift as time passes, the biographer chasing her subject across the centuries in a futile attempt to pin them down.

She discussed her childhood in an affectionate memoir written for Vanessa before her sister's marriage to Clive Bell, and more critically in papers delivered to the Memoir Club, an intimate gathering of Bloomsbury friends whose rules dictated frank self-analysis and forbade the taking of offense. She sat for several portraits by Vanessa, who often painted Woolf with her eyes closed or mysteriously absent, as if to deny the possibility of capturing what lay behind them. In 1932, Woolf was also the subject of a biography, by the novelist Winifred Holtby, who approached her in the hope of writing a critical memoir, setting Woolf's work in the context of her life. Woolf was ambivalent about the process, and claimed that she "roared with laughter" on reading the book. "I couldn't help laughing to think what a story she could have told had she known the true Virginia," she wrote to a friend. But what did she mean by the "true" Virginia? "We're splinters and mosaics; not, as they used to hold, immaculate, monolithic, consistent wholes," wrote Woolf in 1924, reflecting on the patchwork of engagements, public and private, that made up her day; she considered her self a fragmentary, chaotic, and discontinuous identity composed of parts revealed to different people in different ways, and constantly changing.

A few years after the experience with Holtby, Woolf herself took on the task of writing a full-length biography. She agreed, after some hesitation, to write the life of the artist and curator Roger Fry, who had been a close friend for decades, as well as the lover of her sister Vanessa. Woolf was distraught at his death on September 9, 1934, and considered that "nobody—none of my friends—made such a difference to my life as he did." This project—which she began properly in April 1938, entering an "odd posthumous friendship" with the man she had known since 1910—occupied her throughout the first months of war. Lehmann remembered a glum picnic in Mecklenburgh Square with Virginia in September 1939: "While we ate sandwiches despondently in my flat, she confessed that the only way she could find to dispel the restless visions of anxiety that continually oppressed her was to force herself to carry on with the biography of Roger Fry she was preparing, and to re-create herself in her diary." Woolf felt comforted "thinking of Roger not of Hitler," as she sat in the London Library reading reviews of his exhibitions, while far away Chamberlain was negotiating with Hitler. "I dont feel that the crisis is real," she wrote, "not so real as Roger in 1910 at Gordon Square, about which I've just been writing . . . how I bless Roger, & wish I could tell him so, for giving me himself to think of—what a help he remains—in this welter of unreality."

In her Memoir Club paper on "Old Bloomsbury," Virginia remembered Roger Fry first appearing at an evening gathering in an oversized ulster coat, its pockets bulging with books and paintboxes, and being immediately awed by his "knowledge and experience." Fry's influence on the Bloomsbury artists—and on British culture—was cemented by the exhibition *Manet and the Post-Impressionists* which he curated at the Grafton Galleries in November 1910, bringing the work of Matisse, Van Gogh, Gauguin, and Cézanne to London for the first time. The exhibition, Woolf recalled, threw the establishment of gallery-goers and critics into "paroxysms of rage and laughter." The *Daily Telegraph* critic flung his catalogue to the floor in disgust at the paintings; Wilfrid Blunt wrote that "they are the works of idleness and impotent stupidity, a pornographic show." Yet Woolf and Vanessa Bell were thrilled by the possibilities suggested by these colorful, abstract, essentially modern works, which eschewed conventions of Victorian realism in favor of formal arrangements designed to stir the imagination and senses. To Bell, the exhibition proposed new directions in form, color, and light; to Woolf, it opened up new ways of representing subjects, which would shape her approach to both fiction and biography.

Woolf's first two novels, *The Voyage Out* and *Night and Day*, were relatively conventional in form, though both feature heroines frustrated by the ways external expectations fail to reflect their innermost desires. But after reading Fry's book *Vision and Design*, in which he suggested that art and literature could seek "the expression of the imaginative life rather than a copy of actual life," Woolf became convinced that a subject's essence could be more than a factual likeness; that a novel could offer not just a plot but a representation of the "myriad impressions" each mind receives daily. With her third novel, *Jacob's Room*, Woolf felt she had "found out how to begin (at 40) to say something in my own voice." It was to Fry's influence that she ascribed her shift toward a fragmentary style of narrative, featuring multiple points of view and an emphasis on images rather than events, a technique which reached its height in *The Waves* (1931), her great experiment in recording the impressions and thoughts of characters without conversation or external reality at all. "You have I think," wrote Woolf to Fry, "kept me on the right path, so far as writing goes, more than anyone."

When in 1934 Fry's sister Margery had asked Woolf to take on the task of writing Roger's life, she had at first demurred. She recalled E. M. Forster's biography of their friend Goldsworthy Lowes Dickinson which had ignored his homosexuality, a prudishness she considered "quite futile"; in 1935 she agreed with James Strachey on the need for "a full and outspoken life" of his brother Lytton, which would not come until the 1960s. Her thoughts on biography had evolved along-side her view of character in fiction; Woolf had welcomed the rise of the "new biography" amid the social freedoms of the new century, which swapped lifeless panegyric for shorter, more self-aware studies interested in character rather than deeds. But when Woolf agreed to take on the Fry project, she began to realize that this form of writing entailed the sorts of social responsibilities from which she had long believed a writer needed to be free. She felt she couldn't explore Roger's ambivalent feelings toward his family, or his affairs: "How does one euphemise 20 different mistresses?" she wrote in frustration. Fry himself had spoken openly at the Memoir Club about his childhood, but when she discussed with John Maynard Keynes and Lydia Lopokova whether to include an anecdote he had told about getting an erection after administering a beating at boarding school, she was dismayed to be told firmly that the time had not yet come when such subjects could be treated publicly.

With Roger's friends and family looking over her shoulder—and regularly turning up at her door with overflowing boxes "full of tailor's bills love letters and old picture postcards"—Woolf felt burdened by a sense of "joyless and unprogressive" duty which tied her to the documentary evidence. She considered at one point writing it backward, or in the first person, as if trying to trick herself that it was fiction. Soon after his death, she had composed a "private" sketch of Fry, in which she had aimed to present him "almost as a novelist might make a character in fiction"; the subsequent portrait is a hybrid of fiction and biography, joyful, impressionistic, and carefree. But this authorized attempt felt different, and she constantly refers in her diaries and letters to the responsibility as "sheer drudgery," which left her "dazed & depressed." "A bad morning, because I'm dried up about Roger," she wrote in May 1939. "I'm determined tho' to plod through & make a good job, not a work of art. Thats the only way." The diligence of her research is clear from the finished book: she paid tribute to eight generations of his Quaker family, and plowed through bundles of Roger's letters sent home from school, many stained with the juice of the withered buds he enclosed for his botanically minded parents. Though she knew him so well, and witnessed many of the scenes she described, the biography remains for the most part carefully impersonal: to Ethel Smyth, Woolf wrote that "it was an experiment in self suppression," herself appearing only as "the invisible V—the submerged V." Yet the hints of her own experience are those which animate her subject best: she remembers Roger's voice "like a harmonious growl," the way he laughed "spontaneously, thoroughly, with the whole of him," the "gravity and stillness" to his face which made him look "like a saint in one of his Old Masters."

Frustrated by the difficulties of representing another life, Woolf's thoughts turned toward a new project. In April 1939 Vanessa had playfully warned Woolf, who was fifty-seven, that she would soon be "too old" to write her memoirs; now, in Mecklenburgh Square, Woolf began to think more seriously about beginning them. It was a project grounded from its inception in the reality of life under war. Woolf was anxious about losing her memories along with the physical reminders of the past that seemed at risk of imminent destruction: as she lay awake in Mecklenburgh Square, regretting the move and worrying about death, she found herself "going over each of the rooms" in her first home at 22 Hyde Park Gate. To her pleasure, she discovered that snippets of memory, long submerged, could suddenly feel "more real than the present moment," and that she was able to "spin a kind of gauze over the war" by retreating into a world that existed only in her mind.

She worked on a story called "The Searchlight," in which the beams of light from planes overhead spur a woman to recall her Victorian childhood; meanwhile, she gradually assembled these scraps into the beginnings of a piece she called "A Sketch of the Past," which she continued during 1939 and 1940 "by way of a holiday from Roger." "I have no energy at the moment," she wrote, "to spend upon the horrid labour that it needs to make an orderly and expressed work of art; where one thing follows another and all are swept into a whole." If the resulting sketch is halting, full of ellipses, stops and starts, it's a reflection on the very circumstances of its composition, over a period when Woolf was confronting the serious possibility of death at any moment.

In some ways, her memoir-writing was an immediate, pragmatic response to the war: a way of shoring up her legacy against the potential wreckage of an explosion. "Shall I ever finish these notes—let alone make a book from them?" Woolf wondered, acknowledging that, if the war were to be lost, "book writing becomes doubtful. But I wish to go on, not to settle down in that dismal puddle." As the Phony War continued, Woolf traveled back and forth in time, finding that she automatically recalled her life through the houses in which she had lived: from 37 Mecklenburgh Square to her first Bloomsbury residence at 46 Gordon Square, and further back to her childhood homes: Talland House in St. Ives, and 22 Hyde Park Gate. Writing about herself, with no responsibility to anyone else, she thought, would absolve her from the sense of duty she felt with *Roger Fry*, and allow her to write a form of biography more akin in sensibility to fiction: something fragmentary, resisting form or plot, focusing not on an outward chain of events, but—like her novels—on an inner life.

Woolf had always been fascinated by autobiography, and enthusiastically encouraged her friends to write their own. (It was her encouragement that led to Jane Harrison publishing her *Reminiscences* with the Hogarth Press.) In part, this was down to Woolf's endless interest in stories and characters, but more than that, she considered autobiography a potent weapon for women's freedom. She had noted in *A Room of One's Own* that "until very recently, women in literature were the creation of men," but are now—citing as an example "Jane Harrison's books on Greek archaeology"—beginning to "write of women as women have never been written of before." Like H. D., Woolf saw autobiographical writing as a means of countering the narratives so often imposed on women's lives from outside. "I was thinking the other night that there's never been a womans autobiography," she wrote to Ethel Smyth. "Nothing to compare with Rousseau. Chastity and modesty I suppose have been the reason. Now why shouldnt you be not only the first woman to write an opera, but equally the first to tell the truths about herself?" When Smyth began her memoir, in July 1940, Woolf wrote to congratulate her: "Lord how I envy you, compared with my tethered and literal rubbish-heap grubbing in RF, this complete and free handed and profound revelation." Woolf never finished "A Sketch of the Past"—she threw away scraps of notes in fits of efficiency when she was concentrating on *Roger Fry*, and recovered them sheepishly from the dustbin when the urge to procrastinate took over again. She wrote in concentrated bursts of ten minutes at a time, with Roger set aside, thinking guiltily that "this is bosh & stuffing compared with the reality of reading say Tawney." But the project set Woolf thinking in new and productive ways about speech and freedom, and the difficulties of expressing life through language; "A Sketch of the Past" is a nuanced exploration of war and of childhood, but more than that, of life lived under oppression of any kind.

As soon as she began thinking back over her past, Woolf was overwhelmed by the flood of memories: it was immediately clear to her that a linear narrative, such as she had attempted with Fry, would not work. She could not present herself authoritatively, as if her past self remained "miraculously sealed as in a magic tank"; she knew that her childhood memories were partial, and that the significance she ascribed to certain events—such as an intense sense of shame she felt at looking into a mirror—might be false projections. (She connected this tentatively with the sexual abuse she experienced from her half brother, but admitted "I do not suppose that I have got at the truth.") In 1939, she had been "gulping up" Freud—who had been exiled from Vienna in 1938 and ended his life in Hampstead, where both H. D. and Woolf had visited him—and was particularly intrigued by his idea that the self splits as a response to trauma, resulting in multiple possible lives for a biographer to pursue. As she worked, her concentration occasionally interrupted by the noise of strawberry-sellers and organ-grinders wafting up from the square below, Woolf lit upon a form which allowed her to be impressionistic, authentic, and self-aware: she decided to interweave vignettes of the past with diary-like entries on the present, acknowledging—as H. D. also knew—that memoir does not merely preserve history but also shapes it. In a discarded draft, she noted that she wrote "to rescue a real moment from this unreal chaos." But the threat of a world overrun by fascism now lent Woolf a fresh perspective on her strict Victorian childhood under the aegis of her "tyrannical" father, a period with which she had spent her whole life coming to terms.

It's not surprising that, in 1939–40, Woolf was writing again about the way women's lives are shaped and curtailed by social expectations. At the outbreak of the Second World War, the vision of heroic masculinity familiar from propaganda two decades earlier returned to popular discourse, as if the advances in women's position during the interwar period had never happened. Katharine Burdekin's 1937 dystopian novel *Swastika Night* describes a future society ruled by the descendants of Hitler's Nazis where women are considered a subspecies and kept, in pens, solely for the purpose of reproduction: in 1940, the book was reissued by Victor Gollancz's popular Left Book Club, and copies were sold with a note informing readers that this horrific vision of male supremacy was intended to be symbolic, not prophetic. Woolf had long been aware of how significant a threat Nazi rule posed to women's autonomy. Over the 1930s, as she worked on *Three Guineas* and *The Years*, she had assembled a scrapbook of newspaper cuttings revealing Hitler's deplorable attitudes toward women, as well as his hatred of Jews—his idealization of marriage, his anxiety about falling birth rates, his punitive legislation against women's education and work. In *Three Guineas*, written on the verge of war, Woolf denounced the way fascism sought to return society to the Victorian model of public and private spheres, and urged women to challenge this vision by writing: now, she wrote that she was "convinced that it is our duty to catch Hitler in his home haunts and prod him if even with only the end of an old inky pen."

"More and more I come to loathe any dominion of one over another; any leadership, any imposition of the will," Woolf had written in her diary shortly after the end of the First World War. In May 1935, as a second conflict loomed, she and Leonard had visited Germany (Virginia took with her Lawrence's *Aaron's Rod*, which she was reading in the car as they crossed the border from Holland) and had seen firsthand the adoring crowds waving banners and waiting for a glimpse of their Führer. She had reflected on the dangers of exactly the sort of herd mentality that Jane Harrison had denounced in 1914, by which an uncritical community blindly follows a leader bent on destruction. Now, in the midst of war, she remained firm in her belief that the enemy was not Germany but militarism in general, an authoritarian ideology that constrains men and women alike. In an essay called "Thoughts on Peace in an Air-Raid," written from Mecklenburgh Square in August 1940 for an American feminist symposium, Woolf defined "Hitlerism" as a societal problem made manifest: "the desire for aggression; the desire to dominate and enslave," which turned men and women into enemies. The war would be won not by defeating the Germans, she wrote, but by destroying "aggressiveness, tyranny, insane love of power"—all qualities which diminish women in the home as much as in politics. In Mecklenburgh Square, recalling Hyde Park Gate, she began to reflect further on how patriarchal authority, on a domestic level, had deeply affected her own life. "A Sketch of the Past" is a personal history, yet also—like *Three Guineas*—a critique of social structures, an exploration of the way "public and private tyrannies" are inextricably connected. And her chosen form makes this connection manifest. In deciding to blend a record of the present war with recollections of her own past, Woolf was drawing a radical parallel between the personal and the political.

As Woolf recalled her earliest childhood, the images which swam to the surface of her mind were moments of burning emotion, often little more than the deep impression of a color, a sound, a chink of light. She called these "moments of being," which punctuate the "non-being" that is the vast majority of unremembered life. But these hazy visions, strangely timeless and often located in nature, soon faded in Woolf's mind as her memories became more distinct: she began to consider that these represented a brief time before social forces began to shape her. In 1895, when Virginia was thirteen, her mother Julia had died from rheumatic fever, a tragedy followed two years later by the death of another mother-figure to Virginia and Vanessa, their half sister Stella. Having to conform to the expectations of a mourning daughter was Virginia's first experience of a disconnect between her inner and outer self: she and her siblings had to "act parts that we did not feel; to fumble for words that we did not know," while their memories of their mother faded. Now, under the strict eye of her father, "the pressures of Victorian society" weighed upon Virginia: her behavior was governed by a strict set of precepts which dictated what she wore, how her day was divided, which rooms she spent time in, what ambitions she might hold. No longer was Virginia simply a person, receiving impressions of the world as they came to her: she was becoming a woman, and learning her place.

Woolf had remained obsessed by her mother's memory until she wrote *To the Lighthouse:* "I suppose," she now concluded, "that I did for myself what psycho-analysts do for their patients. I expressed some very long felt and deeply felt emotion. And in expressing it I explained it and then laid it to rest." But for years after that she found herself at odd moments arguing in her mind with her father, who had died in 1904. When in 1939 she began to read Freud, she instantly understood "that this violently disturbing conflict of love and hate is a common feeling; and is called ambivalence." The discovery unlocked a surge of emotion. Just as Freud's provocation had shed new light on H. D.'s vulnerability to male influence, his work now convinced Woolf that she needed to confront her father through writing, and in the process to puncture the authority he still somehow held over her. It was not the first time that she had written about him: Woolf's first experience of biography had been a dutiful daughterly contribution to her cousin-by-marriage Frederic Maitland's 1906 *The Life and Letters of Leslie Stephen*, an example of the solemn Victorian panegyric that Woolf came to mistrust. That early work was a flowery portrait of her father, emphasizing his public work as editor of the *Dictionary of National Biography* and historian of unitarian philosophers—research which Stephen himself, not imagining his daughter might have other plans, had once suggested Virginia might continue after his death. Stella's husband, Jack Hills, had warned Virginia, at that time, not to publish "anything too intimate"; like the austere George Frederic Watts portrait of her father that hung at Hyde Park Gate—exactly the sort of old-fashioned art the post-Impressionists railed against—this first biography displayed Stephen in a single pose, as a perfect example of an eminent Victorian gentleman.

But in "A Sketch of the Past," Woolf began to construct a modern portrait, focusing on her father's domestic life, and the effects on his daughters of his "violent temper." Maitland had delicately sidestepped Leslie's rages by referring obliquely to his "pretty shower of coloured sparks"—but Woolf writes, much more frankly, of the "tyrannical" self-absorption he displayed at home after Julia's death, which made Virginia feel "like being shut up in the same cage with a wild beast." Had he lived to old age, she wrote, "his life would have entirely ended mine. What would have happened? No writing, no books;—inconceivable." Woolf had written before, in sketches for the Memoir Club, about the "Greek slave years" that followed her mother's death, when her socially ambitious half brothers ("who had so innate a respect for the conventions and respectabilities") dragged her and Vanessa to endless society parties in an attempt to find them sophisticated matches, while she sat in a corner and refused to engage in polite conversation. Their escape to Bloomsbury, where they no longer had to perform as "young ladies" but could begin to remake themselves as they desired, was—she now wrote—an essential act of rebellion. A new life, in a new house, had given Woolf the confidence to start to write: decades later, she found that in addressing her father she could shake off that "tremendous encumbrance of appearance and behaviour" that her upbringing had instilled within her.

Woolf's major project across her fiction, as well as in her political writing, was to break down these conventions and offer new ways of expressing the self. In her fiction, she had always been interested in the effects on people when their own desires—to paint, to work, to marry—conflict with what society expects; her own life had been a process of unlearning the rules of Victorian society that were supposed to have dictated her future. She decided that her memoir would interrogate the "invisible presences"—gender, public opinion, social status, other people, and what they "say and think"—which work on one subconsciously from outside, pulling one in different directions and creating a gap between one's outer presentation (which Woolf called "the fictitious VW whom I carry like a mask about the world") and the private self. "One's life," wrote Woolf in "A Sketch of the Past," "is not con-

Virginia Woolf in the garden at Monk's House, 1926.

fined to one's body and what one says or does; one is living all the time
in relation to certain background rods or conceptions." Woolf's memoir is a call for a world where women are free to invent themselves, not

forced to follow the preassigned roles and cultural scripts which impose a certain form on their lives. She never finished the project, and it's not certain whether she would have intended it for publication. (The surviving manuscript, of around eighty pages, was published posthumously in 1976.) But this private writing entertained and comforted her during this difficult year in Mecklenburgh Square. Not only did it provide her with a "fidget ground" amid the external tension; it also let Woolf feel that, finally, she was following her own exhortation in *A Room of One's Own* to "kill the angel in the house" and describe, openly, "the passions which it was unfitting for her as a woman to say." Her post-Impressionist autobiography is itself a form of resistance, a way of writing the self which privileges the private, inner world where, throughout time, women's lives have been lived.

The winter of 1939–40 was one of the coldest on record; the electricity at Monk's House failed and the Woolfs had to cook on the open fire, sleep in mufflers, and go without baths, as the pipes were iced up. "I'm using this frozen pause to confront a long last grind at RF," Virginia wrote to Ethel Smyth. "Then it'll be done, but goodness knows when. The family has to pass it. Endless objections I foresee." On February 9, 1940 she wrote that, "though of course I shall get the black shivers when I reread let alone submit to Nessa & Margery, I can't help thinking I've caught a good deal of that iridescent man in my oh so labourious butterfly net." Two days later, she felt that "the authentic glow of finishing a book is on me," and that week completed *Roger Fry* at Mecklenburgh Square. John Lehmann recalled that from that point on Woolf was transformed: "radiant and buoyant, full of teasing malice and the keenest interest in what her friends were doing, and finding a startling new beauty in London—the squares and side-streets in the black-out on a clear night."

Leonard read the manuscript while Virginia was in bed with influenza, and when she emerged he hauled her to the meadows for a "very severe lecture," protesting that the book felt dull and dead. Knowing Virginia's vulnerability, his decision to be so honest with his criticism shows how seriously he took his responsibilities as his wife's publisher, determined to set feeling aside as he pushed Virginia to do her best work. And Virginia was surprised to find herself not upset but impressed by his passion: "so definite, so emphatic, that I felt convinced: I mean of failure; save for one odd gleam, that he was himself on the wrong tack, & persisting for some deep reason—dissympathy with R.? Lack of interest in personality?" But then Vanessa sent a note: "I'm crying can't thank you," before coming to tea and forbidding her sister to change a word. Margery Fry also approved the book, writing "it's him . . . unbounded admiration," though she also sent "some 100 corrections; all to be entered; some to be contrived," which infuriated Virginia: "all the detail that seems to the non-writer so easy ('just to add this about Joan &c') & to me is torture." On June 10, 1940, she sent off the corrected page proofs, delighted to be "free" of the book and satisfied "to have given Nessa back her Roger." She wrote in her diary that she was "rather proud of having done a solid work." But she looked forward to writing once more "entirely to please myself."

After the book was published, Woolf received a disgruntled letter from Vita's son Benedict Nicolson. Nicolson told her that he was struck, on reading the biography, by the "fools paradise" in which Roger and his friends had lived, and suggested that Fry had "shut himself out from all disagreeable actualities and allowed the spirit of Nazism to grow without taking any steps to check it." Woolf, her loyalty stirred, rejected Nicolson's observation in strong terms. Fry's mission, she sharply reminded him, had been to encourage more people, from all walks of life, to enjoy art, bringing to their appreciation not expert knowledge but an open mind. She had always admired Fry's belief that art was important not for its value or its historical context but for the empathy it could inspire; wasn't teaching others to see, think, and feel, she argued, "the best way of checking Nazism?" In her biography, she had emphasized Fry's forbearance during the First World War, and his determination to make his Omega Workshops "a centre in which some kind of civilised society might find a lodging," employing conscientious objectors, producing pacifist plays, and holding concerts in aid of Belgian refugees. Fry's studio, wrote Woolf, was "an arsenal where he forged the only weapons that are effective in the fight against the enemy": free thought and open expression. If they should both survive this war, she asked, would Nicolson give up his job as an art critic and take to politics? "I," she added, "shall be too old to do anything but write."

Nicolson was part of a generation, alongside John Lehmann, Julian Bell, and the new Hogarth poets, who consciously distinguished themselves from their elders by the urgency of their engagement with the chaos around them, and their determination to act on their principles, not simply write about them. Woolf followed their work with interest, and was broadly supportive of their ideas, though bristled somewhat at the implication that she and her friends were now the old guard, perceived as out of touch and faintly embarrassing. When Nicolson wrote back to insist that his quarrel was not with art but with Bloomsbury's elitism and listless detachment from real-world concerns, Woolf objected vehemently. Following a calculated jibe at Nicolson's own academic career at Eton and Oxford, she reminded him of her work with the People's Suffrage Federation, teaching literature to working-class students at Morley College, and chairing the Richmond branch of the pacifist Co-operative Women's Guild, as well as publishing books with Hogarth and doing her best "to make them reach a far wider circle than a little private circle of exquisite and cultivated people." "Leonard too is Bloomsbury," she wrote, her indignation fueling a spate of rhetorical flourishes. "He has spent half his life in writing books like *International Government*, like the *Barbarians at the Gate*, like *Empire and Commerce*, to prevent the growth of Nazism; and to create a League of Nations. Maynard Keynes is Bloomsbury. He wrote the *Consequences of the Peace*. Lytton Strachey was Bloomsbury. His books had a very large circulation and certainly influenced a wider circle than any small group. Duncan has made a living ever since he was a boy by painting. These are facts about Bloomsbury and they do seem to me to prove that they have done their very best to make humanity in the mass appreciate what they knew and saw."

But this accusation of a lack of class consciousness stung Woolf more deeply than her critics might have expected. It was not the first time she had been chastised for failing adequately to interrogate systemic injustice. In his editorial to the February 1940 issue of *Horizon*, Cyril Connolly had attacked Woolf, Joyce, and Proust as "ivory tower-dwellers," claiming that recent Marxist criticism of their work had "set fire to a lot of rotten timber." Throughout this year, she exchanged letters with a Huddersfield millworker named Agnes Smith, who had read *Three Guineas* and wrote to complain that Woolf seemed to "consider working women and the daughters of educated men as a race apart." Woolf's replies haven't survived, but she evidently responded to Smith's challenges seriously, and the pair corresponded for some time on friendly terms; when Smith pointed out that she might herself have written *Three Guineas* had she received access to books, stimulating conversation, and economic freedom, Woolf urged Smith to publish her autobiography with the Hogarth Press. At one point Smith suggested Virginia might like to swap houses for a week, chuckling at the prospect of luxuriating at Monk's House or Mecklenburgh Square while Mrs. Woolf shivered in her tiny kitchen. Woolf had always believed that art was inherently political, but was now forced to confront the uncomfortable truth that her way of life was undeniably the product of inherited privilege, and not necessarily compatible with a commitment to class solidarity.

She picked up these themes in her lecture "The Leaning Tower," delivered to the Workers' Educational Association at Brighton on April 27, 1940 and subsequently published in *New Writing*. There, she praised the new generation of writers working "under the influence of change, under the threat of war" for their commitment to a widening perspective. Insisting that "the novel of a classless and towerless world should be a better novel than the old novel," she ended her lecture with a call for "a stronger, more varied literature," a tribute to public libraries, and a demand for a system of free national education, to ensure that in the future literature may be open to all, not just "a small class of well-to-do men who have only a pinch, a thimbleful of experience to give us." "Let us trespass at once," she declared, including herself—somewhat tactlessly—in the realm of the excluded. "Litera-

ture is no one's private ground; literature is common ground. It is not
cut up into nations; there are no wars there. Let us trespass freely and
fearlessly and find our own way for ourselves. It is thus that English
literature will survive this war and cross the gulf—if commoners and
outsiders like ourselves make that country our own country, if we teach
ourselves how to read and write, how to preserve, and how to create."
It was a stirring speech. But Woolf left Brighton anxious that the audience had not enjoyed it, that "it was hopeless for me to tell people who
had been taken away from school at the age of 14 that they must read
Shakespeare." All the same, she remained convinced, as Fry had been,
that the participation in the arts by people from all classes was essential
for the survival of society. That belief—that this generation needed to
lay the groundwork for a new and more equal order in Europe after
the war—would be central to the projects to which she now turned her
mind.

In Sussex, life continued much as ever before. Out on the Downs,
Virginia "lay under a cornstalk & looked at the empty land & the
pinkish clouds in a perfect blue summer afternoon sky. Not a sound.
Workmen discussing war on the road—one for it, one against. So to
bowls." Leonard made a rock garden, planted violets under the apple
tree, and attempted to resuscitate hedgehogs drowned in the lily
pond; Virginia ate homemade bread (her culinary specialty) with yellow butter sent in the post from Vita at Sissinghurst, and tried to cook
without saucepans, since Leonard had donated all theirs to make airplanes. Throughout these months Woolf experienced a disconcerting—
almost "treasonable"—feeling of private contentment amid the
desolation elsewhere. "Its so hot and sunny on our little island—L
gardening, playing bowls, cooking our dinner: and outside such a
waste of gloom," she wrote to Vita. She contrasted herself with her
brother-in-law Clive Bell, who had glumly admitted he could hardly
bear to live through the war: "We privately are so content. Bliss day
after day . . . No feeling of patriotism."

But this contentment, to Woolf's dismay, was limited to the time she spent in Sussex. "This diary might be divided into London diary & country. I think there is a division," she wrote in February 1940. Her frantic long weekends in Mecklenburgh Square, packed with business and social engagements, were increasingly stressful: she found that she needed the "protected shell" of Monk's House in order to get serious writing done, and that the "incessant interruption" of visits to London was leaving her mind "in a torn state." "You never escape the war in London," she wrote in her diary, finding that she could barely remember the city in peace. In a sketch titled "London in War," she commented on the eeriness and disorientation of living in the city under siege: "Everybody is feeling the same thing: therefore no one is feeling anything in particular. The individual is merged in the mob." In Rodmell, conversely, she found she appreciated the comforting routine of the village, where "everyone does the same thing at the same hour." As she wrote her memoirs, she lovingly recalled the excitement of first moving to Bloomsbury, and the thrill of those days in Gordon or Brunswick or Tavistock squares, where houses were open and crowded with friends, the telephone constantly ringing, everyone brimming with radical ideas and possibilities. Now, walking the streets was a continual danger, maintaining the house a draining responsibility, the city ruled by an atmosphere of silence and suspicion. London, she wrote, "has become merely a congeries of houses lived in by people who work. There is no society, no luxury no splendour no gadding & flitting. All is serious & concentrated. It is as if the song had stopped—the melody, the necessary the voluntary. Odd if this should be the end of town life."

The undercurrent to her recollections of happier times was her ongoing discomfort in Mecklenburgh Square, where the physical threat of destruction was mirrored by Woolf's gnawing sense of disassociation from her old friends and her past. She wrote that "no friends write or ring up"; a "skeleton" meeting of the Memoir Club, held at Vanessa's home, Charleston, that summer, was sparsely attended, while Woolf anxiously wound herself up to believe her friendship with Elizabeth Bowen was over when Bowen failed to reply instantly to a note. Whether as a symptom or a result of the tension Woolf felt in her new house, she found it difficult to concentrate there on her main projects.

She mused in a notebook that she could only remember her past when the present "runs so smoothly that it is like the sliding surface of a deep river," so that one "sees through the surface to the depths." The disturbance of leaving Tavistock Square for Mecklenburgh, combined with the shift of her main home from London to Rodmell, left her anxious that she would never be able to focus her memory for long enough to complete her memoirs. "For this reason—that it destroys the fullness of life—any break—like that of house moving—causes me extreme distress; it breaks; it shallows; it turns the depth into hard thin splinters. As I say to L: 'What's there real about this? Shall we ever live a real life again?' 'At Monk's House,' he says."

In contrast, the Sussex landscape seemed to signal resistance by its stubborn refusal to change. Smoking on the terrace while the owls hooted from the trees, or walking over the frosty marshes in her nightgown at sunrise, habitation suggested only by the lights in occasional windows, Woolf reflected that all was "silent, as if offered from another world. No birds, no carts, men shooting. This specimen against the war. This heartless & perfect beauty." Elizabeth Bowen, who visited Monk's House in June 1940, wrote to Virginia that "I don't think I'd ever imagined a place or people in which or with whom one felt so perfectly happy." In Rodmell, Woolf felt free and peaceful, able to relax and almost forget the war. Partly, this state of calm was a result of their immunity from unexpected visitors. (She quarreled with her sister when Vanessa recommended that Roger Fry's former partner, Helen Anrep, should take a house in Rodmell; Virginia was furious at the encroachment on her private territory, and wrote to Ethel: "Why does this annoy me more than the war?") But it was also thanks to the privacy the Woolfs had, at Monk's House, from their domestic servants, a longstanding source of anxiety for Woolf.

Like most born into Victorian middle-class families, Woolf had always shared her homes with servants, who slept "below stairs" or in the attic, kept at the house's extremities just as they were meant to remain, silent and discreet, at the very edges of their employers' vision. As she worked on "A Sketch of the Past," Woolf recalled the maids at 22 Hyde Park Gate, and guiltily wondered, if the house had seemed to her a prison, how they had coped there. At the time, she had hardly noticed them. At Hyde Park Gate, access to space was directly related to relative power within the household: servants skulked in the "dark, insanitary" basement, while Leslie Stephen's library, known as "the brain of the house," was a large room on the top floor, where the thud of books tossed to the floor would resound in the nursery below. When Virginia and her siblings moved to Gordon Square, they were accompanied by two servants, whose presence rendered the move just about respectable to the Stephens' scandalized relations. Shortly before she moved to 38 Brunswick Square, defying all convention by sharing a house with three unmarried men, Woolf wrote breezily to Ottoline Morrell that "we are going to try all kinds of experiments"; but in the very next line, without noting any incongruity, she added that, of course, "if you have a house you must have servants." While Woolf and her friends prided themselves on rejecting conformity in their household arrangements, Sophie Farrell was still living in the basement and Maud Chart at the top of the house, cooking and cleaning for the socialists discussing sexual liberation in the living room.

But over time, Woolf became increasingly uncomfortable at the irony of arguing for women's economic and emotional liberation while her own freedom to write was contingent on the labor of lower-class dependants. She had always fought to be equal with her brothers, to renounce the shackles of conventional domesticity and make her voice heard in public—but living alongside female servants (some doting, others truculent) reminded her daily that she remained complicit in the very power structures she sought to critique. Their physical presence in her home (which was also, of course, their home, as well as their workplace) made her conscious that her freedom had limits: her responsibilities to them made her anxious, and her dependence on their labor left her feeling infantilized. Guilt mingled with anger, frustration with shame.

In her famous 1924 essay "Character in Fiction," Woolf had argued that the dawning of a new age could be seen in the changing relations between mistress and servant; in Victorian houses, servants hid quietly in their separate quarters, but in modern homes they mingled much more freely, breezing into the parlor to borrow a newspaper or ask advice about a hat. But while Woolf approved, in theory, of the barriers between classes beginning to erode, she privately hated the feeling of being watched. She regularly fantasized about living a "nomadic life" without the material trappings of household maintenance. And at Rodmell, over the 1930s, she and Leonard took practical steps to realize this vision. Throughout her life, Woolf used the royalties from her books to renovate her living spaces into environments where her work could thrive. When *A Room of One's Own* sold twenty-two thousand copies in six months, she used the proceeds to commission a new room at Monk's House, detached from the main building and accessible only from the garden. Other successes paid for new lavatories, an electric fire, a main water system, and an oil stove, a labor-saving device which to Woolf represented sublime release from domestic drudgery. "At this moment it is cooking my dinner in the glass dishes perfectly I hope," she wrote in glee, "without smell, waste, or confusion: one turns handles, there is a thermometer. And so I see myself freer, more independent—& all one's life is a struggle for freedom—able to come down here with a chop in a bag & live on my own."

The fantasy of living completely without servants never became reality—Woolf's enjoyment of cooking did not extend to cleaning—but after 1934, the Woolfs no longer had live-in servants at Monk's House. That year, they bought a small cottage in the village—next door to one they had already bought for their gardener—and advertised for a cook-housekeeper who would receive rent-free accommodation in addition to a salary. It was an expensive solution, and not one which addressed the underlying inequality of the servant system, but it made a significant difference to Woolf's state of mind. Louie Everest, who took the job, worked at the house until lunchtime (leaving the evening meal pre-prepared), and the rest of the day Woolf would bask in the quiet: "all so heavenly free & easy—L & I alone." Now that they were spending more time in Rodmell than ever before, Woolf resented returning to Mecklenburgh Square and the "terrors and constrictions" of working alongside their live-in servant Mabel, with the Hogarth staff bustling around downstairs and visitors liable to interrupt. After the stress of a visit to London, it was a joy to return to Monk's House and experience "the divine relief" of "silence alone with L . . . peace—my private peace—restored."

Woolf often complained that the countryside provided none of the excitement of London, and spoke scornfully of the "contraction" of life she felt there: "There is no echo in Rodmell—only waste air." But without the stimulus of social life, she found she could retreat into her imagination: "take a turn on the terrace, throw away my cigarette & go in to more rambling & discursive sauntering over all the countries of the mind." And the more time she spent in the country, the more she came to see that the village might, after all, provide her with subject and inspiration. "One of the charms of Rodmell is the human life," Woolf wrote in 1920. She had always remained mostly on Rodmell's outskirts, an observer rather than a participant in its community. But as the war confined her more and more to the countryside, Woolf became, somewhat awkwardly, involved in village activity. To some extent, the war had leveled class boundaries: Woolf bumped into her neighbors collecting identical rations from the local shop, participated in first-aid classes in the knowledge that the bombs would choose their victims indiscriminately, joined the committee constructing the air-raid shelter, and attended sessions in the village hall to learn how to escape from burning buildings.

Though she had been coming to the village for twenty years, Woolf had always stopped short of joining the very active local branch of the Women's Institute. This had been established in 1915 as an off-shoot of the Agricultural Organisation Society, and aimed to bring rural women together to socialize and contribute to the war effort; by 1918 it was a flourishing independent organization, with groups meeting across the country. With its motto ("For Home and Country") revealing its emphasis on domestic tradition and patriotic fervor, the WI was a very different community from the anti-nationalist Outsiders' Society Woolf imagined in *Three Guineas*. But in the summer of 1940, the branch president—the "very determined, socially minded" Mrs. Chavasse—decided that all local talent needed to be mobilized to take women's minds off the war, and deputized Woolf's neighbor Diana

Gardner to solicit her membership. Gardner was anxious about the assignment: having read and admired *Three Guineas*, she knew that Virginia Woolf "did not believe in belonging to any group or society," and doubted that the great writer would be interested in the "simple unintellectual gathering at the drafty village hall." On the doorstep, Woolf initially resisted, uncomfortable that the Rodmell WI was run by middle-class women rather than the wives of farm laborers who made up the majority of the membership. But Gardner assured Woolf that the WI was "dedicatedly democratic," and was surprised and delighted when she agreed to join.

"I can't give you all the gossip of Rodmell, because it would need a ream," Woolf wrote in May 1940 to her niece Judith Stephen. "We're acting village plays; written by the gardener's wife, and the chauffeur's wife; and acted by the other villagers." She drew the line at contributing a script herself, though she was involved in the production of plays by two other members—including a daring air-raid comedy titled "False Alarm"—which were performed in August. Woolf was bothered by these plays, which seemed to her to be conventional parodies of middle-class manners; she wished the authors would speak in their own voices. Furthermore, she was frustrated that these working-class women didn't seem fired up by social injustice, and felt distinctly uncomfortable that, rather than demanding to hold her class advantages to account, as Agnes Smith had done, they seemed to be in awe of her and meekly grateful for her presence among them.

Woolf's relationship with the WI was always ambivalent, her theoretical instinct toward class solidarity—manifested in "The Leaning Tower"—often at odds with her private sensibilities. She wrote bitterly in her diary that "My contribution to the war is the sacrifice of pleasure: I'm bored: bored & appalled by the readymade commonplaces of these plays: which they cant act unless we help." These cruel private outbursts are some of the most scathing in Woolf's diaries, and are difficult to read: her vitriol at "the minds so cheap, compared with ours, like a bad novel"; her sneering at her servant for taking "this infernal dull bore seriously"; her regret that by spending so little time in London they had "exchanged the clever for the simple." But this snobbish sense of superiority—never publicly expressed—is intermingled with shy hints of her pleasure at being included: Woolf wrote in November 1940 that the village "now has become familiar & even friendly." That month she was appointed treasurer of the WI, her election reported in the *East Sussex News*. She enjoyed exaggerating her rural credentials to her London friends, hinting at the "violent quarrels" and "incessant intrigues" of village life and claiming that she and Leonard are "thought red hot revolutionaries because the Labour Party meets in our dining room." Woolf's awareness of her hypocrisy does not excuse it. But her uneasy relationship with the WI speaks to Woolf's deep-seated anxiety about her own social position, only accentuated by the strain of maintaining parallel lives in two very different places.

She struggled with the demands of sociability now imposed on her country as well as her city life. ("The WI party tomorrow. My old dislike of the village bites at me. I envy houses alone in the fields.") Nonetheless, whether out of enthusiasm or guilt, she made the effort to petition her friends to come and speak at meetings, and personally made the arrangements for the projection of lantern slides, motoring into Lewes in search of a suitable "Epi-dia-scope." Leonard lectured on a Wednesday evening on "causes and issues of the war," Vita gave a talk on Persia to "20 old ladies in black bonnets," and Woolf's niece Angelica (who was studying acting at the London Studio Theatre) was hauled in to speak on modern drama. Virginia herself addressed a meeting, in July 1940, with a lively reminiscence of the *Dreadnought* Hoax of 1910, in which she and several friends had gone to Weymouth in disguise as an Abyssinian prince and his entourage, and received a tour of Britain's premier battleship. The security breach had leaked to the *Daily Mirror*, prompting questions in the House of Commons, to the horror of Woolf's relations. Her choice of subject was subversive in this context: this sending-up of authority and Empire sat uncomfortably within a meeting preceded by a chorus of "Jerusalem," where the rulebook stated that nothing which "might cause friction or lead to serious difference" should be discussed. But Woolf's talk emphasized the fun of the performance—rummaging through the wares of a theatrical costumier in Garrick Street, spending the day cramming from a

Swahili grammar, the fear of their mustaches blowing off in the wind or drinks dissolving their makeup. The audience was left "nearly helpless with laughter." Woolf slipped out before the celebratory tea, but was secretly pleased with the experience. "I spoke to the Women's Institute yesterday about the Dreadnought hoax," she wrote to Ethel Smyth. "And it made them laugh. Dont you think this proves, beyond a doubt, that I have a heart?"

If Woolf was not drawn to the WI for its social or creative stimulation, her involvement speaks to her increasing desire at this time to feel part of a wider community, to cross class barriers and live in accordance with the principles she had set out in "The Leaning Tower." She had long sought independence, but this didn't mean she necessarily enjoyed isolation: complete individuality, she had written in *Three Guineas*'s closing lines, "has by itself alone no meaning or importance at all. It takes on meaning only in becoming a part of the general life." Contemplating the "severance that war seems to bring," Woolf wrote in her diary that she now found solace in "the community feeling: all England thinking the same thing—this horror of war—at the same moment. Never felt it so strong before." Rodmell's landscape and social life had come to signify a welcome permanence in the midst of uncertainty; there, Woolf began to reflect on the idea of community as a potential salvation in the midst of chaos. In her diary, two years earlier, she had made a cryptic note: " 'I' rejected: 'We' substituted." In *The Waves* she had explored the idea of writing through a shared consciousness, but now—sitting between the cook and the gardener at Labour Party meetings—she began to consider how this polyphonic form could take on more political urgency. An idea for a new novel began to brew: set in an English village where war threatens, where characters stand together in a chorus, yet are absorbed by private fantasies, where amateur theatricals represent an abiding continuity of Englishness, and where airplanes circle menacingly overhead.

"Wasnt it my conscientious grind at *The Years* that killed it?" Woolf asked in September 1939, vowing to take a break from endlessly rewriting single sentences of *Roger Fry*. "I'm brain fagged & must resist the desire to tear up & cross out—must fill my mind with air & light, & walk & blanket it in fog." As she contemplated embarking on a new project, anxious about taking on the "huge burden" of a knotty narrative again after *The Years*, Woolf decided its form would need to provide an antidote to the "grind" of structuring *Roger Fry:* to be "random & tentative," and incorporate all sorts of forms including poetry and drama. She worked on this novel sporadically through 1939, and more concentratedly from May 1940, delighted to be writing "to amuse myself," and at the "relief of fiction after all that fact . . . And I feel so free from any criticism; own no authority." The resulting novel, *Between the Acts*, takes place over the course of a June day in 1939, at a family home in a "remote village in the very heart of England." The house has stood unchanged for centuries, its inhabitants existing within a reassuringly permanent natural landscape: jam is made from the apricot trees planted by a previous generation, conversation is peppered with ancient folklore and superstition, and each year the same flock of swallows returns, dancing "to the unheard rhythm of their own wild hearts." Yet tensions simmer beneath the surface. The novel's imagery is full of foreboding, the peace liable to vanish at any moment like snippets of conversation misheard or declarations tossed to the wind. The newspapers bring rumblings of Europe "bristling with guns, poised with planes," and the characters feel "the doom of sudden death hanging over us." In the house is preserved a family heirloom: a watch, its face shattered during the Battle of Waterloo and its hands frozen in time. History progresses, the book suggests, but the lessons of the past cannot be disregarded.

Vestiges of all Woolf's concerns over this difficult year thread through the novel: how far it's possible to know others, when a knowledge of the past can help equip us for the future, how a society can remain intact amid the threat of invasion from external forces, whether art can heal a fractured community and bring people together across significant divides. The village is gathered to watch a historical pageant performed by local villagers and directed by Miss La Trobe, a woman whose mysterious background, foreign name, and possible homosexuality have caused consternation among town gossips. She is an anxious leader, and the play is not a success; she stands behind a tree, cringing as her actors halt and stumble, fretting as her audience disperses during the interval, and despairing as a rainstorm engulfs the second act. But though her execution is flawed, Miss La Trobe's aims are implicitly connected with the prevailing threat of war: she is driven by an urgent need to impress on the audience their duty to take up their own parts in ensuring a peaceful future. Her vision is of a community which examines itself, and is bound together by a sense of social responsibility.

Woolf's portrayal of a village united, if only fleetingly, by a communal performance, reveals the significant, continuing influence on her thought of Jane Harrison. For Christmas 1923, Harrison had given Woolf a signed copy of her book *Ancient Art and Ritual*, in which she argued that the origins of Greek drama lie in ancient community rituals, their power derived from "the common or collective emotion" the worshippers express toward a shared symbol of devotion. The chorus of actors who form the center of a Greek play, argued Harrison, is an evolution of the ancient band of tillers who would break from sowing and plowing and dance around a sacred object—a maypole, an image of the goddess, or the pile of reaped corn—to ensure fertility for the new season, wearing masks and disguises and dancing to a single rhythm so that, "by the common excitement, they become emotionally one, a true congregation, not a collection of individuals." Over the centuries, Harrison suggested, this community ritual faded in favor of more self-conscious dramas—still performed at religious festivals, in the presence of priests, but where the action was an end in itself, divorced from its original meaning. Writing in the aftermath of the First World War—when H. D. was also focusing, in her inventive translations, on choruses and women's communities as an antidote to individual heroism—Harrison drew a poignant contrast between the old ritual dance in which "the individual was nothing, the choral band, the group, everything," and the leader-oriented tales of tragic drama and epic poetry, where warriors fight in single combat, seeking personal distinction or to avenge a personal grievance. She ended by urging a return to a communal style of art and living; only through rediscovering community values, Harrison suggested, could further wars be avoided.

Harrison's portrait of a time when art played a genuine social role in community cohesion—was political in the most literal way—was suggestive to Woolf: the idea that an instinct to create has always been connected with survival felt relevant to her, as a writer questioning her role in a world now succumbing to violence. Already, she sensed that people were disengaging from books and culture, and was unsure how her work would be received in the postwar future she could barely imagine; she became increasingly preoccupied with the part played by the public, the audience, not only in the formation of future policy, but also in the creation of works of art. From her renewed thinking about community grew another idea, which she developed over subsequent months. In 1932 she had wondered if she could count on another twenty years of writing, and had hatched a tentative plan "to go through English literature, like a string through cheese, or rather like some industrious insect, eating its way from book to book, from Chaucer to Lawrence." During 1940, while waiting for invasion and working on *Between the Acts*, Woolf was already thinking ahead to new projects: she considered an essay on women and peace, and contemplated a biography of her servant Mabel ("how profoundly succulent it wd be . . . her subterranean London life"). But while she was out blackberrying in September 1940, the idea of "a Common History book" resurfaced. The aim, she wrote in a fresh notebook, would be to explore "the effect of country upon writers": to begin in earliest England, and "to find the end of a ball of string & wind out. Let one book suggest another. Keep to time sequence. Pass from criticism to biography. Lives of people. Always follow the genuine scent—the idea of the moment. No 'periods': No text book. Read very widely. Write rather from memory."

Over the final months of her life, Woolf was consumed by research for this hybrid project of creative history, absorbed so fully that she could ignore the noise of air-raid sirens. She wanted to explore the development of the creative impulse from prehistory to the present: to pick up Harrison's suggestion that art used to be a community practice, and place "the universality of the creative instinct" at the center of her literary history. Provisionally titled *Reading at Random* or *Turning the Page*, this would be a democratic story of popular culture, its roots placed firmly in a shared oral tradition. She would show how the story of literature begins with an anonymous singer, "lifting a song or a story from other people's lips, and letting the audience join in the chorus." Woolf would look back to a time when there was no distinction between singer and audience, when culture was shared, not labeled as high or low, and literature was "no man's territory" but rather a common ground—but she would take Harrison's theory even further, using this vision of the past as a blueprint for the future "classless society" she had imagined in "The Leaning Tower."

"Of course I'm 'patriotic,' " Woolf had told Smyth in 1938, "that is English, the language, farms, dogs, people: only we must enlarge the imaginative, and take stock of the emotion." This book was to be about England, but not the martial, self-sufficient Blighty of wartime propaganda. Over the time she was writing *Between the Acts*, London's landscape changed almost daily, as preparations for air raids intensified: windows were shrouded in heavy blinds, pillar boxes were painted yellow on top with a liquid that changed color to warn of gas, and vulnerable landmarks were boarded up or removed for preservation. Woolf wrote movingly in her diary of the surreal quality of the blacked-out city, which seemed "a reversion to the middle ages with all the space & the silence of the country set in this forest of black houses": "Nature prevails. I suppose badgers & foxes wd come back if this went on, & owls & nightingales . . . A torch blinks. An old gentleman revealed. He vanishes. That red light may be a taxi or a lamppost. People grope their way to each others lairs." The end of *Between the Acts* lingers on an image of thick forests swarming with birds, recalling the prehistoric, prehuman landscape depicted at the start of G. M. Trevelyan's 1926 *History of England*. In the novel, a woman of "rather shabby but gallant old age" named Mrs. Swithin is reading a book that merges Trevelyan's text with H. G. Wells's *Outline of History*. While others peruse the newspapers and discuss the impending invasion, Mrs. Swithin is lost in an "imaginative reconstruction of the past": she spends the day "thinking of rhododendron forests in Piccadilly; when the entire continent, not then, she understood, divided by a channel, was all one." While Woolf was writing the book, the whole Ouse Valley flooded, and a lake stretched from the Woolfs' garden to Lewes in the north and Newhaven in the south, appearing to cast the landscape back to a time before the banks were built up. This haunting echo of Europe's communal past was a powerful image for Woolf, the unfractured, peaceful landscape a strong metaphor for the "whole" Miss La Trobe is seeking in her play, and a symbol of hope for a peaceful future.

Now, Woolf decided to open her new book with a passage from Trevelyan, describing early Britain as an untamed forest where hunters would listen in awe to the singing birds, and start to sing to one another as they worked. From there, her book was to form an alternative history of England focused not on "great men," battles, and politics, but on culture, women, and communities—very much in the spirit of Eileen Power's and Jane Harrison's work. It would be a critical equivalent to Miss La Trobe's pageant, in which vignettes from English history illustrate literary culture from Chaucer to the present, interspersed with two romantic farces which revolve around peacetime occupations: gossip, weddings, picnics. One guest, Colonel Mayhew, is furious at the unconventional choice of scenes. "Why leave out the British Army? What's history without the Army, eh?" he harrumphs. But Miss La Trobe's is a version of history, like Eileen Power's, which deliberately emphasizes peace and community over authority and power. Among the books Woolf read or reread that autumn (listing them in her reading notebook) was Power's *Medieval English Nunneries*; she bought a copy of *Medieval People* for 6d in December, and regretted not picking up a new cigarette holder at the same time. Not only was Woolf conjuring for readers a different sort of past, founded on the values of peace and cooperation so sorely needed in the present, but she was also placing herself in a tradition of Mecklenburgh Square women resetting the boundaries of history.

Her scheme also allowed Woolf to return to the question—which had preoccupied both Harrison and Power—of how history is constructed, and what voices it excludes. In *A Room of One's Own*, Woolf describes looking up "position of women" in Trevelyan's index and finding only a smattering of references, mostly to customs of arranged marriage, wife-beating, and the fictional heroines of Shakespeare; she wonders ironically whether a reader is to suppose women have been utterly subservient throughout time, or that they have been consistently held supreme on a pedestal. Reading his chapter headings, focused on wars and kings, she wryly questions why so little room is left for women's real activities in the events which "constitute this historian's view of the past." It was clear to Woolf, as it had been to Power and Harrison, that new historians were needed to offer a different view. "I like outsiders better," she wrote. "Insiders write a colourless English . . . They do a great service like Roman roads. But they avoid the forests & the will o the wisps." Now, just as Eileen Power had done in *Medieval People* and her sketches of medieval women's lives, Woolf sought to fill in these gaps, to follow those "unmarked tracks" which the male historians ignored, and to write, especially, of what was "left out in textbooks." "Keep a running commentary upon the External," she wrote in her notebook. Woolf sketched out a convincing trajectory in which she would follow "the progress of Anon from the hedge side to the Bankside," exploring how communal music-making ceased as class structures developed, before the invention of the printing press created an irrevocable division between poet and audience, meaning art could be consumed in the privacy of one's home. Now, poets could no longer be anonymous, but were conscious of their position in literary tradition, their work shaped by the pressures of the marketplace, the whims of patrons and all the other economic, political and social forces that come to bear on an individual within society. And as Woolf had already outlined so powerfully, these "outside influences" tended to disrupt the work of women and silence their voices. In *A Room of One's Own*, she had imagined that Shakespeare had had a gifted sister, who was thwarted in her artistic ambitions by dismissive relatives and an untimely pregnancy, while her brother was given every possible help and encouragement to allow his talents, no greater than hers, to flourish. Now, thinking back to her Judith Shakespeare, Woolf resolved that her history would not only examine "the germ of creation" but also "its thwarting: our society: interruption: conditions."

Women's work, she had argued, has always been conducted under "conditions that have nothing whatever to do with art": practical questions of whether or not they had children, money, a private space, a supportive husband, servants to help with the childcare and housework. Pondering the fragmented nature of the female tradition—the fact that "the history of England is the history of the male line, not of the female"—Woolf insisted that we cannot account for a woman's success or failure as a writer without first assessing the extent of her handicap. These were the same "invisible presences" she had written of in relation to herself in "A Sketch of the Past"; she now named them Nin, Crot, and Pully, and described them as "always at their work, tugging, obscuring, distorting." Woolf immersed herself in reading about witches, nuns, poets, actresses, servants, governesses, eager to draw these "lives of the obscure" together in an alternative portrait of society, which—like her memoir—would take into account "the immense effect of environment and suggestion upon the mind," and allow women to take center stage "without impropriety."

"Skip present day. A Chapter on the future," she wrote in her notes. Woolf told Ethel Smyth she felt like "a voracious cheese mite which has gnawed its way into a vast Stilton and is intoxicated with eating," invoking an image of her floor scattered with "mouldy dramatists" as she worked her way through English literature. "By the time I've reached Shakespeare the bombs will be falling. So I've arranged a very nice last scene: reading Shakespeare, having forgotten my gas mask, I shall fade far away, and quite forget." Her book—sure to have been artful, esoteric, and radical—was never finished, and survives only in two draft chapters and reams of notes. Yet in its conception, Woolf planned to fulfill what Miss La Trobe's pageant urged others to do: to "look back through our mothers," through the work of women historians and writers she admired, to a time when art drew communities together, in the hope that it might provide consolation and inspiration in the present crisis. "Surely it was time someone invented a new plot," one member of the audience in *Between the Acts* suggests. For Woolf, as for Harrison and Power, this "new plot" might be a world regenerated and brought together by art, which foregrounds cooperation, embraces change, follows the lead of women, and learns the lessons of the past.

The Phony War had dragged on into the first months of 1940; the continued lack of an invasion gave Woolf the sensation of "standing about in a dentist's waiting room." The smallest thrills, such as the grocer dispensing extra tea, became significant amid the "endless boredom" of waiting for attack. Rumors abounded in Rodmell that Germans were parachuting into Britain disguised as monks and nuns. In February, IRA protesters had placed bombs in phone boxes, mailbags, and dustbins, setting panic to the capital, but Hitler made no move. "The war is like desperate illness," Woolf wrote. "For a day it entirely obsesses; then the feeling faculty gives out; next day one is disembodied, in the air." That spring, the anxious limbo finally began to morph into immediate peril as Hitler began a Western European offensive, invading Norway and Denmark in April, and France, Belgium, and Holland in May. Woolf saw, to her horror, that Britain was being "led up garlanded to the altar."

On May 25, she recorded "so far the worst week in the war," during which the BBC announced the taking of Amiens and Arras. "The feeling is we're outwitted. They're agile & fearless & up to any new dodge. The French forgot to blow up Bridges. The Gs seem youthful, fresh, inventive. We plod behind." Nonetheless, she and Leonard continued their games of bowls while, as if in defiance, buttercups and sorrel sprang up in the Monk's House garden—"the very flush of the first summer." But on May 26, the British Expeditionary Force was evacuated from Dunkirk as the German army advanced to the French coast. Trains arrived in London packed full of injured soldiers, in hasty and chaotic retreat. Young men returned to Rodmell with stories of swimming out into the Channel, hoping desperately for a lifeboat, then of walking along the English coast for hours, believing the war to be lost. Wooden stakes were hammered into the fields to prevent German planes from using them as landing grounds. The country lanes were clogged with lorries bearing sandbags and cement. "So," wrote Woolf, "the Germans are nibbling at my afternoon walks."

On June 10, 1940, Mussolini declared war on Britain and France, sparking riots among Soho's Italian community. Four days earlier, Leonard and Virginia had held a despondent dinner party in Mecklenburgh Square, where Kingsley Martin predicted the invasion of Britain within five weeks. "Up till 1:30 this morning," recorded Virginia the next day, "Kingsley diffusing his soft charcoal gloom. Question of suicide seriously debated among the 4 of us—R. Macaulay the other—in the gradually darkening room. At last no light at all. This was symbolic." By June 14, Paris was occupied and Britain isolated. On July 22, the British foreign secretary, Edward Wood, rejected an offer of peace from Germany, and the prime minister, Winston Churchill (who had taken over from Chamberlain in May), announced his resolve, now that invasion was inevitable, to "fight for every inch of London, down to the last street and suburb." The first bombs fell on London on August 22; Churchill immediately ordered a retaliatory attack on Berlin, from which point London became the Luftwaffe's primary target. Vita phoned in horror to tell Virginia that bombs were falling all around Sissinghurst, in Kent: "I'm too jaded," wrote Woolf in her diary that evening, "to give the feeling—of talking to someone who might be killed at any moment." The war had infected her subconscious in a disconcerting and pernicious way, forcing her to think communally rather than as an individual: "We think of weather now as it affects invasions, as it affects raids, not as weather that we like or dislike privately."

On September 7, 1940, the Blitz began, with bombs exploding overnight at London's docks and around Woolwich, West Ham, Bermondsey, Whitechapel, and Limehouse. That night, the dome of St. Paul's could be seen from a distance to be surrounded in flames; five days later a delayed-action bomb buried itself twenty-seven feet deep under the cathedral, taking three days to dig out before being carried away in state. The city's hospitals were besieged, and the roads so pocked with craters that ambulances could hardly make their way through. Underground stations became illegal air-raid shelters; the fire brigade battled night after night, and rescue squads—composed of barely trained volunteers—attempted to restore electricity cables, gas mains, and sewage pipes while providing makeshift first aid to people being dug out from submerged buildings. London was raided on all but three nights to the end of the year, by an average of two hundred bombers each night. Five thousand seven hundred and thirty people were killed in the first month of the Blitz, and by the end of the year the toll had exceeded thirteen thousand. At night, the city was deafened by the noise of antiaircraft guns, the skies bisected by white streaks, ghostly vestiges of distant battles. Londoners grew accustomed to the drone of airplanes, the smell of cordite after an explosion, the sight of pilots gliding down from the sky in parachutes. Restaurants created improvised dormitories for stranded diners; John Lehmann and his friends went pub-crawling in the blackout, floundering through the dark streets high on adrenaline. A dustman reported finding twelve dead cats in Bloomsbury in a week, three in Mecklenburgh Square,

The Hedge-hoppers: woodcut by Diana Gardner showing planes flying over Rodmell, 1940.

and residents speculated that they were being run over in the dark, or that thieves were killing them for their fur. The Woolfs were asleep in Mecklenburgh Square during one of the earliest night raids, but decided not to go out to the shelter in the square's garden: Leonard later recalled that they "thought it better to die, if that were to be our fate, in our beds."

Sussex, on the south coast, formed the German planes' entry point into Britain: bombers sped over the garden of Monk's House so low that the Woolfs, eating lunch outside, could make out the swastikas on their tails as they passed overhead. At night, Woolf would be woken by the low drone as they flew in from the sea; she would lie awake until she heard them returning, having dropped their bombs on London. Often, one plane would hold back and circle the Ouse Valley until the fleet returned, scattering bombs on the Downs and meadows with no apparent policy. A Lewes stonemason who monitored the skies told Leonard that he and his band of spotters were convinced this was a coward afraid of flying over London; when the anomalous explosions ceased one day, they guessed that the rogue pilot had been discovered and dispatched. Once a bomb dropped so close that Woolf's pen jumped from her fingers as she was writing a letter, creating the grim symbol of an inkblot which obliterated her paragraph. Every excursion presented peril: Virginia and Leonard walked out huddled close together, "prudently deciding that 2 birds had better be killed with one stone." "Should I think of death?" she wondered, gazing at the sunset flushing the haystack fiery red. She tried to imagine the feeling of being killed by a bomb: "I've got it fairly vivid—the sensation: but cant see anything but suffocating nonentity following after . . . I said to L.: I dont want to die yet." One evening, while Virginia was writing to Ethel Smyth, she heard the sound of gunfire, and ran outside to see a German plane get shot down over the Lewes racecourse: "a scuffle; a swerve: then a plunge; & a burst of thick black smoke."

Standing behind the barrier between Doughty Street and Mecklenburgh Square on September 10, 1940, watching neighbors jump on smoldering bricks to quell the sparks, Woolf wondered what fate had befallen the inhabitants of these destroyed houses: "the casual young men & women I used to see, from my window; the flat dwellers who used to have flower pots & sit on the balcony." She was "greatly relieved" when the Hogarth secretary advised her and Leonard not to attempt to sleep in Mecklenburgh Square that night, and was mildly alarmed by the attitude of the solicitor Mr. Pritchard, who insisted on remaining at his desk in a leather coat and hat to protect himself from the cold, dust, and rain ("he watches raids from his flat roof & sleeps like a hog"). Returning by car a few days later to assess the damage, the Woolfs were caught in a raid outside Wimbledon and had to retreat to the nearest shelter, where they met a family who had been living there since being bombed out of their home, sleeping on wood shavings while the wind whistled through bullet holes in the corrugated steel. When eventually the Woolfs reached London, they convened with Lehmann at the Russell Hotel and heard the story of that night: the crash of bombs, the sight of a tree where Byron Court had been, the "great cloud of thick grey dust" and the neighbors huddled in doorways in their pajamas. It was some weeks until they could return to the house, and even then it was clear that they couldn't stay there. To her surprise, Woolf remained calm in the face of this disastrous end to her Bloomsbury life, which had begun with such promise but ended up a worry and a burden. She felt a strange "exhilaration at losing possessions—save at times I want my books & chairs & carpets & beds—How I worked to buy them—one by one—And the pictures. But to be free of Meck wd now be a relief. Almost certainly it will be destroyed—& our queer tenancy of that sunny flat over . . . I shd like to start life, in peace, almost bare—free to go anywhere."

For the first time in her life, Woolf was now without a home in London, the city which, to her, had always represented freedom. During her years living out in Richmond, Woolf had felt an exile: she tried to accustom herself to the suburbs, but would idly house-hunt on every visit back to the city, bewitched by its "tumult & riot & busyness." She loved watching the majestic ships pulling into the docks, unloading cargo from all over the world; she loved the allure of Oxford Street's shop windows, and people-watching in Bloomsbury squares, chatting inside with friends while "odd characters, sinister, strange, prowled and slunk past our windows." Woolf associated walking in London with fertile trains of thought—she often referred to "making up" phrases and scenes as she rambled through Bloomsbury or around Charing Cross—and called her visceral creative response to city-walking "street frenzy." She described the city as "reviving my fires" after days spent indoors through illness or bouts of hard work: "London itself perpetually attracts, stimulates, gives me a play & a story & a poem, without any trouble, save that of moving my legs through the streets . . . To walk alone in London is the greatest rest." London, she wrote to Ethel Smyth after the Blitz began, was "the passion of my life": even the uncomfortable tenure at Mecklenburgh Square had not dimmed her love for the city, and her belief in its healing powers. Early in the war she had written: "Odd how often I think with what is love I suppose of the City: of the walk to the Tower: that is my England; I mean, if a bomb destroyed one of those little alleys with the brass bound curtains & the river smell & the old woman reading I should feel—well, what the patriots feel."

In Rodmell in March 1940, lying awake in bed with the starlight pouring through the window, anxious about bombings and Margery Fry, Woolf tried to force herself to think of something "liberating & freshening," and chose "The river. Say the Thames at London bridge; & buying a notebook; & then walking along the Strand & letting each face give me a buffet." Her words echo her 1927 essay "Street Haunt-ing," a paean to the imaginative possibilities of the city, in which a search for a lead pencil—a means of writing—provides "an excuse for walking half across London between tea and dinner." Wandering out, feeling like "an enormous eye" giddy with the "irresponsibility which darkness and lamplight bestow," Woolf celebrates the sense of free-dom and community she feels in London, where "we shed the self our friends know us by and become part of that vast republican army of anonymous trampers, whose society is so agreeable after the solitude of one's own room." Gazing up into lighted windows, she thinks of all the lives being lived in parallel, the characters, stories, and history hidden—for now—behind closed doors. Her words are a rallying cry for the possibility of fiction, of history and biography, and by extension for the pleasure of reading.

> Into each of these lives one could penetrate a little way, far enough to give oneself the illusion that one is not tethered to a single mind but can put on briefly for a few minutes the bodies and minds of others. One could become a washer-woman, a publican, a street singer. And what greater delight and wonder can there be than to leave the straight lines of personality and deviate into the heart of the forest where live those wild beasts, our fellow men?

AFTER THE SQUARE

An incident here and there,
and rails gone (for guns)
from your (and my) old town square.
　　　　　—H. D., "The Walls Do Not Fall" (1941)

After the bombing of Mecklenburgh Square, the Woolfs found themselves suddenly "marooned" in the countryside as if on a desert island, surrounded by "the melancholy relics of our half-destroyed furniture." Petrol rationing prevented much travel, so Virginia used the exile to "cram in a little more reading," seeking to recreate the activity of London through her imagination alone. She found, to her pleasant surprise, that the enforced solitude suited her: she enjoyed gathering apples, bottling honey, and the simple routine of "breakfast, writing, walking, tea, bowls, reading, sweets, bed." Six days after the bombing, the Woolfs dismissed their London servant Mabel Haskins, who went to live with her sister in Holloway; Virginia felt buoyant at "the end of resident servants forever." "One must drop a safety curtain over ones private scene," she told Ethel Smyth; she reflected that living in one place, cut off from outside distraction, made her feel paradoxically freer than before. "By shutting down the fire curtain, I find I can live in the moment; which is good; why yield a moment to regret or envy or worry?"

The problem of 37 Mecklenburgh Square dragged on. Before a second explosion in November 1940 caved in the back of the house, John Lehmann had made arrangements to move Hogarth operations

Mecklenburgh Square (north side) after bomb damage in 1940.

to the Garden City Press at Letchworth in Hertfordshire. (This printer had also taken on the publication of the *Economic History Review*, which Eileen Power continued to edit, chasing up copy and dispatching stern reminders about unpaid subscriptions.) Meanwhile, the Woolfs brought their possessions back from London to store at Monk's House. There they lived "in the devil of a hobble and mess": crockery piled on manuscripts, and Leslie Stephen's bound editions of the classics scattered in heaps around the sitting room. "I've had to empty the whole of 37 Meck Sqre into this cottage," Virginia wrote to Ethel in December 1940. "Oh I can't go into the dreary details—how we went to London and found mushrooms sprouting on the carpets, pools standing on the chairs, and glass to the right left and then a ceiling fell." Leonard wrote to the Bedford Estate asking for a remission on the rent they were still paying on 52 Tavistock Square ("If refused, we mean to tackle the Duke, & ventilate in the papers"), and received a letter in reply saying that the matter was settled, since the house had been utterly destroyed the previous night. The news that Vanessa Bell's studio had been incinerated, with around a hundred canvases lost and "a frigidaire and a statue the only survivors," enhanced the vertiginous sense that their past was receding into oblivion. Yet Virginia felt she had "never had a better writing season." "I want to look back on these war years as years of positive something or other," she wrote, as if embarrassed at putting her own productivity before the common grief.

In November, Woolf had felt confident, even "triumphant" about *Between the Acts*. "I think its an interesting attempt in a new method . . . A richer pat, certainly fresher than that misery *The Years*," she wrote. But by February 1941, when she finished the book, she had changed her mind, and insisted to Leonard—who had read the manuscript and loved it—that it should not under any circumstances be published. They decided to offer John Lehmann the casting vote, and within days he wired to Rodmell to tell Virginia the book was an unqualified success: it possessed, he later insisted, "an unparalleled imaginative power . . . a poetry more disturbing than anything she had written before, reaching at times the extreme limits of the communicable." On March 27, Virginia replied, confessing that she still felt the book "too silly and trivial," that it had been "written in the intervals of doing Roger with my brain half asleep," and that publication must be postponed until at least the following autumn. Leonard attached a covering note to warn Lehmann that Virginia was on the verge of a nervous breakdown. By the time he received the letter, Virginia Woolf was dead.

"I never like or respect my admirers, always my detractors," Woolf wrote in her diary two months before her death. Leonard described her as suffering from "an almost pathological hypersensitiveness to criticism," which meant that the completion of a book and the approach of its publication always placed her under "a terrific mental and nervous strain": she had experienced two of her darkest episodes around the times of publishing *The Voyage Out* and *The Years*, and as she finished *Between the Acts*, the depression that had recurred at intervals throughout her life returned. Toward the end of January she had fallen into a sudden "trough of despair" which lasted almost a fortnight. With previous attacks, she and Leonard had learned that she could avoid collapse if she retreated to bed as soon as the symptoms began.

But this time there was no warning. Convinced that her condition was more serious than ever before, Leonard drove Virginia to Brighton to consult her doctor, Octavia Wilberforce, who advised complete rest: while they were discussing treatment, a German bomber whistled over the roof and crashed its cargo into the sea. The following day, Friday, March 28, 1941, Virginia spent the morning dusting with Louie Everest, then in the afternoon she walked into the River Ouse, leaving short, heartfelt notes for Vanessa and Leonard. Her letter to her husband ended, "I don't think two people could have been happier than we have been."

The news of Virginia Woolf's death shocked the nation. An obituary in the *Observer* described it as "a serious loss to English letters"; alongside the piece was published a poem "in memoriam" by Vita Sackville-West, remembering Woolf as "rich in her contradictions; rich in love." Elizabeth Bowen wrote to Leonard that "a great deal of the meaning seems to have gone out of the world." A coroner gave an interview to the press in which he suggested that Woolf's "extremely sensitive" nature had made her "much more responsive than most people to the general beastliness of things happening in this world today." Leonard, furious, wrote to the *Sunday Times* to reject this account, pointing out that while they had both been devastated by the war, the reference in Virginia's suicide note to these "terrible times" referred not to politics but to the private horror of another breakdown, and the fear that she might never be able to write again.

Accounts of Woolf often view her whole life in the light of her suicide, reading backward from those last dreadful days in search of signs of the darkness to come. But interpretations which present her as a fragile, tormented genius do not do justice to Woolf's strength, humor, imagination, and resilience. In later recollections, friends were at pains to dispel ideas that she was in any way "gloomy and querulous," and instead remembered her wit, her infectious hooting laughter, her love of jokes and gossip, her affinity with children, and her fascination with other people. The year she spent in Mecklenburgh Square, though it ended in her death, was full of activity, friendships new and old, projects, and plans. In September 1940, she had hoped for "another ten years, if Hitler doesn't drop a splinter into my machine": some years earlier she had written in her diary that "between 50 & 60 I think I shall write out some very singular books, if I live," and even two months before she died she was possessed by "a fizz of ideas." During her time in the square, her work was moving in exciting directions, expanding on the themes that had occupied her through her life as she responded to external events: it is a great loss that these books were never written.

Yet Woolf lives on. Through the 1950s and 1960s, Leonard published selections from her essays and diaries at regular intervals; the full diaries appeared in print between 1977 and 1984, edited by her nephew Quentin's wife, Anne Olivier Bell, while Vita's son Nigel Nicolson edited her letters, and Quentin himself published the first biography, authorized by Leonard, in 1972. Later readers have taken issue with his account, which played down her politics and portrayed her as a literary eccentric; subsequent scholars have read her as deeply engaged with the world, her interrogation of the self and society an important precursor to the women's liberation movement of the 1960s and 1970s and its conviction that "the personal is political." Today, Virginia Woolf is the subject of regular homage, in forms ranging from academic studies, exhibitions, and biographies to novels, television series, blockbuster films, and a ballet. And thanks to the National Trust, Monk's House remains preserved for visitors to search for clues to Woolf's character, observing the living room with its walls washed a luminous mint-green, the fireplace tiles painted by Vanessa Bell with a delicate lighthouse, balls studding the lawn as if she and Leonard had a moment ago abandoned one of their fiercely competitive games of bowls. She remains an icon, a figurehead for generations of women to "think back through."

"Oh! That this blasted war were over," wrote Eileen Power in 1939. "The boredom of it is incredible. My mind has been blown out like a candle. I am nothing but an embodied grumble, like everyone else." Power's sabbatical application for 1939–40 had been approved by the

LSE authorities in January, but was canceled in September due to the war. At the start of the new academic year, the LSE moved its activities to Peterhouse College in Cambridge, and Power left Mecklenburgh Square behind. She and Munia Postan, eager for a home to suit their modern marriage, designed a new house to be built especially for them at 2 Sylvester Road in Cambridge, where Power would live and lecture to Postan's students as well as her own, while he remained in London, working for the Ministry of Economic Warfare, which had taken over the LSE buildings.

In the middle of May 1940, Postan was sent to Moscow. Power had been braced for him to be called away on diplomatic business, but his departure—of which she learned from the evening papers—meant that she was alone when she heard the news of the Dunkirk evacuation, which was widely supposed to presage an imminent invasion of Britain. "If only you could be here and all this a nightmare," she wrote to Postan. But her letter did not reach him. On June 9, he was denied entry to Russia and made to turn back; the following day, Italy entered the war. Unable to travel home though Europe, he was forced to embark on a roundabout voyage through Turkey, Greece, and South Africa. Power spent two months waiting, with no idea if her husband was still alive or whether she would survive long enough to see him return. Under pressures hard to imagine, she wrote begging him not to return to Britain if the country was invaded, and promised that "if I emerge alive from this nightmare I shall join you whenever I can, wherever you are." If he returned to find her dead, she insisted that he must remarry and have children if he can—"the poor world will need your brains and character"—and should name any daughter "Eileen Power Postan." "Thank you my own darling," she added, "for making me as happy as a human being can be made and if I never see you again remember that no one could love you more."

Postan did return, sailing from Cape Town and arriving home at the end of July. But their long-awaited reunion was to be cut unbearably short. On August 8, 1940, while out shopping in the Oxford Street department store Bourne & Hollingsworth, Eileen Power collapsed with a heart attack, and died in an ambulance on the way to the hospital. Accompanying her will—which included bequests of jewelry and Chinese gowns to her sisters and an allowance for the education of a friend's daughter—Postan found a letter addressed to him, dated May 30, 1940. "You won't get this unless I am dead," it began, "and how much I hope that you will never get it for I don't want to be dead and I want desperately to pass the rest of my life with you." Power asked him to do two things: first, to finish his own half-written book; second, to publish the manuscript of her Ford Lectures, which she had lodged at her bank for safekeeping. The ending to her short letter recalls Virginia Woolf's last words to her husband: "No man," wrote Power, "could ever have made a woman happier than you have made me."

It is one thing for women to become successful in their own times; it is another to ensure that their work is remembered after their deaths. With the exception of Woolf, whose memory was preserved methodically, in writing about these women I've faced difficulties of burned papers and vanished correspondences, which leave odd gaps in the record or retrospectively accord undue prominence to certain periods or friendships. During her life, Power was well known as a public intellectual, her high standing exemplified by the popularity of her lectures and BBC broadcasts, her eminent position at the LSE, and the international demand for her teaching. "The loss to learning, literature, the world and her many friends is immense," wrote the historian G. M. Trevelyan to Postan in August 1940. "I know of no woman living who was her equal." But after her death, her reputation came to be overshadowed by the men who had worked with her. Power herself may have inadvertently sealed her fate when, in 1938, she decided not to apply for the chair in economic history at Cambridge that J. H. Clapham was vacating. She spoke wistfully of the honor of holding Clapham's chair, and of the benefit to women that her appointment would secure, but she was reluctant to lose the sabbatical that the LSE had promised, and to leave the stimulus of London; besides, she had earmarked Postan for the position since 1932 and knew he would be a deserving recipient. "I am perfectly delighted," she wrote when her husband was given the job. "I never thought the Committee would have the sense. I *do* feel rewarded for choosing London. The P-P household is now commodiously furnished with two chairs!"

In the decades after the Second World War, the methodology of economic history which Power and Postan had pioneered—a scientifically rigorous yet humane approach, applying economic concepts to history and making comparisons across time and place—was hailed as groundbreaking, and Postan's reputation soared. He held the senior chair in history at Cambridge until 1965, a long, illustrious career that culminated in his knighthood in 1980. Their friends from Mecklenburgh Square days—Hugh Dalton, Evan Durbin, Hugh Gaitskell— reached high-ranking positions within the Labour Party after the war, and Postan (then remarried, with two sons) lived at the center of Britain's intellectual life. In 1975, he compiled a collection of Power's essays, published as *Medieval Women*. While this brought her work briefly back to public attention, she was hailed as a women's historian and celebrated for her pioneering life rather than for her work; her interest in international questions and structural inequality in all its forms was left aside. Historians including Maxine Berg (author of an excellent biography, the first of Power to be published) and Natalie Zemon Davis have argued convincingly for her importance in the discipline of economic history, but a 2016 collection of essays subtitled "Revisiting Tawney and Postan" portrays her in passing as a mutual love interest, rather than collaborator and teacher. Since 1980, R. H. Tawney's blue plaque has adorned 21 Mecklenburgh Square; as yet, the house next door bears no memento of the decades Eileen Power worked there, sharing ideas as equals.

Hope Mirrlees spent the Second World War at Shamley Green in Surrey with her mother, aunt, and various evacuees, including T. S. Eliot, by now a close family friend, who came to stay at weekends and wrote parts of *Four Quartets* there. By this point, Mirrlees's own writing had stalled. After Jane Harrison's death, friends had written kindly to Hope, praising her devotion and forbearance. Alys Pearsall Smith was blunter: "For me, it is a very very great loss, but for you it is over-

whelming, & I don't see how you are to bear it." Hope set about organizing the funeral and subsequent memorial service at Newnham (at
which she refused to speak: "I simply *couldn't* talk about her in public").
Writing later to Jane's former pupil Jessie Stewart, Hope lamented the
obituaries she had read ("so abominably patronising & inadequate"),
and praised Jessie for her own more nuanced tribute to their shared
mentor, written for the *Cambridge Magazine:*

> The words of hers that you quote, "What things go on inside
> people that one never knows!" came as a very curious echo to
> my own thoughts. I had been thinking how curious it was that
> the greater intimacy is, the more it becomes a matter of the
> body & of the little things of the surface of life. One only talks
> about things like the soul to comparative strangers, as a sort of
> intellectual exercise, & with, perhaps, a *nuance* of showing off.
> I think whenever a thought had matured we communicated it
> to each other. But I knew nothing of the chemical processes, so
> to speak, of her mind. And whether she had any "intimations
> of immortality" I cannot possibly say—I am inclined to think
> *not.*

Jane Harrison's archive at Newnham College tells the story of
Hope's failed attempt to write her biography, which consumed her
energies for much of the rest of her life. Over thirty years, Hope corresponded sporadically with Jessie Stewart, with whom she at first
intended to collaborate, Hope covering Harrison's personal life and
Jessie providing the intellectual background. But Hope repeatedly
refused to show anyone what she'd done, and in 1943 another former
Newnham student, Victoria de Bunsen, was shocked when Hope
turned up at her house and announced she wished to "wash her hands"
of the project, admitting that she had written nothing at all. In 1959,
Stewart took matters into her own hands, and published *Jane Ellen
Harrison: A Portrait from Letters*, based largely on Harrison's letters to
Gilbert Murray. (Leonard Woolf had regretfully rejected the book for
the Hogarth Press, considering its composition "all over the place.")

Hope was dismayed that Jessie had outlined Harrison's disappointment at Francis Cornford's marriage and hinted at an unrequited love: "I am *horribly* distressed that this has been published," she remonstrated. "Jane would simply have *loathed* it." Her own refusal to finish the project, she insisted, was due to a feeling that she "*couldn't do justice* to the Life without writing about very intimate things which Jane wished forgotten." Whether that meant Harrison's feelings toward men, or their own relationship, remains unknown.

In February 1928, two months before Jane died, Hope canceled the contract for her next novel. An ample cushion of family money enabled her to stop writing completely, such that by the 1940s Anthony Powell could describe Hope as "unmarried, with Bloomsbury associations in early life, though now settled down to a less exacting intellectual condition of comfortable upper-middlebrowdom." A change in religion was also at the root of her silence. In 1929, Virginia Woolf reported rumors that Hope had "grown very fat" and "become a Roman Catholic on the sly": "It is strange to see beauty—she had something elegant & individual—go out, like a candle flame." The following year, Hope left Bloomsbury for Kensington, a move which marked her disappearance from the literary scene. In 1946, she turned down Leonard Woolf's suggestion that Hogarth reissue *Paris* (though she did consent to its republication in the *Virginia Woolf Quarterly* of 1973, but only on condition that passages referring to the Holy Communion and the Virgin Mary, which she now considered blasphemous, should be erased). She had lost touch with Mirsky—who died in a Soviet labor camp in 1939—and Remizov, who also expressed a desire to return to Russia after the war, to the dismay of other displaced writers, who saw this attitude as a betrayal. Following her mother's death in 1948, she emigrated to South Africa; after fifteen years in the Cape of Good Hope, she returned to England in 1963 and lived, surrounded by pug dogs, in Oxford, until she died on August 1, 1978, aged ninety-one. In all this time, it appeared to much of the outside world that she had vanished. When the Hogarth Press decided to reprint *Avvakum* in 1963, they couldn't trace her; nor could the BBC producers who broadcast *Lud-in-the-Mist* in February 1978, and who sheepishly admitted, when she contacted them, that they had assumed she was dead, or possibly fictional: the text was attributed to "an unknown author who wrote under the name of Hope Mirrlees."

In the 1960s and 1970s, Hope Mirrlees did complete two more collections of poetry—formal, mannered verse bearing little resemblance to *Paris*—and the first volume of a projected two-part biography of the seventeenth-century MP and antiquarian Sir Robert Bruce Cotton, which T. S. Eliot had supported her in writing. But this work, like her biography of Harrison, was never finished; nor was a proposed study of Mirrlees herself, by the academic Suzanne Henig, who visited Mirrlees toward the end of her life and promised to spearhead her literary renaissance. At first Mirrlees appeared eager to cooperate, but eventually communication faded out. There were no obituaries on her death. Recently, a popular resurgence—including Neil Gaiman's staunch advocacy of *Lud-in-the-Mist*, and the publication of her collected poems with an extensive biographical introduction by Sandeep Parmar—has returned her to critical attention; perhaps Henig's prophecy—that "*Paris* and *Lud* have earned you a very high place indeed in the history of literature in this century which is yet to be written"—will prove true.

Jane Harrison, meanwhile, has found fewer contemporary champions. Gilbert Murray astutely pointed out in 1953 that Harrison was a pioneer who "stimulated others to go past her"; the style of her books dated fast, and her discoveries came to be swallowed by subsequent, more "accurate" research, enabled by her own work. But her thinking changed history: contemporary scholars have built on the bold approaches her imagination and determination opened up. Among them is the Cambridge don and fellow Newnhamite Mary Beard, who wrote a biography of Harrison in 2000, and in whose study hangs a portrait of Harrison looking "like a benign grandmother." Harrison, writes Beard, remains "an originary and radical thinker, a permanent fixture in the history of scholarship. So crucial is she to our own understanding of why we think (about Greek culture and religion) as we do that it is hard to believe quite how *dispensable* she seemed in the decades that followed her death . . . The scorn for Harrison in the 1940s and 1950s, the faint praise that damned any interest in her as touching (but misplaced) loyalty, now seems little short of ludicrous."

In July 1939, Dorothy L. Sayers joined the Authors' Planning Committee of the Ministry of Information, to offer advice on how authors could best aid the war effort. An internal memo described her as "very difficult and loquacious," and the employment was short-lived. Instead, like many writers, she turned to practical war work, volunteering as an air-raid warden, knitting socks for trawlermen, and adopting two porcupines from London Zoo to raise money for the army. Having not published a Lord Peter Wimsey book for two years, she refused to capitulate to the fans who wrote begging for detective stories to keep their minds off the war. "It has been borne in upon me," she wrote sternly to one well-wisher, "that people are getting rather too much of the detective story attitude to life—a sort of assumption that there is a nice, neat solution for every imaginable problem. I am now spending my time telling people that real difficulties, such as sin, death and the night-bomber, can't be 'solved' like crosswords!" Nonetheless, she relented enough to produce a weekly column for the *Spectator* featuring extracts from the letters and diaries of the Wimsey family, in which Peter, Harriet, and various familiar minor characters discussed their own wartime activities. At first these served as simple, light-hearted propaganda, in the spirit of "keep calm and carry on"—characters offered helpful advice on how to drive in blackouts, the best practice in fire drills, and the educational benefits of evacuation. But by January 1940, the editor put a stop to the series, alarmed at Sayers's increasingly gloomy prognosis and her unwarranted interventions on the paper's editorial line: her bitter criticism of Chamberlain's appeasement policy, her warning at the empty rhetoric of "enduring peace and lasting settlement" ("it's far too like the 'war to end war,'" murmurs Harriet), and her condemnation of the press for its immoral propaganda and its corrupt dependence on advertisers.

After *Gaudy Night*, Sayers published only one more detective novel, *Busman's Honeymoon* (1937), which began life as a play she wrote and produced with her Somerville friend Muriel St. Clare Byrne. Its great commercial success led to a commission to stage a play at the Canterbury Cathedral Festival the following year, and Sayers—delighted at the chance to work on something she considered more serious—poured her energies into *The Zeal of Thy House*, which tells the story of the rebuilding of the cathedral in the twelfth century after a fire. Her aptitude for the dramatic form, and her ability to treat religious subjects in a matter-of-fact style, won the attention of the BBC, who were eager to give her talents a popular platform. *The Man Born to Be King*—a twelve-part drama based on the life of Jesus, from birth to resurrection—was broadcast on Sunday evenings during 1941 and 1942; it caused fierce controversy among Christian groups for allowing a human actor to portray Christ, and for its colloquial language. But Sayers was not bothered by the accusations of heresy: she wanted to remain an artist, free to imagine and critique, not be confined to evangelism or official apologia. She insisted that the human drama and emotional complexity of the Gospels would be wasted if they were read only in a spirit of reverence; she wanted people to gain from her work "the idea that religion is interesting and exciting and practical, and not just a kind of dreary and sloppy emotion about something that has nothing to do with life."

From this point, she achieved a significant reputation as a maverick religious commentator, though she turned down a doctorate in divinity offered by the Archbishop of Canterbury, eager that her secular writing should not be contaminated by association with the Church. She remained exasperated by the "bleating public" and their incessant demand for more Wimsey novels. "I wrote the Peter Wimsey books when I was young and had no money," she told one admirer. "I made some money, and then I stopped writing novels and began to write what I've always wanted to write." She began to use Wimsey when she needed him—he appeared in a tonic advertisement when she had to do repairs at Great James Street, and in another for Horlick's Malted Milk to raise money for the tour of *The Zeal of Thy House* in 1938. He would resurface at intervals just for fun, too: she would write to newspapers or cor-

respondents to correct speculation about the exact contour of the
Wimsey chin, to explain the origin of the family motto, to reveal a
Wimsey cipher hidden in a Shakespeare play, or to regale readers with
the story of a Wimsey ancestor who in the reign of Charles II "boldly
undertook the defense of a pair of Norfolk witches and triumphantly
secured their acquittal." But the Second World War gave rise to a new
passion which would occupy the rest of her writing life. On her way
down to the shelter during an air raid, she grabbed a copy of Dante's
Divine Comedy, and reading in the underground gloom was thrilled and
astonished by his stories, finding in them incongruous humor and stun-
ning emotional depth. She grew convinced that Dante's charm had
been buried beneath bad translations and misconceptions which deemed
him irrelevant to twentieth-century life, when rather his work was "as
public and universal as the Christian faith itself." From 1944, she began
to translate and annotate Dante's work for Penguin Classics. The first
volume of his *Inferno*, published in 1949, sold 50,000 copies in a few
weeks. Sayers considered the project her greatest achievement.

Sayers was always anxious not to be represented as "a detective
novelist, who in middle age has 'taken up' theology and translating
Dante and so on as a sort of irresponsible freak." She wanted to be seen
as a professional, a scholar, not a "gatecrashing outsider," and as such
was swift to emphasize her academic training, the theological preoccupations of her early poetry collections, and her university grounding
in medieval literature and the Romance tradition. "Historically, the
thing is the other way round," she insisted. "I began as a poet and
scholar, wrote detective stories in order to make a living, and have now
gone back, like a spring, to my original bent." If there's a degree of
pomposity here, it's because she had been dismissed before: she had
always taken her work absolutely seriously, but knew that women still
had to work twice as hard as men to prove their worth.

She always found public interest in her personality "intolerable,"
and was wary of her work being reduced to "personal and psychological terms": she hoped there would be no biography for fifty years after
her death, and charged her son with destroying any juvenilia or old
letters that might allow journalists and biographers to "forget the work

in vulgar gossip about the worker." She died suddenly in 1957, at her home in Witham. Only eighteen years passed before the first biography made public the existence of John Anthony, who had remained a secret even from her closest friends. In 1991, Bill White's daughter Valerie—whose mother, Beatrice, had told her about her half brother a few months after Dorothy's death—wrote to Anthony after reading James Brabazon's biography of Sayers, thinking he might like to know more about his father ("both my mother and yours agreed he was a 'charming rotter'!"). But Anthony never received her letter; he had died in 1984, at the age of sixty.

Sayers did return to Peter and Harriet. When, after a couple of short stories introduced a new generation of young Wimseys, readers wrote in to offer Peter and Harriet heartfelt advice on child-rearing, she realized that characters who commanded so much goodwill could not be entirely forsaken. And the theme she had introduced in *Gaudy Night*—whether it was possible for women to avoid a choice between emotional and intellectual fulfillment—remained at the forefront of her mind. In *Busman's Honeymoon*, Sayers had made the newlywed Peter and Harriet negotiate a delicate marital power dynamic, carefully ensuring that neither allows their affection to corrupt their integrity. Subsequently, she began to plan another detective novel, revolving around the theme of power and the way it damages relationships. *Thrones, Dominations* was abandoned, and survives only in several fragments of typescript stored at Sayers's archive at Wheaton College in Illinois, alongside a detailed diagram showing plot lines in green for Wimseys, red for murderer, and purple for victim. (In 1998, the novelist Jill Paton Walsh completed it, remaining faithful to Sayers's preliminary work.) The novel would contrast the Wimsey marriage with that of another couple, whose relationship is founded on the very inequality Harriet and Peter's sought to avoid: Laurence, a rich and distinguished man, rescued Rosamund after her father's fraud reduced her to poverty, leaving his wife in an unbearable position where "every act of love was an act of compliance." The document breaks off before we learn who resorts to murder, but it is evident that Rosamund's residual gratitude to Laurence places a death sentence on her self-respect and on their marriage. In the existing typescript, several amusing scenes see Harriet negotiating her new role as Lady Wimsey, frustrated when people assume she is going to change her name and give up writing, and furious at a visitor who expresses surprise that a whole room in their new home is given over as her study. Sayers might have moved on from detective fiction, but her feminist convictions and her belief in the importance of intellectual freedom continued undimmed to her death.

H. D. was in Switzerland when the Second World War was declared, but returned to London with Bryher, to a flat on Lowndes Square in Belgravia. Although she was appalled by fascism, and dreaded the recurrence of war, she felt a distance from this conflict that she had not experienced during the First World War. She had spent the last two decades roaming Europe, experimenting with psychoanalysis, filmmaking, and the occult, living in various complicated ménages; now that she was comfortably settled in a single place, she felt "more alive and physically stronger than for years." Walking amid the ruins of London, past bombed-out buildings filled with smoke from explosions, H. D. saw in the "orgy of destruction" an intoxicating potential for regeneration. As the bombs fell outside, H. D. sat in her room, composing at speed.

Like Virginia Woolf, H. D. looked back to her childhood as the world combusted beyond her walls. "The past is literally blasted into consciousness with the Blitz in London," she wrote, feeling herself driven inward by "that outer threat and constant reminder of death": to her home in Philadelphia, the memory of her parents and siblings, and the family's Moravian rituals. Her memoir *The Gift*, written between 1941 and 1943, is a celebration of survival and creativity, and of the artistic inheritance passed down by her grandmother, whom H. D. believed to possess second sight. At the same time, she was transforming the figure of her grandmother into an enigmatic prophet (much like one of Jane Harrison's mother-goddesses) who appears in *Trilogy*, a dreamlike modern epic and a poetic manifesto for "new-world reconstruction" which she worked on throughout the Second

World War. In the poem, H. D. posits language as a healing force, bearing within it the possibility for survival and rebirth, and the female poet-speaker as a potential savior of civilization. Her vision recalls Woolf's argument from *Three Guineas*, and the prevailing message of Harrison's and Power's life works: that we need different values, different voices, different forms of knowledge, and, ultimately, different stories, which women must write in order to bring into being a peaceful future.

After a meeting in the spring of 1919 at the Hotel du Littoral in Soho, at which he refused to put his name on Perdita's birth certificate, coldly reminding her that registering the baby as his would be perjury punishable by five years' imprisonment, H. D. did not contact Richard Aldington for nearly ten years. But in February 1929, she heard rumors that Aldington and Arabella had parted after a "violent and final quarrel," that Aldington had sold all his books and begun an affair with their old friend Brigit Patmore. The news came as a shock, reigniting the trauma of their parting, but when she heard that Aldington was asking after her, she began to think of meeting him again, compelled by a strange sympathy. "It may seem odd to you," she wrote to Cournos, with whom she remained occasionally in touch, "but I would like very much to help one or the other of them . . . I know A behaved as only she could, as only R did, but they are both part of our 'youth' for what it is worth and I do want to do what I can . . . It sounds horribly Salvation Army but it is only after one has completely suffered that one can afford to feel that peculiar tenderness." That July, she and Aldington met in Paris. Instantly H. D. felt their old rapport returning; now that their marriage was unequivocally over, they were able to be close "intellectually and spiritually" as they had not been since Mecklenburgh Square days. Resuming contact with Aldington meant that the memories and loyalties of the past were "strangely embalmed" for H. D.: the friendship, she wrote to her friend the illustrator George Plank, "has done much for my 'subconscious' and left me free in other ways, to be more resilient and happy in my own way."

Over the years, H. D. had thought about requesting a divorce from Aldington, but had always been afraid that any publicity would compromise Perdita, and had been reluctant to engage with a potentially volatile Arabella. But in January 1937, she received a "thunderbolt by way of letter," in which Aldington announced that he had fallen "madly in love" with Netta, the wife of Brigit Patmore's son Michael, and wanted to be released in order to marry her. H. D. was skeptical of the relationship, sorry for Brigit, and irritated that the case made Richard look like "a sort of Byron de nos jours" and herself "a noble woman." But she agreed to the divorce, and set to recalling the final days at Mecklenburgh Square as she prepared her witness statement. "I look on it as a damn torturing form of analysis," she wrote to a friend. "It is a strange fatality that I should get my inner life clear with such excruciating pain (the analytical work), only just as I am recovering from that, to have another sort of search light turned on me . . . I suppose that is what the war did to us, took away our youth and gave us eternal youth."

The divorce case offered H. D. a chance to put down another narrative: an opportunity, as she saw it, for "a clear-up of my own inhibitions." H. D. insisted that she would not be "cross-examined and bullied" in the court proceedings, but would offer a single written statement which the judge would have to accept. Her Statement of Facts, dated June 21, 1937, is a curious document, an appendix as rife with inconsistency, artifice, and intrigue as her novels. Anxious to prevent any charge of collusion, H. D. presents herself as a victim of Aldington's brutality, alone and stunned, buffeted between men who used her for sex. The hearing took place on May 13, 1938, among nine other "discretions" in a court which reminded H. D. of an old schoolroom, with huge clocks and desks with inkwells. Afterward, H. D. was exuberant, and described it as a "charming occasion": she had, she told a friend, had to "concentrate and say 'yes' nonchalantly when the KC said, "Is it true that you found your husband and Miss Dorothy Yorke, known as Arabella, in bed together, in an air-raid?' That alone was worth more than the price of admission! . . . It did look like the bestseller run riot into film captions . . . but oddly it was all true." On Wednesday, June 22, the divorce was granted—"'divorce' from so many pasts, not just 1913–1919!" Richard and Netta married days later, and within a month Netta had given birth to Aldington's only child, Catherine.

Aldington and H. D. remained in sporadic but warm contact for the rest of their lives; in an act of supreme generosity, since she had always been furious at Aldington's treatment of H. D., Bryher supported Catherine's education, and Aldington read H. D.'s work in progress, apparently putting aside any sensitivity toward his own portrayal in it. "It's awfully good, Dooley," he wrote in 1953, having read a draft of *Bid Me to Live*, "really good, authentic and concentrated, better than the equivalent chapters in *Aaron's Rod* where Lorenzo was in one of his fits and guying us all . . . It seems to me just as well written as Virginia Woolf, much more interesting and 'human' and truly poetical." The publication of *Bid Me to Live* in 1960 brought H. D. a flurry of welcome publicity: her early works had fallen out of print, and her new releases were seldom given the attention they had commanded in the 1920s. But Aldington's magnanimity was not shared by all players in the drama. John Cournos was seventy-nine when *Bid Me to Live* was published, living alone in New York; his wife, Helen, had committed suicide the previous year, his health and career had declined, and he had resorted to selling off letters from his famous friends in order to survive. In fury at the perceived injustice of the book, he struck up a raging correspondence with Arabella, then living in a residential home in Pennsylvania. Alfred Satterthwaite, Cournos's stepson, recalled that their shared anger was "Olympian, gigantic, inflated with a sure sense of righteousness, of being in possession of the real truth which had been perverted and contorted by H. D." Arabella was resentful at her depiction as an "illiterate bunny-brained whore," while Cournos (who annotated a copy of the novel with sarcastic marginal notes) dismissed it all as "pure bitchiness." For both Cournos and Yorke, on the verge of being forgotten, the book threatened to erase their memories of an illustrious past, which had provided them with a bittersweet sense of status; their correspondence, which soon softened into friendly reminiscence, provided some small succor amid their anger at H. D.

. . .

"When I ask you to earn money and have a room of your own," wrote Woolf, "I am asking you to live in the presence of reality, an invigorating life." It takes some courage and imagination to aspire to an invigorating life, rather than a happy or a successful one; as H. D. wrote in *Bid Me to Live*, "flying in the face of convention" really means performing a tightrope act on "a very, very frail wire." All these women's lives contain periods of ambivalence, sometimes of deep unhappiness; nonetheless, in learning about each of them I have been moved by their determination to carve out new molds for living—varied, multiple, complex, sometimes dangerous, yet always founded on a commitment to personal integrity and a deep desire for knowledge. "There still remains in the minds of many thinking persons," wrote Jane Harrison in 1913, "a prejudice to the effect that only certain kinds of knowledge are appropriate to women . . . the province of women was to feel: therefore they had better not know." The women in this book were hungry for knowledge in all its forms: knowledge of history and literature, knowledge of the wider world, and self-knowledge, no less difficult to obtain. A drive to expand "the province of women" into new realms characterized all these lives, manifesting in their search for education, in their travels, their friendships, their work, and in the way they made their homes. Their pursuit of a fulfilling way to live has resounded through the twentieth century. Today, we speak about "having it all," perpetuating an unattainable ideal of achievement and fulfillment: still, women talk anxiously of how to reconcile their personal lives and careers, of the toll taken by refusing to conform to persistent narratives of how to live, echoing concerns little changed from a century ago.

In a sense, all these chapters tell the same story, that of *A Room of One's Own*, that which Woolf portrayed in her memoirs: of a struggle to be taken seriously, a move to a new place, a quest to find a way of life outside the traditional script. In many ways, the story I've told in this book has been one of community: not only between Bloomsbury women, but also between past and present, and across the wider world. None of these women is a straightforward role model by any means, yet in researching their lives I've been reminded how knowledge of the past can fortify us in the present: how finding unexpected resonances of feeling and experience, across time and place, can extend a validating sense of solidarity. In placing these lives together, I've been particularly struck by small moments which have shown how these figures, too, were quietly bolstered by the examples of other women—including, in some cases, each other. In 1920, when Woolf wrote indignantly to the *New Statesman* to refute Arnold Bennett and Desmond MacCarthy's suggestion that women were intellectually inferior to men, she invoked Jane Harrison's name as proof. Of all these connections and moments of camaraderie, one of the most satisfying is a fleeting encounter I discovered in the course of research. At Cambridge University Library, I saw that Eileen Power had Dorothy L. Sayers noted in her address book, but I couldn't imagine how their paths might have crossed. Across the Atlantic, in Sayers's archive at Wheaton College, Illinois, I found their correspondence. It seems that they were introduced at a party in Oxford, in May 1938, and struck up a conversation about the dearth of literature on Palestine under Roman rule, a subject which Sayers was researching for her play *He That Should Come*, a socially realistic depiction of the birth of Christ. Two days later, Power sent Sayers a notice of a forthcoming book which "seems to me to be exactly what you want," along with recommendations of several other histories, and enclosing her own copy of Vladimir G. Simkhovitch's *Toward the Understanding of Jesus* for Sayers to borrow. Her letter ends with a subtle recognition of like-mindedness between two women scholars: "It was such a pleasure to meet you."

On July 10, 1938, a ball was held in Mecklenburgh Square, transforming its central garden into a wonderland of "baroque fantasy." The grand facade of the east side was illuminated with floodlights and the gardens were decked with colored lanterns; an elegant marquee—built by celebrity stage designer Oliver Messel—hosted two thousand guests resplendent in black tie. Pearly Kings and Queens distributed beer and sandwiches from an antique gazebo, while guests milled around the coconut shies and dartboards, admired jugglers from the queue for the fortune-teller, and careened around the square in a fleet of hansom cabs. The party, organized by the newly established Georgian Group, was a fundraiser designed, as *The Sketch* put it, "to save one of London's most perfect squares from 'vandalism of modern business.'" Over the interwar years, London's green spaces had become increasingly endangered by a "mania for destruction"; the Duke of Bedford's vision of a luxurious and quiet residential estate had swiftly been overruled by wealthy speculators, who saw the open squares and Georgian mansions as ripe for replacement by luxury flats and business premises. In 1926, residents and well-wishers had narrowly shot down a proposal to transfer Covent Garden Market to the fields owned by the Foundling Hospital—which had moved that year to Berkhamsted—and to absorb the gardens of Mecklenburgh and Brunswick Squares into a bustling commercial center. In the wake of this controversy, the Royal Commission on London Squares had been created "to secure these gardens and squares as permanent sources of sunlight and fresh air for the population." Yet Mecklenburgh Square remained in danger.

In 1930, three houses on the south side of the square were converted to form London House, a hall of residence for visitors from the Commonwealth studying at London universities. Founded by F. C. Goodenough, chairman of Barclays Bank, on a wave of imperial idealism inspired by Cecil Rhodes's scholarships, London House was designed to approximate an Oxford college in the heart of London. It aimed to train future leaders of the Empire and to send them back to the colonies as missionaries for British culture. Its hospitality was limited to those "of European origin" (a restriction not lifted until 1945) and to men: ironically, given Bloomsbury's historical tolerance, London House was then as closed to women and students of color as the locked college of *A Room of One's Own*.

During the 1930s, the hall extended its buildings across the square's entire south side, creating room for a library, a great hall, a spacious quadrangle, and hundreds of student rooms. Residents of Mecklenburgh Square—including Eileen Power—protested against the encroachment of this new institution on a residential area, and lamented the detrimental effect of its modern architecture on the unity of Samuel Pepys Cockerell's design. (The architect, Herbert Baker, grumpily retorted that the red bricks and flint tiles "will very soon be as dark and dingy as the houses are at present.") But after the bombs of 1940 left the square in tatters (though London House itself remained intact), the opposition began to resign themselves to its expansion. In March 1950, the Lord Mayor's National Thanksgiving Fund was launched to record the nation's gratitude to the Commonwealth for the food parcels and voluntary aid it had sent to Britain during the war, which had totaled more than £80 million: as a mark of appreciation, donations were sought toward the completion of the London House buildings, and to establish a new hall for women and married students on the north side of Mecklenburgh Square. The fund was advertised on the radio and on billboards, through concerts and exhibitions, with a golf tournament and special sales on Bond Street and Regent Street; it was inaugurated at a banquet at Guildhall, where speakers included Princess Elizabeth, Winston Churchill, and the Archbishop of Canterbury.

To the horror of local residents, donations poured in from businesses and individuals, from members of the royal family, the City of London, the Rhodes Trust, the Nuffield Foundation, and other benefactors. The London County Council served a compulsory purchase order on Mecklenburgh Square's north side, and in June 1950 planning permission was granted—by Power's friend Hugh Dalton, now Minister of Town and Country Planning—for the destruction of numbers 35 to 42 and the adaptation of the rest of the block for student accommodation. The plans caused a flurry of correspondence in the press, where the *New Statesman* gathered contributions under the heading "Death of a Square." Articles described it as "a delightful little urban unit where famous people and humble families have been living side by side for 140 years," and as "one of the finest examples of the architecture of its period that exists in Europe," with houses notable for their "quiet dignity and scholarly character." Some ten thousand families remained on the waiting list for housing in the borough of St. Pancras, yet several longstanding residents, including R. H. Tawney, were evicted to make way for the expansion of London House, which was later renamed Goodenough College. Residents and nonresidents

alike mourned the transformation of the area from an affordable residential district into a campus populated by buildings "of a pompous
and pretentious character, completely divorced from the way of life of
those forced to reside in them." As snow floated down through the
broken roofs and settled in the long-abandoned drawing rooms, troops
of construction workers arrived to rebuild Mecklenburgh Square, and
a new chapter of its history began.

On a chilly afternoon in December, I leave the British Museum and
wander through Bloomsbury toward Mecklenburgh Square. I've been
in the museum's basement examining its collection of admission
records, delighted to find an archive in which all my subjects are represented. There, laid out on my desk in their plastic folders, are their
applications for admittance to the Reading Room, their first announce-
ments of themselves as scholars. There's the neat square handwriting
of Eileen Power, who in a gesture of resolve has crossed out "General
Study" and written "Historical Research" under the heading of "Purpose"; there's Hilda Doolittle, whose 1911 application encloses "recommendation from personal friend, Mr. Ezra Pound." There's Virginia
Woolf, writing from Gordon Square the year after she arrived in
Bloomsbury, and Dorothy L. Sayers, who mentions that she hopes, in
her new home, "to find time to begin a thesis for the Degree of D. Litt:
'The Permanent Elements in Popular Heroic Fiction, with a special
study of Modern Criminological Romance.'" Only Jane Harrison's
does not survive, but a supporting note in her hand, on paper headed
with the 11 Mecklenburgh Street address, accompanies the application
of Hope Mirrlees, made in 1927 ("My object is to work at Russian and
the early Romantic Movement"). A definitive line is scrawled under
her name as Harrison signs an assurance that "in my opinion Miss
Helen Hope Mirrlees is a fit and proper person to be admitted as a
reader in the British Museum Reading Room." Another door opens;
another woman enters the old library, and looks up at the high ceiling,
hoping that one day soon young women will see it as rightfully theirs.

I walk down Great Russell Street, the golden tips of the museum railings glinting in the sunlight as I pass antiquarian bookshops, Korean pitstops, and the offices of Faber & Faber. In Bloomsbury, streets narrate their own legend as you pass through them: plaques, monuments, and faded signs hint at layers of history built up like grime on the facades of old houses. I cross the thoroughfare of Southampton Row, dodge down a tiny side street past a soot-blackened church, and walk through Queen Square to Great Ormond Street, home to Lord Peter Wimsey's policeman friend Charles Parker. As I reach Lamb's Conduit Street, I can see the celebrity photos and rickety piano in Ciao Bella through the window-display of huge panettone bedecked with tinsel, and, beyond, the welcoming lamp of the Lamb pub, where Ted Hughes and Sylvia Plath conducted early liaisons. Approaching the Woman of Samaria, still flanked by a construction site, I double-take at large billboards with triumphant illustrations of the finished building nestled within mock-ups of the present surroundings: a gleaming vision of the future where now there is empty space.

Guilford Street in 1940.

London, for all these writers, was both past and future: a place to encounter history, to observe characters, to be reminded at odd turns of their previous selves, and to forge new friendships. Walking past the Houses of Parliament, St. Paul's Cathedral, the Bank of England and the Old Bailey, the places where "our fathers and brothers have spent their lives," Woolf concluded that the city's public face represents women's exclusion, not their heritage: "though we see the same world, we see it through different eyes." Now, London is beginning to tell a different history: in 2018, a statue of Millicent Fawcett took its place outside Parliament, while Woolf herself is commemorated by a bust in the garden of Tavistock Square. But the legacy of these women lives on not only in static objects, but also in future generations' right to talk, walk, and write freely, to live invigorating lives. And though London isn't always a welcoming place for the marginalized—the lack of affordable housing and the tide of gentrification prices workers out of the center and sweeps away history and communities—there are pockets of the city where we can still recall a radical past, even if its traces now lie hidden. Mecklenburgh Square is one of these.

Today, Mecklenburgh Square is a hub for international students. The garden resounds with the noise of barbecues, tennis matches, and children playing on the slides and in the sandpit: the flower beds bloom, though since the lawns' excavation for air-raid shelters there are still corners where shrubs do not flourish. But at Goodenough College, one more hopeful reminder of the square's past survives. Researchers have established, as far as possible, exactly where Virginia Woolf's study at 37 Mecklenburgh Square would have sat within the modern building. Now, that room is given over each year to a woman student. She arrives in London, nervous or excited about what the city may offer her as she embarks on her new course of study. She crosses Mecklenburgh Square, climbs the stairs, turns the key in the door of her new home, and finds a book sitting on the desk, ready for her to turn the first page: *A Room of One's Own*.

NOTES

Abbreviations for archives referenced:

AC — Papers of Arthur Clegg of the China Campaign Committee. Marx Memorial Library.

Amherst — Aleksei and Seraphima Remizova-Dovgello Papers, Correspondence 1921–48. The Amherst Center for Russian Culture, Amherst College.

Arkansas — John Gould Fletcher Collection. University of Arkansas. MS f63.

Barnard — Dean's Correspondence Folder, BC 05:01. Barnard Archives and Special Collections, Barnard College, Columbia University.

BBC — Eileen Power contributor file. BBC Written Archives. A8573 910. RCONTI Power Eileen Talks 3 1936–40.

Beinecke — H. D. Papers. Yale Collection of American Literature, Beinecke Rare Book and Manuscript Library, Yale University. YCAL MSS 24.

Beinecke GP — George Plank Papers, Yale Collection of American Literature, Beinecke Rare Book and Manuscript Library, Yale University. YCAL MSS 28.

Beinecke JGF — John Gould Fletcher Collection. Yale Collection of American Literature, Beinecke Rare Book and Manuscript Library, Yale University. YCAL MSS 467.

Bodleian — Papers of A. J. Toynbee, Bodleian Library, University of Oxford.

Bryn Mawr — H. D. and Bryher papers. Special Collections Department, Bryn Mawr College Library. M51.

CUL — Papers of Eileen Power and Michael Postan, Cambridge University Library. MS Add 8961.

Girton — Personal Papers of Eileen Power, Girton College, University of Cambridge. GCPP Power E.

Glasgow — Dugald Sutherland MacColl Papers. University of Glasgow. MS MacColl H178.

Houghton AL — Amy Lowell correspondence, 1883–1927. Houghton Library, Harvard University. MS Lowell 19.

Houghton JC — John Cournos letters from various correspondents. Houghton Library, Harvard University. MS Eng 998.

HRC Flint — Frank Stuart Flint Collection. Harry Ransom Center, University of Austin, Texas. MS-1423.

HRC Sayers — Dorothy L. Sayers Collection. Harry Ransom Center, University of Austin, Texas. MS-3715.

Jacques Doucet — Charles du Bos Papers. Jacques Doucet Literary Library, the Sorbonne, Paris. MS 38225.

Kent State — Charles Clinch Bubb and the Clerk's Press. Special Collections Publications, Kent State University Libraries.

LSE — Eileen Power Staff File. London School of Economics.

LSE Robbins — Lionel Robbins Staff File. London School of Economics.

LSE Tawney — Tawney Vyvyan Collection. London School of Economics.

Maryland — Papers of Hope Mirrlees. Archives and Manuscripts Department, University of Maryland Libraries. 74–26.

Morris — Richard Aldington Collection. Morris Library, Southern Illinois University. 1/1/MSS 068.

Newnham — Jane Harrison Papers, Newnham College, University of Cambridge.

Newnham HM — Hope Mirrlees Papers, Newnham College, University of Cambridge.

Sussex — Monk's House Papers. University of Sussex Special Collections.

Wheaton — Dorothy L. Sayers Papers, The Marion E. Wade Center, Wheaton College, Illinois.

Prologue

3   **"three whistling"**—John Lehmann, *I Am My Brother*, pp. 80–81. The following scene is described in detail in this book, from which all quotations here are taken.

4   **A warden**—Report by Incident Officer Richard Hudson. Holborn Record Office, A/01209/2.

5   **"a great pile"**—Anne Olivier Bell (ed.), *The Diary of Virginia Woolf*, vol. 5 September 10, 1940.

5   **"rubble where"**—VW, diary, October 20, 1940.

6   **"a great mass"**—VW, diary, October 22, 1940.

In the Square

7   **"one of the few"**—VW, "London Revisited," *Times Literary Supplement*, November 9, 1916.

8   **"London is"**—T. S. Eliot to his mother, May 20, 1917. Haughton and
     Eliot (eds.), *The Letters of T. S. Eliot.*
8   **"dark, bristling heart"**—D. H. Lawrence, *Aaron's Rod*, p. 69.
8   **"how to go on"**—VW, diary, August 28, 1939.
9   **blue plaque**—It gives her dates in the square, inaccurately, as 1917–18.
10   **illustrious roster**—Mecklenburgh Square has had so many fascinating
     residents over its history that several books could be written taking in any
     combination of them. The Victorian journalist George Augustus Sala—a
     friend of Dickens and Thackeray, whose house at number 46 boasted a
     hall ceiling painted with a gold-bordered mural representing Cupid and
     Psyche—considered Mecklenburgh Square an ideal home: "one of the
     oldest and greenest of full-bottom-wigged squares in front, and a shilling
     cab fare to one's offices and one's club." The Muslim reformer Sir Syed
     Ahmed Khan is commemorated today by a blue plaque at number 21; the
     publisher John Maxwell lived at number 26 with his children and their
     stepmother, the novelist Mary Elizabeth Braddon, author of *Lady Audley's
     Secret.* The artist Ben Nicholson was born in the square, while the poet
     laureate John Masefield lived in Mecklenburgh Square during the 1930s,
     as did Graham Greene in 1938; there he wrote his books *The Confidential
     Agent* and *The Power and the Glory*, and had an affair with Dorothy Glover
     (his landlady's daughter), conducted on the Bloomsbury rooftops while
     they patroled on fire-watching duty. In August 1940, Natasha Litvin and
     Stephen Spender's relationship began after a party on Lansdowne Place:
     they went for a walk in the Mecklenburgh Square garden before sojourn-
     ing to an Italian restaurant to talk "politics and music" into the night.

     There are four women whose stories I would have especially liked to
     include in the book, but eventually decided against—partly for a lack of
     information, and partly to keep the focus on writers. Hilda Martindale
     lived at 20 Mecklenburgh Square for many years, overlapping with Eileen
     Power: a student at Royal Holloway College, in 1901 she became one of
     Britain's first female Home Office factory inspectors. She was made an
     OBE in 1918 for her work in the civil service, on the treatment of
     children and on equal pay for women workers. Helena Normanton, the
     first woman to practice as a barrister in England, lived at 22 Mecklen-
     burgh Square from 1920 to 1928. In 1918, she applied to the Middle
     Temple, but was refused; within a few hours of the passing of the Sex
     Disqualification (Removal) Act in December 1919, she reapplied,
     marching to the Temple from Mecklenburgh Square to claim her rightful
     place. She campaigned for reform to divorce laws, wrote detective novels,
     and was the first married woman in Britain to be issued a passport under
     her maiden name. Though her personal papers were all destroyed, a
     biography, written by Judith Bourne, was recently published.

Lorna Wishart was the youngest of the eight Garman siblings; she married the publisher Ernest Wishart when she was just sixteen, and later became the lover of the poet Laurie Lee. Their affair was interrupted in 1937 by the outbreak of civil war in Spain, where Lee went to fight: she sent him pound notes soaked in Chanel No. 5, and was waiting at Victoria station when he returned in February 1938. They spent the rest of the year in a flat at 35 Mecklenburgh Square—Lorna's children living with a nanny in St. John's Wood—but the period was difficult, and in later years Lee would often use "Mecklenburgh" as a synonym for "miserable." Lorna returned to her husband in November, and later left him for Lucian Freud.

Almost nothing is known about Nancy Morris, who lived at 44 Mecklenburgh Square in the 1930s, but the glimpses of her in the historical record could hardly be more intriguing. She was sister of the painter Cedric Morris, and spent the 1920s in artistic circles in Paris and London. The Bloomsbury chronicler Frances Partridge recalled Nancy's famous parties; one, held at Knole, Vita Sackville-West's country estate, had a hermaphrodite theme, whereby the women wore tuxes while the men strained under the weight of pearl necklaces. At another—perhaps in the square—"about a hundred people stood close together in a stuffy basement, shouting, bellowing rather, into each other's open mouths, and sometimes twining their arms vaguely about one or two necks at once . . . a crowd of truculent Lesbians stood by the fireplace, occasionally trying their biceps or carrying each other round the room." John Mortimer, who met Nancy in the 1940s, recalled a woman who always wore sunglasses and drank champagne; crop-headed, dressed in tweed suits and the castoffs of the Soho restaurateur Marcel Boulestin, who left her his wardrobe in his will. From 1930 she was in a relationship with Alix Strachey, the wife of Lytton's cousin James, who was one of the first psychoanalysts to practice in England and Sigmund Freud's first English translator. "I hope," wrote Alix to Eddy Sackville-West, "you will like her when you meet her, because I have become very fond of her. But she is absolutely uncultured & will remain so, I think . . . And she loves dogs. I even sometimes think she can't distinguish between them and human beings—except that she prefers them."

13   **"Why Are Women Redundant?"**—W. R. Greg, *The National Review*, April 1862.

13   **"Good God"**—EP to Margery Garrett, December 26, 1911. Girton.

14   **"sacred place"**—John Ruskin, "Of Queens' Gardens," in *Sesame and Lilies*, p. 86.

14   **"deeply depressing"**—JEH, "Scientiae Sacra Fames," *Alpha and Omega*, p. 125.

16   **"new beginning"**—Vanessa Bell, *Sketches in Pen and Ink*, p. 98.

16   **"everything was"**—VW, "Old Bloomsbury," *Moments of Being*, p. 47.

16   **"Now we are"**—VW to Violet Dickinson, June 29, 1906. Nicolson and Trautmann (eds.), *The Letters of Virginia Woolf.*

17   **"respectable mummified humbug"**—VW, diary, October 23, 1918.

17   **"think one's own"**—VW, "Leslie Stephen," *Selected Essays*, p. 114.

17   **"passed like"**—VW, "Reminiscences," *Moments of Being*, p. 4.

18   **"to be 29"**—VW to Vanessa Bell, June 8, 1911.

19   **"The room is"**—VW, "Professions for Women," *Selected Essays*, pp. 144–45.

19   **"that Godless Institution"**—Quotation attributed to Thomas Arnold.

20   **"a thought"**—VW, *A Room of One's Own*, p. 28.

20   **"having for its"**—*The Times*, August 24, 1894.

20   **"lived in squares"**—A remark attributed to Dorothy Parker.

21   **"aesthetically speaking"**—C. L. R. James, *Letters from London*, pp. 20, 52.

21   **Australian students**—Among those who chronicled their time in London are Nancy Phelan (*The Swift Foot of Time: An Australian in England*), Nina Murdoch (*Seventh Heaven*), and Louise Mack (*An Australian Girl in London*): "A Boarding-House in Bloomsbury! To some people, no doubt, these words are provocative of horror and dismay. To us they mean freedom, life, novelty, fascination, everything that makes the days worth living."

21   **"learned people"**—Paul Cohen-Portheim, *The Spirit of London*, p. 29.

21   **"Bloomsbury appears"**—Mulk Raj Anand, *Conversations in Bloomsbury*, p. 5.

21   **the Duke of Bedford**—For Bloomsbury's history see Rosemary Ashton, *Victorian Bloomsbury*, and Matthew Ingleby, *Novel Grounds*.

23   **"remote and half-discovered"**—In *Peregrine Bunce* (1842) the satirist Theodore Hook described Mecklenburgh Square as "the bleakest and most inhospitable-looking of squares, in whose road the grass grows all the year around, and where a carriage, or even a pedestrian, is seldom seen . . . this deserted, melancholy square, whose inhabitants, we should imagine, never cracked a joke in their lives." And in Thackeray's 1897 story "The Bedford Row Conspiracy," the address connotes a distinct shabbiness: an upper-class woman's family threatens to cut her off when they hear she is engaged to a young man of Mecklenburgh Square, to which they refer in outrage as "Mucklebury Square."

23   **Mecklenburgh Square**—Named for Queen Charlotte of Mecklenburg-Strelitz, the wife of King George III, and queen of Great Britain and Ireland from 1761 until her death in 1818; a pen pal of Marie Antoinette and an influential patron of the arts. Fanny Burney was one of her ladies-in-waiting.

24   **Samuel Pepys Cockerell**—For the building of Mecklenburgh Square—

and various intrigues involving renegade builders—see Donald J. Olsen, *Town Planning in London*.

24 **"exposed to insult"**—Even in the twentieth century, the location proved off-putting to potential residents. On January 7, 1915, Virginia Woolf rejected a house in Mecklenburgh Square: "a vast place, with a great hall, a sweeping staircase; & we could have a flat at the top—the only objection being that Gray's Inn Road is at the back." She looked over another house in the square but was deterred by the landlady's collections of photographs of royal families of the world; they stayed in Richmond instead.

24 **"indecent and improper"**—Donald J. Olsen, *Town Planning in London*, p. 118.

25 **"so very airy!"**—See also Jean Rhys's 1939 novel *Good Morning, Midnight*, in which Sasha takes a "little health-stroll" around Mecklenburgh Square.

25 **prominent suffragettes**—Among them were the militants Annie Kenney and Rachel Barrett, whose shared flat at 19 Mecklenburgh Square was raided several times by the police. Catherine Pine, nurse and suffragette, lived in the square and cared for four female "war babies" whom Emmeline Pankhurst adopted in 1915.

25 **"ardent but educated"**—VW to Violet Dickinson, February 27, 1910. On January 1, she had written to her Greek tutor, Janet Case: "Would it be any use if I spent an afternoon or two weekly in addressing envelopes for the Adult Suffragists? . . . You impressed me so much the other night with the wrongness of the present state of affairs that I feel that action is necessary . . . How melancholy it is that conversation isn't enough!" She immortalized her experience in *Night and Day*, where Mary Datchet volunteers in a Bloomsbury building shared by numerous relief causes, busy "disseminating their views upon the protection of native races, or the value of cereals as foodstuffs."

25 **"Reform House"**—The premises were shared by the Women's Trade Union League, the National Anti-Sweating League, the Working Women's Legal Advice Bureau, the National Federation of Women Workers (which organized strikes and demonstrations for women excluded from other unions), the Industrial Law Committee (which established an indemnity fund for the protection of women dismissed from jobs for giving evidence to government inspectors), and the People's Suffrage Federation. The top flat—often the site of lectures and fundraising concerts—belonged to the Labour MP Will Anderson and his wife Mary Reid Macarthur, a passionate campaigner for trade unions and workers' rights, who was involved in most of the building's projects. She cofounded the National Federation of Women Workers with Gertrude Tuckwell, who shared another flat in Mecklenburgh Square with Constance Smith, a fellow labor activist and factory inspector.

25 **"colony of workers"**—Gertrude Tuckwell, *Constance Smith: A Short*

Memoir, p. 29. Anderson's obituary in *The Times* described their house in Mecklenburgh Square as "a homely centre for all reformers—not, let me explain, a salon but a home."

27 **"genteel, commodious"**—*The Times*, January 16, 1822.

27 **"high-class service flatlets"**—*The Times*, October 16, 1939; November 26, 1925.

27 **"nests of"**—Thomas Burke, *Living in Bloomsbury*, p. 12.

27 **"sunk in public"**—"The Bohemian in Bloomsbury," *Saturday Review*, September 17, 1904.

27 **"the beloved"**—Emily Hobhouse, "Women Workers: How They Live, How They Wish to Live," *Nineteenth Century: a monthly review* (March 1900).

27 **violent underworld**—Mecklenburgh Square appeared several times in the crime pages of Victorian newspapers, though reportage usually set up a dichotomy between the square's respectable inhabitants and sinister external interlopers, from the servant who pawned all the family's property while they were abroad, to the bogus anchovy-seller, left to wait in the hallway while the maid fetched her master, who made away with two greatcoats.

27 **"people are always"**—DLS, "The Vindictive Story of the Footsteps that Ran," in *Lord Peter Views the Body*.

28 **"in Paddington"**—Jean Rhys, *After Leaving Mr. Mackenzie*.

28 **Bloomsbury signaled possibility**—This sense of freedom is expressed in numerous novels and stories by writers of the period. Woolf's very first short story, "Phyllis and Rosamond" (1906), describes two sisters from a well-to-do South Kensington home who feel "indigenous to the drawing-room," and are offered no education other than preparation for marriage. A visit to friends in "distant and unfashionable" Bloomsbury awakens Phyllis to the potential of reinventing herself in a different place, a different house: "The stucco fronts, the irreproachable rows of Belgravia and South Kensington seemed to Phyllis the type of her lot; of a life trained to grow in an ugly pattern to match the staid ugliness of its fellows. But if one lived here in Bloomsbury, she began to theorize, waving with her hand as her cab passed through the great tranquil squares, beneath the pale green of umbrageous trees, one might grow up as one liked." In Isabella Ford's *On the Threshold* (1895), two student friends move together into cheap Bloomsbury digs, rejecting the comforts of their parental homes in favor of a gloomy boardinghouse, which to them is like "a house in Paradise." *A Writer of Books* (1898) by "George Paston" (Emily Morse Symonds) follows Cosima Chudleigh, an aspiring writer who moves to a Bloomsbury boardinghouse to be near the British Museum; in Violet Hunt's *A Workaday Woman* (1906), the narrator Caroline feels a "sensation of unaccustomed liberty" when she goes to

Bloomsbury to visit Jehane Bruce, who "lives alone in a flat, and pays its rent and supports herself on regular journalism and occasional fiction." In C. F. Keary's 1905 novel *Bloomsbury*, May and Joyce share a room in Mecklenburgh Square itself, described as "the back of beyond," from where they attend art classes, lectures, and revolutionary meetings. In Radclyffe Hall's 1924 novel *The Unlit Lamp*, two women dream of setting up home together in one of the new Working Women's Flats in Bloomsbury ("we'd have a little flat together, and be free and very happy . . . we might be purposeful and tired and happy because we mean something"). Similarly, in Winifred Holtby's 1924 novel *The Crowded Street*, the heroine leaves her small village, where "the only thing that mattered was marriage," to live in Bloomsbury with her friend Delia, who works for "one of the most provocative and militant societies in England," and rails lucidly against "marriage as an end of life in itself, as the ultimate goal of the female soul's development."

28 **"at the centre"**—VW, "Old Bloomsbury," *Moments of Being*, p. 46.

29 **"the Baedeker"**—Bryher, *The Heart to Artemis: A Writer's Memoirs*, p. 174.

30 **"long armistice"**—Richard Aldington, *Life for Life's Sake*, p. 5.

31 **"the war will"**—H. D., *Bid Me to Live*, p. 12.

H. D.

33 **"Hitler gives bread"**—H. D., *Tribute to Freud*, p. 58.

34 **"carefully avoided"**—ibid., p. 134.

34 **"violent purple-patch"**—H. D. to Bryher, May 11, 1933. Beinecke.

34 **"seems to believe"**—H. D. to Bryher, May 18, 1933. Beinecke.

34 **"Evidently"**—H. D. to Bryher, May 13, 1933. Beinecke.

36 **"are of course"**—H. D., "H. D. by Delia Alton," p. 181.

36 **"But Dryad"**—H. D., *End to Torment*, p. 18. Aldington believed this event took place in the Fuller tea shop in Kensington and that he was present—cf. his letter to H. D., November 21, 1958. Beinecke.

37 **"It's just that"**—Interview with Hilda Doolittle by Lionel Durand, *Newsweek*, May 2, 1960.

37 **cocooned in layers**—The novel compresses the events of several months into a single time frame. The letter in which Aldington says "I love you & I desire—*l'autre*" was not sent until well after the Lawrences left Mecklenburgh Square; they were only there for six weeks, but H. D. incorporates her correspondence with Lawrence dating back to 1916.

37 **"not intended"**—H. D. to John Cournos, July 9, (c. 1921). Houghton JC.

37 **impetuous**—H. D., *Compassionate Friendship*, p. 115. H. D. wrote that she left "a bundle" of her letters from Lawrence in a suitcase in the basement of number 44, along with "great stacks" of Aldington's letters,

and the letters she had written daily to Aldington at the front, which he had sent back to her periodically for safekeeping. In 1929, Aldington admitted that he had burned them, in 1920. Zilboorg writes that his charwoman's daughter recalled Aldington asking her mother to burn the "piles and piles of papers" (Caroline Zilboorg, *Richard Aldington and H. D.: Their Lives in Letters*, p. 1).

38 **"Why was it"**—H. D., *The Gift*, p. 4.

38 **"How could I"**—ibid., p. 21.

38 **"morbid"**—H. D., *Tribute to Freud*, p. 164.

38 **"imaginative faculties"**—ibid., p. 121.

39 **"to give her"**—William Carlos Williams, *The Autobiography of William Carlos Williams*, p. 69.

40 **"I don't suppose"**—H. D. to Norman Holmes Pearson, March 12, 1950. Quoted in H. D., *Tribute to Freud*, p. xi.

40 **"You have no"**—Barbara Guest, *Herself Defined*, p. 4.

40 **"Ezra would have"**—H. D., *End to Torment*, p. 35.

40 **"initiators"**—The others (named in *Compassionate Friendship*) are Richard Aldington, John Cournos, Cecil Gray, Kenneth Macpherson, Walter Schmideberg, and Erich Heydt.

41 **"a sort of alter ego"** H. D., Autobiographical Notes. Beinecke.

41 **"like a blue flame"**—H. D., *End to Torment*, p. 8.

41 **"a dreadful little place"**—H. D., Autobiographical Notes. Beinecke.

41 the *Mona Lisa*—Eileen Power, who had recently returned from Paris, wrote to Margery Spring Rice on September 8, 1911: "Isn't it *ghastly* about Monna Lisa? I feel *so* depressed about it, that I wished I had spent all my time padlocked in front of her. Shall we ever see her again? I am convinced that someone is in love with her & has stolen her for that reason."

41 **"Arrive Sunday."**—H. D. to Ezra Pound, September 28, 1911.

41 **"Our reception"**—H. D. to Isabel Pound, December 4, 1911.

42 a short story—H. D., "The Suffragette." Beinecke.

42 **"freedom of mind"**—H. D. to Bryher, December 31, 1918. Beinecke.

42 **"I had to"**—H. D. to Bryher, June 24, 1931. Beinecke.

43 **"extreme vulnerability"**—Brigit Patmore, *My Friends When Young*, p. 65.

43 **"that infernal Bloomsbury"**—H. D., *Asphodel*, p. 62.

43 **"R. & H."**—Ezra Pound to Dorothy Shakespear, May 3, 1913. D. D. Paige (ed.), *The Selected Letters of Ezra Pound*.

44 **"Kensingtonian squabbles"**—Richard Aldington to Amy Lowell, February 1, 1915. Houghton AL.

45 **"nothing that"**—Ezra Pound to Harriet Monroe, undated (January 1915). D. D. Paige (ed.), *The Selected Letters of Ezra Pound*.

45 **"Am sending you"**—Ezra Pound to Harriet Monroe, October 1912. Ibid.

45 **"simply advertising bull-dust"**—Quoted in A. E. Barlow, "Imagism and after: a study of the poetry."

46 **"where friendly people"**—Richard Aldington, *Life for Life's Sake*, p. 140.

46 **"We want war!"**—H. D. to Richard Aldington, October 30, 1959. Beinecke.

47 **conscientious objector**—The area swiftly acquired a reputation for unpatriotic subversiveness: the *Sunday Times* called, only half-jokingly, for Mecklenburgh Square to follow the royal family and Ford Madox Hueffer (now known as Ford Madox Ford) and expunge German origins from its name. David Jones, in his 1937 poem *In Parenthesis*, takes the square as representative of elitist aloofness: "this Conchy propaganda's no bon for the troops—hope Jerry puts one on Mecklenburgh Square—instead of fussing patriotic Croydon."

48 **"black hollow"**—H. D., *Bid Me to Live*, p. 12.

48 **"cold, nun-like"**—H. D., *Tribute to Freud*, p. 116.

49 **"the affinity between"**—Quoted in Francis West, *Gilbert Murray: A Life*, p. 104.

49 **"psycho-physical"**—H. D., Notes on Euripides, Beinecke.

50 **"the child Amor"**—H. D., *Magic Mirror*, p. 55.

51 **"Don't tell me"**—Richard Aldington to F. S. Flint, May 26, 1916. HRC.

52 **"the blundering world"**—H. D. to John Gould Fletcher, undated (1917). Beinecke JGF.

52 **"a mad fanatic"**—H. D. to John Cournos, September 5, 1916. Houghton JC.

52 **"spiritual loneliness"**—H. D. to John Cournos, July 1916. Houghton JC.

52 **"My one struggle"**—H. D. to Amy Lowell, October 31, 1916. Houghton AL.

52 **"I am ready"**—H. D. to John Cournos, September 5, 1916. Houghton JC.

52 **"Hang Flo"**—Quoted in H. D. to John Cournos, September 8, 1916. Houghton JC.

53 **"H. D. has been"**—Richard Aldington to Amy Lowell, August 1916. Houghton AL.

53 **"I have all faith"**—H. D. to John Cournos, September 13, 1916. Houghton JC.

53 **"Korshoon!"**—John Cournos, *Autobiography*, p. 289.

53 **"the very core"**—H. D. to John Cournos, October 3, 1916. Houghton JC.

53 **"If love"**—H. D. to John Cournos, September 8, 1916. Houghton JC.

53 **"If it seems best"**—H. D. to John Cournos, September 5, 1916. Houghton JC.

54 **"If I die"**—Richard Aldington to John Cournos, November 2, 1916. Houghton JC.

54 **apricot-colored walls**—Brigit Patmore, *My Friends When Young*, p. 79.

54 **Alida Klemantaski**—See D. Hibberd, *Harold Monro: Poet of the New Age*.

She wrote to Monro of her annoyance at Cournos continually knocking to see if she was in, and complained that she had had to lock her door to prevent H. D. wandering in unannounced and trying to talk about poetry.

55 **"I am waiting"**—H. D. to Amy Lowell, December 21, 1916. Houghton AL.

55 **"All I want"**   H. D. to F. S. Flint, August 7, 1916. Beinecke.

55 **the *Egoist***—H. D. wrote several long essays for the magazine during her tenure, on Marianne Moore, Charlotte Mew, John Gould Fletcher and William Carlos Williams. She was also an assiduous editor of poetry: to Williams she wrote on August 14, 1916: "I trust you will not hate me for wanting to delete from your poem all the flippancies . . . I don't know what you think but I consider this business of writing a very sacred thing!"

55 **"some most poignant lyrics"**—Richard Aldington to Amy Lowell, January 2, 1918. Houghton AL.

56 **"broken spiritually"**—H. D. to John Gould Fletcher, 1917. Beinecke JGF.

56 **"imminent possibility"**—H. D., "H. D. by Delia Alton," p. 204.

56 **"any stone"**—H. D., *Bid Me to Live*, p. 16.

56 **"We came home"**—H. D. to Norman Holmes Pearson, 1937, published in Diana Collecott (ed.), *Agenda*, p. 72.

56 **"write her cheerful lies"**—Richard Aldington to Amy Lowell, December 8, 1916. Houghton AL.

56 **"For the Lord's sake"**—Richard Aldington to F. S. Flint, January 22, 1917. HRC Flint.

57 **"You really can not"**—H. D. to Charles Bubb, June 1917. Kent State.

57 **"Everyone said"**—Richard Aldington to Charles Bubb, June 29, 1917. Dean H. Keller (ed.), *Bubb Booklets*.

57 **"delightfully lazy"**—Richard Aldington to Amy Lowell, November 20, 1917. Houghton AL.

58 **"A beautiful lady"**—H. D. to F. S. Flint, August 30, 1917. Beinecke.

59 **"as he was"**—H. D., Divorce Statement. Beinecke.

60 **"stage-set"**—H. D., *Asphodel*, p. 126.

60 **"four walls"**—H. D., *Bid Me to Live*, p. 111.

61 **"The truth is"**—Richard Aldington to H. D., May 20, 1918. Beinecke.

61 **"like a person"**—Quoted in Witter Bynner, *Journey with Genius*, p. 145.

62 **"worth anything"**—D. H. Lawrence to Arthur McLeod, December 21, 1916.

62 **"Don't you think"**—D. H. Lawrence to Edward Marsh, January 29, 1917.

62 **"a blasphemy"**—D. H. Lawrence, *Kangaroo*, p. 246.

62 **"I myself"**—H. D. to John Gould Fletcher, 1917. Beinecke JGF.

62 **"very quietly"**—D. H. Lawrence to John Middleton Murry and Katherine Mansfield, March 5, 1916.

62   **Cecil Gray**—This account comes from Gray's own autobiography, *Musical Chairs;* his biography of Philip Heseltine, *Peter Warlock;* and his notebooks, edited by his daughter Pauline. Gray lives on in a variety of fictional avatars: as Cyril Scott in Lawrence's *Aaron's Rod* ("a fair, pale, flattish young fellow in pince-nez and dark clothes"), Mr. Mercaptan in Aldous Huxley's *Antic Hay* ("a sleek, comfortable young man" with "a rather gross, snouty look"), and Maclintick in Anthony Powell's *Casanova's Chinese Restaurant* (a "solidly built musical type" with the air of "a bad-tempered doctor)."

63   **"greatest literary genius"**—Barry Smith, *Peter Warlock*, p. 76.

63   **a publishing company**—This was only one of several schemes conceived by Heseltine and Gray. A concert at the Wigmore Hall in February 1917 devoted to Bernard van Dieren, whose discordant work they considered the height of modernity, was resoundingly mocked in the press; a projected four-week season of opera in a West End theatre never got off the ground.

63   **"a paradisal existence"**—Cecil Gray, *Musical Chairs*, p. 115.

63   **Bosigran Castle**—The house, called the Count House, still stands; it is now a climbers' hostel.

63   **"Remember the revolution"**—D. H. Lawrence to Cecil Gray, June 14, 1917.

63   **"hostile and unsympathetic"**—Cecil Gray, *Musical Chairs*, p. 126.

64   **"vindictive"**—ibid., p. 128.

64   **"thinks and breathes"**—D. H. Lawrence to Cecil Gray, October 17, 1917.

64   **revocation**—Lawrence did not return to Cornwall. In January 1918, he offered the lease of Higher Tregerthen to Leonard and Virginia Woolf, who had expressed interest in the cottage via their mutual friend Samuel Koteliansky. Virginia wrote in her diary on January 23, that "We're in treaty with DH Lawrence for his house at Zennor. It's very distant & improbable at present though sufficiently tempting to make me think of that sea & those cliffs several times a day." This didn't come off, though the Woolfs knew the area well, often staying with their friends Will and Ka Arnold-Forster at Eagle's Nest, on the cliff just above Lawrence's cottage.

64   **"Beyond the tall"**—D. H. Lawrence, *Aaron's Rod*, p. 70.

65   **"very handsome"**—Cynthia Asquith, diary, October 28, 1917. Asquith was sympathetic to Lawrence in his exile: "His health doesn't allow of his living in London and all the money he has in the world is the *prospect* of eighteen pounds for the publication of some poems all about bellies and breasts which he gave me to read." She offered to help him, but doubted the authorities could be persuaded: "after all, the woman *is* a German and it doesn't seem unreasonable."

65 **Earl's Court**—This was not the end of Lawrence's association with 44 Mecklenburgh Square. On July 20, 1928, he wrote to his friend Enid Hilton, who had just moved into number 44: "Did I tell you I believe that is the very house we lived in, in 1917 in the Aldingtons' rooms on the first floor, on the front and Arabella had an attic at the top—it was very jolly, I liked it very much. I hope you can stay there in peace." Lawrence turned to Hilton that year when bookshops began to refuse to stock *Lady Chatterley's Lover*; she enthusiastically collected the stock and distributed copies from Mecklenburgh Square directly to subscribers.

66 **"seem pretty happy"**—D. H. Lawrence to Amy Lowell, December 13, 1917.

66 **"it would be"**—H. D., Divorce Statement. Beinecke.

67 **"someone not in khaki"**—H. D., *Asphodel*, p. 139.

67 **"did not talk"**—H. D., *Bid Me to Live*, p. 116.

67 **"How I must"**—Cecil Gray to H. D., March 13, 1918. Beinecke.

67 **"Poor Dryad"**—Ezra Pound to H. D., March 1918. Quoted in Barbara Guest, *Herself Defined*, p. 93.

68 **"I am not"**—Richard Aldington to John Cournos, April 6, 1918. Houghton JC.

68 **"O, it was"**—H. D. to John Cournos, April 1918. Houghton JC.

68 **"We will go mad"**—H. D. to John Cournos, April 3, 1918. Houghton JC.

68 **"a most unseemly book"**—H. D. to Ezra Pound, July 1, 1938. Beinecke.

69 **"one of the most"**—*Spectator*, July 17, 1926.

69 **"here were two poets"**—Cournos, *Autobiography*, p. 269.

69 **"cold healing mist"**—H. D., *Bid Me to Live*, p. 145.

69 **"Twice last week"**—Richard Aldington to H. D., May 20, 1918. Beinecke.

70 **"We are 'parted'"**—Richard Aldington to F. S. Flint, June 2, 1918. HRC Flint.

70 **"I am so proud"**—Richard Aldington to H. D., June 1, 1918. Beinecke.

70 **"going about London"**—Richard Aldington to H. D., July 7, 1918. Beinecke.

70 **"To you I have"**—Richard Aldington to H. D., August 25, 1918. Beinecke.

70 **"Out of this"**—Richard Aldington to H. D., June 2, 1918. Beinecke.

70 **"cheer up"**—Richard Aldington to H. D., August 3, 1918. Beinecke.

70 **"Damn it, Dooley"**—Richard Aldington to H. D., August 4, 1918. Beinecke.

70 **"Gray becomes"**—Richard Aldington to H. D., August 4, 1918. Beinecke. In the same letter he claimed he had refused to have a child with Arabella for that very reason. Aldington retained a grudge against Cecil Gray; Leonard Woolf recalled that, in 1926, Aldington came to him looking "gloomy and threatening" and complained that one of the

reviewers Woolf had commissioned for *The Nation* had "run off with [Aldington's] wife," and that Woolf should not re-employ him. When Woolf replied that this wasn't reasonable, Aldington never spoke to him again. Gray had reviewed Stravinsky's ballet *Les Noces*, pronouncing it "pretty poor stuff."

71 **"so elusive"**—Cecil Gray to H. D., undated (March 1918). Beinecke.

71 **"sick to death"**—Cecil Gray, *Musical Chairs*, p. 145. Gray didn't meet his daughter for many years, and never publicly acknowledged her existence. In 1922, at H. D.'s request, Brigit Patmore attempted to persuade him to pay H. D. financial support for Perdita; she found him drunk and penniless, smoking hashish with Aleister Crowley, having spent his last money on a bust of Bernard van Dieren commissioned from Jacob Epstein. "He seems divided," she told H. D. and Bryher, "between a hatred and disgust with his own part in it and a consequent weak determination to shut it out completely, and a sort of equally weak desire to make it all right." In December 1936, H. D. wrote to him to request a meeting: "it would not only be laying old ghosts but it would be such fun now to talk about old Lorenzo—God rest his soul—and the others . . . Cornwall has always remained a dream, for which I deeply thank you!" He never replied. Gray married three times and had two further daughters, Pauline and Fabia.

In an afterword to the 1984 Virago edition of *Bid Me to Live*, Perdita tells her own story. As a child, she assumed her father was the "Mr. Aldington" occasionally mentioned by H. D. and Bryher; Bryher told her only that her father was "a very bad man" who "ran away from you"—but grudgingly showed Perdita a copy of Gray's book *Sibelius*, with the instruction not to ask any more questions. When Perdita was a young adult, her mother told her that the affair was "a brief fling, a spunky retaliation for Richard Aldington's infidelities. One of those things, of no lasting import except for my existence." In 1947, she met Gray for the only time. Along with Kenneth Macpherson, Bryher's husband, who had legally adopted her in 1927, Perdita was spending the summer in Capri, at the house of Norman Douglas. The group was joined by Gray and his third wife, Marjorie, also friends of Douglas. Macpherson introduced the pair: "Cecil, my daughter Perdita." Perdita "felt as if I were looking into a mirror." Nothing was said, and she never saw him again. Yet Gray did make a note in his diary: "My best works are probably my daughters, some without opus numbers—not officially acknowledged, but not the worse for that."

71 **"fini, fini, fini"**—Richard Aldington to H. D., September 27, 1918. Beinecke.

71 **sublet her room**—H. D. sublet 44 Mecklenburgh Square to a young woman named Margaret Postgate, who described the flat as "a lovely

first-floor room in Mecklenburgh Square belonging to the poet H. D., with three tall windows, a balcony looking out on the plane-trees of the Square, very inadequate heating and a large population of mice." Postgate subsequently married the economist G. D. H. Cole, with whom she wrote a series of detective novels; the pair were to be part of the detective-writing syndicate Dorothy L. Sayers attempted to form after university. The Coles also knew Eileen Power and R. H. Tawney through their work on the General Strike.

72   **"begun really seriously"**—H. D. to John Cournos, July 17, 1918. Houghton JC.

72   **"a Greek"**—Bryher to Amy Lowell, November 28, 1918. Houghton AL.

72   **"The worst thing"**—H. D. to John Cournos, November 1919. Bryn Mawr.

72   **"I feel it"**—H. D. to Clement Shorter, January 1919. Beinecke.

72   **"My only real"**—H. D., *End to Torment*, p. 8.

73   **"without her"**—H. D., *Tribute to Freud*, p. 49.

73   **"I hope"**—Bryher to H. D., April 21, 1919. Beinecke.

73   **"take, at times"**—H. D. to Bryher, December 18, 1918. Beinecke.

73   **Thinking back**—Perdita Schaffner, "Running," p. 7.

75   **"Every year"**—Barbara Guest, *Herself Defined*, p. 110.

75   **"repetitive thoughts"**—H. D., *Tribute to Freud*, p. 13.

75   **"women did not"**—ibid., p. 149.

76   **"found him some"**—ibid., p. 141.

76   **"a prophet"**—VW, "Notes on D. H. Lawrence" (1931) in *The Moment and Other Essays*, p. 79.

76   **"a fiery, golden"**—H. D., *Compassionate Friendship*, p. 54.

76   **"But there is"**—H. D. to John Cournos, October 31, 1916. Houghton JC.

78   **"I think"**—H. D. to Richard Aldington, February 23, 1949. Morris.

80   **"Feeling sorry"**—D. H. Lawrence to Selina Yorke, December 16, 1918.

80   **"a cat"**—D. H. Lawrence to Emily King, June 14, 1926.

81   **"unrecognisable"**—Quoted in Susan Stanford Friedman, *Penelope's Web*, p. 153.

81   **"which no one"**—Cecil Gray, *Peter Warlock*, p. 120.

81   **"weary and skeptical"**—Cecil Gray, *Musical Chairs*, p. 133.

82   **"a Jesus Christ"**—ibid.

82   **"the threshold"**—D. H. Lawrence to Cecil Gray, November 7, 1917.

82   **"Lawrence does not"**—H. D., *Compassionate Friendship*, p. 114.

82   **"Frieda was there"**—ibid.

86   **"perfect bisexual"**—H. D. to Bryher, November 24, 1934. Beinecke.

86   **"I have tried"**—H. D. to Bryher, November 27, 1934. Beinecke.

87   **"the room grew colder"**—H. D., *Thorn Thicket*, p. 182.

87   **"realised that"**—H. D., "H. D. by Delia Alton," p. 180.

87   **"You must not"**—H. D. to Richard Aldington, January 14, 1953. Morris.

87 **"kick over"**—H. D., *Bid Me to Live*, p. 61.

87 **"This is my"**—H. D., *Thorn Thicket*, p. 23.

Dorothy L. Sayers

89 **As the south doors**—The scene is described in Vera Brittain, *The Women at Oxford*, p. 156.

89 **"but really"**—DLS to her mother, August 18, 1920. Barbara Reynolds (ed.), *The Letters of Dorothy L. Sayers*.

90 **"I gnash my teeth"**—JEH to Gilbert Murray, October 1920. Newnham.

90 **"Of those"**—Vera Brittain, *The Women at Oxford*, pp. 122–3. In *Testament of Youth*, Brittain describes Sayers as follows: "a bouncing and exuberant young female who always seems to be preparing for tea parties, she could be seen at almost any hour of the day or night scuttling about the top floor of the new Maitland building with a kettle in her hand and a little checked apron fastened over her skirt."

91 **"hedged about"**—DLS to Barbara Reynolds, January 27, 1949.

91 **"Dear me!"**—DLS, *The Comediad*. Wheaton.

92 **"brought up without"**—DLS to Maurice Reckitt, November 19, 1941.

92 **"a woman of"**—DLS, "My Edwardian Childhood." Wheaton. Published in Barbara Reynolds (ed.), *Dorothy L. Sayers: Child and Woman of Her Time*, p. 8.

92 **"oblique and distorted"**—Walter M. Gallichan, "The Great Unmarried" (1916). Quoted in Virginia Nicholson, *Singled Out*, p. 37.

93 **"sentimental"**—DLS to Ivy Shrimpton, April 15, 1930.

93 **"Gentlemen—and others"**—Rosamund Essex, *Woman in a Man's World*, p. 11.

94 **"extravagant indoor headgear"**—Vera Brittain, *The Women at Oxford*, p. 123.

94 **"If the trousers"**—DLS, "Are Women Human?," *Unpopular Opinions*, pp. 108–9.

96 **"the best medium"**—DLS to Anthony Berkeley, January 24, 1949. Wheaton.

96 **"I write prose"**—DLS to Catherine Godfrey, July 29, 1913.

96 **"quite a ghost craze"**—DLS to her parents, January 26, 1913.

96 **"immensely exciting"**—DLS to her parents, August 2, 1914.

96 **a military hospital**—See also Siegfried Sassoon, *Memoirs of an Infantry Officer*, and Robert Graves, *Goodbye to All That* for soldiers' memories of Somerville.

96 **"Do you know"**—DLS to her parents, May 26, 1913.

96 **"something real"**—DLS to parents, May 16, 1915.

97 **"wouldn't do any harm"**—DLS to Catherine Godfrey, November 23, 1915.

97   **"growing rusty"**—DLS to Muriel Jaeger, February 6, 1916.

97   **her debut collection**—Her second book of poems, *Catholic Tales and Christian Songs*, was published by Blackwell in September 1918.

97   **"There is no future"**—DLS to her father, January 25, 1917.

97   **"a thorough change"**—DLS to her parents, June 6, 1919.

97   **he later claimed**—Whelpton quotes are taken from an interview in the *Sunday Times*, March 30, 1975.

97   **"The whole thing"**—DLS to her mother, February 27, 1920.

98   **"I really want"**—DLS to her parents, September 12, 1920. Wheaton.

98   **"Certainly no more teaching"**—Paper dated August 17, 1920. Wheaton.

98   **"Our generation is"**—VW, diary June 29, 1920.

98   **"a great generation"**—J. B. Priestley, *Margin Released*, p. 136.

99   **came to shape**—In particular her 1928 novel *The Unpleasantness at the Bellona Club*, in which a former soldier is driven by his demons to a false confession.

99   **"a frightfully paying business"**—DLS to her parents, July 23, 1920. Her proposal is now in a private collection.

99   **"There seem to be"**—DLS to her parents, October 3, 1920.

99   **"I think we could"**—DLS to her parents, September 3, 1920. Wheaton.

99   **"fixed up to take"**—DLS to her parents, October 26, 1920.

100   **"her rents are too high"**—DLS to her parents, December 7, 1920.

100   **"rather beautiful room"**—DLS to her parents, December 3, 1920.

100   **"valiant militant suffragette"**—H. D., *Bid Me to Live*, p. 9. "Early Fabian of the period, herself already period-piece in 1914, in 1917 already pre-war, valiant militant suffragette with brown velvet jacket. She was very tiny. Sometimes she wore her little George Sand jacket with trousers. Her hair was naturally curly, untidy but not dowdy. Mop of gold-brown hair went grey at the temples. Fine wrinkles etched blue eyes. She spoke precisely, with the indefinable je ne sais quoi of the aristocrat. 'I don't like ugly women,' she said, flicking ash from the end of amber."

101   ***Birth of Venus***—In *Miranda Masters*, Cournos writes that the landlady loved Botticelli and every room in the house had a reproduction of one of his paintings.

101   **"full from attic to basement"**—DLS to her parents, December 14, 1920.

101   **"delightful underclothing"**—DLS to her parents, July 27, 1921.

101   **"I have discovered"**—DLS to her parents, December 14, 1920.

102   **"Don't ever think"**—DLS to her parents, December 9, 1920. London restaurants recur in her books, from a memorable lunch at Simpson's in the Strand in *Murder Must Advertise*—"the finest roast saddle of mutton in London"—to moules at Gatti's and turtle soup at the Savoy in *The Unpleasantness at the Bellona Club*.

102 **"felt that"**—DLS to Hilary F. Page, August 10, 1944.

102 **"It's immoral"**—DLS to Muriel Jaeger, March 8, 1917.

102 **"looking rather ungainly"**—Quoted in Barbara Reynolds, *Dorothy L. Sayers: Her Life and Soul* (Hodder & Stoughton, 1993), p. 100.

103 **"a little gold-mine"**—DLS to her parents, October 31 1920.

103 **"of a sort"**—DLS to her parents, November 1920. Wheaton.

103 **"She really seems"**—DLS to her parents, December 14, 1920.

103 **"as a master"**—DLS, "Tristan," *Modern Languages* 1:5 (June 1920) and 1:6 (August 1920).

103 **"a particularly swell"**—DLS to her parents, December 14, 1920.

103 **"She really isn't"**—DLS to her parents, March 15, 1921.

103 **"I don't seem"**—DLS to her parents, December 19, 1920. Wheaton.

104 **"a meeting"**—DLS to her parents, November 20, 1920. Wheaton.

104 **Virginia Woolf**—Woolf records in her diary on January 25, 1921 that she had attended a show the previous night.

105 ***Bonds of Egypt* and "The Priest's Chamber"**—Unpublished manuscripts in a private collection.

105 **"the works of "**—Eric Whelpton interview in the *Sunday Times*, March 30, 1975.

106 **"more a part"**—DLS to Mrs. G. K. Chesterton, June 15, 1936.

106 **"the Holmes tradition"**—DLS (ed.), *Great Short Stories of Detection, Mystery, Horror*, p. 16.

106 **"the nearest modern"**—ibid.

106 **exclusively highbrow**—Detective fiction found several fans among the high modernists, including Ezra Pound, T. S. Eliot, and Gertrude Stein, who wrote an essay titled "Why I Like Detective Stories." Vladimir Nabokov enjoyed *Murder Must Advertise*, and recommended it to his friend Edmund Wilson, a genre skeptic: "Of course, Agatha is unreadable—but Sayers, whom you do not mention, writes well."

106 **"is no longer"**—DLS, "The Present Status of the Mystery Story," *London Mercury*, November 1930.

106 **unpublished essay**—DLS, "Why Is the Detective a Popular Figure?"— in a private collection.

106 **Sherlock Holmes**—Sayers was a founding member of the Sherlock Holmes Society of London, and later wrote a radio script in which the young Peter Wimsey consults the great detective on the question of the disappearance of a kitten.

107 **"all the Sexton Blakes"**—DLS to Muriel Jaeger, March 8, 1920. Wheaton.

107 **"The Adventure of the Piccadilly Flat"**—The manuscript of this story was sold at Sotheby's in 2002, and I have been unable to trace its present location, though its details can be reconstructed from Jill Paton Walsh's report at the Wade Center, and descriptions in Barbara Reynolds's biogra-

phy. I am grateful to Anthony Cardew for showing me the manuscript of the original synopsis in his possession.

107   **bachelor flat**—Wimsey's flat is at 110A Piccadilly, a play on Sherlock Holmes's famous rooms at 221B Baker Street. It is described as "one of the most delightful bachelor rooms in London," with black and primrose walls, featuring a baby grand piano, bookshelves full of rare editions, and Sèvres vases on the chimney piece, and a library looking over Piccadilly.

107   **a masculine adjective**—An ingenious twist which Sayers would later recycle in her story "The Entertaining Episode of the Article in Question."

107   **dashed-off fragments**—A story, "Introducing Lord Peter," and a play titled *The Mousehole*. The first is an incomplete story involving rival journalists jostling for a scoop on the murder of a famous novelist, and introduces Lord Peter as one who "had accomplished many things and identified himself with nothing. He collected old books and old wine, and solved detective problems." In *The Mousehole: A Detective Fantasia in Three Flats*, Sayers placed the bodies of a well-known financier and a mysterious woman not in Wimsey's own flat but in the room above, with the gas on and the keyhole stopped. Enter Lord Peter ("Hobby: other people's business"): "sleek, fair, monocle, dressed in a grey suit, with the exception of his coat, whose place is taken by a luxurious dressing-gown." To the disgruntlement of Inspector Sugg, he immediately recognizes the female victim, and picks up a small object from the floor when the policemen's backs are turned; the story leaves off here. Wheaton.

108   **"a shy Irishman"**—Eric Whelpton interview in the *Sunday Times*, March 30, 1975.

108   **hotfoots to Battersea**—Sayers herself was familiar with the route used by Lord Peter: her cousin Raymond and his wife lived in Battersea, and she visited them several times from Mecklenburgh Square. "I saw Ray and Lucy the other day—stodging out to Battersea all in my smartest clothes in the vilest of weather. Fortunately there is a 'bus which goes all the way."

108   **The novel**—The twist in *Whose Body?* may have come to Sayers some years earlier. In *The Women at Oxford*, Vera Brittain refers to "an Oxford parlor game in which the players each add an incident to make a story. Dorothy Sayers added the naked corpse of an unknown person discovered in a bathtub, and thus provided herself with the plot for a mystery novel."

109   **"conventional to the last degree"**—DLS, "Gaudy Night," in Denys Kilham Roberts (ed.), *Titles to Fame*, p. 75.

109   **is often seen**—Martin Edwards's *The Golden Age of Murder* is an excellent history of Golden Age detective fiction, as are the essays in *The Cambridge Companion to Crime Fiction*.

109   **"It may be"**—DLS (ed.), *Great Short Stories of Detection, Mystery, Horror*, p. 9.

111   **"Things have been"**—DLS to her parents, July 1, 1921.

112   **"One reason why"**—DLS to her parents, December 19, 1921.

112   **"Lord Peter's large income"**—DLS, "How I Came to Invent the Character of Lord Peter Wimsey," *Harcourt, Brace News*, July 15, 1936.

112   **"I simply must"**—DLS to her parents, May 29, 1921. Wheaton.

113   **telephone directory**—Decades later a Mr. Freke wrote to Sayers asking how she chose the name of her murderer. She replied: "I was terrified when I first saw the name on the envelope, thinking that you were intending to sue me for libel." She told him she had never met a Freke in real life but the naming was probably "the result of a pin stuck at random into the London Telephone Directory."

113   **"I'm just going on"**—DLS to her parents, March 15, 1921.

113   **"lots of parties"**—DLS to her parents, July 1, 1921.

113   **"I can't get"**—DLS to her parents, July 16, 1921.

113   **"I'm inviting a friend"**—DLS to her parents, July 27, 1921.

114   **"Just now"**—John Cournos to John Gould Fletcher, December 26, 1921. Arkansas.

114   **"Perhaps I could"**—DLS to her parents, October 30, 1921. Wheaton.

114   **"has consoled me"**—John Cournos to John Gould Fletcher, February 11, 1921. Arkansas.

114   **"prisoners of life"**—ibid.

114   **"these cliques and gangs"**—John Gould Fletcher to John Cournos, April 29, 1920. Houghton JC.

115   **"Few friendships"**—DLS to Leonard Green, August 29, 1919. HRC Sayers.

116   **"a man I wouldn't"**—DLS to her parents, January 2, 1920. He had written three years after the unfortunate proposal, to tell her of his engagement. Wheaton.

116   **"To have somebody"**—DLS to her mother, July 11, 1917.

116   **"sort of abject hero-worship"**—DLS to John Cournos, January 25, 1925.

116   **"a rotten companion"**—DLS to John Cournos, December 4, 1924.

116   **"How stupid"**—DLS to John Cournos, August 13, 1925.

116   **"having tramped"**—ibid.

117   **"You can't be both"**—John Cournos to John Gould Fletcher, May 27, 1921. Arkansas.

117   **"Personally, I think"**—DLS to her parents, October 7, 1921.

117   **"I fear he has"**—DLS to her parents, November 8, 1921. In her 1930 novel *The Documents in the Case*, a character is described as "not a bad old bird, but an alarming bore on the subject of Art with a capital A."

117   **"It makes me"**—ibid.

118   **"full of mouldy sandwiches"**—DLS to her parents, February 14, 1922.

118   **"I've been promised"**—DLS to her parents, November 8, 1921.

118   **"I think of "**—DLS to her parents, February 14, 1922.

118   **"I spend all"**—DLS to her parents, November 8, 1921.

118   **"I shall either"**—DLS to her parents, undated (November 1921).

118   **"I'm afraid he"**—ibid.

118   **"Nobody can feel"**—DLS to her parents, December 19, 1921.

119   **Great James Street**—She had paid annual rent of £65 for one room in
       Mecklenburgh Square; her new digs cost £70 for a sitting room, bed-
       room, and kitchen with the use of a new bathroom and lavatory: "a
       delightful little set." A blue plaque marks the site today.

119   **"actually settled"**—DLS to her parents, June 15, 1922.

119   **"showed signs of "**—DLS to her parents, August 14, 1922. Wheaton.

119   **"I want to"**—ibid.

119   **"he has"**—DLS to her parents, July 24, 1922. Wheaton.

119   **"very confident"**—DLS to her parents, April 4, 1922. Wheaton.

119   **"a lively discussion"**—DLS to her parents, July 27, 1922.

120   **"passionately wanting"**—DLS to John Cournos, August 13, 1925.

120   **"talk about being"**—DLS to John Cournos, December 4, 1924.

120   **"stripped love down"**—DLS to John Cournos, undated (January 1925).

120   **"turned up"**—DLS to her mother, January 18, 1922.

120   **"I had 5 courses"**—DLS to her mother, July 24, 1922. They had red
       wine (which Sayers described as "Spanish Burgundy") and two kinds of
       vermouth, plus five courses: grapefruit rafraîchi, on ice with whipped
       cream, consommé aux vermicelles, beefsteak à l'anglaise with potatoes
       and salad, fruit jelly with cream, and baked mushrooms casserole, with
       coffee and liqueurs.

120   **"John hasn't"**—DLS to her parents, November 28, 1922.

121   **"grave physical"**—June Rose, *Marie Stopes and the Sexual Revolution*, p.
       179.

121   **"every dirty trick"**—DLS to John Cournos, December 4, 1924.

121   **"excluded frankness"**—DLS to John Cournos, undated (January 1925).

121   **"Everywhere, in the hotels"**—John Cournos to John Gould Fletcher,
       November 29, 1922. Arkansas.

121   **"I'm getting more"**—DLS to her mother, January 8, 1923.

121   **"I've been lonely"**—ibid.

122   **"Intellect isn't"**—DLS to her mother, December 18, 1922.

122   **"a revolting slum"**—DLS to her mother, January 8, 1923.

122   **Beatrice White**—The source of this episode, revealed after Barbara
       Reynolds's 1993 biography was published, is provided in an appendix to
       Reynolds (ed.), *Letters*, vol. 2.

122   **"I'm awfully rushed"**—DLS to her mother, November 2, 1923.

123   **let down**—In December 1924, Sayers found herself sitting next to Bill

and another woman in a restaurant; while Sayers tried to discreetly ignore them, the woman spilled tea in Sayers's lap and had to apologize.

123 **"I never meant"**—DLS to John Cournos, February 22, 1925.

123 **"of all motives"**—DLS, "Motives for Crime," *Sunday Times*, August 5, 1934. In Martin Edwards (ed.), *Taking Detective Stories Seriously: The Collected Crime Reviews of Dorothy L. Sayers*, p. 178.

124 **"it would grieve"**—DLS to Ivy Shrimpton, January 27, 1924.

124 **"an infant"**—DLS to Ivy Shrimpton, January 1, 1924.

124 **"Everything I told you"**—DLS to Ivy Shrimpton, January 27, 1924.

124 **"affection rather"**—DLS to Ivy Shrimpton, January 1, 1924.

124 **"I hope he"**—DLS to Ivy Shrimpton, May 2 1924.

125 **one other person**—Cournos was aware of his privileged position and seems to have relished the secret. Among Cournos's papers at Houghton Library is a copy of a newspaper interview with Sayers. Two passages are circled. The first: "As sharp-tongued to bishops as to biddies, Miss Sayers refuses to have her beliefs or her privacy invaded for any reason." In the second, Sayers complains that critics "aren't interested in my translation of Dante; they only want to know the great secret which I must be concealing—the secret of why I'm translating Dante instead of writing more detective stories." Cournos has underlined twice the line "know the great secret which I must be concealing."

In January 1953, Cournos wrote to James Babb of Yale University Library, to whom he had previously sold some letters from the novelist L. A. G. Strong: "I have a singularly interesting series of letters, unusual because they have a unity and a sequence . . . These letters, written by Dorothy L. Sayers to me in the early days of her career, are of a very intimate character, and deal with an episode in her life of interest to any future biographer." He goes on to specify that the letters should not be made available to researchers until both he and Sayers are dead—"I have hesitated to dispose of these letters because of their exceptionally intimate sex character"—then changes his mind: "On second thought I myself don't mind, as the intimate facts concern her." The eleven letters were eventually left to Harvard's Houghton Library, on the proviso that no one should see them until fifty years after Cournos's death. Copies were nonetheless shown to the scholar Carolyn Heilbrun in the 1970s; the papers were officially made available to James Brabazon for his 1981 biography and are included in Barbara Reynolds's edition of Sayers's letters.

126 **"Dear John"**—DLS to John Cournos, August 22, 1924.

126 **"The one thing"**—DLS to John Cournos, October 27, 1924.

126 **"Last time"**—ibid.

127 **"I have become"**—DLS to John Cournos, undated (January 1925).

128 **"interests are"**—ibid.

130   **"everlasting breeziness"**—DLS to Eustace Barton, May 7, 1928.

130   **"with the infanticidal"**—DLS, "Gaudy Night," in Denys Kilham
       Roberts (ed.), *Titles to Fame*, p. 79.

130   **"a drama"**—G. K. Chesterton, *Illustrated London News*, August 19, 1922.

131   **"persuade us"**—DLS, "Puppets or People in Stories of Crime," *Sunday
       Times*, 26 May 1935. In *Taking Detective Stories Seriously*, p. 279.

132   **"a passion"**—VW, diary, January 4, 1925.

132   **"to write a"**—E. C. Bentley, *Those Days*, p. 249.

132   **"breathing and moving"**—DLS, *Trent's Last Case* draft broadcast talk.
       Wheaton.

132   **"in every respect"**—DLS, "Gaudy Night," in Denys Kilham Roberts
       (ed.), *Titles to Fame*, p. 79.

132   **"Bloomsbury bluestocking"**—Sayers created a prototype for Harriet in
       the character of Ann Dorland in *The Unpleasantness at the Bellona Club*: an
       artist, with Virginia Woolf and D. H. Lawrence on her bookshelves, who
       is falsely accused of murder after a failed affair. Wimsey urges her to
       aspire to a different sort of relationship: "You have always thought of
       being dominated by somebody, haven't you? . . . But you'll find that *yours*
       will be the leading brain of the two. He will take great pride in the fact.
       And you will find the man reliable and kind, and it will turn out quite
       well."

132   **"Notwithstanding the usual"**—DLS, "Apology for Peter," *The Book
       Society Annual* (Christmas 1935).

133   **"a major operation"**—DLS, "Gaudy Night," in Denys Kilham Roberts
       (ed.), *Titles to Fame*, p. 79.

134   **"good work"**—DLS, *Why Work?*

134   **"What on earth"**—DLS, "Are Women Human?," *Unpopular Opinions*, p.
       114.

135   **"who are cursed with"**—DLS, *Gaudy Night*, p. 77.

135   **"a passport to"**—DLS, "What's Right with Oxford?," *Oxford Magazine*
       (Summer 1935).

136   **"By choosing"**—DLS, "Gaudy Night," in Denys Kilham Roberts (ed.),
       Titles to Fame, p. 82.

136   **"an Oxford woman graduate"**—ibid., p. 81.

136   *Cat O'Mary*—Wheaton. Published in Barbara Reynolds (ed.), *Dorothy L.
       Sayers: Child and Woman of Her Time*, p. 155. She'd intended to publish
       Cat O'Mary—the "straight novel"—under a pseudonym, Johanna Leigh.

137   **as herself**—Aspects of that unfinished novel recur in *Love All*, a comic
       play Sayers wrote in 1937, in which an unfaithful husband is shocked to
       discover that his wife has written a play while he was away with his
       mistress, and is now living a glamorous and successful life in London,
       with a flat of her own, a West End run, and a constantly ringing tele-
       phone.

137 **not entirely happily**—To her son, who had announced he was to marry for a second time: "I do not know that romantic love is necessarily a good foundation—mutual respect and mutual courtesy are the essentials, and a determination to see the thing through. But I cannot give much advice on the subject, having done rather badly at it myself. However, I did stick it out for over a quarter of a century—and am therefore perhaps inclined to be a little short with the people who *don't* stick it out."

137 **"learning to cope"**—DLS to John Cournos, January 25, 1925.

137 **"quite satisfied"**—DLS to Ivy Shrimpton, March 15, 1926.

137 **"too old"**—DLS to Ivy Shrimpton, January 27, 1924.

138 **Mrs. H. Attwood**—cf. a letter written by Cournos's step-granddaughter, Marcia Satterthwaite Wertime, to the *New York Times*, November 14, 1993.

139 **ongoing fight**—On June 16, 1927, the university council voted to limit the number of women undergraduates to 620, meaning women at Oxford were outnumbered 1:4 by men; in *Unnatural Death*, Sayers made a passing reference to the fact that "Oxford decided that women were dangerous," while in the preface to *Gaudy Night* she apologizes to the authorities for having created "a college of 150 women students, in excess of the limit ordained by statute." Until 1993, Somerville fellows had to resign their fellowships on marriage.

141 **"Whether you advertise"**—DLS to Victor Gollancz, September 26, 1935.

141 **"not really a detective story"**—DLS to Muriel St. Clare Byrne, September 8, 1935.

142 **"a discussion"**—"Crime in College," *TLS*, November 9, 1935.

142 **"For no bribe"**—DLS, "Would You Like to be 21 Again? I Wouldn't," *Daily Express*, February 9, 1937.

142 **"One thing"**—DLS to Hilary F. Page, August 10, 1944.

Jane Ellen Harrison

143 **"John is encamped"**—Quoted in Michael Holroyd, *Augustus John*, p. 364.

143 **"I felt"**—JEH to D. S. MacColl, August 15, 1909. Glasgow.

144 **which she attributed**—Jessie G. Stewart, *Jane Ellen Harrison: A Portrait from Letters*, p. 104.

144 **"seems to me"**—JEH to Ruth Darwin, undated (July 1909). Newnham.

144 **"a very charming person"**—Augustus John to Ottoline Morrell, July 22, 1909. Quoted in Michael Holroyd, *Augustus John*, p. 363.

145 **"odd & disappointing"**—Gilbert Murray to Jessie Stewart, May 1, 1928. Newnham.

145 **bemusement at the choices**—These are unknown, but for the memorial

service at Newnham, Hope suggested reading the third chapter of Proverbs, minus verses 5, 6, 9, 10, 11, and 12, and ending with verse 24: "I cannot think of anything more suitable."

145 **"Who is 'God'"**—VW, diary, April 21, 1928.

145 **"The problem"**—HM to Jessie Stewart, March 29, 1943. Newnham.

146 **"I thought"**—Gilbert Murray to Jessie Stewart, March 26, 1950. Newnham.

146 **"I never understood"**—Gilbert Murray to Jessie Stewart, April 23, 1952. Newnham.

146 **"I send you"**—JEH to Gilbert Murray, October 31 1925. Newnham.

147 **trimmed with fringe**—Reminiscences of Marian Harrison. Newnham.

148 **"ignorant but willing"**—JEH, *Reminiscences*, p. 27.

148 **staying at home**—Reminiscences of Marian Harrison. Newnham.

148 **"the cleverest woman"**—Reminiscences of Mary Marshall. Newnham.

148 **"where all the"**—Quoted in Gill Sutherland, "History of Newnham," www.newn.cam.ac.uk.

149 **"the newest thing"**—JEH, *Reminiscences*, p. 45.

150 **"perambulating lectures"**—Interview with Jane Harrison, *Pall Mall Gazette*, November 4, 1891.

150 **"the lady"**—ibid.

150 **"A woman was"**—Interview with Jane Harrison, *Women's Penny Paper*, August 24, 1889.

150 **"undesirable that"**—Quoted in Mary Beard, *The Invention of Jane Harrison*, p. 62.

150 **"had not enjoyed"**—Jean Mills, *Virginia Woolf, Jane Ellen Harrison, and the Spirit of Modernist Classicism*, p. 19.

151 **honorary degrees**—In April 1895 she received an honorary LL.D. from the University of Aberdeen, the first time a woman had received the degree. Two years later she received an honorary D.Litt. from Durham.

152 **"one woman"**—Interview with Jane Harrison, *Time and Tide*, January 27, 1928.

153 **"the fat and comely one"**—JEH to Gilbert Murray, May 1904. Newnham.

154 **"Zeus is nowhere"**—JEH to Gilbert Murray, April 21, 1901. Newnham.

154 **"the products of art"**—JEH, *Themis*, p. xi.

154 **"a veritable little manual"**—JEH to Gilbert Murray, April 21, 1901. Newnham.

155 **"religious representation"**—JEH, *Themis*, p. 500.

156 **"We are so"**—JEH, *Prolegomena to the Study of Greek Religion*, p. 397.

156 **"Few books are"**—T. S. Eliot, "Euripides and Professor Murray," in *Selected Essays*, p. 62.

156 **"a keen emotion"**—JEH, *Ancient Art and Ritual*, p. 57.

156 **"it just fascinates"**—D. H. Lawrence to Arthur McLeod, October 26, 1913.

157   **"trying to make"**—JEH, *Reminiscences*, p. 26.

157   **"there were *mother*-cults"**—H. D. to Bryher, April 15, 1932. Beinecke.

158   **"and all the"**—VW to Violet Dickinson, October 22, 1904.

158   **"a really Apostolic"**—VW, *Roger Fry*, p. 92.

158   **"excess of sympathy"**—*Saturday Review*, May 4, 1912.

159   **"corybantic Hellenism"**—Harrison knew Duncan, and occasionally read Greek poetry at Duncan's performances.

159   **"such an audacious"**—Jessie G. Stewart, *Jane Ellen Harrison*, p. 88.

159   **"To the orthodox"**—JEH, *Themis*, p. lviii.

159   **"knowing Greek"**—For more on this subject see Yopie Prins's fascinating book *Ladies' Greek*.

160   **"freedom to know"**—JEH, "Homo Sum: Being a Letter to an Anti-Suffragist from an Anthropologist," *Alpha and Omega*, p. 112.

160   **"She was a little girl"**—JEH, "Scientiae Sacra Fames," *Alpha and Omega*, p. 117.

160   **"confine man"**—JEH, "Homo Sum," *Alpha and Omega*, p. 84.

161   **"We must free"**—JEH, "Scientiae Sacra Fames," *Alpha and Omega*, p. 139.

161   **"made their god"**—ibid., p. 142.

161   **"to be set"**—ibid., p. 120.

161   **"With every fibre"**—JEH, "Epilogue on the War," *Alpha and Omega*, p. 223.

161   **"freedom for ourselves"**—ibid., p. 252.

161   **"a notorious centre"**—Quoted in Shelley Arlen, " 'For Love of an Idea': Jane Ellen Harrison, heretic and humanist," p. 178.

162   **"To be a heretic"**—She was a founding member of the Cambridge Heretics, a society for discussion of art, philosophy, and religion. This lecture, "Heresy and Humanity," was read at a 1909 meeting.

163   **burned all her papers**—Annabel Robinson writes that Harrison was "disastrously prevailed upon by Hope Mirrlees to make a bonfire of all the letters and papers she had saved over the years. These included not only all the correspondence she had received from Gilbert Murray, but also letters from Burne-Jones and others of her distinguished London friends. Perhaps Mirrlees's motive was simply to be unencumbered, but there lurks behind this event a more disturbing possibility, also indicated by Mirrlees's later behavior in regard to Harrison: the desire to make a clean break with her past life and to embark on a new one where she, Hope Mirrlees, would be the central figure." Hope herself seems not to have known about the contents of the bonfire: she wrote to Jessie Stewart in 1933 that "I mentioned to Professor Murray as a *possibility* (it occurred to me a few weeks ago) that his answers *might* be among Jane's things stored with Mappy's Mount Blow furniture . . . However, I told him quite frankly that I don't for a moment think they really *are* there. I think Jane

would have said something to me about them if she had kept them. Because at the time that she was tearing everything up she used to show me anything she thought would amuse me—& I certainly had the impression that she was making a complete holocaust."

164   **"to live in"**—The Cornford Letters. Newnham.

164   **motherly mentor**—She hints at this, without naming names, in her essay "Crabbed Age and Youth," in JEH, *Alpha and Omega*, p. 21.

165   **"as if he"**—Jessie G. Stewart, *Jane Ellen Harrison*, p. 112.

166   **"sort of unmarried-married life"**—The Cornford Letters. Newnham.

166   **her health failed**—In 1903, Harrison suffered shortness of breath and fainting, and was told to give up smoking: "Ugh! If giving up drink is like the wrench from a lover whom all the time you despise, giving up smoking is like parting from the best friend, who always comforts and never torments!"

166   **"just now faced"**—JEH to Frances Darwin, 1908–9. Quoted in Robert Ackerman, "Some Letters of the Cambridge Ritualists," pp. 121–24.

166   **"a typical"**—VW to Lady Cecil, September 1, 1925.

167   **"Thank you"**—JEH to HM, July 3, 1910. Newnham.

167   **"that is only"**—JEH to Lina Mirrlees, undated (c. 1910). Newnham.

167   **biographers have**—Robinson suggests Mirrlees had "few of Harrison's intellectual gifts," and writes that "I cannot help suspecting that her friendship with Harrison was fuelled by a craving for fame-by-association, as it were, since there is little else to explain their close relationship." In *The Autobiography of Alice B. Toklas*, by contrast, Gertrude Stein refers to Harrison as "Hope Mirrlees's pet enthusiasm."

167   **long poem *Paris***—Suffused with sights and sounds, *Paris* evokes a stream-of-consciousness walk through the streets on a single day; in a rich collage of allusive fragments, symbols of the city's past and present are mixed in with the speaker's own internal monologue. Mirrlees presents a noisy, surreal vision of modernity, mingling brand names and musical scores, advertisement posters and snippets of conversation, the ghosts of the Père Lachaise Cemetery and the pigeons perched on statues. It is a powerfully evocative snapshot of the city still in mourning for its war dead, yet on the cusp of a new future as diplomats arrive for the peace conference at Versailles. Above all, *Paris* is a tribute to the bustling metropolis and its constantly renewing life force.

168   **"has a passion"**—VW to Lady Cecil, September 1, 1925.

168   **"It's all Sapphism"**—VW to Clive Bell, September 24, 1919.

169   **"spoiled prodigy"**—VW, diary, November 23, 1920.

169   **"knows Greek"**—VW to Margaret Llewelyn Davies, August 17, 1919.

170   **"influence was hardly"**—Hope Mirrlees: biography research. Newnham.

170   **first taken up**—Hope and Jane's Russian teacher was Nadine Jarintzov, who had come to Britain from St. Petersburg in the 1890s. She was a

proponent of sex education, an art critic, and an author, and Harrison wrote a preface to her book *Russian Poets and Poems*: "Madame Jarintzov in her former book made me and every student of Russian her debtor. She expounded for us, she realized as only a Russian could, the Russian spirit. Now she goes further; by her translations she recreates that spirit." The book was published by Blackwell in July 1917, while Dorothy L. Sayers was with the company; "Madame Jarintzov" was present at the dinner party at Basil Blackwell's where Sayers was proposed to by Leonard Hodgson.

170   **"cares more"**—JEH to Gilbert Murray, October 1914. Newnham.

170   **"for our new"**—JEH to HM, August 28, 1914. Newnham. In the *Manchester Guardian* of December 23, 1914, Harrison joined Henry James, H. G. Wells, Constance Garnett and others in signing a letter "To Russian Men of Letters" expressing solidarity "at this moment when your countrymen and ours are alike facing death for the deliverance of Europe."

171   **"It is too fascinating"**—JEH to Gilbert Murray, May 1915. Newnham.

171   **In a lecture**—Harrison began teaching Russian almost as soon as she began learning it, and also argued for Russian's inclusion in the Cambridge syllabus: "An accurate knowledge of the Russian and Greek languages together with an intimate understanding of the two civilisations should furnish a humanistic education at once broad and thorough." She visited Russia only once—in September 1886 with her cousin Marian Harrison, long before her interest in Russian culture had developed—and later regretted that she had spent all her time looking at Greek vases in the Hermitage Museum: "What a fool, what an idiot I was to leave Russia without knowing it! I might so easily have made the pilgrimage to Tolstoy; I might even have seen Dostoevsky . . . Never now shall I see Moscow and Kiev, cities of my dreams." She did once, however, give Turgenev a tour of Newnham. "Dare I ask him to speak just a word or two of Russian? He looked such a kind old snow-white Lion. Alas! He spoke fluent English; it was a grievous disappointment."

171   **"growing richer"**—JEH, "Aspects, Aorists and the Classical Tripos," p. 5.

171   **"If Esperanto"**—JEH, "Epilogue on the War," *Alpha and Omega*, pp. 246–47.

171   **"far famed"**—JEH, "Aspects, Aorists and the Classical Tripos," p. 5.

171   **"which melt into"**—Henri Bergson, *Time and Free Will*, p. 104.

172   **"Each of us"**—JEH, "Unanimism and Conversion," *Alpha and Omega*, p. 48.

172   **"all the recent"**—HM, "An Earthly Paradise," *Time and Tide*, February 25, 1927.

172   **"was where the"**—Gertrude Stein, *Paris France*, p. 11.

172   **the Left Bank**—John Cournos wrote to John Gould Fletcher from Paris,

April 26, 1924, telling him that the Russians drink at the Rotonde café on Boulevard Montparnasse, the Americans and English at the Dôme opposite. "The Russians here look alive; they have every appearance of being virile and of being creatively interested in the life of the time, such as it is; the Americans seem dull, bored, sodden with drink."

173 **"Cubism is now"**—HM to Lina Mirrlees, November 17, 1922. Newnham HM.

173 **"owing to Pellerin's churlishness"**—HM to Lina Mirrlees, November 17, 1922. Newnham HM.

173 **"to wear with"**—HM to Lina Mirrlees, November 2, 1922. Newnham HM.

173 **"Sapphic flat"**—VW to Molly MacCarthy, April 22, 1923. Woolf's reference to their "Sapphic flat" was omitted from the edition of her letters that was published while Mirrlees was alive.

173 **"I feel that"**—D. H. Lawrence to S. S. Koteliansky, May 1, 1917.

174 **"All along"**—JEH to Mary Murray, December 25, 1922. Newnham.

176 **"uses too many"**—JEH to Gilbert Murray, January 22, 1916. Newnham.

176 **During his stint**—Alexei Remizov to John Cournos, June 11, 1924. Amherst.

177 **In August**—Charles du Bos to HM, January 3, 1930: "I am glad that it is Prince Mirsky who is giving the Jane Harrison lecture: the picture of you three working at Pontigny in the 'halle romane' at the Avvakum translation comes back vividly before my mind's eye." Jacques Doucet.

177 **the 1917 Club**—In Dorothy L. Sayers's novel *Clouds of Witness*, Lord Peter Wimsey's sister Mary is a member of the Soviet Club on Gerrard Street, a headquarters indicated by "an orange door, flanked by windows with magenta curtains." The club was "founded to accommodate free thinking rather than high living," and Wimsey's mother complains at her children haunting "low places full of Russians and sucking Socialists taking themselves seriously . . . and given to drinking coffee and writing poems with no shape to them, and generally ruining their nerves."

177 **"the greatest writer"**—VW to Lytton Strachey, September 1, 1912.

177 **"savage-joyful"**—*The Times*, June 24, 1911.

177 **Boris Anrep**—His mosaics featuring his friends, including Virginia Woolf, as Greek muses adorn the entrance hall to the National Gallery.

178 **"whose short curls"**—David Garnett, *The Golden Echo*, p. 6. Garnett considered Harrison, along with Arthur Waley, "the greatest scholar I have known."

178 **"together with Freud"**—D. S. Mirsky, *Jane Ellen Harrison and Russia*, p. 9.

178 **"immensely impressed"**—JEH to D. S. Mirsky, September 1924. Newnham.

178 **"Oh dear!"**—JEH to D. S. Mirsky, November 1924. Newnham.

178   **"draw your inspiration"**—JEH, "Epilogue on the War," *Alpha and Omega*, p. 238. The following quotes are also from this essay.

180   **"our delightful Club"**—JEH to D. S. Mirsky, May 9, 1925. Newnham.

180   **"the size of"**—JEH to D. S. Mirsky, undated (January 1926). Newnham.

180   **"queer little house"**—11 Mecklenburgh Street was the birthplace in 1845 of Henry Sweet, the phonetician who was the model for Henry Higgins in George Bernard Shaw's *Pygmalion*.

180   **"We have taken"**—JEH to Gilbert Murray, undated (September 1926). Newnham.

181   **"a servant is"**—HM to Lina Mirrlees, October 15, 1922. Newnham HM.

181   **already knew**—Jane had met Lytton Strachey in 1909 at a sanatorium at Saltsjöbaden, where they were both undergoing Swedish massage as a cure for various ailments. Jane remembered the meeting with fondness: " 'Take my advice,' he said; 'as soon as they touch you begin to yell, and go on yelling till they stop.' It was sound advice, sympathetically given. I learned then, for the first time, how tender, if how searching, is the finger Mr. Strachey lays on our human frailties." In 1905, she went on a bicycling holiday with Roger Fry in Normandy. He remembered that "it was the fashion then for women to bicycle in bloomers, but Jane had invented a costume for herself consisting of tight breeches and Bishop's apron. She was very pleased with it herself, but the Frogs thought it extremely outré. The following year she almost caused a riot when she appeared in this garb at the Gare du Nord."

182   **"When I knew"**—Leonard Woolf, *An Autobiography*, vol. 2, p. 204.

182   **"Knowing my"**—JEH to D. S. Mirsky, November 21, 1924. Newnham.

183   **"there are few"**—JEH, *Themis*, p. 450.

183   **"full of them"**—Frances Partridge, *Love in Bloomsbury*, p. 60.

183   **"the emotional"**—D. S. Mirsky, *Jane Ellen Harrison and Russia*, p. 10.

183   **"the OO"**—Notebook of Bear Facts. Newnham HM.

184   **in subtle dedication**—Harrison's *Epilegomena* (1921) has an Arabic dedication to Hope; Hope's novel *Madeleine* uses a quote from *Ancient Art and Ritual* as the epigraph for its final chapter.

184   **"fantastic dramas"**—JEH and HM, *The Book of the Bear*, p. xii.

186   **"We chose"**—JEH to Gilbert Murray, undated (September 1926). Newnham.

186   **"The Bear never"**—JEH to Jessie Stewart, December 30, 1926. Newnham.

186   **a long essay**—"Some Aspects of the Art of Alexey Mikhailovich Remizov," reprinted in Parmar (ed.), HM, *Collected Poems*.

187   **"I have lost"**—JEH to Gilbert Murray, August 1924 (misdated 1923 by Stewart). Newnham.

187   **"Slav soul"**—D. S. Mirsky, *Jane Ellen Harrison and Russia*, pp. 9–11.

187   **poverty-stricken exile**—Her last letter to Seraphima, written shortly

before her death, expressed profound grief that her medical expenses had so impoverished her that she could not send the money Seraphima had evidently requested. As late as 1933, Mirrlees sent a small royalty check for the use of Remizov's bear stories in an anthology for schools.

187 **"I had a book"**—JEH to Gilbert Murray, May 16, 1927. Newnham.

188 **"deeply interesting"**—JEH to D. S. Mirsky, January 29, 1926. Newnham.

189 **in-fighting**—Mirsky, who described himself in 1925 as an "anti-communist," became increasingly pro-Soviet. By 1931 he had begun writing a biography of Lenin and joined the Communist Party. He returned to Russia in 1932 under the patronage of Maxim Gorky, but after Gorky's death in 1936, he was arrested and deported to a labor camp, where he is thought to have died in 1939. One of the last pieces he wrote before leaving England was a denunciation of the bourgeois morals of many Bloomsbury writers, including Virginia Woolf, to her dismay ("I'm hated & despised & ridiculed").

189 **"The way walked"**—D. S. Mirsky, *Jane Ellen Harrison and Russia*, p. 4.

190 **"the richest civilisation"**—JEH to HM, January 1921. Newnham.

190 **the work of Dante**—In *Prolegomena*, she had written about an inscribed tablet of thin gold, which she had found in a tomb in Naples in 1902, and which signaled allegiance to the widespread cult of the god Orpheus. The tablet contained instructions for the conduct of the dead in the underworld, ordering the soul to avoid a well called Lethe (named for the goddess who takes away any recollection of mortal sin) and instead drink from one flowing from Mnemosyne (who recovers the memory of good deeds in life, and thus renders immortality). At that time, Francis Cornford had alerted her to a similar story in Dante's *Purgatorio* of the dead being washed on their way to heaven in two rivers named Lethe and Eunoe. She had wondered where this second name (generally considered a Dantean neologism) had come from, and had speculated that it could be a survival of the word "Ennoia," which she had seen on another Orphic tablet. Her research had stalled until she began learning Persian and came across a book entitled *Islam and the Divine Comedy*, written in 1926 by the Spanish scholar Miguel Asín Palacios. Reading this, she grew convinced that Dante's work derived many of its elements from early Iranian tradition, and suddenly wondered whether Orphic ritual ("that strange un-Greek eschatology") might be traced to the same sources. The possibility enthralled her: "Of course it has often enough been suggested that Orphism had oriental elements. But I believe now that in the case of Eunoe—Ennoia—we can clinch the matter with a definite instance." Intriguingly—and inexplicably—a copy of this letter from Harrison to Murray is among Dorothy L. Sayers's papers at Wheaton College.

190 **"upset the whole"**—JEH to Gilbert Murray, August 22, 1926. Newnham.

190 **"Bother my vile body"**—JEH to Gilbert Murray, September 1, 1926. Newnham.

190 **"to re-write the mysteries"**—ibid.

191 **"Nothing Doing"**—JEH to Jessie Stewart, December 30, 1926. Newnham.

191 **"a stream of"**—Hope Mirrlees: biography research. Newnham.

191 **"went right down"**—JEH to Gilbert Murray, January 8, 1928. Newnham.

191 **Thomas Hardy's funeral**—Virginia Woolf, who had prepared a major obituary of Hardy for the *TLS* back in 1919, also attended. During the service her mind wandered, and she began planning the lecture that would become *A Room of One's Own*.

191 **"ungracious"**—Victoria de Bunsen to Jessie Stewart, quoted in Annabel Robinson, *The Life and Work of Jane Ellen Harrison*, p. 304.

191 **"which as a rule"**—HM to Seraphima Remizov, April 28, 1928. Amherst.

191 **"Dear N. V."**—Seraphima Remizov to HM, undated. Amherst.

192 **"crossing the graveyard"**—VW, diary, April 17, 1928.

192 **"It was only"**—HM to Valerie Eliot, January 5, 1965. Woolf's letter actually read: "Anyhow, what a comfort for you to have been all you were to her." VW to HM, April 17, 1928. Maryland.

192 **"delightful old ladies"**—Interview with Jane Harrison, *Time and Tide*, January 27, 1928.

192 **"You cannot be"**—JEH, "Crabbed Age and Youth," *Alpha and Omega*, p. 17.

193 **in *A Room***—Woolf gave the lecture "A Room of One's Own" at Newnham on October 20, 1928; one week later, on Saturday, October 27, 1928, friends gathered at the college to hear Gilbert Murray give the inaugural Jane Harrison Lecture.

193 **"I had not"**—Lytton Strachey to Roger Fry, April 18, 1928. Quoted in Michael Holroyd, *Lytton Strachey*, p. 1026.

Eileen Power

195 **"by the study"**—Albert Kahn Foundation for the Foreign Travel of American Teachers. Reports, volume 1, issue 1, 1912.

195 **"an enlightened French"**—Guy Fletcher, "World History," *Radio Times*, June 21, 1933.

195 **"defeat the objects"**—EP to George Coulton, April 27, 1920. Girton.

196 **"enjoyed the novel"**—EP, diary, December 24, 1920. CUL.

196 **"I would not"**—EP to George Coulton, July 31, 1921. Girton.

196 **"saintly"**—EP, "Mahatma Gandhi's Boycott: another view." CUL.

196 **"I found myself"**—EP, Report to the Trustees, undated. CUL.

197 **"more stridently"**—EP, journal, 1920–1921. CUL.

197 **"the historical textbook"**—EP, diary, May 10–12, 1921. CUL.

197 **"that China can"**—EP, Report to the Trustees. CUL.

197 **"The A. K. fellowship"**—EP to George Coulton, September 5, 1925. Girton.

197 **"I never felt"**—EP to Lilian Knowles, December 24, 1921. LSE.

198 **"the thing which"**—EP to Lilian Knowles, April 3, 1922. LSE.

198 **bevy of journalists**—The scene is beautifully described in Dora Russell's autobiography, *The Tamarisk Tree*.

198 **Margery Spring Rice**—née Margery Garrett, author of *Working-Class Wives*, the classic account of women's lives in the 1930s; and niece of Elizabeth Garrett Anderson and Millicent Garrett Fawcett.

198 **"I thought it"**—EP to Margery Garrett, July 31, 1921. Girton.

198 **"You need not"**—EP to William Beveridge, July 26, 1921. LSE.

198 **"I rather begrudge"**—EP to Amy Lowell, March 1, 1925. Houghton AL. Former students at Girton remembered Sunday-evening poetry readings in Power's rooms, where she would read her favorite poem, Marvell's "To His Coy Mistress," and works by Browning, Brooke, Flecker, Ralph Hodgson, and W. H. Davies.

199 **"I am extremely"**—EP to George Coulton, January 30, 1922. Girton.

199 **Tantalizing fragments**—See Maxine Berg, *A Woman in History*, p. 155. Robeson's wife, Eslanda—who also starred in the film—studied at LSE in the 1930s, where they may have met Power.

200 **"I certainly feel"**—EP to Margery Garrett, July 9, 1912. Girton. Winifred Gaukroger, a former student, remembered most of the Girton dons as "very quaint old birds" who wore "antiquated clothes—a dress with a high neck with buttons from the throat right down to the ground . . . Miss Power, the history don, is quite different from the rest . . . she wears lovely clothes and from the swish she makes evidently wears silk petticoats." Girton.

200 **The obituaries**—R. H. Tawney, address at Golders Green crematorium, August 12, 1940, Girton; J. H. Clapham, "Eileen Power," *The Times*, August 13, 1940; Charles Webster, "Eileen Power," *Economic Journal*, vol. 50, December 1940; G. G. Coulton, "Memories of Eileen Power," *The Cambridge Review*, vol. 52, October 18, 1940.

202 **her salary rose**—When Knowles wrote a testimonial for Power in 1914, she insisted that "Miss Power is by far the best student that has come under my hands in my ten years at the school, & my men are many (& some of them getting their thousand a year now). I hope she will not get the fellowship because then Girton will not keep her & I want her as my colleague & later as my successor."

202 **"because I can't"**—EP to Lilian Knowles, April 3, 1921. LSE.

202 **"like the community"**—EP, "The Problem of the Friars," *The Nation and Athenaeum*, January 18, 1928.

202 **"the virtues"**—JEH, "Homo Sum," *Alpha and Omega*, p. 84.

203 **"is so anxious"**—EP to Margery Garrett, January 6, 1911. Girton.

203   **"a woman's outlook"**—EP, "Women at Cambridge," *The Old Cambridge*, February 14, 1920. In her essay "Are Women Human?," Dorothy L. Sayers wrote of her annoyance at being so often asked for "the women's point of view" on detective fiction: "Go away and don't be silly. You might as well ask what is the female angle on an equilateral triangle."

203   **"extracting all"**—EP to Margery Garrett, August 22, 1910. Girton.

203   **"At her house"**—Judith Listowel, *This I Have Seen*, p. 48.

204   **"The Intractable Princess"**—Girton.

204   **"pirouetting in the"**—EP to Margery Garrett, October 6, 1911. Girton.

205   **"I feel stupid"**—EP to Margery Garrett, August 8, 1910. Girton.

206   **"quite in love"**—EP to Margery Garrett, August 22, 1910. Girton.

206   **"in order to"**—EP to Margery Garrett, August 18, 1910. Girton.

206   **"stumbling along"**—EP to Margery Garrett, May 17, 1911. Girton.

206   **"which divides"**—EP to Margery Garrett, January 6, 1911. Girton.

206   **"exasperating them"**—EP to Margery Garrett, April 7, 1910. Girton.

206   **"asserted that"**—EP to Margery Garrett, February 7, 1911. Girton.

206   **"living la vie Boheme"**—EP to Margery Garrett, August 15, 1910. Girton.

206   **"the most disreputable"**—EP to Margery Garrett, March 26, 1911. Girton.

206   **"feminists, radicals"**—ibid.

208   **full-length published**—Power's first publication was the booklet *The Paycockes of Coggeshall* (Methuen, 1920), based on research at Paycocke's House in Essex, a Tudor merchant's home now owned by the National Trust.

208   **Alice Clark**—For more on these women historians—many involved with Girton and the LSE, and also campaigners for the suffrage and the League of Nations—see Maxine Berg, "The First Women Economic Historians: The LSE Connection," pp. 308–29.

208   **"sounded to the"**—Vera Brittain, *Testament of Youth*, p. 25.

209   **"preachers told them"**—EP, *Medieval Women*, p. 3.

209   **"the middle ages"**—EP, "English Domestic Letter Writers of the Middle Ages." CUL.

209   **"Victorian relegation"**—She reviewed Richard Aldington's translation of *Les Quinze Joyes* for the *New Statesman*, and accused him of "medieval misogyny" because of his complacent remarks on "the inferior and dependent position of women in the Middle Ages."

209   **"to speak of"**—EP, *Medieval People*, p. 18.

209   **"wildly socialistic"**—EP to Margery Garrett, October 17, 1910. Girton.

209   **"the obscure lives"**—EP, *Medieval People*, p. 18. DLS to C. S. Lewis, January 26, 1949: "Does one ever quite get over one's surprise at finding that medieval people were just like people today? That their disputes and quarrels and arguments only need translating out of that extraordinary

dialectical style to become *exactly* the sort of problems that worry you and me? One *knows* they were real people—why does one keep on forgetting it?"

210 **"if less spectacular"**—EP, *Medieval People*, p. vii.

210 **"We still praise"**—ibid., p. 19.

210 **"dew-dabblers"**—EP to Margery Garrett, July 22, 1911. Girton.

211 **Rockefeller Foundation**—Hugh Dalton, *Call Back Yesterday*, p. 109.

211 **cages of chimps**—Stephen Kresge and Leif Wenar (eds.), *Hayek on Hayek: An Autobiographical Dialogue*, p. 82.

211 **converted army huts**—Lionel Robbins, *Autobiography of an Economist*, p. 69.

211 **almost three thousand students**—Ralf Dahrendorf, *LSE*, p. 153.

211 **"circle of rebellious"**—Beatrice Webb, diary, March 20, 1918.

211 **Charles Webster**—Webster was a member of the Honorary Powers—a "most select society" for men who "must be able to recognise the Power idea of a joke at sight"; and who "must at no time have proposed to any of the Power sisters, such proposal constituting an implied slight upon the Honorary surname."

212 **"hotbed of communist teaching"**—1934 letter to the *Telegraph* from Sir Ernest Graham-Little, quoted in Ralf Dahrendorf, *LSE*, p. 280.

212 **"often chafed"**—EP to George Coulton, March 20, 1921. Girton.

213 **chocolate creams**—VW, diary, January 6, 1940.

213 **"I like people"**—EP to Helen Cam, January 6, 1938. Girton.

213 **"cabbage wallpapers"**—EP to Margery Garrett, August 22, 1910. Girton.

213 **"scores of books"**—J. H. Clapham, *The Times*, August 13, 1940.

214 **"I never realised"**—EP to Margery Garrett, November 6, 1910. Girton.

214 **"admired and much-loved"**—EP to George Coulton, September 5, 1923. Girton.

215 **"I've lent"**—EP to Michael Postan, June 25 (no year given). Girton.

215 **"any woman"**—Papers of Dorothy Marshall. Girton.

215 **"a scholar"**—Beatrice Webb, diary, December 8, 1935.

215 **"an idealist"**—VW, diary, November 11, 1917.

216 **"to abolish all"**—R. H. Tawney, *The Choice Before the Labour Party*, p. 6.

216 **"the study, not of"**—R. H. Tawney, "The Study of Economic History," lecture at LSE, October 12, 1932, in J. M. Winter (ed.), *History and Society: Essays by R. H. Tawney*.

216 **"The main business"**—EP, "On Medieval History as Social Study," inaugural lecture delivered at LSE, January 18, 1933. CUL.

217 **"all those Bloomsberries"**—EP to Margery Garrett, September 24, 1914. Girton.

217 **"hankered after"**—LSE Tawney. In the same text, Jeanette goes on to describe 44 Mecklenburgh Square in some detail: "To our delighted

surprise the three lower floors of a house in one of [Bloomsbury's] squares was offered to us at a figure within our competence . . . By some good chance, sunrises exist in very fact in this square; a path has been left through the house-tops for the golden rays. Here in the very heart of the metropolis is a silence so complete as to be audible. There is an atmosphere of past and present that endears the square to the sensitive and imaginative. Internally these dignified edifices have been submitted to much drastic treatment. Externally, their purity of line and color remain. None of these houses are now possessed of their own stables. Where the stables stood, there is now a garage or a shop. The old-fashioned indoor water-closet without outside ventilation, in the form of a cupboard on the top of the stairs, remains to date the primitive civilisation of a hundred and fifty years ago, when one water closet was deemed adequate for a large family, and when there was no bathroom. The stairs are made of that beautiful grey stone, which when polished and left bare, makes an admirable foil for the red of Persian handiwork. The treads are half the height of modern stairs, and the steps twice as wide. It is therefore possible for a long-footed man to go downstairs without turning his foot sideways, or shooting down the stairs. Inaudibly he can go up and down these stairs, for they neither creak nor groan. The handrail is of pure mahogany, polished by years of palm rubbings. You grasp it with affection just for the pleasure of a rare sensation. There are charming leaded lights above the second hall door, which give a 'cachet' of mystery to the house, like successive courts in eastern homes give an air of reserve and strength to the citadel. You are ever intrigued as to what lies beyond. The perfect parlor-maid (where is she?) would close the inner door silently when the front door bell rings. Thus would she protect the inner shrine of the hall from the common gaze, and the inrush of the icy blast, which alas! too often pervades London's squares."

217 **"mental disease"**—R. H. Tawney, *Equality*, p. 198.

218 **"a compost-heap"**—"Profile: R. H. Tawney," *Observer*, January 25, 1953.

219 **"he really is"**—EP to William Beveridge, March 3, 1931. LSE.

219 **"you are continually"**—EP to Michael Postan, January 29 (no year given). Girton.

219 **regular fixtures**—Attendees included Frederick Brown, Robert Fraser, Richard Greaves, Arthur Creech Jones, John Parker, Leonard Woolf, Barbara Wootton. See Postan in W. T. Rodgers (ed.), *Hugh Gaitskell*; Brian Brivati, *Hugh Gaitskell*; and Elizabeth Durbin, *New Jerusalems*.

219 **these informal**—Some of the group's findings formed contributions to the books *New Trends in Socialism* (1935) and *War and Democracy* (1938), edited by George Catlin, and Evan Durbin's book *The Politics of Democratic Socialism* (1940).

220 **"Why are you"**—Vera Brittain, *Testament of Friendship*, p. 132.

220   **"an international authority"**—Leonard Woolf, *An Autobiography*, vol. 2, p. 134.

221   **"The parallel"**—EP to Margery Garrett, July 7, 1917. Girton.

221   **"the greatest ideal"**—Helen McCarthy, *The British People and the League of Nations*, p. 24.

221   **"The hope"**—H. G. Wells to the Chairman of the National Conference on War Aims, December 26, 1917.

222   **"The only way"**—EP, *A Bibliography for School Teachers of History*, p. 9.

223   **The Victorian certainty**—See Richard Overy, *The Morbid Age: Britain and the Crisis of Civilization, 1919–1939*.

223   **"If the League"**—EP, *A Bibliography for School Teachers of History*, p. 9.

224   **"no less imperative"**—EP, Notes on "A League of Nations." CUL.

224   **"the teaching of"**—H. G. Wells, "World Peace," *The Listener*, July 17, 1929.

224   **"so as to widen"**—EP, "The Teaching of History and World Peace," in F. S. Marvin (ed.), *The Evolution of World Peace*, p. 180.

224   **"is one of the most powerful"**—Unpublished essay, "The Approach to Political and Economic Problems in Schools." Quoted in Maxine Berg, *A Woman in History*, p. 223.

225   **"active desire"**—"Formation of the Schools Broadcasting Council" pamphlet. BBC.

225   **"It is fun"**—Hilda Matheson to H. G. Wells, June 14, 1929. BBC.

225   **an impassioned address**—H. G. Wells, "World Peace," *The Listener*, July 17, 1929.

225   **Beryl**—Beryl Power was a speaker and organizer for the National Union of Women's Suffrage Societies; aged twenty-two she was addressing huge outdoor meetings in Hyde Park with Millicent Fawcett. During the war she became a factory inspector, and later a permanent civil servant in the Ministry of Labour. In 1926 she won a scholarship to spend a year traveling in the United States studying the enforcement of labor laws for women and children. She served as a member of the Royal Commission on Labour in India between 1929 and 1931; she became the second of the Power sisters to meet Mahatma Gandhi. During the Second World War she worked in the Ministry of Food, then advised on welfare policy in China as part of the Bangkok-based UN Economic and Social Commission for Asia and the Far East. She was closely involved with the Institute of Race Relations: like her sisters, she believed that "the urgent problem of the relations of the different races and nations of the world holds the key to the future pattern of our shrinking, tumultuous and highly dangerous world."

227   **a cigarette card**—"I keep it in my purse because it's very useful when Eileen and Beryl are given fresh academic and civic honors, I just take it out in their presence and look at it quietly and significantly, to remind them of what *real* fame is."

227 **"one of the most effective"**—Letter to Rhoda Power, December 1934. BBC.

227 **"some definite lessons"**—EP to Mary Somerville, January 27, 1936. BBC.

227 **she and Rhoda**—Guy Fletcher, "World History," *Radio Times*, June 21, 1933. "Two women, sisters, both dark with grey eyes; each with a streak of Puck in her, although in Eileen, as becomes a Professor, it is more restrained . . . It is their job, through book and travel, to interview the ghosts of Kublai Khan and Marco Polo, of some medieval monk in Picardy, some Roman sentinel listening for the Barbarian in the fearful dark; to recreate dead men, to uncover buried cities. And their interviews, their research, their imagination, or the fruits of all three, are called World History, to which Schools listen, and everyone who has left school who can."

227 **"it is, as you know"**—EP to Mary Somerville, March 29, 1936. BBC. In June 1936, the BBC informed her that they had cut a phrase from her lecture as "we rather felt that the missionary societies might object to this kind of statement." Power replied: "I note that you have cut my phrase about the quarrels of the missionaries in the 18th C. As you know, it was this which resulted in the shutting of China to the West and I strongly deprecate these attempts of the BBC to tamper with the presentation of history in order to save the susceptibilities of a class of its listeners. I am, in point of fact, extremely careful to be fair in these matters, and I had therefore deliberately mentioned later in the talk, that 'the missionaries brought schools and hospitals, where the Chinese could learn western learning and be healed by western science.' I have now cut out this reference to the good side of missionary history in China, as I am not allowed to mention its bad side."

227 **"the common contribution"**—EP to Mary Somerville, January 27, 1936. BBC.

228 **"serious attack"**—See Susan Howson, *Lionel Robbins*, pp. 236–8.

228 **a percentage of**—This was 1 percent for lecturers, 2 percent for readers, 3 percent for professors. Among the refugee scholars helped by LSE during the 1930s were Gustav Mayer, Moritz Bonn, Jacob Marschak, and Otto Kahn-Freund. From November 1938, the Co-ordinating Committee for Refugees headquartered at Margaret Layton's home at 5 Mecklenburgh Square—an independent organization dedicated to helping Central European refugees, finding them work and housing, and lobbying the government.

229 **"If we want"**—Albert Einstein, speech, October 3, 1933, published as "Science and Civilisation" in *Essays in Humanism*.

229 **"If, in the case"**—*Spectator*, March 5, 1932.

229 **Muslim countries**—See her article "The Indian Moslems and the

Turkish Nationalists," *The Challenge*, December 8, 1922: "In the world of politics today, grave as are the other political questions left by the war—the reparations question, the resuscitation of dying Austria, the policy to be pursued toward Bolshevik Russia—none is graver than this problem of the relation between the Western powers and Islam, for if it be not settled on terms which are honorable to both, the age of the Jehad and the Crusades may come again."

230   **"an adequate account"**—EP to Mary Somerville, January 2, 1936. BBC.

230   **"merely as a"**—EP, "The Story of Half Mankind," *The Challenge*, September 20, 1922.

230   **"Yellow Peril"**—For an evocative portrait of London's Chinese communities—and of the racism they faced, particularly in finding Bloomsbury lodgings—see Lao She's 1929 novel *Mr. Ma and Son*.

230   **"East is East"**—Rudyard Kipling, "The Ballad of East and West" (1889).

230   **twice in the 1920s**—Robert A. Bickers, *Britain in China: Community, Culture and Colonialism*, p. 52.

230   **"White girls hypnotised"**—*Evening News* front page, October 6, 1920.

231   **Reginald Johnston**—See Shiona Airlie, *Scottish Mandarin*. Life at Puyi's court is dramatized in the Oscar-winning 1987 film *The Last Emperor*, where Johnston is portrayed by Peter O'Toole.

232   **"I remember him"**—EP to George Coulton, December 23, 1922. Girton.

233   **"journalism and odd-jobs"**—EP to Margery Garrett, July 31, 1921. Girton.

233   **"You gave me"**—EP to Arnold Toynbee, February 23, 1930. He told his wife, Rosalind, who remained sanguine: "I don't think she would have been a better wife for you than me, though she would have been quite a good one." Bodleian.

234   **"everyone whose work"**—EP to Virginia Gildersleeve, August 6, 1930. Barnard.

234   **"the difficulty is"**—EP to Virginia Gildersleeve, November 28, 1930. Barnard.

235   **School Textbooks**—In 1932, Power invited Charles Webster to join her in a project to launch an international committee to revise school textbooks: "I think most of the work will be done in the basement of 20 Mecklenburgh Square!"

235   **"no more powerful"**—Speech to the Sixth International Conference of the International Federation of University Women, 1932, quoted in Carol Dyhouse, *No Distinction of Sex?*, p. 171.

236   **"a threat to"**—China Campaign Committee Circulars and Bulletins. AC.

236   **a whimsical essay**—EP, "The Haunted Valley," first published in *The Raven*, May 1, 1922. "The hills bend over it, curving their beautiful abundant bodies to shelter the solitary scholar, escaped from the man-built walls of the city to their protection and their peace."

237 **"War seems inevitable"**—VW, diary, August 29, 1935.

238 **"forget about"**—H. G. Wells to Olaf Stapledon, April 4, 1936.

238 **"almost as much"**—H. G. Wells to *The Times*, May 19, 1936.

239 **"A Manifesto"**—*Manchester Guardian*, November 15, 1938.

239 **"Why did they"**—EP, "The Eve of the Dark Ages: a tract for the times." CUL. In the same folder, along with Power's research notes for the lecture, is C. P. Cavafy's poem "Waiting for the Barbarians," and an article by H. N. Brailsford titled "A Memory of Poland."

239 **assembly in Geneva**—See also her report in the *Spectator*, "Geneva Impressions," December 22, 1939.

240 **"large-scale international trade"**—EP, *The Wool Trade in English Medieval History* (OUP, 1941), p. 1.

240 **"in your little flat"**—EP to Michael Postan, May 29, 1940. Private collection.

241 **"rigorously concealed"**—Raymond Firth to Cynthia Postan, July 1, 1983. Private collection.

241 **"He and I"**—EP to Arnold Toynbee, December 1937. Bodleian.

241 **"I am not"**—EP to Lionel Robbins, December 10, 1937. LSE Robbins.

242 **"furious and miserable"**—EP to Margery Garrett, January 6, 1911. Girton.

242 **"their old interests"**—EP to Margery Garrett, November 6, 1910. Girton.

242 **"The abstract cause"**—EP to Margery Garrett, March 26, 1911. Girton.

242 **"I do think"**—EP to Margery Garrett, January 6, 1911. Girton.

243 **"look upon marriage"**—VW to Leonard Woolf, May 1, 1912.

243 **"One of the greatest"**—EP to Michael Postan, May 29, 1940. Private collection.

243 **"to the extent"**—EP to Margery Garrett, August 22, 1910. Girton.

243 **"We have had"**—EP to Michael Postan, May 30, 1940. Private collection.

243 **"Harriet Vane"**—Recollection of Barbara Clapham, quoted in Berg, *A Woman in History*, p. 194.

244 **"had occasion to"**—Clapham and Power (eds.), *Cambridge Economic History of Europe from the Decline of the Roman Empire, vol. I: The Agrarian Life of the Middle Ages*.

245 **"in spite of "**—EP, *A Bibliography for School Teachers of History*, p. 10.

Virginia Woolf

247 **"no stir in"**—VW, diary, August 24, 1939.

247 **"It's fate"**—ibid.

248 **"rather rashly"**—VW to Vanessa Bell, June 18, 1939.

248 **"a tight wound ball"**—VW, diary, May 14, 1939.

248 **"I long for"**—ibid.

248 **"the horror"**—VW, diary, September 3, 1928. She uses the same phrase in *To the Lighthouse*.

248 **"a grim thought"**—VW, diary, July 13, 1939.

248 **"too tired"**—VW, diary, September 3, 1939.

248 **"The kitchen"**—VW, diary, October 22, 1939.

249 **"a chamber pot"**—VW to Dorothy Bussy, November 5, 1939.

249 **"I've two nice"**—VW to Vita Sackville-West, August 19, 1939.

249 **"How to go on"**—VW, diary, August 28, 1939.

249 **"She is for"**—Quoted in Hermione Lee, *Virginia Woolf*, p. 690.

249 **"a base emotion"**—VW, diary, January 3, 1915.

250 **"preposterous masculine fiction"**—VW to Margaret Llewelyn Davies, January 23, 1916.

251 **"the complete ruin"**—VW, diary, August 17, 1938.

251 **"But what's the"**—VW, diary, September 28, 1938.

251 **"the worst of all"**—VW, diary, September 6, 1939.

251 **"sensible, rather"**—VW, diary, May 15, 1940.

252 **"Over all hangs"**—VW, diary, July 11, 1939.

252 **"betwixt and between"**—VW to W. J. H. Sprott, August 15, 1940.

252 **"our village"**—ibid.

252 **"the usual fight"**—VW, diary, July 11, 1939.

252 **"We lead a"**—VW to Ethel Smyth, February 7, 1940.

252 **"this doomed"**—VW to Angelica Bell, October 16, 1939.

252 **"take my brain"**—VW, diary, July 30, 1939.

252 **"all in the know"**—VW, diary, September 23, 1939.

252 **"He gets up"**—VW, diary, May 25, 1940.

253 **"all spoken of"**—VW, diary, January 19, 1940.

253 **"this war means"**—VW, diary, February 16, 1940.

253 **"A good idea"**—VW, diary, July 5, 1940.

253 **"all set on"**—VW, diary, October 22, 1939.

254 **"driving open eyed"**—VW, diary, October 22, 1939.

254 **"Yes, its an empty meaningless world"**—VW, diary, September 6, 1939.

254 **"This idea struck me"**—VW, diary, May 15, 1940.

254 **Louie Everest**—See Joan Russell Noble (ed.), *Recollections of Virginia Woolf by Her Contemporaries*.

255 **"It's best to"**—VW, diary, September 6, 1939.

255 **"the frying pan"**—VW, diary, October 6, 1939.

255 **"This will see"**—VW, diary, September 23, 1939.

255 **"Leonard says"**—VW to Angelica Bell, October 1, 1939.

255 **"You can't think"**—VW to Margaret Llewelyn Davies, May 2, 1917.

256 **"the only woman"**—VW, diary, September 22, 1925.

256 **"a virgin"**—VW to Violet Dickinson, September 22, 1907.

256 **"As I told you"**—VW to Leonard Woolf, May 1, 1912.

257 **"dailiness"**—VW, diary, July 31, 1926.

257 **"their bonds were"**—John Lehmann, *Thrown to the Woolfs*, p. 68.

258 **"That egotistical young man"**—VW, diary, September 2, 1932.

258 **"create a laboratory"**—John Lehmann (ed.) *Folios of New Writing*, 1940.

259 **stepped back**—Lehmann missed her being present "to discuss the manuscripts that came in, to gossip about the authors . . . to plan new anthologies and new series . . . and to laugh over the day-to-day alarms and excursions in our office life."

260 **"Observe perpetually"**—VW, diary, March 8, 1941.

260 **"roared with laughter"**—VW to Ethel Smyth, October 6, 1932.

260 **"We're splinters and mosaics"**—VW, diary, September 15, 1924.

261 **"nobody—none"**—VW to Mrs. R. C. Trevelyan, September 4, 1940.

261 **"odd posthumous friendship"**—VW, diary, December 30, 1935.

261 **"While we ate"**—John Lehmann, *I Am My Brother*, p. 34.

261 **"I dont feel"**—VW, diary, September 10, 1938.

262 **"paroxysms of rage"**—VW, *Roger Fry*, p. 153.

262 **"they are the works"**—Quoted in VW, *Roger Fry*, p. 157.

262 **"found out how"**—VW, diary, July 26, 1922.

262 **"You have I think"**—VW to Roger Fry, May 27, 1927.

262 **"quite futile"**—VW, diary, September 30, 1934.

262 **"full and outspoken"**—VW, diary, April 5, 1935. She told Dorothy Bussy how impressed she was with André Gide's diaries, which were frank about homosexuality: "Why, if he can say all that, can't I come out with the comparatively modest truth about Roger and his affairs?" She concluded that she found Gide "very French and drastic, and a little stringent. So very French: and here we're so plumpuddingy."

263 **"new biography"**—See her essay "The New Biography," in *Selected Essays*.

263 **"How does one"**—VW to Ethel Smyth, January 20, 1937.

263 **"full of tailor's bills"**—VW to Vita Sackville-West, December 3, 1939.

263 **"almost as a"**—VW, *Roger Fry: A Series of Impressions*.

263 **"sheer drudgery"**—VW, diary, September 25, 1939.

263 **"dazed & depressed"**—VW, diary, August 9, 1939.

263 **"A bad morning"**—VW, diary, May 1, 1939.

263 **"an experiment"**—VW to Ethel Smyth, August 16, 1940.

264 **"going over each"**—VW, "A Sketch of the Past," *Moments of Being*, p. 123.

264 **"spin a kind"**—VW, diary, May 20, 1940.

264 **"by way of "**—VW, "A Sketch of the Past," *Moments of Being*, p. 87.

265 **"Shall I ever"**—ibid., p. 109.

265 **"I was thinking"**—VW to Ethel Smyth, December 24, 1940.

265 **"Lord how I"**—VW to Ethel Smyth, July 9, 1940.

266 **"this is bosh"**—VW, diary, September 3, 1939.

266 **"miraculously sealed"**—VW, "I Am Christina Rossetti," in *The Common Reader*.

266 **"I do not suppose"**—VW, "A Sketch of the Past," *Moments of Being*, p. 82.

267 **"convinced that"**—VW to Judith Stephen, December 2, 1939.

267 **"More and more"**—VW, diary, March 19, 1919.

269 **"the pressures"**—VW, "A Sketch of the Past," *Moments of Being*, p. 104.

269 **"I suppose"**—ibid., p. 93.

269 **"that this violently disturbing"**—ibid., p. 147.

269 **"anything too intimate"**—VW to Violet Dickinson, November 1904.

270 **"like being shut"**—VW, "A Sketch of the Past," *Moments of Being*, p. 123.

270 **"his life"**—VW, diary, November 28, 1928.

270 **"tremendous encumbrance"**—VW, "A Sketch of the Past," *Moments of Being*, p. 52.

270 **"the fictitious VW"**—VW, diary, July 28, 1940.

272 **"I'm using this frozen pause"**—VW to Ethel Smyth, February 1, 1940.

272 **"though of course"**—VW, diary, February 9, 1940.

272 **"the authentic glow"**—VW, diary, February 11, 1940.

272 **"radiant and buoyant"**—John Lehmann, *I Am My Brother*, p. 35.

272 **"very severe lecture"**—VW, diary, March 20, 1940.

273 **"some 100 corrections"**—VW to Ethel Smyth, March 27, 1940.

273 **"to have given"**—VW, diary, March 20, 1940.

273 **"rather proud"**—VW, diary, July 26, 1940.

273 **"fools paradise"**—Quoted in VW to Ben Nicolson, August 14, 1940.

274 **"Leonard too"**—VW to Ben Nicolson, August 24, 1940.

276 **"it was hopeless"**—ibid.

276 **"lay under a cornstalk"**—VW, diary, August 28, 1940.

276 **"Its so hot and sunny"**—VW to Vita Sackville-West, August 29, 1940.

277 **"This diary"**—VW, diary, February 16, 1940.

277 **"protected shell"**—VW to Ethel Smyth, July 6, 1930.

277 **"in a torn state"**—VW, diary, December 8, 1939.

277 **"Everybody is feeling"**—VW, "London in War." Sussex.

277 **"everyone does"**—VW, diary, October 1, 1920.

277 **"has become merely"**—VW, "London in War." Sussex.

277 **"no friends"**—VW, diary, September 6, 1939.

278 **"runs so smoothly"**—Draft for "A Sketch of the Past," dated July 19, 1939. Sussex.

278 **"silent, as if"**—VW, diary, January 20, 1940.

278 **"I don't think"**—Elizabeth Bowen to VW, July 1, 1940.

278 **"Why does this"**—VW to Ethel Smyth, September 25, 1940.

279 **"we are going"**—VW to Ottoline Morrell, November 9, 1911.

280 **"nomadic life"**—LW and VW to Molly MacCarthy, September 28, 1912.

280 **"At this moment"**—VW, diary, September 25, 1929.

280 **"all so heavenly"**—VW, diary, October 12, 1940.

281 **"divine relief"**—VW, diary, October 1, 1939.

281 **"There is no echo"**—VW, diary, March 6, 1941.

281 **"take a turn"**—VW, diary, September 24, 1939.

281 **"One of the charms"**—VW, diary, October 1, 1920.

281 **"very determined"**—Diana Gardner, *The Rodmell Papers*, p. 22.

282 **"did not believe"**—ibid.

282 **"I can't give"**—VW to Judith Stephen, May 29, 1940.

282 **"My contribution"**—VW, diary, May 29, 1940.

283 **"now has become"**—VW, diary, November 23, 1940.

283 **"violent quarrels"**—VW to Margaret Llewelyn Davies, April 6, 1940.

283 **"The WI party"**—VW, diary, December 16, 1940.

284 **"I spoke to"**—VW to Ethel Smyth, July 24, 1940. Diana Gardner recalled the talk as "wonderfully and deliciously funny and I think it appealed to every woman there of all grades of education. It was so magnificently rounded and human and understandable and also very light-hearted."

284 **"severance that war"**—VW, diary, April 15, 1939.

284 **" 'I' rejected"**—VW, diary, April 26, 1938.

284 **"Wasnt it my"**—VW, diary, September 27, 1939.

285 **"random & tentative"**—VW, diary, April 26, 1938.

285 **"to amuse myself"**—VW, diary, September 16, 1938.

287 **"to go through"**—VW, diary, January 13, 1932.

287 **"how profoundly succulent"**—VW, diary, October 10, 1940.

287 **"Common History book"**—VW, diary, September 12, 1940.

287 **"the effect of country"**—*Reading at Random* notebook, September 18, 1940. In Brenda R. Silver, " 'Anon' and 'The Reader,' " p. 373.

288 **"Of course I'm"**—VW to Ethel Smyth, June 7, 1938.

288 **"a reversion"**—VW, diary, October 22, 1939.

290 **"I like outsiders"**—VW, diary, October 26, 1940.

290 **"Keep a running"**—*Reading at Random* notebook, October 3, 1940. In Brenda R. Silver, " 'Anon' and 'The Reader,' " p. 376.

291 **"germ of creation"**—ibid.

291 **"always at their"**—ibid., p. 403.

291 **"a voracious cheese mite"**—VW to Ethel Smyth, November 14, 1940.

292 **"standing about"**—VW to Lady Cecil, March 21, 1941.

292 **"The war is"**—VW, diary, May 20, 1940.

292 **"so far the"**—VW, diary, May 25, 1940.

292 **"the very flush"**—VW, diary, June 3, 1940.

293 **"the Germans are nibbling"**—VW, diary, July 4, 1940.

293 **"Up till 1:30"**—VW, diary, June 7, 1940.

293 **"I'm too jaded"**—VW, diary, August 31, 1940.

294   **Five thousand seven hundred and thirty people**—Laurence Ward
       (ed.), *The London County Council Bomb Damage Maps 1939–45*, p. 20.

295   **"thought it better"**—Leonard Woolf, *An Autobiography*, vol. 2, p. 399.

295   **"prudently deciding"**—VW, diary, October 6, 1940.

295   **"Should I think"**—VW, diary, October 2, 1940.

295   **"a scuffle"**—VW, diary, September 11, 1940.

296   **"casual young men"**—VW, diary, September 10, 1940.

296   **"he watches raids"**—ibid.

296   **"exhilaration at losing"**—VW, diary, October 20, 1940.

296   **"tumult & riot"**—VW, diary, January 6, 1915.

297   **"odd characters"**—VW, "Old Bloomsbury," *Moments of Being*, p. 46.

297   **"street frenzy"**—VW, diary, August 26, 1922.

297   **"London itself perpetually"**—VW, diary, May 31, 1928.

297   **"passion of my life"**—VW to Ethel Smyth, September 12, 1940.

297   **"Odd how often"**—VW, diary, February 2, 1940.

297   **"liberating & freshening"**—VW, diary, March 29, 1940.

After the Square

299   **"the melancholy relics"**—VW to Lady Tweedsmuir, March 21, 1941.

299   **"cram in"**—VW, diary, September 29, 1940.

299   **"breakfast, writing"**—VW, diary, October 12, 1940.

299   **"By shutting down"**—At the end of her diary, written on a separate
       sheet placed at the end of the year, Woolf composed an epitaph for the
       year: "1940 / 37 Mecklenburg Square existed till September. Then
       bombed. We went up every other week & slept there / We had Mabel /
       Roger was published on 25th June / The raids on London began in
       September / France collapsed in June / Raids here began in September /
       There was the fear of invasion / We were victorious over the Italians /
       The Greeks were successful in Albania / Herbert Fisher died / Ray
       Strachey died / Humbert Wolfe died / Hilda Matheson died / Judith &
       Leslie stayed here for August / Ann stayed with us / Mabel left in October
       / Louie takes on the house / We go up only for the day / L arranges the
       vegetable growing / Gives 12 WEA lectures / I am Treasurer of the WI /
       Morgan asked me to stand for LL Committee. I refused."

300   **"in the devil"**—VW to Ethel Smyth, December 6, 1940.

300   **"I've had to"**—ibid.

300   **"If refused"**—VW, diary, September 21, 1940.

301   **"a frigidaire"**—VW to Hugh Walpole, September 29, 1940.

301   **"never had"**—VW, diary, October 6, 1940.

301   **"I want to"**—VW, diary, October 12, 1940.

301   **"I think its an"**—VW, diary, November 23, 1940.

301 **"unparalleled imaginative"**—John Lehmann, *Thrown to the Woolfs*, p. 101.

301 **"too silly"**—VW to John Lehmann, March 27, 1941.

301 **"I never like"**—VW, diary, January 9, 1941.

301 **"an almost pathological"**—Leonard Woolf, *An Autobiography*, vol. 2, p. 106.

301 **"trough of despair"**—VW, diary, January 26, 1941.

302 **"I don't think"**—VW to Leonard Woolf (date uncertain, found March 28, 1941).

302 **"a serious loss"**—*Observer*, April 6, 1941.

302 **"a great deal"**—Elizabeth Bowen to Leonard Woolf, April 8, 1941. Quoted in Elizabeth Bowen, *The Mulberry Tree*, p. 221.

302 **"much more responsive"**—"Cannot Go On Any Longer: Virginia Woolf's Last Message," *Sunday Times*, April 20, 1941.

302 **"gloomy and querulous"**—See Joan Russell Noble (ed.), *Recollections of Virginia Woolf by Her Contemporaries*.

303 **"another ten years"**—VW to Ethel Smyth, September 12, 1940.

303 **"between 50 & 60"**—VW, diary, November 16, 1931.

303 **"a fizz of ideas"**—VW to Ethel Smyth, January 12, 1941.

303 **"Oh! That this"**—EP to R. H. Tawney, autumn 1939. LSE Tawney.

304 **2 Sylvester Road**—The house, fittingly, is now part of the Needham Research Institute for the Study of East Asia.

304 **"If only you could"**—EP to Michael Postan, May 13, 1940. Private collection.

304 **"if I emerge"**—EP to Michael Postan, May 29, 1940. Private collection.

305 **"You won't get"**—EP to Michael Postan, May 30, 1940. Private collection.

305 **"The loss"**—G. M. Trevelyan to Michael Postan, August 18, 1940. Private collection.

305 **"I am perfectly delighted"**—EP to Helen Cam, February 6, 1938. Girton.

306 **"For me, it is"**—Alys Pearsall Smith to HM, April 1928. Newnham.

307 **"I simply *couldn't*"**—HM to Jessie Stewart, September 9, 1928. Newnham.

307 **"so abominably"**—HM to Jessie Stewart, May 1, 1928. Newnham.

307 **"The words of hers"**—ibid.

307 **"wash her hands"**—Victoria de Bunsen to Jessie Stewart, March 17, 1943. Newnham.

307 **"all over the place"**—Leonard Woolf to Jessie Stewart, August 3, 1955. Newnham.

308 **"I am *horribly*"**—HM to Jessie Stewart, June 26, 1959. Newnham.

308 **"unmarried, with Bloomsbury"**—Quoted in Michael Swanwick, *Hope-in-the-Mist*, p. 47.

308 **"grown very fat"**—VW, diary, November 30, 1929.

309   **"an unknown author"**—*Radio Times*, February 9, 1978.

309   **staunch advocacy**—*Lud-in-the-Mist* was reissued by Gollancz in 2018, but her earlier novels remain out of print.

309   **"Paris and Lud"**—On August 17, 1972, Henig wrote to Mirrlees proposing that she write Hope's biography: "You are a great writer and I admire that; and you have known some of the most important writers of the century which makes you a very important person in literary history. Your biography, in a way, would be a kind of pivotal one of the century because all the others could be brought in too . . . Would you feel I would be invading your privacy because you said to me, 'I am a private person' and would it distress you if I asked a lot of personal and possibly embarrassing questions . . . But, of course, though we have not spoken of it, I am sure you know I am aware of A GREAT DEAL MORE about you than I have let on. I have spent too many years studying Bloomsbury not to have learned all the skeletons. And despite our gossiping, I carry many confidences entrusted to me by people who know, rightly, I would never divulge them without their permission . . . I think you are a fascinating, brilliant, erudite person and it would please me immensely if you permitted me to do it. Be assured you could not have a more sympathetic, sensitive or admiring biographer." Newnham HM.

309   **"stimulated others"**—Gilbert Murray to Jessie Stewart, November 5 1953. Newnham.

309   **"like a benign grandmother"**—Mary Beard, *The Invention of Jane Harrison*, p. xiii.

309   **"an originary and radical"**—ibid., p. 162.

310   **"It has been borne"**—DLS to Lady Florence Cecil, March 12, 1941.

311   **"the idea that"**—DLS to Father Herbert Kelly, October 4, 1937.

311   **"bleating public"**—DLS to Nancy Pearn, February 19, 1946.

312   **"boldly undertook"**—DLS to Milton Waldman, December 12, 1938.

312   **"as public and universal"**—DLS, *Introductory Papers on Dante*, p. xv.

312   **"a detective novelist"**—DLS to Eunice Frost, September 1949.

312   **"Historically, the thing"**—DLS to Barbara Reynolds, April 9, 1953.

312   **"personal and psychological"**—DLS to her son, June 7, 1951.

313   **"vulgar gossip"**—In 1954 she wrote to Eric Whelpton, knowing that he was being interviewed about her, requesting that he "avoid the anecdotal" if possible: "the craze for the 'personal angle' and the 'human touch' is rapidly eating away the brains of the common reader and reducing history to the level of the gossip-column and the criticism to something worse."

313   **"both my mother"**—Quoted in Barbara Reynolds (ed.) *Letters*, vol. 2, pp. 437–41.

313   **"every act"**—DLS, *Thrones, Dominations*. Wheaton.

314   **"more alive"**—H. D. to Marianne Moore, September 24, 1940. Beinecke.

314 **"The past is"**—Matte Robinson and Demetres P. Tryphonopoulos (eds.),
H. D., Hirslanden Notebooks, p. 30.

314 **"that outer threat"**—H. D., "H. D. by Delia Alton," p. 192.

314 **"new-world reconstruction"**—"The Walls Do Not Fall," in H. D.,
Trilogy, p. 22.

315 **"violent and final"**—H. D. to John Cournos, February 5, 1929. Houghton JC. The quarrel had taken place during a holiday with the Lawrences.
Aldington stayed in touch with Frieda after Lawrence's death, visiting
her and her new partner in New Mexico. On May 23, 1950, he wrote to
H. D.: "I had a letter from Frieda yesterday, in which she wrote: 'Hilda;
how is she? I shall always be grateful to her.' . . . For what it is worth to
you, what you did for Lorenzo in 1917 is remembered with gratitude by
many who think he is the one great writer in English in this century."

315 **"It may seem"**—H. D. to John Cournos, February 5, 1929. Houghton JC.

315 **"strangely embalmed"**—H. D. to George Plank, May 20, 1929.
Beinecke GP.

316 **"thunderbolt"**—H. D. to George Plank, January 27, 1937. Beinecke GP.

316 **"a sort of Byron"**—H. D. to Frances Gregg, February 10, 1937. Beinecke.

316 **"I look on it"**—H. D. to Jessie Capper, February 1, 1937. Beinecke.

316 **"a clear-up"**—H. D. to George Plank, February 19, 1937. Beinecke GP.

316 **"concentrate and say"**—H. D. to George Plank, May 18, 1938. Beinecke GP.

316 **"'divorce' from"**—H. D. to George Plank, August 3, 1938. Beinecke
GP.

317 **supreme generosity**—In another act of unwarranted kindness, Bryher
also sent money to Flo Fallas. Fallas and Aldington had lost touch after
1918, but met again in London around 1931, and remained in contact
thereafter. In a letter after Aldington's death in 1962, Flo told Bryher that
he "has been a loyal friend—much loved by us—for almost fifty years . . .
It's unbelievable what a blank there is now his letters have ended." She
told Bryher that she remembered H. D. in Devon well: "very tall, fine
eyes and slightly wonderfully madly poetic. She had recently had her baby
and lost it, and so had I. How one wonders how it would have been if
their child had lived. No good, it would never be as we think."

317 **"It's awfully good"**—Richard Aldington to H. D., January 7, 1953.
Beinecke.

317 **"Olympian, gigantic"**—Alfred Satterthwaite, "John Cournos and
'H.D.,'" p. 395.

317 **"illiterate bunny-brained whore"**—In an interview with Walter
Lowenfels, Arabella spoke about the affair for the first time. She described *Bid Me to Live* as "very libelous," and was scathing about H. D.: "I
think she fell in love with Richard inasmuch as she was capable of loving

anybody." She echoed Aldington's lines from the book: "He had married her as a mind, not as a woman." Beinecke.

317   **"pure bitchiness"**—Annotations by Cournos in a copy of *Bid Me to Live*. Beinecke. "What drivel!" "What tosh!" "Execrable English for a poetess!" "Bid Me to Live—the story of a hysteria recollected in hysteria." On October 5, 1960, he wrote to H. D. from New York, sarcastically expressing sorrow that Lawrence "pulled your leg unmercifully" and left her in the unfortunate position of "a woman scorned": "Odd of him, wasn't it, to prefer fat Frieda to you?" He concluded: "I trust your Greek preoccupations do not involve you with the ghosts of Clytemnestra, Medea and other murderesses on the Greek scene who had the good fortune to exist before Freud could analyze them . . . I have an idea, though, that faith in Freud is in itself a complex, perhaps the supreme complex. The harm Freud has done Literature is incalculable. He has killed spontaneity, the drama of intuition as Dostoevsky performed it, doing truthfully and creatively that which writers today do falsely and scientifically. Sounds like a paradox, but any authentic artist will understand me."

318   **"There still remains"**—JEH, "Scientiae Sacra Fames," *Alpha and Omega*, p. 119.

319   **"seems to me"**—EP to DLS, June 1, 1938. Wheaton.

319   **"baroque fantasy"**—*Telegraph*, June 28, 1938.

320   **"to save one of London's"**—*The Sketch*, July 13, 1938.

320   **"mania for destruction"**—Netta Syrett to the *Telegraph*, November 8, 1937.

320   **"secure these gardens"**—*London's Squares and How to Save Them* (The London Society, 1927). A plaque still stands outside the former site of the Foundling Hospital, expressing gratitude to Harold Viscount Rothermere for saving the land "for the use and welfare of the children of Central London."

321   **"a delightful little"**—*The Times*, March 10, 1950.

321   **"one of the finest"**—Douglas Goldring to the *Telegraph*, November 8, 1937.

322   **"of a pompous"**—G. F. Sheere and R. Grainger to *The Times*, March 29, 1950.

324   **"our fathers"**—VW, *Three Guineas*, p. 130.

SELECT BIBLIOGRAPHY

Editions cited are those of first publication, unless quotations refer to a later edition.

Time and Place

Sally Alexander, "A Room of One's Own: 1920s Feminist Utopias," *Women: A Cultural Review* 11:3 (2000), pp. 273–88

Mulk Raj Anand, *Conversations in Bloomsbury* (Wildwood House, 1981)

Rosemary Ashton, *Victorian Bloomsbury* (Yale UP, 2012)

Gaston Bachelard, *The Poetics of Space*, tr. Maria Jolas (Orion, 1964)

Nicola Beauman, *A Very Great Profession: The Woman's Novel, 1914–1939* (Virago, 1983)

Sara Blair, "Local Modernity, Global Modernism: Bloomsbury and the Places of the Literary," *English Literary History* 71 (2004), pp. 813–38

Chiara Briganti and Kathy Mezei, *Domestic Modernism, the Interwar Novel, and E. H. Young* (Ashgate Publishing, 2006)

Peter Brooker and Andrew Thacker (eds.), *Geographies of Modernism: Literatures, Cultures, Spaces* (Routledge, 2005)

Thomas Burke, *Living in Bloomsbury* (Allen & Unwin, 1939)

Catherine Clay, *British Women Writers, 1914–1945: Professional Work and Friendship* (Ashgate Publishing, 2006)

Paul Cohen-Portheim, *The Spirit of London* (B. T. Batsford, 1935)

Susan David Bernstein, *Roomscape: Women Writers in the British Museum from George Eliot to Virginia Woolf* (Edinburgh UP, 2013)

Leonore Davidoff, "Landladies and Lodgers," in Sandra Burman (ed.), *Fit Work for Women* (Routledge, 2013)

T. S. Eliot, *The Collected Letters of T. S. Eliot, vol. 1, 1898–1922*, ed. Hugh Haughton and Valerie Eliot (Faber & Faber, 2009)

Alice Friedman, *Women and the Making of the Modern House: A Social and Architectural History* (Yale UP, 2006)

Paul Fussell, *The Great War and Modern Memory* (OUP, 1975)

Juliet Gardiner, *The Thirties: An Intimate History* (HarperCollins, 2010)

Robert Graves and Alan Hodge, *The Long Week-End: A Social History of Great Britain, 1918–1939* (Faber & Faber, 1940)

Carolyn Heilbrun, *Writing a Woman's Life* (William Norton, 1988)

Matthew Ingleby, *Bloomsbury: Beyond the Establishment* (British Library, 2017)

———, *Novel Grounds: Nineteenth-Century Fiction and the Production of Bloomsbury* (Palgrave Macmillan, 2018)

C. L. R. James, *Letters from London* (Signal Books, 2003)

Maroula Joannou (ed.), *The History of British Women's Writing 1920–1945*, (Palgrave Macmillan, 2013)

Sally Ledger, *The New Woman: Fiction and Feminism at the Fin de Siècle* (Manchester UP, 1997)

Emma Liggins, *Odd Women?: Spinsters, Lesbians and Widows in British Women's Fiction* (Manchester UP, 2014)

Terri Mullholland, *British Boarding Houses in Interwar Women's Literature* (Routledge, 2017)

Virginia Nicholson, *Among the Bohemians: Experiments in Living, 1900–1939* (Viking, 2002)

Donald J. Olsen, *Town Planning in London* (Yale UP, 1964)

Richard Overy, *The Morbid Age: Britain and the Crisis of Civilization, 1919–1939* (Allen Lane, 2009)

Ana Parejo Vadillo, *Women Poets and Urban Aestheticism: Passengers of Modernity* (Palgrave Macmillan, 2005)

Deborah L. Parsons, *Streetwalking the Metropolis: Women, the City and Modernity* (OUP, 2000)

Peter Pepper, *A Place to Remember: The History of London House, William Goodenough House and The Burn* (Ernest Benn, 1972)

Martin Pugh, *We Danced All Night: A Social History of Britain Between the Wars* (Bodley Head, 2008)

Christopher Reed, *Bloomsbury Rooms: Modernism, Subculture and Domesticity* (Yale UP, 2004)

Dorothy Richardson, *Pilgrimage*, four vols (Virago Modern Classics, 1979)

Victoria Rosner, *Modernism and the Architecture of Private Life* (Columbia UP, 2005)

John Ruskin, *Sesame and Lilies* (John Wiley, 1865)

Morag Shiach, "London Rooms," in Lisa Shahriari and Gina Potts (eds.), *Virginia Woolf's Bloomsbury, vol. 1: Aesthetic Theory and Literary Practice* (Palgrave Macmillan, 2010)

Anna Snaith, *Modernist Voyages: Colonial Women Writers in London, 1890–1945* (CUP, 2014)

J. C. Squire, *A London Reverie: 56 Drawings by Joseph Pennell* (Macmillan, 1928)

Gertrude Tuckwell, *Constance Smith: A Short Memoir* (Duckworth, 1931)

Martha Vicinus, *Independent Women: Work and Community for Single Women, 1850–1920* (Virago, 1985)

Jerry White, *London in the Twentieth Century: A City and its People* (Viking, 2001)

H. D.

Richard Aldington, *D. H. Lawrence: Portrait of a Genius, But . . .* (Heinemann, 1950)

———, *Death of a Hero* (Chatto & Windus, 1929)

———, *Life for Life's Sake: A Book of Reminiscences* (Viking, 1941)

Cynthia Asquith, *Lady Cynthia Asquith Diaries 1915–1918* (Hutchinson, 1968)

A. E. Barlow, *Imagism and After: A Study of the Poetry* (Durham University thesis, 1975)

Bryher, *The Heart to Artemis: A Writer's Memoirs* (Collins, 1962)

Witter Bynner, *Journey with Genius* (J. Day, 1951)

Helen Carr, *The Verse Revolutionaries: Ezra Pound, H. D. and the Imagists* (Jonathan Cape, 2009)

Nephie J. Christodoulides and Polina Mackay (eds.), *The Cambridge Companion to H. D.* (CUP, 2011)

Diana Collecott (guest ed.), *Agenda* 25:3–4: H. D. Special Issue (1988)

———, *H. D. and Sapphic Modernism 1910–1950* (CUP, 1999)

John Cournos, *Autobiography* (G. P. Putnam's Sons, 1935)

———, *Miranda Masters* (Knopf, 1926)

Charles Doyle, *Richard Aldington: A Biography* (Palgrave Macmillan, 1989)

Carl Fallas, *The Gate Is Open* (Heinemann, 1938)

Elaine Feinstein, *Lawrence's Women: The Intimate Life of D. H. Lawrence* (Flamingo, 1994)

John Gould Fletcher, *Life Is My Song: The Autobiography of John Gould Fletcher* (Farrar & Rinehart, 1937)

Cecil Gray, *Musical Chairs: An Autobiography* (Home & Van Thal, 1948)

———, *Peter Warlock: A Memoir of Philip Heseltine* (Jonathan Cape, 1934)

Pauline Gray, *Cecil Gray: His Life and Notebooks* (Thames Publishing, 1989)

Eileen Gregory, *H. D. and Hellenism: Classic Lines* (CUP, 1997)

Barbara Guest, *Herself Defined: H. D. and Her World* (Doubleday, 1984)

H. D., *Asphodel* (Duke University Press, 1992)

———, *Bid Me to Live* (Virago, 1984)

————, *Collected Poems 1912–1944*, ed. Louis L. Martz (New Directions, 1983)

————, *End to Torment: A Memoir of Ezra Pound, with the poems from Hilda's Book by Ezra Pound*, ed. Norman Holmes Pearson and Michael King (New Directions, 1979)

————, *The Gift*, ed. Jane Augustine (University Press of Florida, 1998)

————, "H.D. by Delia Alton," *The Iowa Review* 16:3 (Fall, 1986)

————, *Helen in Egypt* (Grove Press, 1961)

————, *HERmione* (New Directions, 1981)

————, *Hirslanden Notebooks*, ed. Matte Robinson and Demotes P. Trypohnopoulos (ELS Editions, 2015)

————, *Magic Mirror, Compassionate Friendship, Thorn Thicket: A Tribute to Erich Heydt*, ed. Nephie Christodoulides (ELS Editions, 2012)

————, *Paint It Today* (NYU Press, 1992)

————, *Palimpsest* (Houghton Mifflin Harcourt, 1926)

————, *Tribute to Freud* (Carcanet, 1985)

————, *Trilogy* (New Directions, 1973)

Dominic Hibberd, *Harold Monro: Poet of the New Age* (Palgrave Macmillan, 2001)

Dean H. Keller (ed.), *Bubb Booklets: Letters of Richard Aldington to Charles Clinch Bubb* (Typographeum, 1988)

Mark Kinkead-Weekes, *D. H. Lawrence, vol. 2: Triumph to Exile 1912–1922* (CUP, 1996)

Donna Krolik Hollenberg, "Art and Ardor in World War One: Selected Letters from H. D. to John Cournos," *The Iowa Review* 16:3 (Fall 1986)

D. H. Lawrence, *Aaron's Rod* (Penguin, 1995)

————, *Kangaroo* (Penguin, 1950)

————, *The Letters of D. H. Lawrence, 1901–1930*, ed. James T. Boulton et al, eight vols (CUP, 1971–2001)

Frieda Lawrence, *Not I, But the Wind: D. H. Lawrence as Seen by Mrs. D. H. Lawrence* (Viking, 1934)

Robert McAlmon and Kay Boyle, *Being Geniuses Together 1920–1930* (Hogarth Press, 1984)

Adalaide Morris, "H. D.'s 'H. D. by Delia Alton," *The Iowa Review* 16:3 (Fall 1986), pp. 174–9

Nanette Norris (ed.), *Great War Modernism: Artistic Response in the Context of War, 1914–1918* (Fairleigh Dickinson UP, 2015)

Brigit Patmore, *My Friends When Young: The Memoirs of Brigit Patmore* (Heinemann, 1968)

Ezra Pound, *The Selected Letters of Ezra Pound, 1907–1941*, ed. D. D. Paige (New Directions, 1971)

Alfred Satterthwaite, "John Cournos and 'H.D.,'" *Twentieth Century Literature*, vol. 22, no. 4, pp. 394–410 (Duke UP, 1976)

Perdita Schaffner, "Running," *The Iowa Review* 16:3 (Fall, 1986)

Barry Smith, *Peter Warlock: The Life of Philip Heseltine* (OUP, 1994)

Susan Stanford Friedman (ed.), *Analyzing Freud: The Letters of H. D., Bryher and Their Circle* (New Directions, 2002)

Susan Stanford Friedman and Rachel Blau DuPlessis (eds.), *Signets: Reading H. D.* (University of Wisconsin Press, 1992)

———, *Penelope's Web: Gender, Modernity, H. D.'s Fiction* (CUP, 1990)

Vivien Whelpton, *Richard Aldington: Poet, Soldier and Lover, 1911–1929* (Lutterworth Press, 2014)

William Carlos Williams, *The Autobiography of William Carlos Williams* (MacGibbon & Kee, 1968)

John Worthen, *D. H. Lawrence: The Life of an Outsider* (Allen Lane, 2005)

Caroline Zilboorg (ed.), *Bid Me to Live* (University Press of Florida, 2011)

———, *Richard Aldington and H. D.: Their Lives in Letters, 1918–61* (Manchester UP, 2003)

Dorothy L. Sayers

E. C. Bentley, *Those Days* (Constable, 1940)

———, *Trent's Last Case* (Nelson, 1913)

James Brabazon, *Dorothy L. Sayers: A Biography* (General Publishing Co., 1981)

Vera Brittain, *Testament of Youth* (Gollancz, 1933)

———, *The Women at Oxford: A Fragment of History* (George G. Harrap, 1960)

John Cournos, *Babel* (Boni & Liveright, 1922)

———, *The Devil is an English Gentleman* (Farrar & Rinehart, 1932)

Martin Edwards, *The Golden Age of Murder* (HarperCollins, 2015)

——— (ed.), *Taking Detective Stories Seriously: The Collected Crime Reviews of Dorothy L. Sayers* (Tippermuir Books, 2017)

Rosamund Essex, *Woman in a Man's World* (Sheldon Press, 1977)

Ruth Hall, *Dear Dr. Stopes: Sex in the 1920s* (Penguin, 1981)

Richard Hand and Michael Wilson, *London's Grand Guignol and the Theatre of Horror* (Exeter UP, 2007)

Susan J. Leonardi, *Dangerous by Degrees: Women at Oxford and the Somerville College Novelists* (Rutgers UP, 1989)

Virginia Nicholson, *Singled Out: How Two Million Women Survived Without Men After the First World War* (Viking, 2007)

Layne Parish Craig, *When Sex Changed: Birth Control Politics and Literature Between the World Wars* (Rutgers UP, 2013)

J. B. Priestley, *Margin Released* (Heinemann, 1962)

Martin Priestman (ed.), *The Cambridge Companion to Crime Fiction* (CUP, 2006)

Barbara Reynolds, *Dorothy L. Sayers: Her Life and Soul* (Hodder & Stoughton, 1993)

Jane Robinson, *In the Family Way: Illegitimacy Between the Great War and the Swinging Sixties* (Viking, 2015)

Annie Rogers, *Degrees by Degrees: The Story of the Admission of Oxford Women Students to Membership of the University* (OUP, 1938)

June Rose, *Marie Stopes and the Sexual Revolution* (The History Press, 2007)

Muriel St. Clare Byrne, *Somerville College 1879–1921* (OUP, 1921)

Dorothy L. Sayers, *Clouds of Witness* (Unwin, 1926)

———, *The Documents in the Case* (Gollancz, 1930)

———, *Gaudy Night* (Hodder & Stoughton, 2003)

———, "Gaudy Night," in Denys Kilham Roberts (ed.), *Titles to Fame* (Nelson, 1937)

———, introduction to DLS (ed.) *Great Short Stories of Detection, Mystery, Horror* (Gollancz, 1928)

———, *Have His Carcase* (Gollancz, 1932)

———, *Introductory Papers on Dante* (Methuen, 1954)

———, *The Letters of Dorothy L. Sayers*, five vols, ed. Barbara Reynolds (vol. 1: Hodder & Stoughton, 1995; vols 2–5: Dorothy L. Sayers Society, 1997–2000)

———, *Lord Peter Views the Body* (Gollancz, 1928)

———, *Love All* (Tippermuir Books, 2015)

———, *Murder Must Advertise* (Gollancz, 1933)

———, *The Nine Tailors* (Gollancz, 1934)

———, *Poetry of Dorothy L. Sayers*, ed. Ralph E. Hone (Dorothy L. Sayers Society, 1996)

———, *Strong Poison* (Gollancz, 1930)

——— and Jill Paton Walsh, *Thrones, Dominations* (Hodder & Stoughton, 1998)

———, *Unnatural Death* (Benn, 1927)

———, *The Unpleasantness at the Bellona Club* (Benn, 1928)

———, *Unpopular Opinions* (Victor Gollancz, 1946)

———, *Whose Body?* (Boni & Liveright, 1923)

———, *Why Work?* (Methuen, 1942)

Alzina Stone Dale (ed.), *Dorothy L. Sayers: The Centenary Celebration* (Walker & Co., 1993)

Eric Whelpton, *The Making of a European* (Johnson, 1974)

Jane Ellen Harrison

Robert Ackerman, "Some Letters of the Cambridge Ritualists," *Greek, Roman and Byzantine Studies* 12 (Spring 1971), pp. 113–36

Shelley Arlen, *The Cambridge Ritualists: An Annotated Bibliography* (Scarecrow Press, 1990)

———, "'For Love of an Idea': Jane Ellen Harrison, heretic and humanist," *Women's History Review* 5:2 (1996)

Mary Beard, *The Invention of Jane Harrison* (Harvard UP, 2000)

Rebecca Beasley, "Modernism's Translations," in Wollaeger and Eatough (eds.), *The Oxford Handbook of Global Modernisms* (Oxford Handbooks, 2012)

Rebecca Beasley and Philip Ross Bullock (eds.), *Russia in Britain, 1880–1940: From Melodrama to Modernism* (OUP, 2013)

Shari Benstock, *Women of the Left Bank: Paris 1900–1940* (University of Texas Press, 1987)

Henri Bergson, *Time and Free Will*, tr. F. A. Pogson (Allen & Unwin, 1910)

Dora Carrington, *Carrington: Letters and Extracts from Her Diaries*, ed. David Garnett (Jonathan Cape, 1970)

Galya Diment, *A Russian Jew of Bloomsbury: The Life and Times of Samuel Koteliansky* (McGill-Queen's UP, 2011)

Laura Doan, *Sapphic Modernities: Sexuality, Women and National Culture* (Palgrave Macmillan 2006)

T. S. Eliot, *Selected Essays* (Faber & Faber, 1951)

David Garnett, *Great Friends* (Macmillan, 1979)

———, *The Golden Echo* (Chatto & Windus, 1953)

Michael Glenny and Norman Stone (eds.), *The Other Russia: The Experience of Exile* (Faber & Faber, 1990)

Jane Ellen Harrison, *Alpha and Omega* (Sidgwick & Jackson, 1915)

———, *Ancient Art and Ritual* (Williams & Norgate, 1913)

———, *Aspects, Aorists and the Classical Tripos* (CUP, 1919)

——— and Hope Mirrlees, *The Book of the Bear* (Nonesuch Press, 1926)

———, *Epilegomena to the Study of Greek Religion* (CUP, 1921)

——— and Hope Mirrlees, *The Life of the Archpriest Avvakum, by Himself* (Hogarth Press, 1924)

———, *Prolegomena to the Study of Greek Religion* (CUP, 1903)

——, *Reminiscences of a Student's Life* (Hogarth Press, 1925)

——, *Themis: A Study of the Social Origins of Greek Religion* (CUP, 1912)

Michael Holroyd, *Augustus John* (Penguin, 1976)

——, *Lytton Strachey* (Penguin, 1971)

Caroline Maclean, *The Vogue for Russia: Modernism and the Unseen in Britain 1900–1930* (Edinburgh UP, 2015)

Jane Marcus, *Virginia Woolf and the Languages of Patriarchy* (Indiana UP, 1987)

Jean Mills, "The Writer, the Prince and the Scholar: Virginia Woolf, D. S. Mirsky, and Jane Harrison's Translation from Russian of *The Life of the Archpriest Avvakum, by Himself*—A Revaluation of the Radical Politics of the Hogarth Press," in Helen Southworth (ed.), *Leonard and Virginia Woolf, The Hogarth Press and the Networks of Modernism* (Edinburgh UP, 2010)

——, *Virginia Woolf, Jane Ellen Harrison, and the Spirit of Modernist Classicism* (Ohio State UP, 2014)

——, "'With Every Nerve in My Body I Stand for Peace'—Jane Ellen Harrison and the Heresy of War," in Justin Quinn Olmstead (ed.), *Reconsidering Peace and Patriotism During the First World War* (Palgrave Macmillan, 2017)

Hope Mirrlees, *Collected Poems*, ed. Sandeep Parmar (Carcanet Press, 2011)

——, *The Counterplot* (Collins, 1924)

——, *Lud-in-the-Mist* (Collins, 1926)

——, *Madeleine: One of Love's Jansenists* (Collins, 1919)

D. S. Mirsky, *Jane Ellen Harrison and Russia* (Heffer, 1930)

Frances Partridge, *Love in Bloomsbury: Memories* (Little, Brown, 1981)

Sandra Peacock, *Jane Ellen Harrison: The Mask and Self* (Yale UP, 1989)

Yopie Prins, *Ladies' Greek: Victorian Translations of Tragedy* (Princeton UP, 2017)

Marc Raeff, *Russia Abroad: A Cultural History of the Russian Emigration, 1919–1939* (OUP, 1990)

Annabel Robinson, *The Life and Work of Jane Ellen Harrison* (OUP, 2002)

Roberta Rubenstein, *Virginia Woolf and the Russian Point of View* (Palgrave Macmillan, 2009)

Marilyn Schwinn Smith, "Aleksei Remizov's English-language Translators: New Material," in Anthony Cross (ed.), *A People Passing Rude: British Responses to Russian Culture* (Open Book, 2012)

——, "Bears in Bloomsbury: Jane Ellen Harrison and the Russians," in Maria Candida Zamith and Luisa Flora (eds.), *Virginia Woolf: Three Centenary Celebrations* (Porto, 2007)

——, "Bergsonian Poetics and the Beast: Jane Harrison's Translations from the Russian," *Translation and Literature* 20:3 (2011)

G. S. Smith, *D. S. Mirsky: A Russian-English Life, 1890–1939* (OUP, 2000)

————, "Jane Ellen Harrison: Forty-Seven Letters to D. S. Mirsky, 1924–1926," *Oxford Slavonic Papers* NS XXVIII (1995)

Gertrude Stein, *Paris France* (Scribner's, 1940)

Jessie G. Stewart, *Jane Ellen Harrison: A Portrait from Letters* (The Merlin Press, 1959)

Michael Swanwick, *Hope in the Mist: The Extraordinary Career and Mysterious Life of Hope Mirrlees* (Temporary Culture, 2009)

Francis West, *Gilbert Murray: A Life* (Croom Helm, 1984)

Alex Zwerdling, *Virginia Woolf and the Real World* (University of California Press, 1986)

Eileen Power

Shiona Airlie, *Scottish Mandarin: The Life and Times of Sir Reginald Johnston* (Hong Kong UP, 2012)

Michael Bentley, *Modernizing England's Past: English Historiography in the Age of Modernism, 1870–1970* (CUP, 2005)

Maxine Berg, *A Woman in History: Eileen Power 1889–1940* (CUP, 1996)

————, "The First Women Historians: The LSE Connection," *Economic History Review* 45:2 (1992), pp. 308–29

William Beveridge, *Power and Influence: An Autobiography* (Hodder & Stoughton, 1953)

Robert A. Bickers, *Britain in China: Community, Culture and Colonialism, 1900–1949* (Manchester UP, 1999)

Vera Brittain, *Testament of Experience: An Autobiographical Story of the Years 1925–1950* (Gollancz, 1957)

————, *Testament of Friendship* (Macmillan, 1940)

Brian Brivati, *Hugh Gaitskell* (Richard Cohen Books, 1996)

Peter Brock and Thomas P. Socknat, *Challenge to Mars: Essays on Pacifism from 1918 to 1945* (Toronto UP, 1999)

George Catlin, *New Trends in Socialism* (Dickson & Thompson, 1935)

———— (ed.), *War and Democracy: Essays on the Causes and Prevention of War* (Routledge, 1938)

Martin Ceadel, *Pacifism in Britain 1914–1945: The Defining of a Faith* (Clarendon Press, 1980)

Paul Costello, *World Historians and Their Goals: Twentieth-Century Answers to Modernism* (Northern Illinois UP, 1993)

George G. Coulton, *Fourscore Years: An Autobiography* (CUP, 1943)

Ralf Dahrendorf, *LSE: A History of the London School of Economics and Political Science, 1895–1995* (OUP, 1995)

Hugh Dalton, *Call Back Yesterday: Memoirs, 1887–1931* (Muller, 1953)

———, *The Fateful Years: Memoirs, 1931–1945* (Muller, 1957)

Elizabeth Durbin, *New Jerusalems: The Labour Party and the Economics of Democratic Socialism* (Routledge, 1985)

Evan Durbin, *The Politics of Democratic Socialism: An Essay on Social Politics* (Routledge, 1940)

Carol Dyhouse, *No Distinction of Sex?: Women in British Universities, 1870–1939* (UCL Press, 1995)

Albert Einstein, *Essays in Humanism* (Philosophical Library, 1950)

John King Fairbank, *Chinabound: A Fifty-Year Memoir* (Harper & Row, 1982)

Lawrence Goldman, *The Life of R. H. Tawney: Socialism and History* (Bloomsbury, 2013)

Susan Howson, *Lionel Robbins* (CUP, 2011)

E. R. Hughes (ed.), *China: Body and Soul* (Secker & Warburg, 1938)

Reginald Johnston, *Twilight in the Forbidden City* (CUP, 1934)

Stephen Kresge and Leif Wenar (eds.), *Hayek on Hayek: An Autobiographical Dialogue* (Routledge, 1994)

Judith Listowel, *This I Have Seen* (Faber & Faber, 1905)

Marjorie McCallum Chibnall, "Eileen Edna Le Poer Power (1889–1940)," in Jane Chance (ed.), *Women Medievalists and the Academy* (Wisconsin UP, 2005)

Helen McCarthy, *The British People and the League of Nations: Democracy, Citizenship and Internationalism, c.1918–48* (Manchester UP, 2011)

William H. McNeill, *Arnold J. Toynbee: A Life* (OUP, 1989)

Kingsley Martin, *Editor: Autobiography, 1931–1945* (Hutchinson, 1968)

———, *Father Figures: Autobiography, 1897–1931* (Hutchinson, 1966)

F. S. Marvin (ed.), *The Evolution of World Peace* (OUP, 1921)

Kate Murphy, *Behind the Wireless: A History of Early Women at the BBC* (Palgrave Macmillan, 2016)

Ben Pimlott, "The Socialist League: Intellectuals and the Labour Left in the 1930s," *Journal of Contemporary History* 6:3 (1971)

Michael M. Postan, *Fact and Relevance: Essays on Historical Method* (CUP, 1971)

———, "Time and Change," in William A. Robson (ed.), *Man and the Social Sciences* (Allen & Unwin for LSE, 1972)

Eileen Power, *A Bibliography for School Teachers of History* (London, 1919)

——— and Rhoda Power, *Boys and Girls of History* (CUP, 1926)

——— and J. H. Clapham (eds.), *The Cambridge Economic History of Europe from the Decline of the Roman Empire, vol. 1: The Agrarian Life of the Middle Ages* (CUP, 1941)

———, *Medieval English Nunneries, c.1275–1535* (CUP, 1922)

———, *Medieval People* (Methuen, 1966)

———, *Medieval Women* (CUP, 1995)

———, *The Paycockes of Coggeshall* (Methuen, 1920)

——— and R. H. Tawney (eds.), *Tudor Economic Documents* (Longmans, Green & Co, 1924–7)

———, *The Wool Trade in English Medieval History* (OUP, 1941)

Mary Prior (ed.), *Women in English Society 1500–1800* (Routledge, 1985)

Lionel Robbins, *Autobiography of an Economist* (Macmillan, 1971)

W. T. Rodgers (ed.), *Hugh Gaitskell 1906–1963* (Thames & Hudson, 1964)

Bertrand Russell, *The Autobiography of Bertrand Russell*, three vols (Allen & Unwin, 1967, 1968, 1969)

———, *The Selected Letters of Bertrand Russell, vol. 2: The Public Years, 1914–1970*, ed. Nicholas Griffin (Routledge, 2001)

Dora Russell, *The Tamarisk Tree: An Autobiography*, three vols (Virago, 1977, 1980, 1985)

Michael Sherborne, *H. G. Wells: Another Kind of Life* (Peter Owen, 2010)

R. H. Tawney, *The Choice Before the Labour Party* (The Socialist League, 1934)

———, *Equality* (Allen & Unwin, 1929)

———, *History and Society: Essays by R. H. Tawney*, ed. J. M. Winter (Routledge, 1978)

———, *Religion and the Rise of Capitalism* (John Murray, 1926)

Ross Terrill, *R. H. Tawney and His Times: Socialism as Fellowship* (Harvard UP, 1973)

Andrew Thorpe, *A History of the Labour Party* (Palgrave Macmillan, 2015)

Beatrice Webb, *The Diary of Beatrice Webb*, vol. 3, ed. Norman and Jeanne Mackenzie (Virago, 1984)

H. G. Wells, *The Correspondence of H. G. Wells*, four vols, ed. David Smith (Routledge, 1997)

Diana Yeh, *The Happy Hsiungs: Performing China and the Struggle for Modernity* (Hong Kong UP, 2014)

Natalie Zemon Davis, "History's Two Bodies," *American Historical Review* 93 (1988), pp. 1–30

Virginia Woolf

Gillian Beer, *Virginia Woolf: The Common Ground* (Edinburgh UP, 1996)

Vanessa Bell, *Sketches in Pen and Ink: A Bloomsbury Notebook* (Hogarth Press, 1997)

Martha Celeste Carpentier, *Ritual, Myth and the Modernist Text: The Influence of Jane Ellen Harrison on Joyce, Eliot and Woolf* (Gordon and Breach, 1998)

Patricia Cramer, "Virginia Woolf's Matriarchal Family of Origins in *Between the Acts*," *Twentieth Century Literature*, vol. 39, no. 2 (Duke UP, 1993), pp. 166–84

Melba Cuddy-Keane, "The Politics of Comic Modes in Virginia Woolf's *Between the Acts*," *Modern Language Association*, vol. 105, no. 2 (1990), pp. 273–85

Roger Fry, *Vision and Design* (Chatto & Windus, 1920)

Diana Gardner, *The Rodmell Papers: Reminiscences of Virginia and Leonard Woolf by a Sussex Neighbor* (Cecil Woolf, 2008)

Victoria Glendinning, *Leonard Woolf* (Simon & Schuster, 2006)

Alexandra Harris, *Virginia Woolf* (Thames & Hudson, 2011)

Clara Jones, *Virginia Woolf: Ambivalent Activist* (CUP, 2016)

Hermione Lee, *Virginia Woolf* (Chatto & Windus, 1996)

John Lehmann (ed.), *Folios of New Writing* (Hogarth Press, 1940)

———, *I Am My Brother* (Longmans, Green & Co., 1960)

———, *Thrown to the Woolfs: Leonard and Virginia Woolf and the Hogarth Press* (Weidenfeld & Nicolson, 1978)

———, *Virginia Woolf and Her World* (Thames & Hudson, 1975)

Alison Light, *Mrs. Woolf and the Servants: An Intimate History of Domestic Life in Bloomsbury* (Penguin, 2007)

Patricia Maika, *Virginia Woolf's* Between the Acts *and Jane Harrison's Conspiracy* (UMI Research Press, 1987)

Jane Marcus (ed.), *Virginia Woolf and Bloomsbury: A Centenary Celebration* (Palgrave Macmillan, 1987)

Susan Merrill Squier, *Virginia Woolf and London: The Sexual Politics of the City* (North Carolina UP, 1985)

Gina Potts and Lisa Shahriari (eds.), *Virginia Woolf's Bloomsbury, vol. 2: International Influence and Politics* (Palgrave Macmillan, 2010)

S. P. Rosenbaum (ed.), *The Bloomsbury Group: A Collection of Memoirs and Commentary* (University of Toronto Press, 1995)

Joan Russell Noble (ed.), *Recollections of Virginia Woolf by Her Contemporaries* (William Morrow, 1972)

Sandra D. Shattuck, "The Stage of Scholarship: Crossing the Bridge from Harrison to Woolf," in Jane Marcus (ed.), *Virginia Woolf and Bloomsbury: A Centenary Celebration* (Palgrave Macmillan, 1987)

Brenda R. Silver, "'Anon' and 'The Reader': Virginia Woolf's Last Essays," in *Twentieth Century Literature*, vol. 25, no. 3/4 (Duke UP, 1979), pp. 356–441

———, *Virginia Woolf's Reading Notebooks* (Princeton UP, 1983)

Anna Snaith, *Virginia Woolf: Public and Private Negotiations* (Palgrave Macmillan, 2000)

Frances Spalding, *Roger Fry: Art and Life* (University of California Press, 1980)

Laurence Ward, *The London County Council Bomb Damage Maps, 1939–45* (Thames & Hudson, 2015)

J. H. Willis, *Leonard and Virginia Woolf as Publishers: Hogarth Press 1917–41* (Virginia UP, 1992)

Leonard Woolf, *An Autobiography, 1880–1969*, two vols (OUP, 1980)

Virginia Woolf, *A Room of One's Own* and *Three Guineas* (Vintage Classics, 2016)

———, *Between the Acts* (Hogarth Press, 1941)

———, *The Collected Essays of Virginia Woolf*, four vols (Chatto & Windus, 1966–7)

———, *The Common Reader* (Hogarth Press, 1935)

———, *The Diary of Virginia Woolf*, five vols, ed. Anne Olivier Bell (Hogarth Press, 1977–84)

———, *Jacob's Room* (Hogarth Press, 1922)

———, *The Letters of Virginia Woolf*, six vols, ed. Nigel Nicolson and Joanne Trautmann (Hogarth Press, 1975–82)

———, *The Moment and Other Essays* (Hogarth Press, 1947)

———, *Moments of Being: Autobiographical Writings*, ed. Jeanne Schulkind (Pimlico, 2002)

———, *Mrs. Dalloway* (Hogarth Press, 1925)

———, *Night and Day* (Duckworth, 1919)

———, *Orlando* (Hogarth Press, 1928)

———, *Roger Fry* (Hogarth Press, 1940)

———, *Roger Fry: A Series of Impressions* (Cecil Woolf, 1994)

———, *Selected Essays*, ed. David Bradshaw (OUP, 2004)

———, *To the Lighthouse* (Hogarth Press, 1927)

———, *The Voyage Out* (Duckworth, 1915)

———, *The Waves* (Hogarth Press, 1931)

———, *The Years* (Hogarth Press, 1936)

ACKNOWLEDGMENTS

In writing about this London square, I've benefited from the generosity and expertise of people across the world. I've pursued these women to Paris and Sussex, to America and to Cornwall (where I tried to stay as close as possible to the house where H. D. lived with Cecil Gray, and ended up staying at a farmhouse which, as it turned out, Virginia Woolf visited in 1910). Writing is always a collaborative enterprise and my research has been informed by that of many predecessors, whose works are listed in the bibliography; I'm also immensely grateful to the many scholars who have patiently answered questions, helped with leads, shared their own research with me, and shown so much enthusiasm for this project over the four years I've spent working on it.

Thank you to all the librarians and archivists whose work has made this book possible: to the staff at the University of Arkansas; Barnard College, Columbia University; the University of California, Los Angeles; the BBC Written Archives; the Beinecke Library, Yale; the Bodleian Library, Oxford; the British Library; the British Museum; Bryn Mawr College; Cambridge University Library; the Camden Local Studies and Archive Center; Cornell University Library; Girton College Library; Glasgow University; the Harry Ransom Center, University of Texas at Austin; the Houghton Library, Harvard; the Jacques Doucet Literary Library; the Keep; the Lilly Library, Indiana University; the London Library; the London Metropolitan Archives; LSE Library; the Marx Memorial Library; the University of Maryland; the University of Reading; Southern Illinois University, and the Women's Library at LSE. Special thanks to Anne Thomson at Newnham College, Triin Vallaste at Amherst College, Laura Schmidt, Elaine Powell Hooker and Marjorie Lamp Mead at the Marion E. Wade Center,

Gilbert O'Brien of the Georgian Group, Rachelle Arthey and Isobel Harcourt from Goodenough College; and Seona Ford of the Dorothy L. Sayers Society (for afternoons exploring the extensive archives held in her garage).

Thank you to Hannah Rosefield, Tyler Curtis, Rosie Clarke, and Edward Town for accommodation during my U.S. research trip; and special gratitude to Marilyn Schwinn Smith, fount of information on John Cournos, Jane Harrison, Bears, and so much more, for hospitality in Amherst and wonderful conversations and emails. Thank you to Alasdair McKinnon for help with Russian.

Of all my subjects, it's fitting that Dorothy L. Sayers has provided the most entertainment and mystery throughout the research process: I'm extremely grateful to Anthony Cardew for showing me the synopsis for an unpublished Sayers story in his possession, and to Martin Edwards for inviting me to a dinner of the secret Detection Club, where I witnessed a candlelit initiation ceremony using the very words Sayers wrote in the 1930s. It's been a great pleasure to correspond with Dan Drake, possessor of an array of unpublished Sayers manuscripts, and I'm very grateful to him for sending scans of several tantalizing pieces of her early writing.

I've been extremely lucky to meet Basil Postan, who has allowed me to quote from previously unseen letters from Eileen Power to his father Munia; I'm hugely grateful to him for his support, and to his brother Alexander Postan.

Another great privilege of research was to meet the late Jeremy Hutchinson, QC, then aged 101; he regaled me with stories of his own stint at 42 Mecklenburgh Square in the 1930s, of his friendship with Virginia Woolf, and of the delights of Holborn's music halls.

Thank you to my brilliant agents, Caroline Dawnay and Sophie Scard, for their belief in this project from the very beginning; working with them has been a joy. Thank you to the judges of the 2015 Tony Lothian Prize, and to all at the Biographers' Club. Thank you to everyone at Faber: to Mitzi Angel, who commissioned this book and whose advice was formative at an early stage; to Laura Hassan for such generous editing and Rowan Cope for expertly seeing it through to publication; to Josh Smith, John Grindrod, Kate Ward, and others. Special thanks to Ella Griffiths for perpetual support and wise conversation. Thank you to Tim Duggan and William Wolfslau at Crown; to Silvia Crompton for copyediting, to Hilary McClellen for fact-checking, and to Mark Bolland for the index.

I wouldn't have written this book without the support of Edmund Gordon: helping with research on his biography of Angela Carter taught me an enormous amount about archives, storytelling, and structure. Thank you to Peter Stothard for his generosity and encouragement when I was first starting out in book reviewing. I'm grateful for the support of friends and colleagues, especially to Nicola Beauman and Lydia Fellgett at Persephone Books—where the idea for this book originated—and to Ben Eastham and Jacques Testard at *The White Review*, whose example has shown me how to be a better editor and, by extension, writer. Huge thanks to friends who read parts of the book in progress—Sandeep Parmar, Ben Eastham, Patrick Langley, Clara Jones—and very special thanks to Edmund Gordon, Alice Spawls, and Matthew Rudman for reading the entirety; all their comments have deepened my thinking and improved the book immeasurably. Above all, thank you to my mother, Alison. This book is for her, and in memory of my grandparents.

TEXT PERMISSIONS

LIST OF ILLUSTRATIONS

INDEX

Numbers *in italics* denote pages with illustrations; MS denotes Mecklenburgh Square.

Power, Eileen (*cont.*):
WORK:
and Manchurian crisis, 229; on medieval nunneries, 199, 208; on medieval people, 358–9; on medieval women, 208–10, 358; pacifism, 220, 223–4, 227, 244; politicizing of research, 216, 222, 228, 239–40; Postan collaboration, 218–9, 240; posthumous reputation, 305; and public status, 203; school textbooks plan, 363; Sorbonne research, 206–7, 209, 333; supports expelled scholars, 228–9; Tawney influence, 215–8; on wool trade, 210, 219, 240
WRITINGS: *A Bibliography for School Teachers of History*, 223, 245; *Boys and Girls of History* (with Rhoda Power), 226; "The Eve of the Dark Ages: a tract for the times," 239, 364; "The Haunted Valley," 364; "The Indian Moslems and the Turkish Nationalists," 362–4; "The Intractable Princess," 204; *Medieval English Nunneries*, 289; *Medieval People*, 210, 223, 306; *Medieval Women*, 306; notes and unpublished lectures, 202; *The Paycockes of Coggeshall*, 358; "The Story of Half Mankind," 230; "Women at Cambridge," 203
Power, Philip, 204
Power, Rhoda, 205, 213, 225–6, *226*, 241, 369; *Boys and Girls of History* (with EP), 226
Priestley, J. B., 98
Proust, Marcel, 172, 275
psychoanalysis, 30, 85, 168, 189, 218, 269, 324; *see also* Freud, Sigmund
Punch, 169
Pushkin, Alexander, 184
Puyi, Emperor of China, 232, 363

The Quorum, 115
Qur'an, 190

Radio Times, 227
Randall, Amy, 71
Raverat, Jacques, 174
Reith, John Reith, 1st Baron, 225
Remizov, Alexei: arrival in Paris, 175; and Avvakum translation, 177; bakes cake, 180; and *The Book of the Bear*, 184, 185, 186, 372; Cournos translates, 176; desires return to Russia, 308; and emigré publications, 188; meets JEH and Hope, 183–4; toy animals, 184; *The Clock*, 176; *Posolon*, 184
Remizov, Seraphima, 175, 176, 177,180, 186, 191, 354–5
Reynolds, Barbara, 342, 345, 346
Rhys, Jean, 28; *Good Morning, Midnight*, 330
Richardson, Dorothy: *Pilgrimage*, 28
Richmond, Surrey, 234, 251, 255, 257, 274, 296
Ridgeway, William, 159, 161, 163
Robbins, Lionel, 211, 228, 241
Robeson, Eslanda, 357
Robeson, Paul, 199
Robinson, Annabel, 350, 351
Rodmell, *see* Monk's House
Roerich, Nicholas, 175
Rogers, Annie, 93
Rome, ancient, 77, 227, 239, 319; Pantheon, 20
Rothermere, Harold Harmsworth, 1st Viscount, 373
Rousseau, Jean-Jacques, 265
Rowe, Dorothy, 94, 113
Ruskin, John, 14
Russell, Bertrand, 25, 161, 198, 205, 225
Russia: British fascination, 177, 187; Cournos job, 58, 67, 176; emigré publications, 188; exiles in Paris, 146, 173–7, 352; grammar, 171; and Hogarth Press, 178; JEH trip, 352; Mirsky's volte-face, 355; Moscow Art Theatre, 174; 1917 revolution, 30, 67, 173, 177, 219, 226;

ABOUT THE AUTHOR

FRANCESCA WADE has written for publications including the *London Review of Books, Times Literary Supplement, Financial Times, New Statesman,* and *Prospect.* She is editor of *The White Review* and a winner of the Biographers' Club Tony Lothian Prize. She lives in London.